D1230539

FATHERHOOD
A Sociological Perspective

Consulting Editor

Marvin Bressler, PRINCETON UNIVERSITY

FATHERHOOD

A Sociological Perspective

BY

LEONARD BENSON

North Texas State University

NEW YORK

RANDOM HOUSE

FIRST PRINTING

 Published in New York by Random House, Inc. and simultaneously in Toronto, Canada, by Random House of Canada Limited.

Library of Congress Catalog Card Number: 68-21549

Manufactured in the United States of America by The Haddon Craftsmen, Inc., Scranton, Pa.

DESIGN BY VINCENT TORRE

FOR

Warren, Roger, and Marian

PREFACE

Like all primary social roles, fatherhood is acted out in a great variety of situations and fulfills a number of different social functions. It is bound by few formal requirements and thus has almost endless possibilities. Most people acquire a general conception of fatherhood from personal experiences with their own fathers and those of their friends; in a reasonably full life, one is likely to find himself in an enormous range of situations involving the role of father. Its catholicity and scope make it of interest to all: everyone is familiar with it; everyone knows something about it; and everyone is, in his own way, an expert on the subject. The folklore of fatherhood does in fact serve its purpose rather well, providing a wide assortment of knowledge, myth, and conjecture by which to answer those questions about fathering that are most frequently raised.

But, when asked to write a scholarly paper on the subject, both graduate and undergraduate students in my family sociology classes have frequently complained that reliable information is very hard to find. I reply that they are mistaken; the literature on fatherhood is voluminous, and a vast amount of information collected by research workers is available. Nevertheless, students seem to have trouble finding it.

Slowly I came to the realization that the scattered materials about paternity have never been brought together in any systematic way. This book represents an attempt to correct the situation, although it is not meant to serve only as a review of the literature. It is an effort to place the useful theories and research knowledge about fatherhood into a coherent framework by which extremely diverse materials can be integrated, and inconsistent and troublesome data viewed in sharp relief. This, then, is a sociology of fatherhood based on the accumulated data about fathers and on the principles of parenthood that have been developed by leading students of the family, fatherhood, and masculinity.

No attempt has been made to review the flood of discursive and hortatory literature or to present a critical assessment of the methodology of each of the many research reports cited. Studies are evaluated primarily in terms of the significance they assume in the context of their relationships with one another. I have found that works that help to explain major problems or that plausibly contradict the conclusions of other studies are usually of greater value than conclusions based on impeccable methods whose content is only tenuously related to the significant issues.

It might be appropriate in a work on fatherhood to trace the historical conceptions of paternity, searching for their legal, ecclesiastical, literary, and artistic roots, but that would be a major project in itself. No good history of father has yet been written. Writers who have tried to read a cyclical pulsing of maternal and paternal styles into succeeding historical eras, such as Carle Zimmerman (1947) and G. Rattray Taylor (1953), have inevitably met with failure. Evolutionary theories about the family, Lewis Henry Morgan's (1877) for example, have gained more recognition, but no greater acceptance. This is one area in which scholars are not likely to become lost in an avalanche of details, since historical facts about fatherhood are rather too scarce than too numerous. Hence no effort will be made to account for the rich variations in fatherhood over time within the world's countless paternal legacies, such as those of the Chinese father, the Pygmy father, the Communist father, the Jewish father, or the Catholic father.

I wish to thank the Faculty Research Council of North Texas State University for the generous financial assistance granted to me during the preparation of this manuscript. The editorial assistance of Mrs. Sylvia Moss of Random House is greatly appreciated. I am also indebted to Professor Marvin

Bressler, consulting editor, for the many helpful suggestions he has made throughout the book. Professors Harry R. Dick and David H. Malone read portions of the manuscript, and I am grateful to them for their suggestions and criticism.

Denton, Texas L. B.

CONTENTS

PART FOUR
Prognosis

PART ONE

Fatherhood in Perspective

Father, Family, and Society

Mother is the primary parent. She is first by popular acclaim, in actual household practice, and in the minds of students of family life, although the child draws even more research attention than mother. Jerome Kagan (1964) concluded that most studies of psychological development report richer data on children than on parents or on parent-child interaction. But material on mother is much more extensive than that on father and, as the inference suggests, grandmother is a more alluring subject than granddad.

When one considers how many fathers there are and the many problems they have in common, it seems rather surprising how little notice they receive. Very few people, if any, devote their careers to the study of fatherhood or to the distribution of information for the purpose of assisting men in their capacity as fathers. Polite inquiries are made about a man's children now and then, and he is happy to show their pictures, but we do not really expect him to say or even know much about them. His wife is the person to consult; the man of the house and his male cronies discuss other matters. The American father is almost invisible, perhaps even at home.

Motherhood is quite another matter. It is a much more intensely cultivated role, and its importance is diffused throughout the woman's most absorbing affairs. Womanliness is still often equated with motherliness and succorance; manliness is hardly ever identified with fatherhood, especially in modern industrial societies. Even the emergence of industrialism has not deprived women of their maternal claims, although it has permitted them to stake out some new ones.

A recurrent problem of civilization is how to define sex roles satisfactorily, as Margaret Mead (1953) has observed, but this is not a problem that we work at with self-conscious determination, certainly not in the case of the male role. Other kinds of problems spark the great debates and prompt the truly dramatic decisions. Nevertheless, father is widely acknowledged as the weak link in the chain of family interaction, and it is not surprising that the social design for fatherhood varies from place to place and time to time more extensively than does that for motherhood.

By their very prominence several features of American family life obscure our concern for paternity. Clearly man is the chief breadwinner and woman is the principal homemaker in the family division of labor. The man's occupational role and his wife's role as mother occupy center stage, making it difficult to become greatly concerned about either the man's father role or the woman's occupational role. Even in this comparison, however, father comes off second-best. The working wife and mother receives much more attention than does man as father.

It is apparent that the problems of women *as women* arouse our most anxious concern, while those of men rarely stir our passion for reform. Only recently have women in large numbers become deeply ambivalent about the virtues of motherhood; this conflict is occasioned by gross changes in their education and occupation patterns. Women have been variously described as "the lost sex," "the second sex," "the superior sex," "the subjugated sex," and as "a tribe of hapless adherents to a mystique rather than to the realities of modern life." Men have their problems, too, but few people have attempted to blame them on the nature, or on the debasement, of masculinity. M. F. Ashley Montagu's contentious book on "the natural superiority of women" (1953) is an exception, and Myron Brenton (1966) contends that masculinity in the traditional sense is disastrously inappropriate for modern man; to most people, however, manliness is an unquestioned virtue.

Perhaps the claim can be made that, in order to maintain a minimal level of social well-being, mother cannot possibly be neglected or taken for granted to the extent that father can. Mothers may be spontaneously alert to their maternal responsibilities because of the mother-infant relationship, as many people have argued, but society takes no chances; girls are schooled in their duties long before they become pregnant and are constantly reminded of these responsibilities as they pass through the childbearing years. By comparison, boys are left unadvised about their approaching parental duties, except when they are facetiously counseled to avoid them. As we might expect, males do not discipline themselves for "father work" during or after they grow up, but society manages to endure.

Robert Lane (1959) found that father simply is not as conspicuous in his parental role as mother. Jules Henry (1963) says the American father is widely regarded as a beloved but playful imp and need not be taken too seriously, while Irene Josselyn (1956) notes that he is often considered little more than mother's helper in child rearing. The relatively greater importance of mother in child care is reflected in the fact that the mother's life routines are more completely altered in the case of a "subnormal" child than are father's (Schonell and Watts, 1956); she is more skillful in handling retarded children than father (Tallman, 1965), but she is also more thoroughly traumatized at the birth of such a child, especially if it is a girl (Farber, 1960).

Some reading material has been dedicated to the continuing education of father, exhorting the man to do a better paternal job, even suggesting how, but it is remarkably scarce compared to the literature of advice, instruction, and edification for women. Of course the literary market in this case reflects an underlying division of interest. Women are eager for such copy, men are not, which is significant because almost all social activities that are considered important and challenging now have a publisher's market. Advice for teen-agers, for the aged, for all the professional occupations, and even for hobbyists is readily available. Obviously fathers do not clamor for help, although Margaret Mead (1963) once stated that modern American men are more interested in being fathers than in having careers and jobs. She supplied no supporting evidence, however; one can question her argument if for no other reason than that men who neglect their work usually have a superior to account to, which is not true for those who neglect fatherhood. The wife may keep up a stream of chatter on the subject to be sure, and she may be her husband's de facto superior, but she is not established as such by social conventions. Fatherhood is a pastime that does not call for training, discipline, or high-priority effort. Pressures upon men to take stock of themselves as fathers are fitful and unorganized at best.

Possibly all of this has something to do with the fact that fatherhood is neglected in social research. We study men's work roles, their political behavior, religious philosophies, and leisure habits, and we talk earnestly about their athletic records, but their role as father has exceptionally low priority for methodical inquiry, record keeping, and conjecture. One review of the literature revealed about fifteen times as many publications dealing with the mother-child relationship as with that between father and child (Eron, *et al.*, 1961). Furthermore, information about fathers is usually obtained at second hand, from either their wives or their children. Father himself is rarely consulted.

Research into mother's role is relatively easy to conduct, of course. She is easier to reach through the school, and she has more time than father in which to cooperate. Many difficulties must be faced in the study of mother-child relations, as Marian Radke Yarrow (1963) has demonstrated, but father-child studies are even more demanding. Lillian Robbins (1963) found that as a rule the memory of parents with regard to their child-rearing experiences was not very good, but that the memories of fathers were less accurate than those of mothers.

Although problems of the solo mother (divorcees and widows) have not been investigated very much, there has been at least some research in this area. Solo fathers have rarely been studied (Freudenthal, 1959), reflecting the fact that most American children stay with their mothers in case of divorce. Where patriarchal traditions remain strong, as among Moslems in the Middle East, children generally stay with the father (Beck, 1957), which is a workable arrangement because the extended family is a dependable, multipurpose social unit, and the father can call on female kinsmen to perform maternal functions.

Erving Goffman (1961) notes that social scientists tend to neglect the many roles that persons play with detachment, shame, or resentment; the father role would seem to be one of these. It is not characterized by shame to be sure, but some resentment and considerable detachment apply. On the other hand, Irving Tallman (1965) argues that fathers receive comparatively little empirical attention because the theoretical framework employed in child-rearing research does not attach any critical significance to the father's role.

Perhaps we automatically turn to the study of mother rather than father because of a vivid combination of favorable images of both mother and the mother-child relationship. The figures of Mary and maternal tenderness are preserved in Christianity from the Judaic tradition, for example, along with the unsympathetic elements of patriarchal rigor and harsh legalism associated with fatherhood. It becomes hard to tell whether our indifference to father and attraction to mother is caused by a factual appraisal of family life or by an overwhelming verbal tradition. Is it a product of the conditions of life or of the rhetoric of family living that we have inherited?

Apparently the feeling is widespread that the basic psychosomatic make-up of men provides them with little aptitude for child rearing. We are prone to think that women are naturally endowed for child care; that it is their native disposition. But women are physiologically structured for childbearing and infant nurturance, not necessarily child rearing. Whether they have some innate aptitude in this regard, aside from their specific fitness for suckling, is not known. (In studies of macaque monkeys, Harry Harlow [1958] found that "contact comfort" with the mother, or with a surrogate mother, was very important for survival of the infant monkeys in the early years and was also strongly associated with a sense of security. Lactation, by contrast, was a variable of negligible importance. The mothering monkey is important, but not essentially because of her suckling abilities. In fact, continuing studies have suggested that the play group, not the mother, is the most irreplaceable social entity needed to assure the proper adaptation of growing monkeys.)

The fact that father is assigned the role of breadwinner rather than that of caring for the child guarantees that boys will not develop and cultivate skills appropriate to child care. The primary skills of fathers are often beyond the understanding or even appreciation of contemporary children, and their style in social relations is usually conditioned by the demanding, singularly adult world of "work." Men are characteristically less patient with children or with immaturity and incompetence of any kind, unless that is precisely what they have been trained for. Then, as in related areas of work that are routinely identified as feminine, men characteristically develop the skill to an even higher level than women.

For whatever reason, mother's role in child rearing does inspire more research than father's, which leads in turn to a still greater emphasis on the mother. Yet rarely is a critical test of the relative importance of mother and father attempted, nor is father found to be of no importance at all. A situation results that is common in other areas of behavioral science that base their findings on "statistically significant" distinctions; areas of successful investigation are cultivated ever more intensively, which in its cumulative effect amounts to an overreaction to rather small differences in percentages. Once our belief in the importance of mother's role is upheld, we have a kind of empirical justification for studying her role in even greater depth. More and more research is done that increases our knowledge of her significance, and the fact that we know little about father contributes to our continued ignorance of his function.

Nor do social theorists find father challenging, although, as we shall see, he has not been neglected altogether. In Robin Williams' (1965) highly respected analysis of American society, he weaves together countless sociological theories and concepts in an attempt to describe and explain the American social pattern, yet the book contains hardly any reference to fatherhood. Talcott Parsons, whose relevant works will be cited in many places in the present book, refers to fatherhood as "one of the obvious keystones of the social structure" (1954), but motherhood seems to have a more important position in his thought. Father is believed to have an impact primarily by his influence upon the family system rather than by directly affecting the child—a "global" impact that is very hard to pin down.

Mother has the major parental role in the child's first few years and is considered the basic humanizer; she implants in children their most fundamental values and attitudes (Parsons, Bales, *et al.*, 1955; Sears, 1957). An especially significant literature has accumulated linking mother to mental health (Sullivan, 1953; Garner and Wenar, 1955; Harris, 1959). Her role in anxiety formation is crucial, since anxiety is often regarded as the source of functional mental disorders and is inherent in the anticipation of punishment, withdrawal of love, and isolation. It is widely believed that the formative period for the individual's anxiety pattern occurs in the earliest years of life and especially in the context of mother-child relations. In a study of similarities in symptoms of personality disturbance between parents and their children, E. L. Phillips (1951) found mother-child similarities in 71 percent of the cases, while correspondences between father and child occurred in only 48 percent. Elsie Adams and Irwin Sarason (1963) suggest that mothers' anxiety patterns are more closely related to their children's than fathers' are, especially in relation to daughters; they claim that patterns of anxiety for fathers and daughters are totally unrelated.

The influence of parent-child relations on the development of schizophrenia has been studied extensively, and again, if either parent is singled out as the predisposing agent, it is usually the mother. Abnormalities in mothering have also been used much more impressively than those in fathering to explain male alcoholism. For that matter, an alcoholic mother is considered to be a greater danger to the child than an alcoholic father, and this invidious difference could be extended to almost all comparisons of maternal and paternal defects. Mothers are not held directly responsible for mental retardation, but their role in this regard is usually magnified; fathers are rarely even mentioned (Jordan, 1962).

To the extent that interpersonal experience rather than heredity is stressed in accounting for personality development, and the early years of childhood are accorded great determinative significance, mother's parental role is necessarily the more important one. A warm, intimate, and continuous relationship with mother—one in which both mother and child find satisfaction—is thought to be essential for the well-being of the infant and the young child (Bowlby, for example, 1952). A large body of literature points up the undesirable effects of maternal deprivation, which, if it occurs in infancy, is difficult to counteract later on by any means.

There is no comparable literature on paternal deprivation. When it is argued that children thrive better in bad homes than in good institutions, the importance of mother is usually being defended, not the importance of father. Mary Ainsworth (1962) suggests that, like Harlow's monkeys, the human infant may be "innately monotropic," attaching himself primarily to one person: mother.

But there is at least some evidence to the contrary. Bettye Caldwell and Julius Richmond (1964) could find surprisingly few behavioral differences between a group of babies reared in a monomatric (one mother figure) environment and those reared in a predominantly polymatric (more than one mother figure) environment. The generally successful Israeli Kibbutzim are another case in point. Noticeable in recent years is a growing tendency to recognize change and even discontinuity in the psychological characteristics of people over time, at least to a greater degree than we once thought possible (Kagan and Moss, 1962). The first years are not solely determinative, and hence father's role in character formation is not permanently preëmpted by mother's nurturance of the infant.

Whereas the professional literature on the importance of mothering is eminently worthwhile, there is a strong tendency for it to be sentimentalized as it is translated into popular thought. We become convinced that mothers are needed to supply love, and both mother and love become sacrosanct in the process. They call for hushed respect and insure all good things. The "mother-and-love approach" to mental health is stretched far beyond its legitimate psychiatric boundaries, although it does not really solve all the problems asked of it even in this restricted area. At best, it is a convenient starting point for a broader theory of socialization; a more precise account of the role of father is needed to help explain the complicated processes of growing up in modern society (Murrell and Stachowiak, 1965).

In fact, father has not been neglected altogether. His name appears over and over again in the case records of mental patients, for example. One student concluded that in both men and women failure to identify with the father was more closely associated with tendencies toward abnormality than failure to identify with the mother (Sopchak, 1952). Herman Lantz (1958) collected some data that suggest that the nervous stability of the father may be more significant than that of the mother for psychosis in the child. According to Ian Gregory (1958), evidence is inconclusive that the loss of the mother is necessarily more significant than that of the father in the development of psychiatric disorders. Although the father has proved important for the emotional health of his children in any number of studies (especially as a warm but firm authority figure), the significance of the relationship between parents has also been cited, in particular the dangers inherent in a family in which the father has greater dependency needs than the mother (Becker, Peterson, and Hellmer, 1957; Westley and Epstein, 1960a, 1960b; Peterson, Becker, Shoemaker, *et al.*, 1961).

Despite these indications of father's importance, the fact remains that mother receives much the greater share of attention.

We have emphasized the marginal or neglected role of fathers, but sometimes they are pictured as a positively bad lot. An analysis of daytime radio serials indicates that fathers are portrayed as troublemakers more often than mothers are, and they are also shown to be "weak" and "bad" more often

(Foster, 1964). Father's image ranges from that of the hapless man-boy who needs constant care and supervision to that of an authoritarian monster. He is undoubtedly pictured as an objectionable character on television more often than occurs in real life, but this can probably be said for mothers too. Inadequacy, witlessness, and absurdity are staple qualities in the family situation comedy. In reality, the sin father is most commonly accused of is passivity; we are not sure just what he should do to promote the well-being of his children, but we are convinced he should avoid indifference or passive compliance to the will of a dominating mother. One major father role, in fact, would seem to be to deflect the energy of just such a woman.

Perhaps because mother is expected to play the more positive parental role, she is a more conspicuous target for censure than father; if the child goes wrong, mother is usually blamed. This is true especially in the twentieth century as father has become more anonymous. Dorothy Beck (1957) points out that the traditional Moslem father, by contrast, is thoroughly disgraced if his daughter should conceive out of wedlock, and his savage anger toward her is considered quite normal. In recent years we may be somewhat less prone to accuse either parent of "ruining" the child—because of our greater awareness of surrounding cultural forces—but father, in particular, has enjoyed immunity. It might help redress the balance if someone, preferably a woman, could popularize "anti-dadism" as much as Philip Wylie (1942) once scandalized "mom."

Father and Social Theory

Father is not a very impressive figure in American life, and, in slighting him, American social theorists may simply confirm the fact that the behavioral sciences can be influenced by cultural predispositions. An alternative explanation, of course, is that the concept of father has little or nothing to add nor any power of illumination to offer to social theory; such a position is not easily rejected.

The roles of the father and the family are customarily considered by social theorists to be passive ones that react to the pressures of other, more basic social phenomena. They are not part of the vital nuclei of culture that generate new social forms; primarily, they reinforce the status quo. In fact, changes in family behavior are accepted only reluctantly as a rule, with a flourish of moral indignation. Change typically is initiated by people who are playing economic or political roles, or, nowadays, scientific roles, which are only indirectly linked to family activities. It is true that kinship considerations intruded into the areas of cultural vitality to a greater extent in man's earlier history, but even in the past a distinction could usually be made between the father as family man and the man as inventor or social reformer.

Thus, the position of father in social theory centers on his role as an agent of social stability. This rather conservative function is stressed repeatedly; father is virtually never viewed as an instrument of social change. When father is used as an explanation for reform or social invention, it is the impact he has upon his son that is considered to be the dynamic force, not the innovations that he makes in the father role per se. Thus it has been contended that reformers are bred by certain types of fathers, especially tyrannous and arbitrary ones.

Erik Erikson (1958) has suggested that sons of such fathers will react to frustrations later in their lives in accordance with the patterns evoked in childhood by the frustrating father. But this of course is not a fully developed theory of social change, creativity, or innovation; nor would Erikson argue that it is. His theory would have greater utility if it could identify the social or historical circumstances that predispose men to be tyrannous or arbitrary fathers in the first place and if it could explain those instances in which arbitrary authority results in creative rebellion rather than submission. As we shall see, contemporary research has linked paternal tyranny to various kinds of problem behavior, but almost never to creativity and innovation.

Freud's view is more consistent than Erikson's with the character of father's function, though one must not take Freud too literally. He considered totemism a form of indirect father worship and thus, in an oblique way, an agency of social control. He believed it was derived from a magnification and elaboration of the status of father, who even in death stands for *authority* and serves as a conservative tool of social obedience (Freud, 1918). Freud repeatedly stressed the role of father as the source of the superego, serving as a moral control over his children's behavior; he thought father had much less control over the formation of id and ego, except as mediated by the superego. Father, for example, is a threatening figure to his children much more often than he realizes. He excites high levels of anxiety when the children are young, assuring the presence of tension and hesitancy in countless situations, and this leads to inhibitions and the emergence of a pattern of cautiousness in their lives.

We will never know how many of the millions of low-order panic reactions experienced by people every day can be traced to earlier relationships between father and child, but through subtleties of perception and interpretation, father's emotional habits do evoke lifelong response patterns. Mother, typically "softer" in her functions, is probably less often the source of severely inhibiting or paralyzing conditioned reactions. She also has an opportunity to mold the child to her ways in infancy; the father as threatener is superimposed upon her more basic pattern and is therefore more likely to appear as a terrorizing intruder, but one who speaks as authority and therefore *ought* to be obeyed. (It is said that children in France are threatened with vague, dark creatures, always male, each of whom is interpreted as an image of the dangerous aspect of father, who may carry the children off in a sack and possibly eat them [Abel, Belo, and Wolfenstein, 1954].)

In man's capacity as father he has rarely been party to reform campaigns or revolutionary movements. *Men* do of course play roles as visionaries, but *fathers* do not. Instead, father is a constant and awesome bulwark against change. Mother qua mother may speak against the status quo in behalf of injustices done to her children and her loved ones, but father becomes a politician or some other distinctively nonfamily spokesman when he takes up a cause.

The literature of anthropology, sociology, and history contains astonishingly few indications that father has had any discernible role as innovator even in family life itself, although he has undoubtedly served as a mediator between families in disputes. The community in simple societies is, in a sense, a mere extension of the family, but such societies are characteristically oriented toward tradition, not novelty. Change, if noticeable, is likely to be instigated by totally unanticipated circumstances and is thus a matter of necessity. It is neither planned nor subject to any conscious mediation, and father's role in it is therefore fortuitous rather than socially structured.

The role of father in theory may best be clarified by reviewing a leading contemporary analysis of the family as a social system by Talcott Parsons, Robert Bales, *et al.* (1955). First, it is recognized that the family is found in all societies and is the basic unit of social control. It handles a multitude of human problems; some concern only members of the family, others bear upon the adaptation of the family to its larger environment. Thus the family can be viewed as a self-contained social microcosm, but also as a subsystem within a more inclusive social order. In the former sense it faces the problem of maintaining its own integrity; in the latter, the problem of accommodating to a more complex, external order. In either case it must care for its children, train them in the basic modes of social cooperation, orient them to more specialized adult tasks, and provide a social framework for managing the tensions of its members.

In simple societies having large, extended family systems the individual is surrounded by kinsmen and the distinction between internal and external problems is faint. With increasing technical complexity and the need for a mobile labor force, villages become cities and the small nuclear family becomes relatively isolated from its circle of consanguine kinsmen. (This point has been the subject of debate in recent years and will be discussed in more detail in Chapter III.) Thus, as society industrializes, a sharper division of concern between the inner life of the family and its need to accommodate to pressure from outside becomes apparent.

Organization within the family revolves around two axes:

age, upon which an authority structure is established, and sex, according to which responsibilities are divided. Authority automatically falls to the older members of the household as long as they can remain active, and responsibilities are always divided between the sexes. In the overwhelming majority of societies for which there are adequate data, the roles of father and mother are functionally different; father is primarily responsible for the instrumental and executive tasks that relate the family to its larger social environment, while women specialize in meeting expressive needs and routine tasks within the family (Zelditch, 1955). Although this pattern varies from one social setting to another, as we shall see, father is usually the prototype of adult masculinity for both his son and his daughter, and virtually all major values attaching to the masculine role are integrated within the symbolism of fatherhood (Parsons, 1954).

This point of view has received support from many sources. Taking his lead from Frédéric Le Play, John Mogey (1957) argues that the key to family equilibrium in the contemporary small family, as in virtually all family arrangements, is the nature of the paternal role. Le Play (1879) long ago formulated the proposition that social stability depends upon harmony between family and society, which is rooted in a particular type of family organization. The family pattern he stressed was called the "stem" family, in which property is passed from one generation to the next, thus supplying the link between generations. A prominent feature of this system is the authority of the father, the essence of which is his power to bequeath family possessions in one piece to a successor, his son. Mogey drops this point, but retains the idea that father is a key to both family and social stability. He contends that the societal expectations of fatherhood must be altered in accordance with changing social conditions and traces some of the changes that have occurred with the rise of industrialism, to which we shall return.

The significance of father for social solidity is found primarily in his role as the overseer of family integrity, equanimity, and endurance, and is predicated on the assumption, virtually unchallenged, that a stable family system is essential to the well-being of society. The family is the social unit to which the majority of people orient most of their behavior most of the time; its basic routines and satisfactions anchor and enhance individual and group behavior in the many non-family roles people must play. Child training within the family provides the foundation upon which the entire process of social learning is based. Hence, it is necessary to have a stable family system in order to provide unity and strength in the community at large.

William Goode (1960b) has extended this proposition by calling attention to the fact that only within the family can the individual be observed in terms of the *total* configuration of his life roles. Only here can the sum of his performance as a person be judged. For this reason the family is the social institution capable of exerting the most meaningful pressure upon individuals to organize their entire set of roles into the most effective pattern or constellation possible. Outside of the family the individual is seen for only short periods of time and in the performance of specialized activities; spouses, parents, and children have an opportunity to see one another in full measure. Anything that may contribute to the sustained level-headedness of the family unit is of fundamental social importance, and the role of father assumes its greatest relevance in just this capacity.

For father to be effective in maintaining family stability, he must have some authority; he must be able to control certain kinds of actions of members of his family. In a sense, he is society's man in the household, since he represents the larger social order to a greater extent than his wife does. Authority is granted to father partly because of the age factor, since he is usually the oldest member of the family, but his authority is also delegated by the laws and ideals of society and reinforced by a web of venerable social habits. The pattern is vital in the life of virtually every human being and is acted out principally by close kinsmen and immediate friends of the family. Father's power is thereby made authentic in terms of daily social usage; it is *legitimate*.

It is never used simply to police the family and settle disputes, however, nor is it often used in this way; father's existence symbolizes legitimate authority and this provides the leverage by which he can exercise control before the fact, "anticipatory social control." Family members can foresee his judgments and are constrained to act correctly according to their conception of his wishes.

The authority vested in father is not always made explicit of course. We are sometimes shocked, in fact, when it is, as in the case of American reactions to the Soviet viewpoint on this matter. One of the most influential men in the Soviet Union in the field of character education, Anton Makarenko, has based much of his work on the assumption that the authority that parents exercise over their children is delegated to them by the state. Parental responsibility in Soviet thought is considered but one aspect of a broader public duty. Eleanore Luckey (1964) has called attention to this fact, and regards it as most astonishing. But it is not really so strange. We in the United States *implicitly* assume that parental authority over the child is delegated by society and that it is one aspect of a broader parental obligation. The development of the juvenile court system at the turn of the century was based on the historical concept of *parens patriae,* which in essence imposes upon the state, through the juvenile court, the responsibility of fatherhood when the real father cannot perform his duty.

In Mexican-American families the father often considers it his explicit duty to police the family in order to preserve its public image as an integrated and honorable unit. He holds himself responsible primarily because society holds him responsible and assumes that he can indeed exercise control (Madsen, 1964). In the theology of the Mormon Church father is explicitly designated as *the* authority within the household. His power is justified by his role as family religious leader which, in turn, is the basis for church government. Father is thus the connecting link between church and family (Christopherson, 1956).

Preserving our assumptions about paternal authority in an unformalized state may allow for greater flexibility in the social control of both parents and children, but it also means that a great deal of authority is extended to parents without holding them accountable, except under the most extreme circumstances. The confusion of authority at home leads to its confusion in the community at large. Hence, the fact that the social basis for parental authority is ambiguous does not mean that it does not exist, but it does have consequences for the way it is used and for the way parental behavior is judged.

As an authority within the family, father keeps watch over his group in their strictly domestic concerns, but he is also expected to exercise control over their extrafamilial affairs. Family members must adapt to environmental demands, and it helps if their behavior is based upon a reasonably accurate understanding of the alternatives available; speaking generally, there is no substitute for the advice and guidance of older men in this regard. Their greater experience in the nonfamilial affairs of the community ordinarily equips them for such a role better than any other member of the household. The typical father is more strategically involved in the outside world than his wife; he stands at a crucial point of articulation between the family subsystem and that of the wider society, which is the primary basis for his symbolic significance and the main reason that he is the family's chief representative of the nonfamily world (Parsons, 1954).

As an example, Parsons contends that the major value premise of the American occupational system is its emphasis upon work competence, independent of family background, whereas a key value in family life is that each member of the family has a claim on its resources in terms of his needs, without reference to his skills. Hence the occupational system and the family system are founded on different value premises, but each sphere must be accommodated to the other. Because father participates in both worlds more often and more completely than mother, he is usually more qualified to make concrete decisions enabling just such an accommodation. Because he is active in both worlds, father is also more easily embarrassed by any deviance from community standards on the part of members of his family. For example, while a mother tends to regard a severely retarded child as a "challenge" to her expressive skills, such a child is more likely to be perceived as threatening by his father, who is more sensitive to the deviant role that the families of retarded children are forced to play in the community (Tallman, 1965).

Father is a protector of the basic principles of social cooperation—not so much of the kindergarten faith, which is mother's domain, but of the critical perspective, which occasionally borders on the cynical, and has obstinate dilemmas to deal with and harsh language to use. But it is basically traditional. In Baudelaire's phrase, fathers are "quoters of precedents." The authority father has sustained over the centuries, his right to be family spokesman, has been preserved largely because he can be counted on to make the traditional, conservative judgment, rather than the novel one. This is the sense in which father knows best.

One final point. Although father has been regarded as a key to social order in this discussion, there is also evidence that a smoothly operating society facilitates, and may be essential for, paternal stability. Groups that are not integrated into the stable socioeconomic order—many Negro groups in the United States, for example—cannot sustain a reliable paternal role. Kingsley Davis (1940) has called attention to the role of social change in undermining certain kinds of parental authority; he notes that the quality of parent-child conflict is conditioned by very broad social patterns. Revolutions, counterrevolutions, wars, postwar periods, and depressions have often crippled father's ability to stabilize the family. It cannot be argued, however, that father's inability to maintain family order under these critical circumstances is a strategic factor in the study of generalized social unrest; no serious student would blame community crises on the failure of fatherhood. His failure is symptomatic, not causal. As Norman Ryder (1965) has pointed out, the family is the primary agent of child rearing to the extent that the relationships portrayed in it closely resemble those of the community into which the youth must move. When a society breaks out of the mold, the family and its father figure no longer suffice for the tasks of socialization, and "boys grow up to resemble the times more than they do their fathers." We are forced to acknowledge that father's family stewardship is subject to larger social forces.

Man: The Instrumental Sex

As we have seen, the concept of fatherhood cannot long be separated from that of masculinity. Throughout this book certain assumptions will be made about the nature of manhood, and it will help to make them explicit at the outset.

Men are larger and stronger than women, of course, and superior in activities that require muscle power; women are uniquely endowed for pregnancy and the nurturance of infants. Beyond such obvious physiological differences, all distinctions must be meticulously qualified, but sex-linked roles, and manners appropriate to each, are deeply rooted in all the nations of the world. Even motor habits—ways of sitting, standing, walking, gesturing—are sexually differentiated. For this reason sex traditions that are learned almost always *seem* to be inborn.

Of inestimable value in sociology is the distinction between men and women in terms of two fundamentally different modes of behavior: expressiveness and instrumentalism. *Expressiveness* is characterized by a basic predisposition toward pleasing others, responding to them in rewarding ways in order to receive pleasurable responses in return. When friends get together, for example, their interchange ordinarily follows an expressive pattern, and they enjoy simply being with one another. In this mode, pleasant interpersonal relationships are ends in themselves: they are consummatory in nature, rather than investment relationships. Their main purpose is to afford satisfying experiences with no thought for future goals.

The *instrumental* orientation, on the other hand, evokes a disciplined pursuit of goals transcending the immediate situation and encourages resistance to any emotional involvement as an end in itself. In a sense, instrumentalism is the inhibition of expressiveness. It fosters affective restraint along with a desire for achievement, acceptance of objective standards for performance, and task fulfillment. Thus it serves an adaptive social function, while expressiveness fulfills the need for morale and cohesion and serves an integrative function. One can think of both instrumentality and expressiveness as universal patterns, found in all cultures, but molded in unique ways by the particular pressures of each.

Both theory and research suggest that girls are encouraged to cultivate expressiveness, while boys are urged to adopt an instrumental approach to life. In a cross-cultural survey of fifty-six societies, Morris Zelditch (1955) classified the father as instrumental in forty-eight societies and expressive in eight, while he listed the mother as instrumental in six and expressive in fifty. William Burch (1965) has shrewdly observed that even in the American world of camping out the feminine role is to sustain and encourage, to be an appreciative audience for masculine endeavors. The male returns from fishing, hunting, or whatever to be admired by an updated version of the "brave but gentle pioneer mother," modeled after all Hollywood Westerns.

Research on sex differences has shown repeatedly that women are more sensitive to interpersonal relations than men and more responsive to the norms of the groups to which they belong: girls are "person-centered," boys tend to be "thing-centered." Mirra Komarovsky (1953) has observed that social pressures are exerted upon girls to be gentler and more emotionally demonstrative than boys. Women are almost always poor poker players, probably because poker is intensely competitive and allows no place for kindness, sympathy, or an ingenuous show of emotions. In a study of three-person groups, Ralph Turner (1964) reports that men tended to settle disputes in terms of bargaining strength, by which a coalition of two could dominate. Women sought consensus and welcomed the opportunity to relinquish an advantage. Girls seem to be more willing to abide by arbitrary, even inhibiting, peer-group codes than boys (Henry, 1963). The boy is given greater leeway—by parents, and even by the male gang—*not* to be one of the boys, to be a loner. Since girls stress interpersonal relationships so heavily, being "one of the girls" is more thoroughly satisfying to them than being "one of the boys" is to boys (and men).

The urge to be autonomous is not an essential function of instrumentalism, but it does imply a willingness to renounce expressive loyalties and parochial commitments. It is a facet of the heritage of a double sex standard, whereby males, from earliest childhood, are given greater freedom than girls to probe, explore, and test their own inclinations, and to do these things in greater privacy (Komarovsky, 1950).

Jules Henry (1963) has argued that man is the symbol of "law, restraint, industry, severity, and aloofness—the superego values," while woman stands for "closeness, warmth, softness, yielding, and guile—the values of the id." Yet if there are two major modes in our literary conception of childhood, as Leslie Fiedler (1960) suggests—original sin and innocence—girls are attributed innocence; boys, original sin. This, of course, is also part of our double sex standard—or, more accurately, triple standard: one standard for men, one for "good" women, and one for "bad" women. Girls may be good or bad, but boys must be bad, at least a little bad, in order to be good. Boys are expected to test the limits of propriety, to see what they can get away with, and they prove themselves by occasionally getting into trouble, a corollary of their freedom. Girls prove themselves by taking no chances.

Although we often think of creativity as an expressive function, that is not necessarily the case within the present context. Female expressiveness turns to a concern for group harmony and centers on group experience. But creativity in almost any field is a lonely endeavor, which provides a clue to why women have been less creative than men in many areas (Rossi, 1964). The publication of a book, the painting of a significant picture, or the initiation of a scientific breakthrough are all products of many lonely hours of thought; such isolation is more characteristic of the instrumental than of the expressive mode. Jessie Bernard (1964) argues that even the scholarly work of modern academic women is generally less creative than that of men because women either can not or do not want to be innovators and because the people (men) who must certify their contributions think of them as less than full-fledged colleagues.

Even the learning process for girls seems to involve a greater expressive emphasis. Girls require more satisfactory affiliations and are more often affected by the interpersonal context of the situation in which learning takes place. It has often been noted that girls are superior in verbal abilities while boys excel in the use and manipulation of numbers. Harold Leavitt (1965) reports that the female naïveté concerning numbers is related to their interpersonal style and is reflected in the way they cope with group games requiring numerical skills. Females are very sensitive to the reactions of each other within the group; males are more likely to employ logical processes in the solution of such problems. David Lynn (1962) suggests that boys tend to operate on their own and to learn by problem solving—by acquiring a goal, restructuring the field, and abstracting principles—while girls learn more often by imitation within the context of their group memberships.

Thus, female intellectuality tends to be more narrowly channeled than that of boys. The intellectual life of boys is channeled, too, of course, but many more channels are available. In fact, while intellectual mastery for boys is not clearly related to sex identification (Kagan and Freeman, 1963), the forms available to girls are rather routinely stereotyped as feminine. Most female novelists, although certainly not all of them, like to keep their focus narrow; Jane Austen, the Brontë sisters, Sarah Orne Jewett, and Françoise Sagan exemplify the tendency. The range of intellectuality found among males is greater and affords a much broader scope for divergent interests—too broad to identify with masculinity as such. Many interests pursued solely by men are identified with the human condition, not with manliness.

This greater concern for principles of universal application reflects the instrumental orientation of boys. To girls, learning is likely to be an end in itself; boys, on the other hand, think less in terms of the immediate importance of learning and more about its long-range utility (Lynn, 1962). This is not because boys are specifically taught to think of learning as a means to other ends, but rather because the general male style of instrumentalism seems to predispose boys to this orientation. It is the product of countless indirect cultural pressures.

One consequence of this outlook is that intellectual work itself is more often identified as a male than a female pursuit. Girls, it would seem, are subtly called upon to inhibit "principled" learning; as they grow older they may even suppress the intellectual abilities they have already developed when competing with boys. Both Paul Wallin (1950) and Mirra Komarovsky (1946) found that a substantial proportion of college girls at least occasionally "play dumb" on dates. In one study, women college students consistently rated men as superior to or "more worthy" than females (McKee and Sheriffs, 1957). Males, in fact, are more likely than females to flaunt any intellectual advantage they may have in order to control their feelings of insecurity (Beigel, 1957). Although not usually stereotyped as a masculine trait, the need to be intellectual is apparently more masculine than feminine.

Differences between men and women can be explained partially in terms of the processes that establish the differences. For example, Jules Henry (1963) contends that the unique peer-group activities of boys provide a key to their masculinization. He reasons that, generally speaking, boys are involved in team sports as they grow up, while girls are not. Girls play some team games, of course, but much less than boys. Nor does superior performance provide the basis for the self-esteem of girls: they are more often immersed in the social activities of their peer group and are more dependent upon acceptance within it.

The team sports to which boys devote themselves stress competence in cooperation along with hard and fast rules by which the game must be played. Boys learn these rules as moral imperatives and are trained to regard them as facts of life. Strict codes for personal conduct and the need for skilled teamwork become basic life premises for boys. Most important of all, each player's performance is judged by unimpeachable standards of excellence known by all and visible to all. Older men call attention to the code's subtleties, and the boys themselves can see that better players are distinguished from the poorer ones by objective criteria. In addition to the visual cues to good performance, statistical records are often kept, such as batting averages, passes completed, and free throws missed.

Girls, on the other hand, grow up within an atmosphere of *arbitrary exclusiveness*. They are absorbed with life in a small group that is held together by poorly understood sentiments, sentiments that engender cliquishness and jealousy toward other, similar groups of girls. Such a pattern is not unknown among boys, of course, but it is counterbalanced by the objective and yet highly moralistic standards of the game itself. To the extent that a group's purposes are vague, undirected toward any special interest, and purely "social," the ranking of the members will be based upon personal characteristics such as amiability, good-naturedness, charm, and in general, "personality" (Berelson and Steiner, 1964). Without unassailable rules for teamwork and performance, and without objective rules for judging behavior, girls develop arbitrary rules of exclusiveness by which to maintain their integrity.

The fact that instrumentalism is the basis for both teamwork and autonomy obviously poses a dilemma that must be worked out by each boy in his own way. The desire for autonomy creates a tension when teamwork is called for, but the two qualities are not totally unrelated nor are they completely in conflict. Although instrumentalism often calls for teamwork, it also calls for the elimination of unnecessary affect, and that helps to resolve the dilemma. A viable autonomy pattern involves emotional neutrality in teamwork. To be effective, the man must have skill and keep his feelings in check.

Boys can in fact achieve their greatest awards through athletics—in contests against other boys they do not even know. Girls receive their greatest satisfactions through participation in social affairs and the cultivation of beauty (Coleman, 1962). Striving among girls is directed especially toward pleasing boys; boys strive in a much less parochial manner. In fact, girls tend to become thoroughly engrossed in the winning of male favors. Since they are judged in large part by their ability to attract boys, they are confronted with the problem of pleasing boys they may not even like. As David Riesman says (1964), girls would be better off if they had a "moral substitute" for boys.

While girls are reared in an expressive tradition, the quality of their interpersonal relationships tends to be superficial. Perhaps this is anomalous only in a moral sense, since it follows a social logic. The fact that girls are brought up to be more concerned with interpersonal relations than with personal achievement does not logically preclude the fact that the interpersonal relations they do cultivate are quite often superficial.

The sex distinctions noted here extend to very general differences in male and female activities in the United States. The social participation of men in American society is caught up in work, business, and government, where performance is judged by universal standards of competence, while women are somewhat more immersed in interpersonal relations of a parochial nature. Even when women work their activities tend to be confined by contrast with men's. Women are concentrated in only a few occupational categories and work is usually a secondary pursuit for them, not the major condition by which they are judged. There are as many types of men as there are major occupational categories, and the identities they put forward are usually occupational titles, while women usually identify themselves by their family names (Gross and Stone, 1964). A job title signifies a status; names are subjective and mean little or nothing in mass society. The possessor must be judged by his immediate behavior and the claims he makes for himself.

Thus, the social milieu to which the woman adapts tends to be smaller and more parochial; its inhabitants are more arbitrary in their judgment of individual performance than the inhabitants of the man's social milieu. Female expressiveness is reflected in a rather wayward effusiveness. Rose Giallombardo (1966) found that the prevailing conception of women as being undisciplined is even imported into the female prison world; concepts such as fair play and courage lack meaning to the female inmate, but the pattern is quite different in men's prisons where inmate loyalty and the concept of the "right guy" are usually very strong.

Of course, a magnification of sex differences is inevitable in the study of sex traits. Moreover, some of the differences between males and females that have been discussed concern areas of life in which the contrasts between the behavior of boys and girls are most pronounced. David Riesman (1964) comments that when college girls consider themselves less inner-directed than boys, it may simply mean that the boys they know are expected to show initiative on dates; it may not reflect general differences between girls and boys at all. In fact, there are many facets of boys' behavior that girls know very little about, and vice versa.

Philip Slater (1961) argues that although mothers may be generally more expressive than fathers, in many homes mother is both more expressive and more instrumental than father *vis-à-vis the children.* Mother is the salient parent in both regards, despite the fact that one might rank her as more expressive and less instrumental than her husband *generally speaking.* Slater also argues that expressiveness and instrumentalism are in some respects incompatible. To the extent that they conflict with one another, it would seem undesirable for mother to specialize in one and father in the other. Empirical studies do indicate that where middle-class parents differ markedly from one another the emotional adjustment of their children is impaired (Lazowick, 1955; Wechsler, 1957; Manis, 1958).

Slater argues most convincingly against the "human limitations theory of role differentiation," the idea that people are rarely able to cultivate *both* expressiveness and instrumentality. People can, in fact, combine the two modes in their life style; one is never all one or the other. Indeed there is a rather distinctive expressive-instrumental syndrome for both men and women.

Males are *expected* to combine expressive and instrumental qualities (Johnson, 1963); they are called upon to play the dissimilar roles of breadwinner and husband, the former stressing instrumentalism and the latter demanding greater expressive emphasis. When he becomes a father, the man plays still a third role that combines instrumentality and expressiveness to a greater extent than either the breadwinner or husband role.

The woman is not ordinarily expected to juggle expressiveness and instrumentality in such complicated ways. But she *is* expected to juggle the two modes in accordance with a uniquely feminine configuration. Women devote themselves to the nurturance of children, by which they develop expressive patterns, but each mother must also "look out" for her brood. The functional setting of instrumentalism for mothers is the family, in which they concern themselves with the maintenance of the household, the care of the children, and the use of resources available to the family. Father's instrumentalism involves less housekeeping and childbearing chores; it revolves around the procurement of basic resources—in a money economy, money.

Women are probably more instrumental in their relations with men than the latter are with women. In the process of growing up women learn to work subtly through men, whereas men rarely practice the fine art of indirectly manipulating women. Many women take pride in having a capable husband who is, in a sense, a primary resource to be "husbanded" and "managed." By general social expectations, the girl seeks to have a loving relationship with a man who is self-propelling, but she is also expected to urge him on if he does not push himself. The more aggressive he is, the more comforting and nurturant she is expected to be. The cultivation of expressiveness by women enables and, of course, promotes an accommodation to their secondary status.

The "go-getting" man, on the other hand, must beware of true expressiveness, because it can sidetrack him from his work. The quality most often attributed to highly masculine men is aggressiveness, which, like authoritarianism, is associated with a positive distrust of female qualities (Allen, 1954). The male instrumental orientation is, or tends to be, an invidious one, breeding a sense of superiority over those who are "weak" and compliant. Thus, antifeminism is established as part of the syndrome of masculinity, but femininity does not embrace antimale attitudes (Hartley, 1959). The woman who is truly hostile toward men abandons her sex role and adopts an inverted form of masculinity.

Humanization and Domestication: The Paternal Link

Father not only has an instrumental contribution to make in preserving social order, he once played a decisive role in the very establishment of the human type of family. His role in this regard is now widely acknowledged by anthropologists, and theories extolling the primal role of mothers have been modified in the light of contemporary knowledge.

We can never know, of course, precisely how the human

family was first formed. It had to have an origin somewhere, somehow, but suppositions as to how and when it began are necessarily based on limited information. Archaeological data tell us virtually nothing. Inferences must be made from what we know about human culture and from what we know about the behavioral border line between the life patterns of apes and men. The first father in the human sense was probably not a member of Homo sapiens, but some rather clever tool-using male belonging to a near-man species that is now extinct.

The *human* family system can exist only within a species capable of semantic language—that is, capable of using symbols. Only then is it possible to create concepts of "mother," "father," "son," "daughter," and an ever wider range of kinship terms shared by members of the group. We have no evidence that such a symbolic creature would, or could, have invented a "subhuman" concept of mother or father; certainly the most primitive members of our own species have had fully developed and extremely complex kinship concepts.

Of paramount importance in the genesis of kinship was the invention of fatherhood. The universal participation of a father figure in the human family is not founded upon instinct, glandular or hormonal controls, or upon any genetically induced paternal behavior; it cannot be traced directly to organic necessity. Rather, the role of husband and father depends upon customs and traditions that, once established, must be taught to each new generation. The domestication of father required the creation of symbolic controls—social rules—for the paternal role, by which the male progenitor (or his surrogate) became a cooperative member of the family, sharing food, shelter, and materials for clothing with the female and their mutual offspring. Other primate males may be "paternally interested in infants" (Hockett and Ascher, 1964), and they will protect females and the young against predators, but only the human male shares food with women and children and works in cooperative projects with them.

Males of other species occasionally fight to possess females, but they do not nurture them, and while those of some nonprimate species will share food with females and infants (Spuhler, 1959), their manner of living in this respect is not comparable with primate social life or human family life. None of the *male* mammals have developed a method for feeding infants except Homo sapiens (Bates, 1963), although male marmosets premasticate food for their young (Coon, 1962). Among primates other than man, the female cares for her offspring and fends for herself. Whatever training the children receive is given almost exclusively by the mother, while the father's relationship with his progeny is primarily one of tolerant indifference. The male's continued sexual interest in the female may be all that keeps him "in the family," but it is Homo sapiens who makes female sex fidelity a moral matter.

Adult male gorillas, "silverbacks," occasionally groom infants (Schaller, 1964), and females often lean or rest against dominant males; infants are also attracted to the powerful males and sit by them or play on them. Guarding the infant from harm during day-to-day existence, however, is entirely the responsibility of the mother. The comfort and security that the infant derives from close physical contact with the mother, even after she has ceased to provide food, is probably essential to its physical and mental well-being; contact with the father may be of some use in this connection, but it is rather doubtful.

Charles Hockett and Robert Ascher (1964) have called attention to the increased need for father to help in the rearing of children as a result of the evolutionary enlargement of the hominid brain. They point out that, in the transition from hominoid to hominid tool using, that is, from apelike to more human patterns, the development of language and upright posture probably created a selective advantage in favor of larger brains. But larger brains mean larger heads, and even today the infant's head is the chief troublemaker in childbirth. To some extent this difficulty can be combated by expelling the fetus relatively early in its development, creating a selection in favor of earlier parturition in pregnancy. The brain of the human infant is thus only about a quarter of its adult size, and the human baby is very immature by comparison with other primates. But this, in turn, produces a longer period of helpless infancy, a deeper attachment to the mother, and perhaps requires that the mother be bipedal and capable of holding the baby (Washburn and DeVore, 1961). Infancy and childhood then become periods of maximum plasticity during which the complex, extragenetic heritage of the community can be acquired. The helplessness of infants necessitates prolonged and more elaborate child care, and it becomes highly convenient to mothers if adult males are willing to help. In fact, male assistance in child care was probably crucial to hominid survival. Moreover, some of the skills that young males must learn in a group that is dependent upon cultural adaptation can only be acquired from the adult males. All these considerations strongly suggest that the domestication of the father in the very earliest stages of human development was necessary if the species was to survive.

Carleton Coon (1962) has speculated about these developments in a way that bears quite directly on the humanization of fatherhood. He contends that hominids with greater intelligence had a selective advantage primarily because of their superiority in securing women. With hominization, "women getting" increasingly called for the intelligence and finesse that improved brains could supply, qualities that were also required by males who must meet the social standards of human fatherhood. The children of such men would be very likely to inherit cerebral and endocrine advantages. Men with larger brains would also be able to tolerate and adapt to the stresses of a complex social order, which requires the ability to deal with the idiosyncracies of other individuals and thus generates the capacity to attain group objectives through adaptive social intercourse.

Coon contends that this selective process among hominids favored both "stress tolerance" and superior intelligence. Stress tolerance is the ability to live with a large number of individuals and to interact with them without conflict; it enables the individual to keep trying in complicated and frustrating interpersonal situations. Above all, it involves self-control and rapid adjustment to the status customs of a variety of individuals. It is not merely a learned ability, according to Coon; it involves brain mutations, but perhaps more importantly, it requires a certain kind of endocrine system. M. R. A. Chance (1961) has also suggested that the ability to adapt to social requirements

—especially the faculty of maintaining one's place in a hierarchy of power without foolishly challenging a more powerful male—taxes the discriminating power of the primate brain and could have played a potent part in the evolution of our mental capacities.

Chance's proposition is exemplified among the great apes, who generally live in little kingdoms including a dominant male and several females, juveniles, infants, and a few subordinate adult males. The nature of the dominant male and the structure of the dominance hierarchy seem to set a limit upon the number of adult males that can coexist in the group. Once a status equilibrium is established, it is challenged only rarely. Conflict among male gorillas, for example, occurs very infrequently (Schaller, 1964); they seem to be well adjusted to one another and rarely make errors in behavior that defy the dominance pattern and lead to strife. But the group is very small, and the males almost always keep their distance from one another. The same cannot be said for the macaques and baboons studied by Chance. In their competition for supremacy, the ability to control the expression of motives at high levels of social excitement is the crucial factor; Chance believes this ability played a role in evolution before the period of maximum cortical expansion. Equilibrium at this presymbolic level allows for only a narrow range of social cooperation.

Konrad Lorenz (1966) argues that aggression is more carefully controlled in most animals than it is in man. Members of two different animal species frequently fight to a fatal finish. Members of the same species seldom go so far; at the last minute, the animal taking a beating makes a gesture of submission, and that gesture compels the victor, no matter how furious, to spare the victim's life. Lorenz speculates that it was so hard for one primitive man to kill another that nature never bothered to develop an instinctual safeguard against homicide. Then, with the aid of his powerful brain, man discovered weapons, and a creature created for flight was abruptly transformed into one capable of attack.

Nevertheless Coon, using the Australian Tiwi as his model, argues that early male hominids had to have considerably greater intelligence and tolerance of stress than the monkeys and apes in order to accommodate to the status customs of their species. If a male was successful, he would live at the center of activity in his group and gain the prestige needed to have several wives. Less successful men might survive, but in relative solitude. Since a man can have several wives while a woman can be impregnated by only one man at a time, the man is able to have many more children than the woman. Selection thus favors characteristics borne by the male, and the dominant male would have a strategic position in the course of evolutionary development. The key is his "women-getting ability," a function of both stress tolerance and superior intelligence. Moreover, those qualities that were specifically selected because of their usefulness in securing women might also have facilitated the essentials of a human kind of family nurturance. They provided man with the symbolic and tolerance capabilities that promote cooperative work habits within the family group.

This approach, however, cannot be regarded as a substitute for Sherwood Washburn's (1959) generally more acceptable explanation of the rapid increase in the size of the hominid brain. Washburn explained how a threefold enlargement of the brain could have taken place during the relatively brief period of the Pleistocene, from about 550 cc. in the Australopithecine to 1,500 cc. in modern man. This is an incredibly rapid evolutionary change and can only be explained by a comparable change in the hominid condition. Washburn ascribes the selective advantage of an expanded brain to a critically important development in the behavior of man during this period: man's fabrication and use of tools. The new adaptive pattern bestowed a great advantage upon men with larger brains who were more adept and inventive in the use of tools, and the pattern created a selective superiority for such men.

It also established a new basis for male authority because the innovation of hunting large game with tools could only be carried out by adult men (Washburn and DeVore, 1961). The male role as economic provider had certainly appeared by the Middle Pleistocene, based on the cooperative killing of big game *to be shared* with the women and children. Nonhunting members of the band had to adapt to the hunting requirements of the fathers, who in turn could be expected to apportion the products of the hunt. It was apparent to all that these men must be given complete authority for the accomplishment of their work, so dangerous and yet so vital to the entire group.

Coon's theory is by no means incompatible with this one, however, and is in fact a useful adjunct to it; as Coon suggests, the same qualities that gave superior power in the use of tools could also have afforded an advantage in mating. In this way a process is isolated—mating superiority—that explains how the advantage of a larger brain was transmitted to succeeding generations.

In addition to symbolic behavior, the nurturing, cooperative behavior of the male, along with the observance of incest taboos, constitute what is distinctively human in the family of Homo sapiens (Mead, 1953; Sahlins, 1959). The founding of incest taboos was probably a function of the social norms invented for fatherhood. The primary incest taboo, that against mother-son mating, seems to be inextricably related to the integration of father within the family social unit. In order to draw father in and hold him, it was probably necessary to regularize sex relations between husband and wife, ruling out any possibility of sex relations between mother and son.

One should not infer that the woman promised fidelity in order to get her man or that early man was wise enough to recognize the social importance of the incest taboo. The necessity of this taboo for family survival was by no means apparent. But any hominid group that did not hit upon the prohibition of incest simply failed to sustain the minimum level of social cooperation and economic sharing needed for group survival. Furthermore, without the extension of the mother-son taboo to father-daughter and brother-sister sex relations, the harmful effects of inbreeding in a small, slow-breeding population might have been disastrous (Aberle, *et al.*, 1964). Nor would the population have had the cooperative advantage of kinship bonds between the diverse primary families that incest taboos guarantee. The incest taboo, which forced marriage outside the nuclear family, is an associative mechanism that cements relatively small groups together within wider unities, as Yonina Talmom (1964) has demonstrated in a study of mate selection in the Israeli Kibbutzim. Only with the early development of such taboos could the human group survive, and its development was contingent upon the invention of social codes for fatherhood.

Thus, fatherhood was a strategic invention in the development of human culture. Margaret Mead (1953) may be correct when she claims that most women will want to have and care for children unless they are taught—"outraged"—not to want them, but this certainly cannot be said for men. Even human females, by contrast with other primate females, are greatly freed from hormonal controls over sexual behavior and parenting. Replacement of the female oestrus cycle, with its rhythmical rutting season, by the human menstrual cycle and continuous female sexual receptivity must have accompanied the hominid evolution. But because of the inevitable importance of the mother's role in infant care, mother-infant nurturance follows a similar pattern the world over—much more than that between father and child. Foreign students in the United States, especially from countries where the father retains strong patriarchal prerogatives, often observe that the American mother is not greatly different from mothers they know back home, despite her free-swinging ways when she is away from the children, but the American father, who is often rather weak and indifferent, violates their most fervent conception of fatherhood.

We have seen that "father" played an important role in the earliest establishment of the human family. His main continuing functions are to provide material resources for his family and to serve as an adaptive and stabilizing domestic influence, reflecting the instrumental orientation of men and their key position linking the family to its larger social environment. But men in their capacity as fathers are not visionaries, and they do not ordinarily speak in favor of new social developments. If father knows best, it is because the conventional wisdom happens to remain relevant in the midst of social change.

CHAPTER II

The Dimensions of Fatherhood

Certain paternal roles are given special emphasis in all societies, and there are inevitably preferred styles by which to play them. Virtually all fathers are expected to work, for example, but the social significance attached to their work varies enormously. Anxiety and stress vested in the occupational role in America breeds a corresponding masculine style: the driving, success-oriented, failure-frightened father. But since there are many avenues to success and many stages of adequacy this side of failure, even this pattern may take different forms. Moreover, the father who is alienated from his own job may still be success-oriented in a manner dictated by the American achievement ethic, through identification with the success potentialities of his children.

Because the father role is a basic one in social affairs, its performance simultaneously fulfills expectations in several overlapping dimensions of society. Fathers in a wage economy are expected to spend time earning income to be spent by their families, and thus the man, as father, works for his family and, as employee, for his boss. Each man brings his own individuality to this complex set of roles and hence develops his own fathering style.

In this chapter we shall describe and explain the primary dimensions of paternal behavior in terms of the requirements of society. The actions of fathers can be viewed as a collective response to social necessity, not simply a collection of responses of individual men each acting in terms of his own self-generated personality traits. Thus, the community establishes general expectations for fathers, but it also generates innumerable social agencies that help fathers to do what is expected of them, to reward them for living up to expectations, and to rebuke them when they fail. Even paternal ego states are socially patterned.

Since the impulses of men are conditioned by the social order, that is, by their historical experience together, a purely psychological approach to the explanation of fatherhood in particular or social regularities in general cannot rise above tautology. In fact, much of our behavior can only be explained by the unique pressures of the immediate situation; both general role prescriptions *and* personality traits are often beside the point, as Erving Goffman (1959) has shown. But a strictly situational approach, recognizing that no two situations in life are exactly alike, does not lend itself to the study of the general functions of father or to the cultivation of a historical view of his role.

Unfortunately, fatherhood has rarely been a subject of interest to historians. Nor have students of the family been in the habit of thinking of father in a historical way, distinguishing, let us say, between primitive, peasant, medieval, Renaissance, and modern fathers.

One must bear in mind that what some fathers do and what all fathers do, or what fathers can do and what they ordinarily do, are quite different things. Some fathers engage in family acts that are totally unfamiliar to most adult men. A great many fathers may be crucial in advancing their children's search for "the height of the times," but this does not seem to be a self-conscious effort of the majority of men. We shall be concerned with both the universal and the incidental aspects of fatherhood, but above all we want to recognize which is which.

As an organizing device, it is possible to isolate two general dimensions of fatherhood that overlap to some extent and constitute the universals of paternity. Each dimension consists of a clustering of paternal roles serving an important social function found in *all* cultures, although in each case the clusters are patterned differently. The first is the *survival* dimension, in which father acts to sustain the physical livelihood and value premises of his family, and, indeed, those of society and the species. The second is the *expressive* dimension, in which father ideally contributes a sense of security to his family and adds a sense of pleasure or significance to its activities.

The Survival Dimension

Father engages in a number of activities in behalf of the survival of his family and, ultimately, in behalf of the preservation of society itself. The typical man must reproduce and, as father, help sustain the life of his offspring during their dependency. He teaches his children certain basic skills for survival, models for them his unique means of accommodating to life, copes with a variety of real or potential family crises, and cooperates with other people, nonkinsmen as well as family members, in the routine tasks of survival.

Reproduction Reproduction is father's most obvious function, and yet only in the earliest stages of man's cultural development, if ever, has it posed a problem for man's survival. Almost all men are biologically capable of having children since there is a strong evolutionary bias against those who cannot; all men have had fertile fathers. But now we know that men are about as often the cause of infertility as women and that the explanation must be found in nonbiological considerations. A man's ability to perform the biological role in parenthood is much more dependent upon his "emotional frame of mind" than is the case for his wife's ability (Phadke, 1958). Unlike women, men must reach a climax in sex relations in order for conception to occur, which calls for the proper psychological components of sexual arousal. But even this requirement has never constituted a problem for the survival of mankind.

There is, in fact, much less danger of biological discontinuity today than was true in the past, and fear of it from the point of view of society at large is almost nonexistent. It has become quite anomalous to think of intercourse and reproduction as religious deeds calling for special foods and stimulants when the male's sexual powers begin to lag, as was recently the pattern among Moslem husbands (Beck, 1957). We do not worry about keeping the human race going any more; that is, we no longer think of this as a fertility problem. Fertility magic has been replaced by scientific birth control and perhaps by the fear of nuclear extinction.

Among the advocates of bold action in the face of population growth, Bentley Glass has argued that the problem is so serious that persons should now be required to obtain a license before having children. If they passed a test at a "genetic clinic" to determine their chances of having defective offspring, they would be permitted to marry and have two children. Glass would allow a tax exemption only for the first child; a third child would add to the family's taxable income. Penalties for unlicensed births would be severe; Glass suggests sterilization as a fitting punishment.

Margaret Mead (1967) believes we now need two different forms of marriage. The first would be "individual marriage": young people would live together without having children (with the aid of the pill) and could easily dissolve the union if it became tedious. The other would be "parent marriage," more difficult to obtain: here the couple would be allowed to rear children (Mead seems to condone occasional adultery to relieve the inherent monotony of such an arrangement).

It may be that in the future people will have fewer children, and an increasing number of people, in response to genetic counseling, will have none at all. The eminent biologist Robert Morison (1967) envisions the day when adults may feel as pleased with themselves for *not* having children as they now feel for having them. Along with other scientists, he has suggested abandoning the family as the unit of human reproduction and thus separating the phenomena of sexual attraction from those of reproduction. He feels that this combination is becoming incompatible, but acknowledges the persistence of a gigantic problem: finding new ways to care for infants and children in an atmosphere that lacks the traditional reinforcement of sexual and emotional drives.

It should be added, however, that freedom to become a parent is one of the least interfered with freedoms we have. In the prevailing climate of opinion it is sacred and above open debate. Should it become a live issue, and perhaps it will in a generation or so, we may find that many of the discussants are actually more concerned about the social and psychological potentialities of young couples than about their genetic weaknesses.

In any case, the average man in industrial societies does not regard the siring of children as a central life interest. He does not possess the traditional urge to conceive in great numbers, and he is not obsessed with the desire for a son to continue his name and family line. Today many grandfathers do not seem to regard the birth of a grandchild as the source of biological renewal; at least they are less likely to than grandmothers (Neugarten and Weinstein, 1964). The diminished concern for male babies is part of the complicated chain of developments that has brought about an upgrading of the status of women along with the need for relatively fewer pregnancies to sustain any population level. The rise of science, modern medicine, public-health efforts, and effective birth control enable community survival through a low birth rate and long life expectancy. Clearly these conditions, in which the problems of immediate survival have largely been solved, induce parents to stress the quality of their children rather than their quantity.

Contingent upon these changes is the fact that more is expected of a man now than merely the ability to reproduce. In the nineteenth century, "sexual responsibility" referred to the wife's duty to submit to her husband's sexual advances (Davis, 1963). Now women, too, are supposed to enjoy sex, not simply provide it, and husbands are urged to assist them in their pleasure. The marriage manuals tell married men to nurture their wives' erotic sensibilities, and Albert Ellis (1963) has boldly extended this advice to unmarried men. (The new view apparently has not reached the very poor yet, where sex is still the man's pleasure and the woman's duty [Rainwater, 1964].)

In a sense, not agreeable to all to be sure, virility has been enriched, and a sexual code at least partially separating sex and reproduction, even separating sex and marriage, has already been popularized. The democratization of sexual expression as an art to be cultivated has thus been associated with elimination of the fertility problem.

Although we can now speak in a superior way about the splitting of sex and reproduction, the father's biological role has not always been correctly understood, and it has even been ignored. The Arapesh, for example, thought the child was conceived gradually, a product of steady accretions of semen from the father and blood from the mother. Trobriand Islanders apparently did not understand the causal relationship between coition and conception until the arrival of Europeans. Because of ignorance of the male's role in reproduction, almost all early people, including the ancient Hebrews, believed that barrenness was the fault of the female. In matrilineal societies there may be little need or concern for determining paternity, while in some fraternal polyandrous groups the elder brother is automatically designated as father, or a ceremonial act performed by the mother may be used to identify him.

Misconceptions and ignorance still persist. Even where the reproductive process is studied scientifically the establishment of biological paternity is subject to question and remains ambiguous to this day. Our contemporary science of genetics cannot tell us who the father is, only that a certain man could or could not be the progenitor.

It is significant, nevertheless, that modern knowledge of both reproduction and the psychodynamics of sex is quite useful in overcoming sexual fears and incapacities among married couples (Friedman, 1962). Genetic or heredity counseling is becoming available, although very few people yet know of its existence or where to seek help. Artificial insemination has also become feasible, in spite of our suspicions of it. It is by no means crucial for social survival, however, nor does there seem to be any need yet for "test-tube babies," which we can not produce anyway. With no shortage of infants and, in fact, a surplus born to unmarried mothers, we can afford our bias against artificial insemination, especially since the bias encourages adoption (Vernon and Boadway, 1959).

But some people are thinking about the future. Hermann Muller (1963) suggests establishing banks for storing the sperm of gifted men, perhaps millions of sperm from each man. It would then be possible for a woman to be artificially inseminated with the genetic properties of an exceptional man, one who may have lived years before. She could have her pick.

Implicit in this discussion is the proposition that the big changes in patterns of human reproduction have occurred only recently, with the growth of industrialization. Studies of the differences between primitive and peasant societies do not support generalizations about the differentiation of father's reproductive activities, except perhaps in the case of the marriage of more than one man to a single woman. Polyandry is found only in nonliterate societies, or as a "backward" enclave in peasant societies; it has no viability in industrial communities. If normal sex ratios are assumed, polyandry can sustain only a low birth rate and is thus self-limiting.

Polygyny is found in both nonliterate and peasant societies, especially among men of high status, but it always becomes incompatible with industrialization. The biparental pattern of rearing children is inevitably weak in a polygynous system, since care of the children is assumed almost completely by mothers. Admittedly, some of our own basic values concerning fatherhood and male dominance were initiated under polygynous circumstances, perpetuated for example in the Old Testament account of the ancient Hebrews. But polygyny has thrived primarily outside the territory associated with Western Christianity and is invariably brought under attack by industrial development due to the upgrading effect of the latter upon men of low status and upon women in general.

In a sense, industrialization democratizes fatherhood, although the evolution of Homo sapiens itself has had that general effect; by contrast with human males, nonhuman mammalian males reproduce only if they happen to be relatively strong and aggressive. (In the course of man's technological development grandfatherhood too has been democratized, since the average father now lives to see his children marry

[Glick, 1955].) The genetic implications of the democratization of fatherhood are beyond the scope of this book; suffice it to say that there seems to be no reason to worry about being overrun by the progeny of "inferiors" (Dobzhansky, 1967). The trend is toward greater variability in the human physique (Brace and Montagu, 1965), which may very well be a good thing. But for man, especially modern man, the key to effective performance is probably not so much the physical state of the body as the quality of the intellect, and that is a function of educational facilities, not eugenics.

Material Support The human community needs fathers, but not just their sperm; all societies expect more of "father" than the biological sine qua non of impregnation. Writers of science fiction have plotted fanciful stories in which the biological work of men is their only "family" act, but an imagination grounded in studies of man's historical experience cannot truthfully conceive of a society that lets fathers off so easily. Perhaps Philip Slater (1961) was being facetious when he argued, as did Robert Briffault (1931), that the only time two parents are necessary is when the child is conceived. At least some further effort in behalf of physical nurturance and material assistance is required of men. In fact, the major function of the concept of legitimacy is to clarify male responsibilities in the care and support of children. Illegitimacy represents a threat to the orderly division of society into economic and social units based on kinship and to the orderly distribution of male responsibilities in this regard.

The invention of paternity—that is, the creation of a set of rules obligating men to assist mothers and to provide for infants and children—is required for a human type of family system. The biological father, the male progenitor, is not as important as the social or nurturant father precisely because the latter has a family role to play after conception.

Although all cultures have ways of establishing fatherhood, they do not necessarily imply that the man so designated be the biological progenitor. Children may be raised in the home of the wife's relatives, reducing the husband and biological father to the status of a privileged visitor. Men may provide for their sisters as well as their wives, or instead of their wives, and the brother may also be given the dominant position in the family of his sister (Opler, 1950). Stepfatherhood is found in all cultures.

In matrilineal societies, where the man lives among his wife's people, the biological father is generally not as important as he is in patrilineal groups. Women in matrilineal societies take care of the household, and the social functions of father are often handled by male kinsmen.

Judith Blake (1961) has described the matrifocal family structure in Jamaica in which the husband is quite often absent. Women are relatively free to engage in sex relations with transitory males who have virtually no role in raising the resultant offspring; they are taken care of by the mother's family. But men are by no means relieved of all family obligations. *Husbands* can come and go, their minimal function being procreation, but these men must assist in their mothers' and sisters' families.

In patrilineal societies, on the other hand, women are not relieved of their responsibility as mothers, especially in the early years, while husbands have important family obligations other than reproduction. Since loss of the mother through divorce is a greater possibility in patrilineal societies, and also a more critical loss, wedding rituals are usually highly developed as a means of strengthening the marriage bond and lowering the divorce rate.

Many anthropologists have noted that three roles define the father-son relationship in patrilineal societies: the son, his father, and the son's mother's brother. George Homans (1962) points out that in such an arrangement the father often has "jural" authority over the boy: he has the right to give orders and the son is obliged to obey them, but their relationship is marked by formality and restraint. Relationships between the boy and his mother's brother are more often characterized by informality. The uncle, though the boy's superior, frequently plays the role of intimate friend, adviser, and helper to the boy. (A similar pattern is sometimes found in matrilineal societies, except that the roles of father and maternal uncle are reversed.) Thus the biological relationship between father and son is superseded by a more important social relationship that includes a third male. Gerald Berreman (1962) has supplied "monandry" as a name for this relationship; he suggests that "monandry" occurs when the role of social father is one man's exclusive responsibility, and "polyandry" occurs when the role is shared. Thus Berreman wrenches "polyandry" from its more conventional usage. In Berreman's terminology the United States would be a "monandrous" society.

There are strong sanctions in all societies against "just anybody" being the nurturant father of the child. In our own society this is reflected in the careful supervision of legitimate adoption proceedings and also in the fact that artificial insemination with the use of the husband's semen is much more acceptable than the use of an anonymous donor's semen (Vernon and Boadway, 1959). We equate the biological father with the social father. But semen from an anonymous donor is in turn much more acceptable than semen from someone other than the husband whose identity is known to the family. It would intensify problems of the social father in our family system if the biological father was a known third party.

Although the family division of labor may be complex, the most common social expectation is that a father figure will supply the raw materials for family and social survival, while mother's more characteristic duty is to prepare them for immediate use. This traditional division of work remains quite apparent today, in spite of the fact that father increasingly helps to prepare family resources for consumption while mother often serves as resource (or income) producer. In fact, throughout history mother has been more thoroughly in charge of her domain than father has been of his. Mother had an important role in food gathering in the earliest human societies; she was the important food producer in hoe cultures and, occasionally even in agricultural societies. As Mabel Rollins (1963) has shown, mother was often an income producer in rural and small-town America before she left home to work in the city. By comparison, father has been considerably less important in the conventional women's activities of child care, food preparation, and housekeeping. The unique fathering trait of the human male is his habit of sharing food with his family; his "breadwinner" role is but a facet of this fundamental food-sharing activity.

In almost all societies the family whose father cannot perform his subsistence function is seriously handicapped, and father is still the potentially weak link in the chain of material support. No doubt there have been families with inadequate fathers in all kinds of societies; they have been much more common in peasant cultures than we are prone to acknowledge, as Oscar Lewis' writings have revealed, and such fathers are relatively numerous among Negro families in the United States today. But the early industrial period in Europe and America stands out as the most severely disorganizing period for father in the history of Western man. The most critical breakdown of paternal nurturance patterns occurred as the factory system was emerging in the seventeenth, eighteenth, and nineteenth centuries. This was the period of cheap labor, long working hours, and the emergence of the urban working classes. Overworked and underpaid, the man was no longer a symbol of authority, and often could not retain the respect of his family. Although women and children worked for low wages too, fathering stability was undermined more than that of any other domestic role as home and work were separated and men lost the historical basis for their strategic familial influence (Mogey, 1957).

In a broader context, the key historical distinction concerning father's support function is between subsistence and money economies, separating in a general way nonliterate and peasant societies from modern industrial ones. In subsistence societies, father secures resources directly for his family, especially through hunting, fishing, and agriculture. In money economies he works for wages; he earns rather than makes a living and thus becomes the breadwinner in the modern sense.

Whether the economy is based on subsistence work or wage labor, father's work has always been the key social role linking the family and the larger community. The family's status in the community of families is established by father's work, and the material well-being of his family reflects the social significance of that work. Retention of the family's position is contingent upon father's continuing performance. Boys learn as they grow up that they must make a family effort, which is the primary strategy of social control over males in virtually all the cultures in the world. The socialist alternative—production for a collective of nonkinsmen—has yet to become a primary source of motivation, even in ostensibly socialist societies (which is not to say that it can never succeed). Because father is held accountable for the well-being of his family, he can require members of his family to subordinate their personal plans and interests to the needs of his work. Thus his role is assigned to him by prevailing social assumptions, and, through the corollary family authority vested in him, his family is subject to the social controls of the economic system.

With industrialization, values based upon individual achievement gain in favor, and kinship as a basis for the assignment of work and status is reduced in importance (Goode, 1963). The family budget system is formalized as the money economy takes over and it becomes necessary to develop new social strategies for providing for families whose males are inadequate providers: mothers must work for wages too, and welfare agencies are established. The chief agent of social control within the typical family is still father—the breadwinner—and his dependability continues to rest upon his possession of a skill that is in urgent economic demand. But the means of acquiring such a skill has become more complicated and difficult, and many fathers fail to qualify.

Associated with the rise of the money economy and its complex commodity and labor markets is the fact that large numbers of men and fathers are more easily managed by directors of great economic enterprises. As a result of father's manipulability, the management of the entire economic system is greatly facilitated. Rather sudden changes in the resource potential of families and in their well-being become feasible. Both the distribution of money and the distribution of services in kind are brought under more centralized control. Thus, fatherhood is increasingly a dependent social role, subject to the decisions of administrators and legislators who act as representatives of a variety of social interests, "the family" being only one.

Commitment to Order Father is in a strategic position to contribute to two essential aspects of social organization (Cohen, 1959): he can help make clear to his children certain general rules governing social interaction, and he can promote a desire in the children to live by these rules. Although we like to think that each person decides for himself how to act and what to believe, indoctrination is a universal family, and father, function. Whatever innate wisdom children may be said to have, they are not automatically equipped to know what is best for themselves in choosing among cultural alternatives. Fathers may not know what is best either, but children cannot have equal access to all aspects of culture in any case, and fathers are in a position to exercise considerable control over what reaches their children. Because indoctrination maintains essential "rules of the game," "pattern maintenance" in Talcott Parsons' phrase, it necessarily serves a survival function.

Due to the continuous and intense emotional nature of the parent-child relationship, what we learn from our parents tends to become ritualistic and dogmatic. Parents program the subconscious behavior and attitudes of the child. By comparison, what we learn from others is received in a more pragmatic way, and the individual is freer to pick what he can use and ignore the rest. The parental imprint is indelible, although the values of fathers, in the process of transmission to their sons, may be transformed into something quite different from what the fathers had in mind (Inkeles, 1963; Elder, 1964).

Father serves in the capacity of teacher, censor, and promoter, not simply because he is vested with authority, but because he is usually in a strategic position to make decisions vitally affecting his children. Furthermore, his competence is different from mother's, and his knowledge usually turns to more general considerations. Mother's interests and expertise are typically restricted to household activities and matters of everyday routine; father can deal with "global" problems of purpose if any member of the household can, and he has a broader perspective on the balance between cosmopolitanism and provincialism.

Thus he has a hand in transmitting very general cultural orientations to his children, but he is also useful in passing on those patterns found only in certain groups within the larger society; Catholic fathers in the United States, for example, act out general American values shared by all as well as those social principles unique to the American Catholic community. If a child is strongly attached to his father, he will usually become attached to the larger organizations with which his father is identified (Spaulding, 1966). Ethnic as well as religious and racial groups may very well continue to serve an "identity-bestowing" function for a long time to come (Glazer and Moynihan, 1963), although not much is known about father's specific role in this process; it is apparently neither very direct nor a consequence of self-conscious design (Radke Yarrow, Trager, and Miller, 1952). We know that the "culture of poverty" is transmitted from parent to child and includes orientations and sensibilities encompassing the role of father that help to perpetuate a style of impoverishment quite distinct from that of people who have never been poor (Schneiderman, 1964).

Father's influence on the social climate within which his children's many experiences occur is perhaps most important. It establishes the conditions for his basic value, or moral, function: to develop a generalized commitment to social order. His existence personifies for his children the inevitability of rules, and these rules become as natural as his presence. Of course the rules are implicit in the ordered behavior of almost everyone who enters the life of the growing child, but father commonly comes to "stand for" the absolute necessity of social order more than any other person. Even the social pattern that mother establishes is typically legitimized by the larger, more insistent parent lurking in the background.

The fact that society contrives to safeguard father's authority serves as only one of his controls. Father does not govern his children simply because people think he ought to, nor is that the only reason he can get away with it. His power rests on certain personal characteristics possessed by almost every adult male and is implicit in the relationships that typically develop between the father and his children.

He is bigger and stronger than his children, for example, and therefore he looms—he literally towers—over them. He speaks with a deep voice, modulated to give incontestable emphasis when he really means business; mother's efforts to create the same effect are usually feeble by comparison. In his deportment, father is almost certain to appear as an ominous force while his children are small. (Children characteristically perceive adults to be more menacing than adults themselves can appreciate. Most of us cannot remember how small we once were or how it felt.) Father can pick up the child and put him exactly where he chooses for several years after mother has lost this power; he can physically restrain the child longer, even terrorize him. In this way father is the embodiment of a basic form of social control: coercive power. And therefore some people can never see their fathers as mortal men.

Father already knows the ropes in his community, of course, and therefore has an immense advantage over his children. He can make decisions. His life is usually ordered in a fairly effective way; if it is not, his authority is almost certainly weakened. He is *socialized* as his children are not, and they need him much more than he needs them. For this reason, and because of his superior size and knowledge, plus the fact that he is the adult male they see most often, the children almost inevitably organize a major part of their personal energies in response to his life style; they identify with him. Even when father is not present the child knows that father must be somewhere, that he cares about what happens, and that he himself will feel better if he lives up to father's standards. In this way father's symbolic presence carries the authority of *respect*. Of course maintaining respect becomes more difficult as the children grow older and acquire independent means of appraising their parents, but by then the commitment to social order has been made.

As an object of identification, father's routine behavior is endowed with the properties of social control. The child has no choice in the matter; he becomes like his father by the nature of the intimate and repetitive interaction between man and child. Reflecting father's expectations, a "conscience" is internalized at the same time that the child is borrowing his father's mannerisms. But father's authority extends beyond the identification process, and because it does he can exercise control in situations where the child's inner restraints are inadequate. Father is an agent of both internal and external control, and the child responds to him in terms of both his respect for the man and his respect for the man's power.

In addition to father's functions within the family, the concept and imagery of fatherhood in the community at large has the power to induce people to commit themselves to social causes, which, without family symbolism, would be too abstract to capture their imagination. Thus, the nation-state becomes the fatherland, and loyalty to the state takes on some of the characteristics of filial loyalty. Priests are called "father," as is God, the Great Parent. Society needs a man in the household for very practical reasons, and it has made use of the image of a superfather for social purposes encompassing entire nations.

But now we find it increasingly difficult to use fatherhood as an all-embracing icon. As society becomes more complex, it becomes less possible for any one person to symbolize its order. Consequently personalized representations of society are diffused, different ones being used in the social spheres of religion, politics, education, work, recreation, and science. The clergyman as a father figure competes with the college professor, the physician, the coach, the politician, the lawyer, and so on. It is just possible that as the father's powerful role in the family has diminished, quasi-fathers must take over to an ever greater extent in the larger world—in the professions and bureaucracies, and in the images created for mass persuasion.

Robert Morison (1967) has called attention to the anomaly that parents have retained their position as moral authorities for their children although their place as authorities in purely informational and scientific matters has been replaced by those outside the home. The family is a fine mechanism for transmitting conventional wisdom in a relatively static society, he argues, but a poor one for assimilating and transmitting new knowledge essential to survival in a rapidly moving world. The farm boy, for example, cannot learn farming in any comprehensive way from his father any more. Morison contends that this dualism between the family and modern knowledge surely cannot last.

It would seem, however, that it can—and must last. The

family provides the prime motivational and moral basis for seeking scientific advancement (or the desire to run a farm) and at the same time is the main source of moral continuity in the community. Science does indeed generate its own morality, but it can supply neither a flawless nor a total product. Science tackles and resolves man's problems a little at a time; the moral framework of life is much more inclusive than that part of life for which there are clear-cut scientific answers. It is in the broad area of moral ambiguity that the legitimate moral function of the family flourishes. Thus, Morison is quite correct when he suggests that it is ridiculous to argue that parents should, through their right to veto the fluoridation of water, be allowed to decide whether or not their children shall have dental caries; but it does not follow that parents should have no rights at all with regard to the management of their children. Science and its morality are not yet wise enough to replace the home.

Although modern parents have been stripped of the assurance that they know what is best for their children and are not even sure what is not good for them, parents cannot abandon their role in encouraging certain values and activities upon their children. This parental function remains not merely a parental privilege, but a responsibility. Parents now often find that their job is not to train and care for their children directly but to make decisions concerning which agencies should do the job for them, and which ones should be allowed to exercise an influence. Parents are necessarily culture brokers for their children before the "age of consent"; they encourage and facilitate access to some parts of culture, censor others, and unconsciously or ambivalently screen out still others in response to their own preferences and sensibilities.

But the role of the modern father in this regard has become relatively less important. Mother now plays a larger role in screening cultural influences in the lives of her children as she moves more freely in civic affairs and is no longer totally engrossed in household functions.

Survival Skills and Personal Styles Father's role in the transmission of basic eating, sleeping, elimination, work, and health habits to his children falls within the survival dimension. These habits constitute the practical, everyday resourcefulness needed to keep the individual and his primary social world intact. Just how they are conveyed remains somewhat mysterious, although the role of mother, especially in the establishment of "infant disciplines," has been studied extensively. Father's role has been almost thoroughly ignored.

Nevertheless it certainly seems that father influences mother's activities in this regard for good or ill, and that he transmits to his son certain motor skills and body controls associated with masculinity that are ultimately related to male work performance. Father is the male adult whom the children see most often; he is more likely than anyone else to symbolize *manhood* to his children as a living reality, and at least as likely as mother to be a model for simply being human.

None of father's imitable habits go undetected by children, nor does his style and facility in the use of language fail to affect their verbal habits. Even his diffidence, his unique combination of timidity and temerity, is likely to be refractively imitated by the child, although with a different effect on son than daughter (Paivio, 1964). The child must learn survival skills, but he must also develop a personal style that is compatible with the recurrent themes of his culture. Hopefully the child will lay claim to some niche of particular usefulness in his community. Most fathers have achieved a serviceable individuality themselves and can therefore help their children acquire one; children whose fathers have failed in this regard are not so fortunate. As an agent of personality development, father bridges the gap between the maintenance of cultural patterns and the continuity of distinctive skills within them.

A parallel can be seen between the processes of biological and social continuity. Each father perpetuates his own physical type according to the principles of genetics, enabling a reproduction of the range of physical varieties within the breeding population. Each father also perpetuates his unique qualities, but according to the principles of socialization; this enables the transmission from one generation to the next of the total range of skills, interests, and personal styles within each culture. Each child is very much like his parents in manners and physical type; collectively, the current population resembles the previous one, and a continuity of general patterns composed of distinctive individualities is maintained, although never perfectly (Wrong, 1961).

The preservation of father's social specialty is in fact more crucial to society than the preservation of his physical type, although biological patterns are undoubtedly the more stable of the two. Fathers today are not much different organically from what they were in the Stone Age.

The preservation of specialties seems to be an area in which the interests and skills that parents exhibit in their actual behavior are much more important than any "empty" wishes they may have for their children. It is fairly easy, for example, for parents who themselves have musical expertise to instill musical interests in their children. The same is true for reading habits and scholarly curiosity. As Jerome Kagan and Marion Freeman (1963) have observed, the parent who is involved in intellectual pursuits can foster a more intense intellectuality in his child than one who preaches the importance of academic excellence but does not practice it himself and does not really know how.

The point at issue seems to apply to behavior of a very general and complex nature. By the way father relates to his wife, for example, he serves as a model for the husband role in the eyes of his children. We don't know exactly how it is done, but we do know that parents pass on some part of the formula for marital accommodation to their children. If they have succeeded in marriage, their children are more likely to succeed.

The transmission of personal qualities includes undesirable traits; fathering seems to have something to do with criminal recidivism, for example (Litwack, 1961). Fathers who do time in jail somehow predispose their sons to that vulnerability, not through imitative and identification processes as a rule, but through their inability to stabilize the family and to serve as a constructive object of imitation and identification.

The paternal specialty of greatest significance, at least the one that has been studied the most, is the man's work skill. The more or less automatic succession of the son into his father's line of work is most evident in areas where work remains a family affair and in occupations that are not included in the nation's formal training system. Thus, for example, farming is passed on from one generation to the next to a much greater extent than other occupations. The traditional father-son work pattern is also quite evident in certain marginal occupational lines; carnival skills, for example, are still passed from parent to child for the most part.

It is apparent that as the father's skills become only indirectly related to problems of physical survival, his role as teacher and expert is greatly reduced. Industrial societies are less dependent upon the time-honored motor skills and body controls for survival, and hence other learning tasks for the boy are now more important, especially his need to develop a rather generalized linguistic, or symbolic, competence such as that taught in the modern school system. The contemporary father is much less likely than his preindustrial counterpart to indoctrinate his son in the primary work lore that he has mastered; he doesn't have the time to do it, and he probably wouldn't know how if he had the time. Hence professional teachers have taken over.

The sons of professional men exemplify the contemporary pattern of father-son continuity. They are much more likely to follow in their fathers' footsteps than the sons of men in clerical, sales, or service work (Current Population Reports, 1964), but the fathers do not teach professional work lore in any direct way. Instead, they encourage their sons to get appropriate education (and they are in a position to assist them along the way). In part, father-son continuity in the professions is the result of successfully urging appropriate aspirations upon boys; the career goals of adolescents in the higher social classes are more ambitious and more realistic than those in the lower classes. They reach a little higher, and their aspirations are combined with preparations that are quite in keeping with the goals they have set. It seems likely that a major reason for this is the effectiveness—and attractiveness—of the father as a model for what the son would like to become.

Although Talcott Parsons (1964) has referred to the increased "capitalization" of the modern household due to the spread of home ownership and other forms of domestic affluence, it seems more correct in the present context to say that the family has been *de*capitalized. The family was once a producing unit, and its capital, in the form of land, equipment, and skills, was transmitted from parents to children. Now the family is a consumer or budgetary unit, and only in the upper classes and the upper levels of the middle classes is wealth handed down in significant quantities. The primary strategy available to most middle- and some lower-class families is to help their children do well in school and to provide for the encouragement of their talents. Father is increasingly called upon to assist and support his wife in the effort to develop a viable (or vendible) personal style in the children. The role of parents becomes one of facilitating their children's educability; most parents are not in a position to bequeath either a marketable skill or the kind of capital that is external to the training potential of the child.

The family does retain an important "patronage" function, however. Young people with career ambitions of a marginal nature—those wishing to become artists, for example—are not supported in our industrial system as are promising young men who want to be physicists or doctors. They have a longer period of dependency and may never be able to make a living in their chosen fields. The family serves a useful function in many cases by supporting offspring in the pursuit of specialties not encouraged or subsidized by the culture at large (Schapiro, 1964). Such individuals are more likely to receive comfort and support from mother than from father. Father is almost always stereotyped as the less congenial parent when the child, especially the son, chooses an unusual or unremunerative vocation, and we know that stereotypes are self-fulfilling.

There is evidence that today many adolescent boys simply do not want to do the same kind of work their fathers have done (Epperson, 1964), although these reactions may be no more negative than in the past; historical data on this point are not available. It does seem that father's work is less likely to be idealized now, especially the work of semi-skilled and clerical employees, the very kinds of work that emerge so plentifully in industrial nations.

Father's role in transmitting practical technical skills has become marginal; he transmits do-it-yourself lore and enthusiasms about recreation to his son, if anything at all, and a large part of his repertoire of skills, ideas, and information are abandoned, or merely ignored, by the family line. Even father's obiter dicta must compete with the marginal observations of teachers and celebrities and may be overshadowed by the carefully tailored phrases of a favored college professor.

Father's position is in some respects analogous to the historical plight of hunting. Once hunting was a crucial activity; now it is "sport," engaged in as a token of masculinity or in search of the magic stuff of maleness. Hunting skills are no longer survival skills, and they may or may not be passed on to the son. They certainly need not be, which is true of much of father's lore in the modern city.

But it remains true that certain kinds of leisure activities are still preserved primarily because the lore and the pleasure in its use are transmitted from father to son. Fishing is a good example; few fishing addicts have nonaddict fathers. Many men may put more genuine effort into leisure skills than into those with which they earn a living.

We must remember, however, that mothers have the major role in supervising play when children are young. Father may be greatly concerned about what his children do in their free time, but mother is the one who has to make arrangements, serve as chauffeur, see that the piano lessons are done, and so on. Even so, father's intellectual interests, hobbies, skills in singing, collecting coins, making pottery, and so on—have a reasonably good chance of being preserved in the life style of his children. In fact, he may influence his daughter almost as much as he influences his son; contemporary fathers seem to have an enlarged role in the socialization of their daughters that is proportional to their loss of control over the training of their sons.

This can be said in spite of the fact that the father may be more important in the early years of his son's training now than at certain times in the past. Our history books tell us that in the Middle Ages boys of the upper classes served as pages to women until a rather advanced age in the childhood cycle, perhaps up to the age of fourteen, and only then were allowed access to the arts of knighthood by the men whom they served as squires. Father may spend more time with both his young son and daughter now than he once did in Western history; mother is the one who has been most tellingly replaced by the school and by other outside influences, such as television, in the early years of childhood.

Handling Crises Still another facet of the survival dimension involves the handling of family crises. Routine strategies for maintaining order are ordinarily followed, and, once established, these procedures rarely claim the conscious attention of family members. But when order breaks down or is openly challenged the need for a new approach assumes an immediate, deliberative significance, and father is customarily expected to help meet the crisis. In fact, it is common for him to take charge, unless he himself is the prime reason the critical condition exists.

When the child becomes sick, for example, mother usually handles the case. If it is a tough one, however, father may be called in as a consultant. Indeed, pediatricians usually work through the mother; she in turn consults father, and hence, characteristic of father's role in crises, he tends to become involved only after the situation has advanced beyond mother's ability to handle it alone.

Family crises are extremely varied, and no attempt will be made to classify them in detail here. In very broad perspective, there are those that arise from within the family, such as severe husband-wife conflicts, and those that intrude upon the family from outside, such as father's call to military service in wartime or a natural disaster disrupting the household. Severe health problems begin as internal concerns, but usually lead to problems of external relations as well. Crises from within the family itself, other than health problems, often indicate that father has failed in some way, since the routine function of father is not to handle crises, but to see that they are avoided. Thus, because internal troubles often imply some degree of paternal inadequacy, and father is the traditional key to family stability, they are the most difficult ones to manage.

Crises thrust upon the family from outside are less disruptive as a rule. Charles Fritz (1961) contends that the social disorganization that occurs in disaster, for example, is essentially a disorganization of secondary community relations. Except momentarily, it does not disorganize established family activities. Primary-group life is in fact strengthened in disaster as a rule and provides the nucleus out of which the community can once again reconstitute itself. The induction of father into military service, on the other hand, is a special case that can drastically impair the equilibrium that a family has already established. It introduces troubles associated with new living arrangements, which would never have appeared but for the war emergency. (Due to a kind of "undernourished-hopes syndrome," couples suffering in an unfortunate marriage often cannot conceive of happier circumstances. Only external pressures can make them see the possibilities of better alternatives through divorce or separation.)

The precise role of father in crises has received hardly any scientific study. The "sturdy-oak ideal" remains virtually universal and seems to carry with it the image of father as a strong and steady hand in adversity. This is especially true where patriarchal values are strong, as in peasant societies. A distinct expectation of the Pakistani father, for example, is that he will take charge in an emergency and settle all major family crises (Brieland and Brieland, 1957). Social expectations of father in both nonliterate and industrial societies seem to be more variable than those in the peasant setting, although this is a very gross generalization. In modern nations, greater scope is given to women in handling critical situations; this is also true in many of the diverse cultures classified as primitive.

The child's reaction to a disastrous event is molded to a very considerable extent by his parents' response to it (Silber, Perry, and Bloch, 1958). To young children, for example, the death of President Kennedy was less salient than the accompanying but more immediate emotional reactions of their parents and teachers (Wolfenstein, 1965). In very tense and unfamiliar situations the child constantly checks parental reactions for clues to the meaning of each new development. The sick child, for example, defines his condition in terms of his parents' reassurances and anxieties, however poorly informed the parents may be (Davis, 1963). This is largely a subliminal process, and hence father is a point of reference in crises not simply because he is present, but also because of his superior knowledge and strength, and because he possesses the advantage of established habits. He seems to know what he is doing and what is going on most of the time; hence his response to a crisis will seem more authoritative than it actually is, even when he acts quite irrationally.

The most critical historical era for father seems to occur during the transition from peasant to industrial society. The early industrial period is accompanied by an increase in family crises as families move to the cities and as a new pattern relating domestic life to work outside the family is being established, but father cannot meet these crises with customary lore and skills. Furthermore, the early industrial period places father in unfamiliar work surroundings and he can rely less on his wife to be of help in coping with his own problems. It remains true even today, as Robert Blood (1958) has pointed out, that farm fathers are more likely than those in the cities to receive help from wives in their work.

Cooperation With Others We have referred to father as the primary link between the family and its larger social environment. Father stands as an intermediary between the interests of society and those of his family, and he has a role to perform in satisfying the just claims of his wife and children in their constant entanglement with the surrounding social world. Father ordinarily helps to decide just what these claims should be and how they can best be protected.

Parents, of course, are the most emotionally involved adults (sometimes the only ones) in a position to provide and fend for their children. Other adults may become concerned and step in to help when parents call for assistance or fail to act, but parents themselves have the prime obligation to see that their children's needs are met and that their hopes and talents are nurtured. In this sense, both mother and father are culture brokers for their offspring.

Because the father is especially important for the adaptation of members of his family to external demands, he becomes relatively more important in helping them adjust to the institutions of society as they grow older. The child gradually turns away from his mother and childhood dependencies in favor of active adjustment to the larger, nonfamily reality. The longer couples have been married, and the older their offspring, the more the father cooperates with the mother in disciplining the children and in guiding their leisure activities (Geiken, 1964). The father who does not increase, or at the very least maintain, his participation in the activities of children as they mature is symptomatic of serious family malfunctioning.

But father is no longer the undisputed mediator between his family and the external world. Mother has gained relatively more control over the adolescent than she once had, even as both mother and father have lost parental powers along with a general trend toward the emancipation of youth. Mother is the spokesman for children in dealing with contemporary professionals such as teachers and doctors, and she is the one who manages the consumption needs of the household (Dybwad, 1952).

Indeed, mother herself frequently serves as a mediator between father and the children, certainly more often than father plays the peacemaker role. This is especially true of families with a high level of marital integration (Farber, 1962): mother intercedes between father and child and is protective of both insofar as their relationships with one another are concerned.

At the same time that the modern mother's interests and parental prerogatives have become more encompassing in the later years of childhood, father has become more involved and influential in the earlier years, as we noted earlier. But again, in the most critical cases father is the less dependable parent. In families of low social status, for example, father is typically less effective in using community resources available to his family than mother is. Bruce Hollingsworth (1966) studied a county welfare agency in Dallas and found that lower-class fathers rarely participate in securing family welfare assistance. If initiative is required, contact with agencies is initiated by the mother; it is she who goes to the agency periodically to receive help (although in some cases if the father is able to go, the family is not eligible for relief).

In a sense, industrialization makes the role of father as mediator much more ambiguous. He must deal less with kinsmen, cooperate more intensely with his wife, and cooperate to a greater extent with nonkinsmen. Modern children are brought up to accept extrafamilial intrusions upon their privacy in the name of "help"; school counselors, for example, are now licensed to probe for problems in children, which is provoking a variety of reactions from parents and citizens at large. It has been suggested that we are producing a generation of people who practice easy confession and are altogether too receptive to "professional" (not necessarily valid or advantageous) explanations of who they are and what they aspire to become (Kitsuse and Cicourel, 1962). This may be deplorable, but we should not forget that kinsmen of undetermined competence have performed these functions for centuries.

As parents grow older, mediation roles are reversed and children become the emotionally involved adults acting in behalf of the best interests of their parents. Some parents ignore their duty, just as some children neglect parents in their time of need; the study of parental cruelty has been neglected until rather recently, and the study of filial cruelty has not been touched. But there is a German proverb: "One father takes care of ten sons better than ten sons take care of one father."

The Expressive Dimension: Paternal Love

Fathers can do a number of things that help to keep feelings of anxiety and insecurity on the part of their children in check and that contribute to a more or less continuous feeling among family members that life is worthwhile. The father's expressive "work" includes such activities as providing bodily comfort to the children, showing love and respect for them, playing with them, and giving their lives a sense of immediate significance. He promotes a measure of security in his children by being interested in them as no other man is and by his very presence as countless problems arise and are settled. (We might add that father is granted a major role in naming his children, especially sons, which now carries an appreciable charge of expressive significance; it once had its prime importance as a symbol of social status.)

All these expressive roles provide for the management of tensions within the family, which is itself the primary *social* agency for tension management. They have been explored more extensively in novels than in scholarly monographs—not more systematically, but with more dramatic impact.

Expressive relationships between father and children are not the same as those that link husband and wife, but in both cases the unique "expressive" quality is satisfaction (or dissatisfaction) with the immediate relationship—some emotional feeling or sensual response ranging from ecstatic pleasure through simple contentment to repulsion and horror.

Although the survival dimension is by definition the most crucial one, without a minimal expressive ambience survival obviously lacks any reason for being or any sense of inevitability. The underlying expressive concern of parents for their children is the reason that they will make personal sacrifices and suffer inconveniences to assure that each child's survival needs are met. Expertise in the subtleties of one's culture is usually rewarded with a secure place in the community; when parents, in their efforts to discipline children, say "This will hurt me more than it does you," they are often enough telling the truth (although their efforts may be ineffective).

We have noted that father's material support function was undermined in the early phases of the industrial revolution. Had he been able to provide basic expressive satisfactions during this period it seems likely that the revolutionary sentiments that emerged so strongly would not have gained the power they did. But the economic dislocations of the industrial revolution made it difficult, if not impossible, for working-class parents to instill emotional complacency in their children. It might be added that if working-class children in modern America are complacent by historical standards, an important reason is that their lives are not made miserable by the almost unbearable indignities inflicted upon their fathers. Negro children are not so complacent, and their fathers' sufferings must account for this in no small way, mediated of course by reactions to their mothers.

A Sense of Security and Attachment The first conditions of security are supplied by mother, who is the primary source of warmth and physical comfort for children. In Eric Berne's (1964) clever analysis, the general term for intimate physical contact is "stroking," and mother is the child's first "stroker." A stroke, says Berne, is the fundamental unit of social action, referring to almost any act of recognition or awareness of one person by another; an exchange of strokes constitutes a transaction. Mother satisfies the child's earliest need to be stimulated in her transactions with the child, but this pattern is gradually transformed into a need for recognition—not merely stimulation—and can no longer be gratified by mother alone. Father becomes important for the satisfaction of recognition-hunger as the child grows away from mother.

While mother feeds, cleans, and clothes the infant, she soothes it with her voice and cuddles it with her body. In a sense, this is a survival function since its absence impairs the child's ability to play normal social roles later on. Harry Harlow and Robert Zimmerman (1958) have shown that among monkeys in captivity the mother is primarily a warm, kinetic refuge from insecurity and is of considerably less essential significance as a source of food. Among humans, too, it appears that there are alternatives to the mother's feeding function, but no alternative to the sustained physical presence of a mothering one in the life of the infant.

There is no evidence that father's physical contact with the child provides any special "paternal" quality, and, whereas father can substitute for mother in this function, and there are alternatives to breast feeding, throughout the cultures of the world his role is most often supplementary. Clearly father is not as important as mother for the child's earliest sense of security; he is not even necessarily more important than the infant's brothers, sisters, or maternal kinsmen. (A special case is found in the Israeli Kibbutzim, where peer groups and nurses have a prominent role in this regard, sometimes eclipsing that of either father or mother.) Generally speaking, if the mother does not perform her bodily comforting duties adequately, for other than health reasons, the chances are that the father will not either, which is consistent with the proposition that the father is the weak link in the family. Where family disorganization is pronounced, the father usually contributes less to its limited organization than does his wife, inadequate as she may be, in both the survival and expressive dimensions. The fact that fathers are generally less accepting of their children than mothers (Burchinal, 1958) is probably due in part to the limited bodily contact that fathers have with them during the first year.

It is also probably correct to say that the modern father has more intensive nestling and comfort-giving relations with the infant than the peasant father in preindustrial societies. The maintenance of social distance between little children and their fathers is a well-established pattern in most peasant societies; it has been reported that the medieval father in Northern Europe was not even supposed to be seen with his young son (Chrisman, 1920). Fathering in this regard is a quite variable function in nonliterate societies, and hence comparisons between "primitive" and modern paternal practices on this point are virtually impossible.

After infancy, the security enshrouding the child due to mother's tender concern for its bodily needs must be sustained in other ways, especially by the intense personal attention that parents show for the child's broadening social interests. Father's role now becomes relatively more important. He usually supplies a measure of emotional support for his children by comforting them in times of pain and embarrassment and by applauding them in their minor successes as well as in their truly impressive triumphs. His presence gives life a sense of significance transcending the individual reality of the child—a routine sense of attachment that we come to take for granted, but are occasionally reminded of in the bewilderment or terror expressed by little children when they are "lost." Father can be a confidant, intimately discussing the experiences of his children and thereby enlarging or deepening their significance, and he may simply enjoy being with the children just as they enjoy being with him. But father still does not feed them; he does not comfort them when they are hurt, welcome them when they come home from school, or guard the refrigerator and dispense its contents.

Since father does not provide the more routine comforts, he has to work harder than mother to be of expressive significance to his children, especially in the positive, pleasure-giving sense of the term. He is almost forced to invent and improvise signs of affection by bringing things home, taking the children to circuses and parades, telling them stories, playing games, making jokes, and so on, although he runs the risk of becoming little more than a stunt man in the process. As expected, fathers who take their children places and are frequently willing to "have fun" with them are especially well liked (Henry, 1963). If father attends almost *anything* with his children, the occasion usually becomes a much more important one than it would be otherwise. Children are quite accustomed to mother's companionship on mundane visits to the dentist, to buy shoes, and the like; therefore her presence cannot add the luster of a paternal companion.

Several qualities characteristic of virtually every father take on a special significance in the life of the child. Father's age and sex, for example, identify him according to institutional definitions as man instead of woman or child, and his activities as husband and father typically carry a thematic significance representing an extremely important expressive dimension found in nearly all the cultures of the world. Father is more likely than mother to convey a kind of authoritative concern for his children, due to his size, strength, the depth of his voice, and all the symbolic carryovers of patriarchy that still flourish so widely. Father's presence typically assures a kind of protectiveness for which we have no measure, but which is a bit different from that guaranteed by the presence of mother. He is a model of *male* expressiveness, and thus the child has a personal relationship with a man who embodies all the culturally supported connotations of *fatherhood*. These constitute an existential property of family life itself, and rather independent of the way a given father happens to play the father role. As with the security associated with father's presence, male expressiveness is most obvious when it is lacking, that is, when the child has no father.

In a sense, father's role is only meaningful as a reciprocal of mother's role, especially in modern societies, which place so much emphasis on emotional interaction between married couples. The expressive relationship that parents have with their children is always conditioned by the nature of their association with one another. Mother and father may, for example, embolden one another in the face of family crises and parent-child relations, or their relations with one another may contribute to a mutual inability to cope with such family problems. Even as they talk to one another, those facets of the conversation that are overheard by the child become a part of the total pattern of reward, comfort, punishment, and threat that gives life meaning for the child.

Leo Bartemeier (1953) contends that the role of the father during infancy is fulfilled largely in his relationship with the mother, not the child. Paternal neglect at this time is most characteristically neglect of the wife. The father's most important contribution can be made by promoting the woman's emotional security and stability; she will then be a more effective mother and this leads to a higher level of emotional health in the children (Westley and Epstein, 1960b).

In fact, an important expressive function of fathers is to counteract some of the excesses of motherly love that women often show for their children. The problem of preventing boys from becoming emotionally dependent upon mother arises in most societies and can be handled in various ways; for example, in some cultures, puberty rites help to keep this tendency under control (Norbeck, Walker, and Cohen, 1962). Father himself, however, can probably be even more useful in preventing mother from overloving, or expressively absorbing, her children. Nathan Ackerman (1958) argues that husband-wife conflicts are transposed in complex ways into parent-child conflicts and that there may be a kind of seduction of the child by a sexually disappointed mother. But even if mother has no strong emotional feeling for her husband—even if she rather dislikes the man—convention requires that she devote some attention to his emotional needs as well as to those of the children. Father, as an object of mother's attention, if not affection, divides maternal love, allowing the children to become independent with a minimum of remorse and pain (Hill, 1945).

Of course if there is alienation between husband and wife, the mother may direct her libidinal energy toward her children all the more, whether the couple separates or not. On the other hand, it is possible, perhaps likely, that if the couple does not separate the father can help the children break away from "loving maternal protectiveness"; he can, for example, prod the children to make their own decisions, and he can support them as they challenge the mother's manipulative efforts. Fathers are often allied with both sons and daughters against maternal domination, not only out of concern for their children's independence, but out of concern for their own.

There may be a paternal counterpart for "momism," but it has received little attention, probably because it is so rare. In fact, the most prevalent counterpart of excessive maternal love is not too much paternal love, but excessive paternal severity. Mother is often called upon to protect the children from a harsh father and to protect a volatile-when-fatigued father from his provocative and foolhardy kids. Father is much less likely to be faced with the problem of arranging a modus vivendi for expressive relations between mother and the children.

The expressive dimension of fatherhood carries an emotional significance for father himself, not just for his wife and children. Part of the subjective reward for father—the pay-off if he does his job well—is a certain inimitable fatherly feeling, found especially where there are traces of a patriarchal tradition. This is quite a different sense of identity than is characteristic of any of the archetypal sentiments associated with motherhood. It is a consciousness of being the provider, the cornucopia figure, the "big daddy," the dispenser of largesse (gifts, money, pardons, knowledge): the source of all good things, and wisdom too.

This archetype is not merely the basis for a subjective paternal feeling, however. Its performance and attendant satisfactions are part of the social expectations of fatherhood, and mother as well as the children are pleased if father can meet its demands. Thus, it is not simply an ego builder for father; it is an aspect of the traditional basis of respect for father, and one that still serves as a conventional measure of family well-being, although modern men are called upon to set it aside at times and roll on the floor with their children. Even then father is usually conscious of his size and strength and romps not as age mates romp, but as only a daddy can.

But we now recognize that fathers themselves *need* expressive relations with other members of the immediate family in a form rarely acknowledged in the past. The expressive needs of father, along with the decline of his authority, create in the extreme case a father who is marginal to the central functions of his household, one who is more dependent upon his family than in charge of it. Jules Henry (1963) sees the modern father as a seeker of love from his children and also as a kind of fool who willingly lets his children get away with things they are not supposed to do. Henry calls him "the beloved imp-father," "imp" suggesting impulse release and fun. As such, father is the essence of "patterned evasion," by which he conspires with his children to uphold the pretension that they are not breaking rules (often those set by mother) that both he and the children know in fact are being broken. Expressive relations with the children become the means by which father finds refuge from both an exacting job and a demanding wife.

The Rise of the Expressive Dimension The survival duties of the contemporary father certainly seem to have declined relative to his expressive chores. The shift from instrumental to expressive family activities has been recognized by many writers, perhaps most effectively by Ernest Burgess and Harvey Locke (1953) in their claim that a patterned contrast exists between the "institutional" family of rural society and the "companionship" family of contemporary cities. Only in the expressive context has father become truly more crucial than ever before.

Not only does the domain of expressiveness loom larger as a part of fathering, but it is also of greater importance within the total life space of the man. To be sure, father now has a greater expressive role vis-à-vis his wife than his children, since with them he is still assigned a basically instrumental role, but there is more opportunity for him to maintain expressive relationships with his children than before and more need for him to do so.

In nonliterate and peasant societies, most expressive relationships between husbands and wives are shallow and unstable. The modern family has become smaller and relationships within it are necessarily more intensive. The sheer frequency of interrelationships between each pair in a family of four, for example, is much more than twice the number possible in a family of eight. And many of the utilitarian roles formerly managed by the family are transferred to outside agencies as the family loses its self-sufficiency.

Even as relationships in the contemporary community come to be characterized by greater impersonality and a reduced emphasis on kinship, there is more intense emotional interaction within the smaller, socially dependent family. Indeed, one reason the family has a more important expressive function in the rearing of children is because there are so many more potential sources of disillusionment for them, such as greater competitiveness in school along with formalized procedures for judging success and failure. But, because there is greater discontinuity between the meaning of life on the family level and the community level, domestic emotions become isolated, even alienated, from those of the larger social life. A challenge to parents, perhaps especially a challenge to fathers in this context, is to use whatever ingenuity they may possess to keep the gap in meaning between these two spheres from becoming any greater than it needs to be.

Nathan Glazer and Daniel Moynihan (1963) have pointed to the difficulties that confront families when they attempt to maintain the traditional system of paternal aloofness in contemporary America, as seen in the case of Puerto Ricans in New York. The father in the traditional Puerto Rican home demanded respect and obedience from his children, but in reality he had little to do with them. He considered it beneath his dignity to participate in the management of the home and assumed as his prerogative the right to be off by himself whenever he wished. This traditional pattern cannot be maintained in the United States without rather severe consequences. When families from peasant circumstances are thrust into industrial cities, the adjustment they must quickly make dramatizes the changes that appeared almost imperceptibly in the long historical transition from one era to another.

Perhaps the expressive effectiveness of the family has actually progressed too slowly in the twentieth century. Parents may be more "loving" now, but they still do not always create an adequate expressive home life for their children. We think of the family as the refuge, the place where the person receives warmth and affection in contrast to the competition and bureaucratic indifference he meets outside. But this is not necessarily the case. The home may be cold and unloving, while the outside world may in fact provide warmth. One reason some women work away from home is because they do not find their home life rewarding enough; the nature of the work itself is rarely a major attraction, nor is the paycheck in many cases, but work groups can be as expressively satisfying as families, and occasionally even more so. Moreover, various community agencies, even those that are rather highly bureaucratic, sometimes supply expressive services in addition to their instrumental ones, and often by design—in response to an acknowledged need. Jules Henry (1963) has observed that elementary-school teachers frequently use a rhetoric of love as the basis for classroom discipline. The reward for good behavior in school is not just passage to the next class, but signs of affection from a motherly teacher.

Perhaps the child needs this kind of motivation because of inadequate expressive support at home, although another interpretation is also possible: the schools may simply reflect our contemporary concern for affectionate interpersonal relations, and demands made upon modern children may call for a greatly enhanced expressive foundation from which to start. Thus, family life and pedagogical theory are altered simultaneously; as home life becomes characterized by an atmosphere of warmth and affection, the early years at school assume a similar distinction. This explanation is probably the best one for general purposes, but the "expressive inadequacy of the family" theory has justifiable applications, too. The kind of striving required of contemporary children calls for a compassionate and expressively active father.

Father is subject to a series of demands in both the survival and expressive dimensions of life, demands that change as historical conditions change. One particularly difficult era occurs during the transition from feudal and peasant cultures to the modern industrial state. In the early stages of industrial development the survival functions of father are subject to severe pressures, and in country after country the ability of working-class men to provide for the material comfort of their families has proved to be especially difficult.

As economic conditions improve, however, it would appear that the expressive needs of the family exert relatively greater and more unaccustomed pressures upon father. Men in advanced industrial nations are now in the process of adjusting to these pressures. The contemporary father's own expressive needs have grown more insistent at the very time that his wife has become a conspicuously independent woman. But cooperation between husband and wife is now more crucial to family stability than ever before. We turn to this problem in Chapter III.

CHAPTER III

The Father-Mother Team

A number of new conditions that bear upon fatherhood accompany industrialization: new birth and death patterns, the growth of cities and bureaucracies, the upgrading of masses of people into the highly self-conscious middle classes, the cultivation of the independent man *and woman,* and of course the popularization of psychology. In the midst of such extravagant changes, child rearing becomes a complex process beyond the limited powers of parents to control or comprehend fully, and the family becomes the locus of much more intensive emotional interaction. Emile Durkheim (1965) argued that the dominant theme in the history of the family has been the reduction in the number of members in each family unit along with a corresponding increase in family ties.

Expressive concerns have expanded in almost all facets of human life relative to those that concern survival. In particular, the broad social changes associated with industrialism expose the traditional, extended family system to stresses it cannot handle. A number of conflicts commonly met by modern families can no longer be managed by the cooperative efforts of people who are obligated to each other by kinship ties alone. Activities once performed by the kinship unit are shared with schools, courts, corporations, professions, and scores of ad hoc community agencies.

In Durkheim's view, the family becomes smaller as the social environment expands, and individuation—the freeing of the individual from rigid, traditional controls—proceeds with this expansion. The family tends to become a little social world where special "primary-group" rules apply; the nonfamily world is a larger world where much more formal and bureaucratic standards are adhered to, but one that people, especially fathers, must nevertheless cope with daily.

For many the family has become a refuge from the "real world," and as a refuge it provides ego support for the individual as never before, but it seems to offer no effective social strategy for solving modern community and national problems. Although parents serve as mediators between their children and the external world, there is a discontinuity between family life and the great impersonal mix of city, state, national, and international affairs. Parents are destined to "lose" their children to this outside world, though they will, of course, enjoy the tenuous bonds of telephone calls, letters, visits, Christmas cards, and a measure of filial nurturance in their old age.

The ego needs of children are changed as more time and energy must be invested in the training of each one of them, and it is no accident that a rhetoric of *individualism* has emerged along with the increased investment. People need to feel that they are important as individuals, although from the point of view of society and its purposes each individual is in fact expendable. The ideology of individualism helps maintain the fiction that each person is a special case, and the family continues to be the primary institution for nourishing our ego needs. Mother love remains the key to this necessary distortion of the human ego, but mother has never been able to carry the burden alone, and her problems have multiplied.

Where social interaction occurs mainly among kinsmen, the responsibilities of father encompass his own children, but they often extend to all children with whom he normally has contact. Among certain New Guinea groups, for example, adult men act towards all children as fathers—as teachers and correctors—and do not develop the intense and exclusive emotional concern for their own children characteristic of American fathers (Salisbury, 1962).

As family life becomes a compartmentalized aspect of society, fatherhood becomes a compartmentalized aspect of manhood and motherhood becomes a smaller part of the total life of women. But there is an important difference since, as we have seen, the expressive role of father within the family has actually expanded; it is his instrumental role that has been diminished and defamilized. By comparison with those of men, the expressive family functions of women have been reduced in importance, while their instrumental functions have at least held their own and seem to have increased.

In response, modern parents seem to be more insecure in their parental roles and less able to disguise their uncertainties. This is most true of the contemporary mother (at least we know more about her anxieties), although father's parental security has been disturbed too. We have mentioned that parents are no longer sure just what is good and what is bad for their children. Our commitment to a *science* of family life aggravates the normal concern of parents as they confront the inevitable imperfection of their children and must reflect on their own inevitable mistakes. As Leslie Fiedler (1960) has put it, "Who, in this context, is not guilty as charged, whatever the charge? Who has not slipped up in toilet training, discipline, selection of books, supervision of TV? Who has not at some moment seemed to reject his child?"

And yet the comparatively small, independent family becomes the most effective familial arrangement as industrialism expands. Talcott Parsons (1943) argued a quarter of a century ago that the smooth functioning of a progressive society, requiring the free flow of human resources, is contingent upon the flexibility and freedom of movement made possible by a system of isolated, "nuclear" family units. The large, extended family system is indeed historically associated with agriculture; smaller, independent families are more often found in hunting and gathering societies or in modern industrial nations where most people, although reliant upon agriculture, are not engaged in it (Nimkoff and Middleton, 1960).

The strength of kinship controls is not reduced because people rebel against them, but because they become anomalous in the urban, industrial setting. Greater physical mobility is needed, reducing kin contacts; social-class mobility is also intensified, weakening the kin hierarchy; urban and industrial services replace or undermine services formerly lodged in the kinship system; and opportunities are based more on individual achievement than on kin favor, because highly specialized skills are needed and the kinship system simply cannot manage to fill the many key social positions (Goode, 1963).

In fact, the tenacity of kinship bonds tends to impede industrial development, at least for a while. In Nigeria, for example, the demands of home ties make the accumulation of wealth extremely difficult. Since the person's first loyalty must be to his homeland and family, requests for money by kinsmen cannot be easily refused, and they start early. Money that might be used for investment in a business or for savings in a bank is spent instead on traditional gifts to chiefs, elders, and sick kinsmen, although some money may go for the educational expenses of young male relatives (Plotnicov, 1965).

The phenomenal industrial growth experienced in America was surely fostered by conditions that scattered members of the family; physical mobility has always been pronounced in the United States by world standards because it has been relatively easy for citizens to leave home and find opportunities elsewhere. The mobility of immigrants had an important role to play in the growth of the nation, of course, effectively cutting children off from their parents and grandparents (Croog and New, 1965). Mobility both generated the new nation and forced the decline of the large family unit; it offered a selective advantage to people who had no particular desire to remain near their kinsmen (or perhaps even to remember them) and who could solve their problems outside the large family network. American history, however, is only a special case. Industrialization, in whatever form it develops, undermines the extended family system.

Thus, the family ceases to be the only source of social continuity for a much larger part of the population. The individual, for example, can now define himself, his past and his future, in terms of a career in some corporation and in terms of the stability, security, and opportunity it offers. The firm, the government agency, the university—*the organization*—offers an entirely new sense of belonging, one that kinship cannot supply. Durkheim (1965) exaggerated when he contended that only one group is now close enough to the man to hold him tightly and comprehensive enough to allow him a broad social perspective: his occupational or professional group. It is the only social unit, he argued, able to perform the economic and moral functions that the family has become increasingly incapable of performing.

The family as an institution finds itself in a position somewhat comparable to that of the church; the important new agencies of continuity for the masses of people are nation-states, professional societies, and industrial bureaucracies. By comparison, the family and the church have lost ground. In fact, there is now less concern for any continuity that stresses tradition rather than progressive innovation. Under the circumstances, the father must cooperate with his wife more and kinsmen less, and both he and the members of his family find themselves caught up in larger organizational activities that are not controlled by people who are family or kinship representatives.

The Perseverance of Kinship

But familism is by no means obsolete. It still enshrouds the lives of children in their most formative years: they learn their first words within a family setting; they acquire their first conceptions of age and sex roles here; and responses to their first awkward efforts occur at home. The sheer number of these familial transactions, in the millions, is overwhelming. For adults, too, the family remains the primary social unit for rendering life worth living. Almost all writers acknowledge that despite dramatic changes the family continues to be essential for social survival and that father is still a basic source of strength, unity, and economic security within it. But a change of great importance has occurred nonetheless.

In the light of recent interest in the continued functions of the extended family in industrial society, some further discussion is necessary. The persistence of kinship obligations within an environment that is comparatively hostile to them has important implications for fatherhood. For example, Marvin Sussman and Lee Burchinal (1962) argue that a full understanding of the family as a social system is possible only by rejecting the concept of the isolated nuclear family. They repudiate Talcott Parsons' hypothesis and claim that the proposition that the nuclear family is the most adaptive arrangement for modern conditions has led to misleading if not false conclusions about both the family and society in general. If their position is correct, we may presume that fatherhood too has been distorted.

Other students have joined the attack. Frank Furstenberg (1966) argues that the family is not merely a dependent variable in the complicated relationship between economic system and family; he claims that the extent to which the industrial system affects family life has been greatly exaggerated. Sidney Greenfield (1965) contends that there is no necessary relationship between the small, nuclear family and industrialism. Any relationship that exists, he claims, probably results from the fact that the small, nuclear family happened to exist in Northern Europe prior to the industrial revolution. Eugene Litwak (1960a, 1960b) suggests that a modified extended family system is not inconsistent with the high levels of geographic and occupational mobility found in industrial societies, and in fact is even more appropriate than the small family system. He maintains that industrial pressures force the extended family to accept and promote social and spatial mobility and that the kinship group provides significant aid to nuclear families without interfering with bureaucratic wage and salary programs. Improved communication systems, he points out, have reduced the disruptive forces of geographical distance. Sussman and Burchinal (1962) also argue that kinship practices may actually facilitate individual achievement among family members.

Many writers have pointed out that the small conjugal family (that is, the core family of parents and children) is rarely completely isolated from its kinsmen in the modern city. The

Jewish nuclear family, for example, whose members often retain a close relationship with relatives in the extended family, has the lowest average number of offspring of the three large religious groups in America. In fact, Lee Robins and Miroda Tomanec (1962) contend that the smaller the nuclear family, the greater the number of obligations fulfilled outside with relatives. But the assumption that the time and effort people spend in family interaction remain relatively constant during historical changes is a risky one. Many people have more leisure time now than they would have had in an earlier period, and they may use it at home watching television, or visiting grandmother, or playing golf, or in any number of ways. There is certainly no compelling reason to assume that the ratio of family to nonfamily activities will remain constant.

One of the strongest arguments that can be made in favor of the extended family is the fact that many modern couples share very few intimate cronies other than kinsmen. In one study the most frequent number of agreed-upon friends (other than kinsmen) was two, and the average was only three (Babchuk and Bates, 1963). Not only were there few mutual intimate friends, but pronounced disagreement often occurred among couples in deciding who their friends were. Kinsmen as intimates are still very likely more numerous than friends for many couples, and certainly there is greater agreement as to who they are, although there may be no consensus as to who the most intimate ones are.

The inability of friends to replace kinsmen at the present time is apparent in the behavior of the family in crises. After reviewing the research literature on this subject, Enrico Quarantelli (1960) concluded that disaster victims most frequently turn to their extended families for help. However, he also calls attention to the fact that the larger the scope of the disaster, the less probable it is that the kin group will be the most effective source of help. Social agencies undoubtedly provide assistance in serious disasters to a greater extent now than in the past. Thus, the trend is toward more encompassing and effective nonkin agencies, even though relief and support from relatives remain essential in the more common family emergencies.

Leonard Blumberg and Robert Bell (1959) have noted that rural migrants to the big, anonymous city are encouraged by urban circumstances to create ethnic, "hillbilly" areas in which kinship ties continue to be very strong. But they also discovered that migrants who achieve upward social mobility tend to modify or drop many of the old family ties. Harry Schwarzweller (1964) found that close identification with family origin tends to keep the young rural migrant from becoming an effective member of the urban, industrial community. Close ties with the family of one's childhood help to compensate for a feeling of "rootlessness," but if the ties persist, strains are generated that interfere with urban adaptation. Only in the early stages of the migrant's career are extended family ties helpful.

One might argue that our most vivid experiences, other than those with parents and siblings, continue to occur with grandparents, uncles, aunts, nieces, and nephews. These are possibly the most impressive adult "characters" in our lives, because they are real—unlike the constant parade of shallow personalities on television—and their behavior is not stereotyped, which so often happens in the case of teachers, doctors, salesmen, and so on. But many of the people we meet in secondary contexts are in fact more impressive, more memorable, than our relatives. Knowledge about kinsmen, even about the ones that are typically closest to us, is very limited in modern society. Sydney Croog and Peter New (1965) found that many Americans have little or no knowledge of the occupations of their grandfathers, a discovery that is consistent with the image of a rather isolated nuclear family. The data of these investigators also suggest that people in the higher socioeconomic levels know more about their grandfathers than people of lesser status do. Only fathers who have attained impressive occupational positions are likely to be remembered for more than one generation!

But the role of grandparents is unquestionably the prime survivor of the extended family system. They remain closer to members of the nuclear family than any other relatives do, followed by aunts and uncles, then cousins (Robins and Tomanec, 1962). Great-aunts and uncles are very rarely included among the relatives with whom nuclear family members have close relations. Hence, the chief tie between the nuclear family and the extended family is the tie between adult couples and their parents. A pattern of assistance and communication between these two generations is the life line of the modern kin network (Sussman and Burchinal, 1962).

Certainly parents help their children after they leave home if they can, offering financial aid and emergency assistance, making tactful gifts, giving constructive advice and encouragement, and providing a wide range of services, such as babysitting (Sussman, 1953; Moss and MacNab, 1961). Marvin Sussman and Lee Burchinal (1962) argue that financial aid is available to an increasing number of families because of the higher per capita income of recent years; they contend that parental assistance to married offspring has weakened the financial autonomy of the nuclear family unit, *though it has not replaced the norm of autonomy* (the italics are the author's). Moreover, Bert Adams (1964) notes that parental financial aid is usually indirect so that there is no appearance of usurping the young father's position as provider. He found that financial aid in the middle classes begins immediately after marriage and soon diminishes; the rendering of services, too, reaches its peak during the preschool years of the grandchildren.

In fact, the larger kin group *very* seldom makes specific decisions for the nuclear family. Kinship is now supportive rather than coercive; the immunity of the nuclear family to kinship control is guaranteed by strong social conventions. Assistance from the larger family supplements rather than displaces the basic activities of the core family. It should also be recognized that the primary tie of the kin network, parental aid to the young married offspring, is itself based on neither a legal nor a cultural norm, but rather upon ad hoc feelings and sentiments linking parents and children (Sussman and Burchinal, 1962). Thus, kinship bonds are much more tenuous than they were in an earlier historical period.

Ideally, children in our society are progressively emancipated from their parents in the process of growing up. But parents remain more emotionally attached to their adult offspring than the children are to their parents (Streib, 1965). A tension between generations is inevitably created by the interplay between this new theme of emancipation and the traditional theme of filial respect, an ambivalent desire to maintain kinship ties and to keep the conjugal families separate (Glasser and Glasser, 1962).

Ambivalence is reflected most clearly in residential patterns. Paul Reiss (1962) found that relatives quite often wish to live closer together than they actually do, but not too close. The ideal of an independent nuclear family is strongly institutionalized, but an effort is usually made to avoid prolonged or pronounced isolation from kinsmen; nevertheless, a sizeable minority of elder couples prefer to live alone, away from their relatives (Beyer, 1962). Common residence is strongly disapproved, and Alvin Schorr (1962) has argued cogently that this negative reaction is now often exaggerated beyond good judgment.

About one out of four homes in America is still a "three-generation household." Widowed grandmothers in particular often live with their children, and inadequate housing along with low income are the most common reasons (Sheldon, 1958). It is only with great reluctance that older people give up their autonomy and become members of their children's households (Gleason, 1956). Thus, the three-generation family must be considered a special case; it is no longer typical or ideal. It may well be that it persists because in Robert Frost's phrase, "home is the place where, when you have to go there, they have to take you in."

Although grandparents typically make regular social visits to their children's families, they neither have nor want responsibilities for the care of grandchildren (Albrecht, 1954), and they derive vicarious satisfactions from the accomplishments of these children to a markedly lesser extent than do the parents (Neugarten and Weinstein, 1964). Indeed, the ideal would seem to be for older relatives to avoid an active and regular part in raising or providing for grandchildren unless unusual circumstances arise. Max Kaplan (1960) compares the contemporary grandparent to the second-generation immigrant of forty or fifty years ago: they are both marginal. Their positive roles within the family are defined largely by the needs of the nuclear family, not by the interests of the extended family.

Mother, incidentally, rather than father, bears the burden of keeping up the flow of information among kinsmen and acting as the representative of the nuclear family in fulfilling obligations to relatives. She does most of the letter writing and more than her share of the telephoning. Parents of the wife give more frequent assistance to the couple than parents of the husband do (Adams, 1964), while maternal relatives are closer than paternal relatives, and female relatives in general closer than male relatives (Robins and Tomanec, 1962). Since women are usually more involved with their parents than men are, one might argue that mothers, rather than fathers, are now the chief *practical* link between the nuclear family and the kinship network. Thus, the traumatic impact of any disruption of this network is greater for them. Because the mother often has no occupational skill as a basis for forming a new cluster of relationships, her social life remains denuded for a longer period of time than her husband's when she is separated from the larger family group (Rainwater, 1964).

Of course the attraction of the extended family lingers on. Most of us retain some contact with it, and our "sense of family" includes a sentimental attachment to the large kin group. Perhaps most of the greatest literature from the past conveys this sense of family, and it retains an appeal for us even today. But it seems more difficult to produce literature in that genre now. Family dissolution in modern fiction is less likely to be pictured as the passing of the family clan; it is more likely the story of an ill-fated marriage. The impact of a novel dramatically exposing the breakdown of a large family, such as Faulkner's *The Sound and the Fury,* depends not only upon the reader's sense of family, but on an implicit recognition of the relationship between family and society in social change. In our imagination at least, the strong, extended family belongs to the old order.

Our conclusion is that the traditional family system has indeed been severely modified. Although not completely isolated from the kin group, the nuclear family is now much more independent of it, which is true even though kinship may have assumed some new functions. It has lost many more. Three developments in particular have been noted: (1) the responsibilities of the extended family have been altered; (2) other social agencies have emerged to handle various matters formerly handled by the extended family; and (3) the nuclear family has become the focal point for both expressive and instrumental family interaction. As Talcott Parsons pointed out, the nature of family commitment has assumed a new form and content. Loyalty to one's nuclear family, not to the extended family group, has become the person's most compelling family obligation.

The Rise of the Father-Mother Team

A constriction of the father role accompanies this broad change, and John Mogey (1957) was probably correct when he said that it is almost impossible to understand the emerging nature of fatherhood without placing it in the social and historical context of declining family functions. He noted that in the early stages of the factory system father had to work away from home for long hours and returned to his family tired and unable to exercise firm control. As a result, this was a period of considerable family instability, reflecting general forms of social unrest. Currently, however, Mogey contends father is being reintegrated within the family: he earns more than his forebears, he works shorter hours, he gets more support from state welfare programs, and his wife often works away from home too. Family stability in the course of this evolution requires new expectations of father, and modern society does indeed make new demands upon him.

Ernest Burgess and Harvey Locke (1953) argued that there is now greater change in our conceptions of parental roles from one generation to the next than there was in the past, largely because of disruptions in the continuity of family practices. Their point was not that the small family system calls for repeated changes in parental practices, but that the *transition* from an extended system to the nuclear structure is a period of profound parental adaptation. (Mogey adds that the concept of fatherhood is the most rapidly changing role in this transformation, although there would seem to be no way to verify his impression.)

What happens, of course, is that the family itself has a less comprehensive role to play than before, and its reduced status establishes the primary context conditioning what can be expected of father. He becomes more totally involved in family affairs, but affairs of the family make up a smaller part of life. Perhaps for this very reason a new animating spirit enhances certain of father's roles. The decline of the large family system, for example, tends to bring father as a human being into greater prominence and clearer focus for his children. They have a closer look at the *man* as social distance between the generations is reduced. Father is no longer the overwhelming authority, nor is he quite so distinctively the mainspring of family self-sufficiency. He almost becomes one of the rank and file.

Both his internal and his external roles are altered. In the case of the latter, change is most apparent in cultures moving very rapidly from village life to urban life, telescoping changes that occurred slowly elsewhere in a long historical transition. For example, traditionally the leader in Turkish villages was also the head of an expanded kinship group. The village itself consisted almost solely of kinsmen. All political power flowed through the family structure; the village had no other functioning political organization. But in recent times, with the appearance of cash crops and a money economy, village leadership based on kinship alone has been unable to maintain its position (Pierce, 1964). Not all fathers have reduced social functions of this nature, of course, but some do, and an impressive aspect of fatherhood is lost.

With industrialization, the community of citizens even more than the community of kinsmen becomes the important social unit with which the nuclear family must cooperate. And the mother-father team becomes much more significant as the center of conciliation between children and society. Father must cooperate with mother more, and with other relatives comparatively less.

Where the kin network is of critical importance, as in nonliterate societies, marriage is in fact quite typically an unstable relationship (Goodsell, 1934; Murdock, 1950), and conjugal relationships are emotionally shallow. Neither Don Juan, Tristan, nor St. Paul would be able to understand the intimate sharing of confidences—the sheer friendship—between modern husbands and wives. Even in classical Greece the marriage bond was only very rarely a focus of attention. Alvin Gouldner (1965) has pointed out that in Homer, as in most classical Greek literature, no ordinary words were used that specifically meant "husband" or "wife." A man was called many things—"man," "father," "warrior," "nobleman," "king," "hero,"—but he was almost never called "husband."

The relationship between husbands and wives in nonliterate and peasant societies is usually distant, formal, and impersonal; it does not involve the intimacy and sharing that is characteristic of the modern companionate ideal. It is not uncommon for the woman in tropical Africa, for example, to feel like an alien in her own marriage; her enduring emotional ties are with kinsmen, not spouse (Paulme, 1963). The major strains within the household in Zinacantan, Mexico are between brothers, or between mother-in-law and daughter-in-law (Cancian, 1964). Occasionally the husband gets drunk and beats his wife, after which she may take the children home to her mother for a while. The element of conjugal affection is not totally absent from marriage as a rule, but the degree of personal disrespect that is tolerated is almost incomprehensible to citizens of the United States; it precludes the close companionship now deemed essential for effective family life.

Even sex relations, or perhaps especially sex relations, reflect this fact. In general, the greater the joint organization of marital roles, the more importance the couple will attach to being able to work out a mutually satisfying sexual relationship (Bott, 1957). In societies where the roles of husband and wife are segregated, the couple will not usually develop an ardent sexuality, and the wife will not consider sex relations with her husband as an attractive source of gratification (Rainwater, 1964). The fact that there is a greater degree of sharing, communication, and joint participation in social relations in the middle and upper classes in the United States may account for the fact that the satisfaction women derive from their husbands' "love and affection" increases steadily with social status.

A close sexual relationship has no particular social function where marital roles are segregated since the duties of husband and wife are organized on a separate basis; no useful contribution can be made by activities that promote their ability to cooperate as a separate pair. It is even possible that a high degree of marital intimacy in an extended kinship system is disruptive since it can conflict with the demands of important kinsmen other than spouse. William Goode (1959) argues that romantic love does tend to cause problems where the large family system is strong, and measures are often taken to inhibit its expression.

In fact, the sternness of the struggle for survival in many preindustrial societies places a premium on the ability of people to stifle emotional response. A rather striking contrast between the "impersonal" as against the companionate marriage is still found in traditional farm families as compared with urban households in the United States. In a study of Mennonites, J. Howard Kauffman (1961) concludes that emerging family patterns are composed of interpersonal relationships of a distinctly "higher quality" than those found in the more traditional and authoritarian families.

Today there is greater stress on the husband-wife team as the social unit responsible for care of the child, as well as greater emphasis on certain formalities in the establishment of marriage. Hyman Rodman's (1961) work in Trinidad, where the kin network remains strong, calls attention to two alternatives to the standard marriage existing there: "friending" and cohabitation. In "friending," the man visits his woman at intervals to have sex relations and contributes to the support of any children thus conceived; children are given his surname, but he can disown them and neglect his obligations with virtual impunity. The second alternative simply involves cohabitation of the couple; they live together but are not legally married and may remain economically independent of one another in important ways. These alternatives to marriage occur more frequently than marriage itself in Trinidad because marriage imposes relatively heavy economic obligations on husbands and fathers in a society in which poverty is endemic. The culture of poverty is of course most characteristic of peasant societies and the underprivileged sectors of industrializing societies. With higher economic status, marriage procedures are established, which is part of the trend toward the greater importance of the father-mother team.

The family has become smaller as the surrounding community has enlarged and diversified; father's role is almost inevitably constricted along with the narrowing of general family functions. But this constriction is a selective process, since the father's expressive role usually expands at the same time his instrumental role is being reduced. The latter remains of critical importance in spite of its diminished scope, however, just as the extended family is not totally destroyed. In some ways grandparents may have become more important than they were before. Nevertheless, in the modern city the father-mother team emerges as the key cooperative unit within the family and it provides the basis for a stable domestic life. Expressive relations within the family are heightened, marital relations are more intensive, and the quality of relations between mother and father becomes more influential in the lives of their children.

CHAPTER IV

The Passing of the Patriarch

Trends in paternal authority are also linked with the decline of the large family system and with virtually every new social development that has contributed to that decline. The father's strategic position is weakened as the function of "blood relationship" diminishes relative to other strategies for maintaining community order.

Most of our leading ideas about family authority are derived from the value premises and myths of patriarchy. But the term "patriarchy" is used quite loosely, having referred to a wide assortment of conditions by different writers, and with a great variety of purposes in mind (Bowerman and Elder, 1964). Let us simply acknowledge that patriarchal ideologies have persisted into the twentieth century in all the major cultures of the world. One guiding principle is found in all of them: father is granted certain prerogatives in determining the activities of members of his family. Father's wishes are expected to take priority over those of his wife in a wide range of matters of common interest, although ad hoc compromise is inevitably called for. Even when the wife is allowed to handle certain matters as she chooses, such as household details, her wishes are usually molded by an education stressing female deference to men. Little girls learn to live by an ideal of family relations that men, the principal spokesmen for society, have articulated throughout history. In a man's world, women work through men and must learn to make them like it. (Patriarchy in special circumstances may extend far beyond the rather mild form expressed here. In a study of paternalism in Japan, Bennett and Ishino [1963] do not regard it simply as a kinlike social form whereby fathers are given powers to maintain order and preserve traditional values, but as a highly dynamic one in which the *kobun*—the child-status person—can be exploited for selfish purposes by the *oyabun*—the parent-status person.)

Although women are called upon to defer to men in most parts of the world, the sex factor is usually qualified by the age of the persons involved. Women have authority over boys, for example, and old women may have authority over young men. In Zinacantan, Mexico, each household member expects obedience from all younger members, with one exception: women do not have authority over slightly younger men who are not their brothers (Cancian, 1964).

But even when the formal rules of society clearly subordinate women, they may occasionally declare their independence. Denise Paulme (1963) reports that in a number of recurring situations in tropical Africa a woman can at least obliquely defy her husband's authority. A woman can also assert herself if her husband fails to meet minimum standards of masculine conduct. The man may give his wife many routine orders, but she is quite commonly consulted on major decisions; this seems to be an almost universal practice in the cultures of the world. William Madsen (1964) reports that children in traditional Mexican-American families learn early in life that their mother can influence father in strange and subtle ways; when in trouble they seek their mother's aid because she can appease father.

Thus, the wife may exercise her will at times, even where patriarchal sentiments are strong, but the appearance of a wise and strong fatherhood is usually not violated. Situation comedies on television in the United States frequently capitalize on the familiar pattern: mother succeeds in winning her way by tricking father into suggesting precisely what she wanted all along; mother and the children then compliment their loveable pushover for his thoughtfulness—a happy, heartwarming ending indeed. (This has proved to be such a standard comedy success in the United States that one can only assume it appeals to both women *and men.*)

Among primitive groups, patterns of paternal authority have been quite variable, although active, adult men in the earliest hunting societies were probably granted great powers in their relatively small groups. Patriarchial practices reached their highest influence and widest prevalence in the extended families of peasant societies. Challenges to the patriarchal system are repeatedly made as peasantry lingers on, but only with industrialization do they become irresistible. Even then, the rhetoric of patriarchy is abandoned only slowly.

Almost all observers agree that the scope of father's authority has been reduced in response to the wholesale social changes associated with industrialism and that there are now strong pressures upon father to modify the demands he makes on both his wife and his children. One skeptical voice, that of Ezra Vogel (1961), suggests that there may be no necessary correlation between industrialization and the decline of paternal authority. He claims that patriarchal power in preindustrial Japan has been greatly exaggerated, but the data he presents indicate that Japanese women are in fact gaining greater independence due to the conditions brought about by industrialization.

All evidence points to the recent emergence of an egalitarian marriage pattern along with the reification of a democratic family ideal, especially in the United States (Johannis and Rollins, 1959). When William Ogburn and Meyer Nimkoff (1955) asked eighteen "family experts" to name the most important recent changes in the family, twelve mentioned a decline in the authority of husbands and fathers, a very high level of agreement in a field characterized by controversy. Russell Middleton and Snell Putney (1960) studied college professors and skilled workers, both Negro and white, and found the egalitarian pattern of family decision making to be clearly the most prevalent in all four groups. According to Edward Devereux, Urie Bronfenbrenner, and George Suci (1962), the scarcity of truly patriarchal families has made it almost impossible to study the effects of extreme types of family structure on personality development. Glen Elder (1965) compared information from the oldest and youngest persons in each of five samples from the United States, West Germany, Great Britain, Mexico, and Italy: he found that parental dominance has decreased appreciably over the last fifty years. The decline is very pronounced in the United States, Great Britain, and West Germany; less marked in Italy; and negligible in Mexico. In each case, trends were consistent with historical patterns of social and economic change during this fifty-year period.

The trend extends to grandparents. Grandfather is no longer the final arbiter in reaching tough family decisions, nor is he still an acknowledged source of family wisdom. He frequently assumes the role of "fun seeker" with his grandchildren and attempts to exercise very little authority (Neugarten and Weinstein, 1964), while the characteristic attitude of grandchildren toward him is quite often one of "privileged disrespect" (Townsend, 1957). Only where economic power and prestige rest with the aged are relationships between grandparents and grandchildren likely to be formal and authoritarian; where the grandparents are denied family authority, they cultivate an equalitarian or an indulgent relationship with their grandchildren (Apple, 1956). Ruth Cavan (1962) suggests that the modern grandfather must operate within a maternal, companionship pattern rather than the traditional patriarchal arrangement, but she also adds that grandfathers have no great difficulty finding satisfaction and maintaining pride within this context.

Father is now expected to be supportive in his relations with children; he is doing quite well if he succeeds in being a pal to his son and a courtier to his daughter. Ideally, as we have noted, the quality of "expressiveness" is developed by men as well as women in contemporary society and by fathers as well as mothers in their parental capacity. As mother and father functions become more similar, boys become relatively more submissive and dependent, or so Urie Bronfenbrenner (1961b) cogently argues, and thus a self-perpetuating cycle is established.

The Impact of Industrialism

No single event or social condition can be held responsible for the modern father's status. The more exaggerated separation of home and work that accompanied industrialism was a major force. The sheer length and burdensomeness of work was also important; it fatigued the working-class father and stripped him of the physical strength and prestige essential to the conservation of authority. The new industrial city provided no strong or independent social position for the proletarian father; his very anonymity in the burgeoning city foiled almost all means of holding him accountable, since the power of shame as a social control is dependent upon the individual's possession of a community identity in which he can take pride. As a result, father became weak and passive in many cases (Mogey, 1957), or retained his authority in an arbitrary and cantankerous way.

The trend away from patriarchy is not simply a trend toward husband-wife equality, however, nor is it merely a redressing of the balance of conjugal power. Changes in family authority are part of a much more comprehensive modification of the complex pattern of social discipline and community management. Authority patterns are altered throughout the entire range of social action; not only are women and children allowed more opportunity to express themselves, but the distribution of power among classes and social institutions is altered.

In this transition, authority, like responsibility, is segmented and parceled out among many different individuals, institutions, groups, and organizations. The modern father's most highly developed sphere of authority, his career competence, may not even be appreciated by his wife and children, since they do not actually see him at work. Nor does the modern father retain the ancient authority wielded by men in nonliterate societies in their capacity as storytellers and preservers of an oral tradition (Riesman, 1964). As knowledge and the affairs of men become highly specialized, skilled technical performance is only visible to work associates, and competence can be properly judged only by nonfamily members.

By contrast, the nonliterate or peasant father could not escape the judgment of his kin, a fact usually to his benefit. His skills were manifest and their critical importance was self-evident. In his study of Japan's new middle classes, Ezra Vogel (1963) found that the wife now knows much less about her husband's daily work than she would have in an earlier generation. Helena Lopata (1965) discovered that surprisingly few American women in her study expressed any interest in what their husbands do when they are away from home. The husband's work is not a significant part of their lives, except as it is manifested in a paycheck and a time schedule. Jules Henry (1963) found that one of the reasons contemporary children "like" their fathers (if they do) is because he shows an interest in their activities and will occasionally take time out to enter their world, on their terms. Rarely does a child express appreciation for his father because the child can be with him or help him in his work.

Nor does father's occupational remoteness strengthen his image. Lack of knowledge about father's work may give him an air of mystery, but it rarely contributes to his authority. In fact, since the father's work is neither observable by family members nor considered secret, he lacks the aura of mystery that adult males belonging to all-male societies often had in nonliterate tribes. The contemporary secret society for men by no means imbues father with the exotic enhancement of old; it may only make him appear silly.

Children are more likely to admire or respect fathers who "let them do things" than those who help them in school work, or than those who are exceptional because of some commitment, talent, or skill (Henry, 1963). There is little evidence to suggest that children appreciate the pressure exerted upon them by demanding parents—unless it is moderated by a sustaining and warm relationship.

Thus the very things that endear father to his children tend to undermine his authority. In fact, the persistence of patriarchy within the family is now often symptomatic of child-rearing pathologies. Father-dominated families are currently pictured as settings for incompetent and dependent boys, but whether strict or permissive, the extremes in parental discipline are associated with lack of intimacy and confidence between parent and child (Middleton and Putney, 1963). Mother may team up with the children to evade father's sternness and thus circumvent any harsh demands he may make, or she may be too cowed by her husband to help the children effectively. The autocratic father is not likely to promote high educational aspirations in his son (Bowerman and Elder, 1964), and this inability renders his style incongruous in a society dependent upon the higher learning.

But the autocratic father is in fact a rarity. Since the man must be away from home so much of the time, mother necessarily assumes an important role as authority and disciplinarian, especially as the children grow older. Using data from daily records kept by mothers, Edward Clifford (1959) concluded that mothers now do most of the disciplining in the home, and they discipline primarily to preserve orderly household routines. Joan Aldous (1961) also found that mothers are most often named as the governing parent by their children. Mother, by herself, supervises the children more often than mother and father together, and the two supervise them together more often than father does alone.

Even though the focus of discipline is routine behavior, and mother has probably always been the more important parent for such matters, she is less likely to be relegated to the administration of mere details in the contemporary small family (Bossard and Carter, 1958-1959). Her authority is not so sharply subordinated to her husband's as far as general family activities and goals are concerned. Whether father actually did most of the disciplining in the traditional large family system is not known for sure—it seems unlikely—but he certainly was more often the *salient* taskmaster. Glen Elder and Charles Bowerman (1963) found that as family size increases, father is even now more likely to be considered the family spokesman on child-rearing matters and to act as chief disciplinarian, although this seems to be primarily a middle- rather than a lower-class phenomenon; if father is present in the lower classes, he is usually an authoritarian type independent of the size of his family.

Despite gains by mother, it would appear that the total joint authority of both husband and wife has been reduced by the impact of industrial society. Marion Levy (1949), among others, has suggested that an important concomitant of industrialization is a decline in the authority of the family over its younger members. Children increasingly can, and must, make decisions for themselves without reference to family considerations, and many other models for human behavior besides parents and kinsmen become visible, some of whom must appear superior to the child's parents. Professionally trained people who deal with children, for example, present only their best, practical qualities; by comparison, the parent is a rank amateur.

The utility of father's authority in certain matters, such as choosing mates for his children, is quite apparent in societies in which each new marriage is, for many very practical purposes, an addition to an already functioning kinship group. In our own system, marriage establishes a new family that must operate more or less independently, and the exercise of power in mate selection by father, or by father and mother, becomes an intrusion into affairs that are not, properly speaking, their business. In Martinique, the father's approval may be requested to permit his daughter to live with a man even in the absence of a regular marriage ceremony (Horowitz and Horowitz, 1963). American parents ostensibly retain the right to prevent their children from marrying before the legal age, but even this power has become a weak one (Gover and Jones, 1964). The legal authority of parents is not what counts; it is the *quality* of their influence. Modern parental sovereignty is a perfect example of informal, as distinguished from traditional or bureaucratic, control.

The idea that children must be carefully controlled and indoctrinated has been replaced, little by little, by the idea that each child should explore and learn as much as possible by himself, which is reflected in a shift toward greater sensitivity to the unique needs of each child (Kell and Aldous, 1960). Parents are no longer encouraged to believe that they can manage their children on the basis of traditional disciplinary dogma and are often told that they should not try. The very fact that parents receive conflicting advice from friends, journalists, and authorities on child rearing, and are surrounded by contradictory parental models, undermines their ability to exercise authority in a self-assured manner (Davis, 1940).

The whole process of growing up, it may be added, is supposed to be an enjoyable one. In a discussion of the contemporary "fun morality" Martha Wolfenstein (1955) has described a drastic shift from strict to permissive recommendations in the child-guidance literature of the past thirty years. As a matter of fact, the new hedonism is a highly moral one, retaining social responsibility as a prime consideration. If our theory is correct, the happy, explorative child of today is the mature, trustworthy executive of the future (although contradictory findings in the study of business leaders by W. Lloyd Warner and James Abegglen [1955] must give us pause).

Industrialism was not the direct cause of this relaxation of controls, although it supplied the predisposing conditions. The sustained and conscientious study of child rearing, which emerged only after industrialism was well under way, was the more immediate cause. A foundation for the trend away from dogmatism in infant care had been laid even before the Freudian era (Vincent, 1951). But we have only slowly discovered that tradition cannot be relied upon to tell us the most appropriate or effective ways to rear children. Unfortunately, modern research into human behavior has not revealed precisely what we should encourage our children to do; rather, it has admonished us that needless restrictions and inhibitions have been used too frequently in the past. As we have become aware that the traditional taboos were often neither effective nor salutary, and certainly unsuited to the new industrial setting, one by one the time-honored restraints have been spotted and exorcised; the decline of paternal authority parallels the progressive debunking of traditional wisdom.

Often father can neither explain nor defend sensibly the traditional positions when they are challenged. In many cases he does not even try; he tells the child he will understand when he is older or refers him to an encyclopedia. Father cannot be expected to understand the far-flung and contradictory character of values and practices surrounding his little family.

No one person can, and the manageable areas of knowledge become smaller, more specialized, and more estranged from one another all the time. One of the truly new developments of recent centuries is the emergence of a world view that condones the expression "I don't know." Preindustrial man could hardly think in such terms, because there was an answer to everything through magic and religion, known by the older men. Science demotes all three—magic, religion, and older men—and as science becomes popular, people distinguish between the known and the unknown, the knowable and unknowable, and begin to think in terms of "the present state of our collective knowledge." Father can only help a child to adapt to this reality, he cannot possess modern man's collective knowledge.

If there are means by which the exercise of influence in the family is culturally legitimized, it seems safe to say that they are no longer derived to any important degree from inherited ideologies. They are worked out on a much more pragmatic basis and in terms of contemporary social conditions. William Kenkel (1959), for example, in an attempt to gain empirical knowledge about the impact of "traditional family ideology" upon the behavior of husbands and wives, could discover no consistent or logically predictable pattern.

Not only does tradition no longer legitimize a discernible power pattern in the home, but the form of the small family in the United States offers virtually no protection for *any* authority. This is true of both its internal structure and its surrounding social supports. The type of authority that is institutionalized in mores and laws, the "jural" type, is surely gone (Mogey, 1957). There are no devices for underscoring family authority such as are found in other areas in life, in the corporation for example, or among families in peasant societies. Oscar Lewis (1959a, 1959b) concluded from his intensive study of Mexican family life that only men who are aging, impotent, homosexual, or "bewitched" are unable to carry out the authoritarian role of the husband in the strongly male-oriented Mexican culture.

By contrast, a man wields power in the contemporary household only if he has the personal characteristics to pull it off or because of a unique pattern of domestic relationships, not because society backs him up with strong support (Freilich, 1964). The weaknesses of patriarchal arrangements now outweigh advantages, as wives of any but the most resourceful fathers can attest, and the new ideal of companionship serves as the major ideological solvent for the old concept of paternal authority.

Discipline in the Small, Pragmatic Family

The sheer number of relationships that can occur within a family is greatly enlarged as its size increases, and the chances for conflicting loyalties and interests multiply proportionately. As the level of potential conflict is heightened, parents are likely to be less flexible and more authoritarian, and to rely more frequently on strong child-rearing controls (Elder and Bowerman, 1963). The child is expected to assume a passive role more often, especially in relations with father, and expressions of praise, approval, comfort, and acceptance are likely to be reduced in frequency for each child. Indeed, the need to formalize and centralize leadership in response to increasing group size has been observed in a variety of "task-oriented" experimental groups.

Conversely, the position of father as the family's "directive symbol" becomes more problematical as family size is reduced. Almost any kind of discipline has deeper emotional implications in a small group or family, and parents in such families seem to have greater anxieties about their children. It may very well be that the recent emphasis upon the need for the child to be wanted by his parents is a functional adaptation to the nuclear family pattern; G. R. Hawkes, Lee Burchinal, and B. Gardner (1958) found that children in small families do rely on their parents more for emotional security than children in large families do. The latter find security in relations with each other, while children in small families must look to their parents for intimacy and a sense of acceptance.

But should the parent be authoritarian, the consequences are magnified in the small family. An autocratic father or a nagging mother may be much the same in character as these types in the large family, but the context changes the nature of the children's reaction. A father who exerts a great deal of pressure on his children has far less impact on six than on one (Amatora, 1959). Moreover, a father with only one child may want that child to have many qualities that he admires in a person; a father of five need not expect so much of each child and may in fact delight in the striking differences among his children. In the small family a child can hardly be shielded from, or find escape from, a father's imperious control. The relationship between each child and the father is more intense, and the father's character is more likely to suffuse all family relationships. It is possible in the large family to have both more isolated members and more coalitions among the children. The father may be more authoritarian under these circumstances, but actual leadership is diffused and differentiated. Thus a "strong" father in the small family may have a greater salutary influence on his children, but potentially he also has a greater harmful effect.

Almost all available evidence indicates that oral methods of discipline and verbal reasoning tend to be used more often in the small family than in the large (Elder and Bowerman, 1963), which is but a specific example of the general tendency for the management of people in small groups to be based less upon command and physical duress and more upon flexible, pragmatic ingenuity. Father is still somewhat inclined to withhold privileges, while mother is the prime user of oral admonitions (Bossard and Carter, 1958-1959), but both employ a greater range of techniques than parents in large families do, and both rely more on knowledge of the strengths, weaknesses, and vulnerabilities of the children involved. Although manipulation itself has become suspect, we do not consider the person who influences others through the cunning use of rewards as deplorable as the crude authoritarian type; in fact, the shrewd manipulator is often admired.

Spanking and slapping as means of discipline are regarded with suspicion, especially in the middle and upper classes (Elder and Bowerman, 1963). Here psychological punishment, the reward orientation, and pragmatic control techniques are most highly prized, and it is here that the small-family system has been most completely accommodated. Class differences are apparently most pronounced, however, in the case of mothers. Compared to mothers in the lower classes, and to fathers in general, mothers in the middle and higher socioeconomic levels are least inclined to regard "obedience to parents" as a virtue (Kohn, 1950; Kantor, *et al.*, 1958; Sewell, 1961).

Middle-class fathers have opportunities to express power motives outside the home and partly for this reason are not likely to be driven to the exercise of domestic power (M. Hoffman, 1963b). The father's only chance to assert his will in the lower classes may occur on the family stage. In general, a more egalitarian approach to discipline is found in the middle classes, no doubt entailing some jockeying for power by the spouses, while in lower-class families the husband is prone to act imperiously toward both his wife and his children.

But parents in the middle classes are often more punitive than they realize; they use "reason" to control their children, but when that fails, as it often does, corporal punishment is by no means taboo (Dubin and Dubin, 1963). The frequency of this recourse is easily underestimated, as is the fact that even when reasoning succeeds, the child may have been swayed by an unstated threat of punishment.

Reasoning itself involves conditioned cues and is not devoid of the element of intimidation. The child perceives each control situation in terms of his previous experiences, which Elisabeth and Robert Dubin call the "serial reinforcement of sanctions." Even parents who consider themselves permissive customarily expect plain old-fashioned obedience more than they will admit and can become enraged by prolonged, willful disobedience. Aggression toward parents is rarely tolerated (Sears, Maccoby, and Levin, 1957), and apparently is not becoming more acceptable (Leslie and Johnsen, 1963). Parents are still apt to meet aggression with aggression, at least when the aggressive behavior comes from their children, although the same parents may find aggression toward others by their children a promising sign that the children are learning how to take care of themselves (Dubin and Dubin, 1963).

As might be expected, some facets of child rearing have reacted to the new dispensation of permissiveness more readily than others. The greatest change seems to have occurred in the acceptance, on a verbal level at least, of sexual curiosity by children. Indeed, a lively sex interest is encouraged in the current publications on sex education; it is considered healthy, which may be the most significant way modern parents are distinguished from the many sexually permissive parents in nonliterate groups: We have a theory! Advice in child-development texts clearly suggests that parents should be calm, unruffled, and nonpunitive in the midst of all sorts of challenges to their authority and that they should not consider the wisdom received from their own parents to be sacrosanct.

The increased tolerance of sexual inquisitiveness on the part of mother is an ambivalent one, however, and there is reason to assume that ambivalence is common among fathers too. Gerald Leslie and Kathryn Johnsen (1963) found that mothers were quite aware of their own anger when children were aggressive toward them, but these women believed they were more forbearing with regard to sex play than they actually were. Sexual broad-mindedness seems to operate more typically at the level of opinion than in our routine dealings with children.

Of course the exercise of parental authority has a more piercing emotional effect nowadays because of our reservations about authority in general. Antiauthoritarianism is "in the air," especially in current political thinking. Attitudes of youth toward the legitimacy of parental authority are by no means sharply defined, but our repeated promotion of the ideal of personal freedom and concern for the rights of the individual, not excepting the individual child, inevitably undermines traditional parental prerogatives. For this reason, permissiveness in child rearing reflects an underlying reaction to authoritarianism in the realm of politics and national government; antiauthoritarianism as a political ideology fosters antipatriarchy as a family ideology. The relaxation of paternal controls has been attractive in its own right, but it is also a rider on general ideological trends and stands to gain because the exercise of traditional authority is so easily routed in the modern family.

Patriarchy and the Sturdy-Oak Syndrome

As society changes, continuities linking the old to the new are inevitable, and hence certain facets of patriarchy can be expected to linger on. In fact, many people wish to maintain even greater continuity with the past, and have pleaded for the revival of a more authoritarian father to combat the ambiguities created by paternal weakness and general social upheaval. Parents are often admonished to set limits upon their children's behavior as a means of helping them make sound judgments on their own. Adolescents do seem to be more self-confident and independent in decision making if their parents explain the rules they are expected to follow in a clear, intelligible, and firm way (Elder, 1963). The rhetoric of patriarchy per se may have an appeal for contemporary society, but its application is another, less timely matter.

Our expectations for husbands and wives are still influenced by the traditional concepts of patriarchy: thus, for example, obstinate husbands are almost always more socially acceptable than stubborn wives. The father who fights for his dignity through the exercise of misguided authority is likely to receive our sympathy; in a comparable plight mother seems villainous. In the "mother manipulates father" comedies, the manipulating wife must be, above all, feminine—for all her trickery. But it remains true that, although ill-tempered women are clearly out of place in modern suburbia, they are not any more so than male troublemakers. In fact, the suburban shrew is probably a more common stereotype to most people than any male counterpart they can imagine.

But various studies suggest that fathers are still more likely than mothers to be dominant in the home. William Dyer and Dick Urban (1958) found evidence in support of the generally recognized trend toward parental equality, but they also found that the notion that father is the "head of the family" was sometimes retained. Yi-Chuang Lu (1952) found that fathers were most often judged by their children to be the ruling parent. Jerome Kagan (1956) found the same pattern; fathers in his study were also considered by their children to be less friendly, more punitive, and more threatening than mothers. There is strong evidence that where power wielded by parents is clearly unequal, father is more often the dominant influence. In a sample studied by Charles Bowerman and Glen Elder (1964), the extreme patriarchal family was more than three times as prevalent as the matriarchal extreme, nor were the mothers in the wife-dominated families considered to be as autocratic as the fathers who dominated. Joan Aldous (1961) also reports fathers to be harsh and unbending more often than mothers. When father has the upper hand, he is likely to use it as a "commander." The quality of female control is tempered by an almost inescapable heritage of maternal nurturance.

Nevertheless, the domineering mother, even if she is less autocratic than her paternal counterpart, is symptomatic of greater family tension than the overbearing father. Where extreme father dominance occurs, and the man is the principal agent of pressure and discipline in child rearing, mother usually retains an important family role, as she has for centuries. She is likely to be viewed by her children, by her husband, and by herself as the chief source of nurturance and emotional support for her children (Devereux, Bronfenbrenner, and Suci, 1962). In cases of extreme mother dominance, on the other hand, the mother is usually reported as the principal agent of both discipline and support, and father drops into the background as a slack and powerless figure. Maternal dominance is associated with high levels of marital conflict and inadequacy, indifference, or sheer wrong-headedness on the part of father. The father-ascendant pattern is overwhelmingly preferred.

Wives in father-dominated homes, as one might expect, are more satisfied with their family life than either wives or husbands in households controlled by mothers. Nathan Hurvitz (1965) reported that wives who are conservative, traditional in their outlook, and who advocate deference to the male, are even more likely to be happy in marriage than those with democratic orientations. Of course conventional women may find it impossible to say they are unhappy, but this pattern certainly suggests that we have not completed the move from the traditional to the equalitarian point of view or to a social order that fully supports and rewards marital parity.

Men are now asked to bring patience, understanding, and gentleness into their human dealings (qualities formerly reserved for women) yet they must still be strong in their relations with women (Hacker, 1957). In the ideal case, the man is self-confident and directive, yet solicitous and supportive of the weak (Lane, 1959). He is expected to be a sturdy oak—big, strong, and comforting, more self-controlled than his wife, and better able to cope with psychological pressures. Symptoms of mental illness, for example, are usually less tolerable in men than in women (Phillips, 1964).

Clearly, strength is better than weakness, and human warmth better than aloofness and inaccessibility. Together, strength and warmth enhance the desirable elements of each. Nevertheless, studies suggest an inverse relationship between the two. As fathers become more affectionate, they become less authoritarian (Bronfenbrenner, 1961b), and the most desirable balance between the two qualities is difficult to achieve.

Due to a combination of circumstances, the sturdy-oak syndrome is especially attractive, and practicable, in the middle classes. Here the father usually wields power more effectively than his lower-class counterpart and assumes more family responsibility, both alone and with his wife. Evidence from various sources—not just American—indicates that father's power in the family tends to vary directly with the economic rewards and social prestige of his work (Strodtbeck, 1958; Blood and Wolfe, 1960; Bronfenbrenner, 1961b). John Mogey (1957) reported a study in Paris showing a striking variation in the power and authority of French fathers by social class. Bourgeois fathers, by contrast with those in the working classes, were more likely to control the family budget, monitor the list of family friends, and decide where the family would spend its annual holiday, especially when their wives did not work.

Middle-class fathers also exercise power in a different way from those in the lower classes and within a context of closer interpersonal relations. In particular, their power is tempered by supportive measures; their commands are combined with a greater knowledge of what can reasonably be expected of the immature and greater patience with the perversities of childhood (M. Hoffman, 1963a). Despite his conformist image, the middle-class father is less annoyed by his children if they are unlike other children than fathers in either the higher or the lower classes (Nunn, 1964). But, although his control efforts are marked by the use of reason and strategies of compromise, his teen-age children are still likely to consider him the dominant parent in the home.

Nevertheless, an impressive body of evidence points to a greater than average retention of the ideal of paternal power in the lower classes, both in individual families and in neighborhood clusters. The lower-class father is more likely to attempt to wield power in the family, but with a minimum of supportive gestures (Duvall, 1946; Kohn, 1959; Straus, 1964); retaining the worst features of the patriarchal tradition, he tends to be domineering, autocratic, authoritarian, and probably quite arbitrary. The pattern seems to hold no matter what index of social status is used (Elder, 1962b), and whether the informants are parents or children. The lower-class husband may not succeed in mastering his wife—he fails quite frequently—but it is taken for granted that he will try, and he often worries that his wife will turn to extramarital sex in retaliation for his efforts to dominate (Rainwater, 1964).

The authoritarian bearing of the lower-class father toward his wife in turn propels her to greater aggressiveness toward the children, with the result that adolescents in this milieu are actually more likely than middle-class youth to report mother as the dominant parent (Bowerman and Elder, 1964). Obligations assumed by mothers are more total in the lower social levels; the mothers have a more consistent relationship with the children, while fathers, despite their "power assertiveness," cultivate the fine art of avoiding domestic responsibility, which is but one of a set of traits in the lower socioeconomic levels reflecting a pronounced reservation about fatherhood, if not outright rejection of the role (Kohn and Carroll, 1960; Komarovsky, 1964). Although father may be defined as the final authority, by default he usually has less influence over the daily family routine than his wife, or her mother, to whom she often looks for guidance.

Traditional expectations with regard to husband and wife roles also remain particularly strong among boys (Dunn, 1960). Alver Jacobson (1952) found that males in general were significantly more conservative or favorable to male-dominant positions than women. Jacobson also found that divorced men had the most male-dominant attitudes of all, while divorced women led the field in endorsement of feminine-egalitarian attitudes. The difference between the mean scores on Jacobson's measure of attitudes toward power in marriage for the divorced couples was approximately four times as great as that between scores for married couples. Since divorced women are more likely than women who have never married to marry divorced men, this contrast gives one pause; either clashes over authority are exceptionally intense in remarriages or such couples have learned to work around the issue.

The very perception of authority patterns appears to differ between men and women. Robert Hess and Judith Torney (1962) found that boys in their sample were inclined to see father in the ruling position at home, while girls were more apt to think mother was boss. Girls were also more likely to perceive egalitarianism in the relationship between parents than boys were. In a study by Theodore Johannis and James Rollins (1959), more teen-age boys than girls viewed their families as patricentric; in spite of the fact that both mothers and daughters tend to exaggerate the traditionalism of fathers, girls more often reported either egalitarian or democratic decision making in their families (Steinmann, 1958).

It is possible, of course, that homes in which there are boys tend to be particularly father-dominated, which would explain these data as well as the theory that boys tend to be more perceptive of authoritarianism than girls. It is also possible that differences in perception can be traced to the fact that mothers devote relatively more time to the control of daughters, while fathers concentrate on their sons. We cannot say yet which is the correct answer, but each view supports the proposition that traditional authority orientations are more prevalent among males than females.

Such orientations may also be stronger among Catholics than Protestants. Catholic children report less egalitarianism in relationships between their parents than do non-Catholics; they tend to see either father or mother as "boss" more often than Protestants do (Blood and Wolfe, 1960). Glen Elder (1962b) found a somewhat similar pattern in his research, but he points out that it is the Catholic father, not the mother, who is more authoritarian. Throughout its history, the Catholic Church has stressed nurturance and compliance in motherhood; it has never accorded mother a strong, controlling position.

In earlier times "devoutness" was associated with patriarchy, an association that may linger especially among Catholics and Jews. Perhaps religiosity and respect for father go hand in hand, both part of a more inclusive value system. Judson Landis (1960) found that the feeling of closeness to father by both sons and daughters is more positively associated with parental religiosity than is closeness to mother. Where religious sanctions are strong, it may very well be that father has been instrumental in making them strong, and an aspect of these very sanctions is respect for father. Thus, the decline of religiosity becomes symptomatic of the erosion of paternal authority (or vice versa).

But Landis also provides evidence of an association between religious piety and the contemporary stress on parental equality; devoutness was found to be associated with the egalitarian family pattern, while indifference to religion was associated with the extremes of a father- or mother-dominated home. This was true of both males and females and applied to about the same degree among Catholics, Protestants, and Jews. Perhaps the most valid generalization with regard to the relationship between religion and paternal authority can be formulated in this way: Religious sensitivity reflects the age in which we live—in a patriarchal age, paternal power assumes religious significance; in an age of sexual equality, the same value becomes suspect.

Current trends clearly favor sexual equality. Father's authority in the household has been reduced along with general changes in the pattern of work and social power in the modern community. Father's domestic power declines relative to mother's, but both parents have relatively less control over their children as outside authorities are allowed a larger role in the care and training of youth. Nevertheless, traces of patriarchy are retained in the form of the "sturdy-oak syndrome," and fathers, more often than mothers, are still dominating figures in the home. In the ideal case, father is self-confident and directive, yet protective of those weaker than himself, and better able than mother to cope with the more difficult family crises caused by unexpected events originating outside the family.

PART TWO

The Man as Parent

The Marital Prelude to Fatherhood

The first task for father is adaptation to marriage. Before he has a child, even before a child is conceived, the husband and would-be father must make some accommodation to conjugal life. This is only indirectly a problem of fatherhood, of course, but there are indeed preparatory fatherhood duties if the man is to bring some measure of proficiency to the role, let alone excellence. Becoming a parent is a critical transition in one's life, as E. E. LeMasters (1957) has shown; it is a greater one if it is superimposed upon marital troubles (Dyer, 1963). All favorable adjustments before children are born increase the couple's ability to cope with later family stresses, while unresolved problems contribute to future failures, compound earlier ones, and strain the environment in which children are to be reared. At the very least, delays in adjustment increase the probability of difficulties.

There is no evidence to suggest that having children improves or enhances a couple's ability to handle marriage problems. The relatively high divorce rate among childless couples is the consequence of a high separation rate in the first years of marriage, when childlessness is most likely, and is not due to any increments of marital virtuosity brought about by the presence of young children. When a twosome becomes a threesome, the number and variety of possible conflicts are in fact increased. A spouse may sacrifice his own interests and pride more readily "for the sake of the children," but new problems turn up. All too often children precipitate crises that "for their sake" solutions fail to resolve.

The pattern of parent-child relations is conditioned by the tensions that already existed between husband and wife before the birth of the child. Because the total field of involvement and annoyance has been enlarged, earlier tensions usually become less salient, but they do not disappear. Earl Koos (1950) found that family crises resulting from strained parent-child relations occur more than twice as often as those resulting from strained husband-wife relationships, and it seems likely that this ratio is maintained as the children grow older. Unfortunately, husband-wife relations do not benefit as much from the children's maturation as parents of troublesome infants inevitably hope. Kathryn Powell (1963) offered the discouraging suggestion that marital relationships may often develop new vulnerabilities when children reach adolescence.

Father's Marital Challenge

Much more penetrating knowledge than we now possess must be gathered before we can fully understand the behavioral conditions linking marital adjustment to parental performance, parent-child relations, and the child's personality. Terms such as "marital adjustment," "marital happiness," "marital accommodation," and "marital success," although suggesting matters of genuine human concern, are not used much more meaningfully now than they were forty years ago. We still cannot agree on what they mean or what their most profitable definitions should be.

"Marriage accommodation" is a particularly useful term when discussing the health of a marriage, however, because it implies that couples do not usually resolve all their problems, but rather that they must accommodate to something less than perfect adjustment. Accommodation in marriage encompasses three processes: *mutualization, idealization,* and *marriage enchantment.* Each originates before the couple is married and each is gradually patterned, continually modified, and thoroughly steeped in marriage itself.

Through *mutualization* the man and woman acquire habits and routines by which their activities become interdependent and coordinated. Each relinquishes a measure of autonomy and reduces involvement with "third parties," and the two become accustomed to taking one another into account when planning for the future—for the coming evening, the next day, the next weekend, or the next year. Rhona Rapoport (1963) refers to the early stages of marriage as the time of change from "self-orientation" to "mutuality." This period actually begins even before marriage, since some commitment by the couple to a life of mutual interest and concern must be made before they marry.

Idealization is the process by which the couple develops a heightened pleasure in one another; each magnifies the other's strengths, reduces awareness of weaknesses, and perhaps sees virtues in the other that are not really there (Waller, 1937). At least some idealization seems to be necessary if couples are to meet the minimum standards of romance in our society.

Enchantment involves two processes: the increase of hope or confidence that marriage itself—that is, the institution of marriage—is desirable (development of this precedes even the courtship stage for girls), and growth of the conviction that marriage with the current partner will be a most enthralling state.

Thus, in courtship, couples mutualize their activities, develop idealized images of one another, and become increasingly enchanted with the prospects of their marriage.

Little is known about interrelationships among the three processes, but we can assume that when couples enter marriage, their idealization of each other and their enchantment with marriage are at high levels of intensity. Their mutualization of life activities, however, is adapted to the routines of courtship much more satisfactorily than to those of marriage, since the couple is just embarking on joint living arrangements.

In fact, inordinately high levels of idealization are linked with narrow patterns of mutuality: the more time couples spend together in a wide range of activities, the less likely they are to maintain idealized images of one another. Therefore problems of mutualization will assume the greatest significance after marriage; they are the ones that will affect, more often negatively than positively, the revised state of idealization that accompanies experience in marriage. They are also the problems of greatest importance for the performance of father.

Mutualization is thus the key problem in marriage accommodation and is to be the primary concern in this chapter. The most pressing challenge confronting father can be stated most effectively as the temptation to disengage himself from vital concern for the state of his marriage and for the daily affairs of his family. What is most important for father is not so much accommodation to marriage per se as retention of an abiding sensitivity to and concern for the quality of his family life.

The concept of "familism" has been the subject of much confusion (Rogers and Sebald, 1962), but it is usefully defined as a state of mind in which the well-being of the family—whether that of the nuclear or the extended family—takes priority over other things. Evidence collected by Purnell Benson (1952) indicates that common interests in certain things, especially similar concerns for family life, are essential for marital adjustments; however, dissimilar interests in a variety of activities, such as the use of television, need not cause serious conflict. The key to success is the couple's mutual involvement in home life, children, and the establishment of some kind of expressive relationship; the contemporary father's task is to retain a strong family commitment, especially a vital place in the family division of labor, in spite of the loss of conjugal and familial powers once associated with the male family role. This is a variation of the universal problem of harnessing father to the family yoke.

Philip Slater (1961) has written about the social limits to what he calls "libidinal withdrawal"; he calls attention to the fact that it can be dangerous for intensive erotic and love orientations of the individual to be turned inward upon marriage and family life. If romantic introversion should become the common marriage condition, he argues, then the striving of citizens in behalf of the larger collectivity might become too weak to sustain important community, state, national, and international efforts. William Goode (1959) has also developed this interesting theoretical point, and Talcott Parsons (1964) argues that there is an intrinsic connection between erotic attachment and disengagement from broader social interests. But there is an even greater possibility that the "libidinal energies" of the male may *not* be sufficiently or adequately turned inward upon his family. In fact, these male energies are not automatically focused upon any social purpose in an effective way, certainly not in recent history. Women are expected to turn their energies inward upon the family, and usually do, but men are expected to turn their energies both inward and outward. The greatest danger in the case of both sexes is that they will exaggerate the prevailing expectation for their sex, not that they will fail to respect it. Thus, women tend to become overcommitted to their parochial household affairs, and men tend to become preoccupied with their careers.

Marriage and Parenthood

In the absence of concerted research into the relationship between marriage adjustment and the performance of the couple as parents, we are prisoners of our unverified insights and can only hope they spring, in David Riesman's phrase, from a "seasoned subjectivity." Considerable work has been done concerning the effects of marital tension upon the "adjustment" of the child, but results are contradictory. Lois Hoffman and R. Lippitt (1960) have reviewed a number of such studies: they suggest that measures of adjustment of the married couple and those of the child are almost never made independently, which explains at least part of whatever correlations have been reported. The adjustment of parents, for example, is often judged by their offspring, and perhaps children who get on well with their parents cannot help but think their parents live in harmony with each other.

Negative evidence concerning the effect of marital adjustment on parental performance is impressive, although by no means conclusive. Orville Brim, Roy Fairchild, and Edgar Borgatta (1961) could discover no correlation between husband-wife relationships and child-rearing patterns. Lee Burchinal, Glenn Hawkes, and Bruce Gardner (1957) found no correlation between father's marital adjustment and certain facets of the personalities of his children, and very little between mother's adjustment and characteristics of her children. Graham Blaine (1963) contends that children can shrug off much more family discord than most adults realize. William Westley and Nathan Epstein (1960b) could find no indisputable relationship between the quality of parental sex relations and the level of emotional health among children. They did claim, however, that the nature of family organization—the patterning of its relationships—was more important for the mental health of children than the state of the parent's mental health per se. But Charles Bowerman and Glen Elder (1964) contend that conjugal relations are separable from parent-child relations; their data consistently indicate that parental power in parent-adolescent relations provides a better explanation of the variation in school achievement drives among youth than the structure of husband-wife relations does. Similarly, Helena Lopata (1965) claims that many American women regard their roles as wives and mothers as distinct from each other and that fathers have lower priority in the eyes of most women than do their children!

Nevertheless, it seems reasonable to assume that an unstable marital relationship will impair the coordination necessary for effective child rearing, as many students of family life have argued (Baruch, 1937; Baruch and Wilcox, 1944; Nye, 1957a). Just as any tension in the staff of a mental hospital is immediately reflected in the conduct of the patients, tension at home is rarely lost on the children (probably less often than Graham Blaine suggests). This is especially true of the modern small family system, since the key to stability in the nuclear family, by contrast with that in the extended family of earlier times, is the effectiveness of the husband-wife team.

There is, in fact, no scarcity of evidence linking marital adjustment to effectiveness in child rearing. Wallin and Vollmer (1953) found that parents who are well-adjusted to one another are more likely to have strong, satisfying relationships with their children. They take pleasure in associations with the children, and in turn their offspring are likely to find satisfaction. No clear indication of a causal relationship emerges from this study, however, since the conditions enabling parents to find pleasure in one another are usually the same qualities enabling them to have gratifying relationships with their children.

Bernard Farber and Julia McHale's (1959) work indicates that consistency in child rearing, which students of family life first learned to recommend and are only now learning to identify, is at least partly a function of marital harmony, that is, agreement between spouses on marital values and role expectations. Philip Slater (1961) suggests the same thing. J. Howard Kauffman (1961) found that among Mennonites harmonious parent-child relations were associated with high marital adjustment scores. Snell Putney and Russell Middleton (1961) concluded that college students, especially girls, were more likely to conform to the religious beliefs of their parents when the parents were in substantial agreement with one another. They have alerted researchers to the fact that it is not enough to investigate individual parental attitudes toward child rearing; one must consider the pattern of interaction between parents and its effect on the decisions they make. Thomas Langner and Stanley Michael (1963) found that parental quarreling affected the mental health of children even more adversely than educational, religious, or ethnic differences between spouses. Ezra Vogel (1960) is still another research-oriented student of the family who has stressed the importance of the parents' marital configuration, not simply the psychodynamics of each parent as an individual, for the emotional health of the children. The child is often a pawn of parents in conflict, Vogel argues, and may even be used as a means of preserving an unstable marriage. Emotional disturbance in the child can result when the child internalizes the conflicting demands of parents, especially when such demands spring from disorder in the marriage (Vogel and Bell, 1960).

Judson Landis (1962a) found that a feeling of closeness by the child to both parents is a more accurate index of family integration than the child's feeling toward either the mother or the father. He also found that this sense of closeness to both parents is associated with cooperation between parents in their efforts to control the child.

These studies lack a truly cumulative impact because the various researchers have defined marital adjustment in different ways, and they use different indices of child-rearing effectiveness. But the research does suggest a relationship between the quality of marital relations and the conditions of childhood.

In fact, the roles of mother and father are, in a social sense, only meaningful as reciprocal roles. Although both imply a primary association with offspring, in our imagery of family life the father-child relationship is assumed to cross-stitch that between mother and child, just as activities, affections, and interests between mother and father are assumed to intersect. "Mothering behavior" is not simply the product of the mother's nature, but is influenced by her relationships with father, her marital frustrations, and by the father's attitudes toward the children. Mothering is as much a function of the woman's position in the family structure as it is an expression of her personality, and this is surely true of fathering as well.

On formal grounds alone it would seem to be important for the modern couple to attain a minimal level of marital accommodation. In their relationships with one another they must maintain a balance between practical considerations and sentiment in order to establish a basis for consistency as well as cooperation in child rearing, and such a balance is no longer sustained by the simple expedient of being conventional. Tradition cannot prescribe roles for husbands and wives, although, as mentioned earlier, instrumentalism is still most often attributed to the husband and expressiveness to the wife. But mutual expressiveness is implicit in the modern conception of husband-wife relations, and it is quite apparent that husbands are now expected to have both instrumental and expressive talents. Marital accommodation becomes an adaptive process that requires flexibility. If keeping tension under control is desirable while children are being reared, the contemporary husband-wife team must *achieve* a relatively high level of adjustment with regard to both work and sentiment.

Moreover, fathers (and mothers) who are capable of warm, expressive marriage relations, and who are also able to establish a satisfactory division of utilitarian roles, are more likely to inculcate such qualities in their children. The transmission of these qualities is probably even more important—though less apparent—than the ethnic, racial, and socioeconomic status that parents pass on.

Of course, some marriages may be based on essentially instrumental arrangements, offering very little in the way of expressive satisfactions. A couple may find rewards in living together even though there is no warm feeling between them, except occasionally during sex relations, or whenever they can share some sentiment based on their mutual interest in the children. Some couples like to argue, challenge, badger, and even hurt one another, and can be counted on to come back for more (Berne, 1964). Perhaps the very survival of a marriage gives the couple some satisfaction through identification with the expressive pleasures presumed to exist in unbroken marriages, and the children may also share in these pleasures. But rearing children under such circumstances seems to be fraught with dangers, if only because the children themselves are likely to recreate the same family pattern when they marry.

Companionship has become a more important part of marital adjustment than it was in marriages on the farm, where husband, wife, children, and occasionally boarders or other kinsmen made up a work team, and children were brought up within a context of essential family labor. Work to be done is no longer the immediate reality facing children as they grow up; the ambience established by the unique web of personal relations within the family is now a crucial social condition in the life of the child. Though secondary insofar as our urban occupational order is concerned, the need for marriage adjustment on the part of the male has become much more important as a result.

In Chapter III we called attention to the fact that, with industrialization, the father-mother team becomes the center of both family management and the expressive life, while the larger kinship unit is reduced in importance. Ideally, marriage becomes a deeper, more stable emotional relationship, and deviations from the ideal are more likely to cause trouble. More is now required of the couple than the stoic ability to put up with each other, or the willingness of the wife to suffer a man as long as he gets his work done.

Male Reluctance

One reason that the man as husband and father poses a mutualization problem in marriage is because he was not carefully groomed for paternal roles as he was growing up. While girls look forward eagerly to marriage, boys are more likely to grimace at the thought. This childhood difference lasts through the teens, leaving young men more willing than their girl friends to skip marriage altogether; the pattern is even more pronounced among boys in the lower classes (Christensen, 1961a).

Negro males are particularly reluctant to marry. Carlfred Broderick (1965) found that, during the age period from ten to thirteen, white children followed the traditional pattern: girls were far more romantically inclined than boys. Negro boys, however, showed a high level of preadolescent heterosexual interest and involvement. The anomaly was then compounded because white males become somewhat more willing to marry as they progress through their teens, while the reverse is true for Negro men; they are progressively disenchanted. These differences reflect the relative commitment of the two racial groups to middle-class social norms and their different opportunities within the middle-class order.

Returning to general sex differences, men give different explanations from women for not wishing to marry, especially economic or educational reasons; women are more likely to say there is no satisfactory mate in prospect (Rose, 1951). Having found the "right girl," a man is still prone to find reasons extrinsic to the relationship for not marrying. His girl friend is more often single-minded in her desire to enter the married state and enjoy the family life it brings. Men, regarding reservations about marriage as a mark of their sex, are more likely to call the wedding off if they are ambivalent, disturbed, or suspicious about what they are getting into. They are more likely than women to find reason for caution and to look for another girl or wait for a better time.

But during courtship the young man does of course find excitement and pleasure in his new romantic interest. Let us assume that mutualization, idealization, and enchantment all progress in a normal manner; the man and woman "fall in love," and they marry. The proposition to be explored is that problems of marital and parental adjustment for the husband are qualitatively different from those for his wife and that this difference remains a source of friction throughout their family life (Havighurst, 1957).

First, men rarely experience the fear of never marrying, and if they do, it is not with the intensity known to women. The woman thinks incessantly about her forthcoming marriage and is likely to discuss it at great length with her mother and friends, much more than her boy friend does. There is good reason to believe that the more talking she does with various people about sex and family roles, the more consistent her familial attitudes are likely to become (Kammeyer, 1964). If this principle holds true for men, as it probably does, it follows that men, talking less about their courtship experiences, would have less distinct and less consistent expectations about what is likely to occur after the wedding. Although the girl may have faced some disturbing questions, if only because she has thought for so long about her courtship, she is inclined to go through with the wedding anyway, entering marriage with greater ambivalence than men ordinarily experience. As a result, she is more thoroughly prepared for the reality shocks to come.

In spite of his greater reluctance to marry, or perhaps because of it, the man is more likely to be disappointed with his spouse after marriage. Roland Tharp (1963), for example, noted a greater discrepancy between what men hoped for in marriage and what they get than among women. The sheer naïveté with which men enter matrimony probably explains this fact. They are not alone, but their marital ingenuousness commonly exceeds that of women. Paul Hilsdale (1962) found that as a rule neither men nor women enter marriage with unduly romantic images of one another, but they do have a naïve faith in their ability to work out all problems, mainly because they feel they will be able to talk to each other about their difficulties. They have, he says, an "almost infantile confidence in the medicinal powers of mere communication." The male may have no greater confidence in communication than the female, but he is more prone to think, mistakenly, that the interpersonal problems of marriage are easily solved. This is a rather unconscious transplantation of the spirit of engineering, found rather commonly among men, to family life. Girls have an advantage because they are closer students of interpersonal relationships and are disposed to study boys as they grow up, while the boys superciliously ignore girls.

Greater family naïveté is the price men must pay. They are usually less prepared for marriage than women, having thought about it less, and are more shocked by its revelations. If, however, men are no more disheartened by the recognizable indignities of marriage than women, or perhaps even less so as we shall see, it is because there are other roles, their careers especially, that absorb so much of their thoughts.

The Initial Shock and Beyond

A certain amount of shock and disenchantment typically follows marriage; it may appear even during the honeymoon. The transition to marriage is associated with more disillusionment than any other courtship transition, especially for the husband (Hobart, 1958). Any misperception or misinformation in the process of selecting a mate must bring about some disappointment as the mistakes are discovered, and a few errors are almost certain to be made. No one is able to perceive complicated personality processes perfectly, especially those in which he is passionately involved, but the idealization occurring during courtship adds immeasurably to our deception. As a matter of fact, idealization seems to be a necessary *mis*perception process, required because of our current stress on love as the basis for marriage; it propels the couple toward matrimony as nothing else can. Sidney Greenfield (1965) argues that this is the primary function of romantic love, since there are compelling reasons in a society that stresses rational decision making to opt against marriage, especially in the case of the male. The love complex induces people to make a family effort; the romantic trappings characteristic of courtship help to assure that the lovers' faults will not be discovered before the wedding and that the marriage rate will remain high.

Even under the very best courtship conditions certain facets of the partner's nature cannot be fully appreciated or perfectly forewarned against. These are the components of personality that become visible only after the wedding, when changes in the circumstances surrounding the couple almost inevitably occur. The new context breeds a new perspective. Getting married is associated with a high level of mobility, for example, not only because the marriage requires a new household, but also because the "just marrieds" are in the most mobile age group in the population. Even the appearance of new acquaintances in the life of the couple may illuminate heretofore unnoticed personal traits, and the newlyweds are still establishing their circle of most congenial friends.

A common source of disillusionment after marriage, especially among teen-age couples, is the set of unrealistic expectations that are brought into married life. Robert Herrmann (1965) found that young couples frequently think they will be able to have immediately what it took their parents years to accumulate; husbands in particular are quite willing to buy cars that consume an unreasonably large part of the budget. In the United States, where marriage hopes are kept at a high level by the outrageously optimistic mass media, and from which the more realistic, often cynical, life lore shared by close friends cannot protect everyone, disillusionment may be particularly distressing. People who are most at the mercy of television's image of universal happiness are probably most susceptible; those who enjoy a circle of friends to counter the alienation fostered by slick popular culture have a distinct advantage.

A rather specific reason for male disillusionment in marriage is created by the "sex-looks syndrome." As Winston Ehrmann (1959) has shown, boys are attracted to romanticism in adolescence only *after* developing a strong erotic orientation in their relations with girls. Therefore, at the very outset marriage has a special sex-linked imagery and significance for them. The most compelling initial push toward marriage for boys is the sex drive, which is molded in the preadolescent and early adolescent male peer groups.

But as girls are growing up they are taught a complex of modesty, reticence, and rejection of sexual interests that often continues into marriage. Ordinarily girls are not rewarded by the important people in their lives for being passionate (Rainwater, 1964). Their greatest worry is that they may not marry; their most enchanting hope is that they will someday have healthy babies. Thus, while the average teen-age boy is thinking erotic thoughts, the girl daydreams about her future husband and the children she will soon be having. The pattern continues in college, where sororities underscore the female style; they are oriented to the task of husband getting much more than fraternities concern themselves with wife getting. Sororities also exercise a much more inhibitive influence with regard to the premarital sex interests of their members (Scott, 1965).

In fact, men have a symbolic, even a mythic, significance for women quite unlike that which women have for men. The female is either *sex partner* or *mother* in the male's most vivid imagery. To a woman, on the other hand, the man is a potential link in the family chain; he is an essential partner making the desired state of motherhood possible. As Helena Lopata (1965) has demonstrated so effectively, women consider the role of mother much more important than that of wife; it would almost appear that to many women men are a necessary evil. By contrast, the man who conceives of his girl friend as a kind of catalytic agent enabling fatherhood is a rarity indeed. This is true in spite of the fact that men who escape the father role are always in the minority, and they usually suffer reduced status unless they engage in important, compensating community activities.

The girl's physical attractiveness is the basis for her fascination and her sex appeal; boys encourage one another to seek sexual release in dating with attractive girls, while the girls are more likely to be looking for "love." Even as unmarried men grow older they tend to retain the image of an ideal wife with the same erotic qualities that fascinated them in their youth, as can be inferred from Paul Glick's (1957) study of the increasing age differential between bride and groom as the age of the groom advances. This difference between men and women in initial courtship motivation becomes the basis for different processes of marital disillusionment for the sexes; men are more likely to be disappointed by the erotic content of their marriages, while women may feel that their dreams of romance have not been fulfilled.

Thus, fatherhood, like marriage itself, is less important to men than motherhood is to women, in spite of the fact that maternity causes severe limitations on women's activities. William Saroyan (1964) is not the only person who claims to have known many men who were adamantly opposed to having children. A. E. Hotchner (1966) quotes Ernest Hemingway (called Papa by his intimates): "To be a successful father, there's one absolute rule: when you have a kid, don't look at it for the first two years." In societies and social circles where women learn to read and thus are encouraged to seek psychic mobility, disaffection with motherhood does appear, but usually not in a critical way until one or two children are born. Women are more receptive than men to the idea of artificial insemination (Vernon and Boadway, 1959), but this merely reflects what Clifford Kirkpatrick (1955) calls women's greater "parental urge." (Kirkpatrick, incidentally, does not claim that this urge is the product of inherent sex differences. He discusses in detail various factors that affect its intensity.)

Fortunately, there is some convergence of erotic and love interests in later adolescence (Ehrmann, 1959); boys gradually become more romantic as they progress through the courtship cycle and girls become somewhat more erotic. But it may be years, a decade or more, before the intersection of these interests allows the couple maximal gratification in intercourse (Kinsey, Pomeroy, and Martin, 1948) and a feeling that they have balanced love and eroticism.

Physical appearance and sex, which have a major role in enticing males into heterosexual relations, become much less important in marriage itself. Unless bolstered by other attributes, they "wash out" quickly and merge with many considerations that received little attention before. Females, on the other hand, place relatively more emphasis on the quality and extent of mutual relations during courtship and on the male's potential ability as a breadwinner. These facets of the couple's relationship remain important, and judgments made about them, as well as attractions based upon them, are likely to hold up somewhat better in marriage. Thus, the male disillusionment generally operates more swiftly (Pineo, 1961) because of the kind of optimism from which it springs.

But the couple's mutualization is under attack after marriage in any case. Peter Pineo (1961) found that particularly great losses are shown in the area of "sharing of interests and activities." The pattern of mutuality the couple has developed must change when they start living together. During courtship the sharing of leisure activities is emphasized precisely because other kinds of intimacy are not permitted. Just as idealization is often overdone during courtship, couples frequently "overengage" at this time, doing things together that do not give both, or perhaps either, of them very much pleasure. After marriage, these sham activities are weeded out. Domestic and occupational involvements loom larger and may automatically result in less emphasis on the sharing of leisure.

Thus, disillusionment is brought about by the inevitable difficulties of interweaving long-established life habits as much as by the couple's need to develop new routines in order to cope with unaccustomed situations. The strengths and virtues of each spouse are now subjected to severe tests, and weaknesses that were previously minimized (due to idealization) are raised into sharper relief.

Ironically, marital deterioration is especially likely to occur where conjugal roles are not rigidly prescribed by society. As Clifford Kirkpatrick (1955) has observed, human beings can stand almost any situation that is inevitable and clearly defined; adjustment to social roles varies directly with the clarity with which they are culturally defined. The main strength and greatest potential weakness of the flexible, "partnership" type of marriage idealized in contemporary America is that it permits rich, full relations between husband and wife, *if* they are well suited to one another. Compared with an American couple, for example, the Australian husband and wife seem to share fewer activities and to participate less often in joint decision making. Their lower level of mutualization is not the result of personal impulse but of different social expectations. Their marital roles are clearly prescribed and do not stress partnership in the American sense of the term. The consequence, according to Lincoln Day (1964), is a reduction in opportunities for friction, which is probably one of the reasons for the lower divorce rate in Australia. (Certainly not the only one. Day does not argue that the nonpartnership type of marriage will always produce the lowest divorce rate, but in terms of the overall configuration of American as against Australian family systems, this becomes an important factor.)

Ordinarily the couple will make some sort of peace with the recurrent conditions that persist in their marriage which are less than completely satisfying. This, of course, is an accommodation to disillusionment, which is not an exclusively marital phenomenon. If it were, successful adjustment in marriage would be much less common than it is. Most of us learn to handle disillusionment in various aspects of life before we marry, and accommodation in marriage is but a special form of our generalized resignation. Nevertheless, marriage confronts many people with a kind of disillusionment that is acutely distressing, and the alternative to making a private truce is marital *deterioration.* The failure to compromise and conciliate differences turns the three accommodation processes on their heads. Idealization becomes alienation, and the spouses begin to see only egregious qualities in one another. Mutualization becomes disengagement, and the spouses disentangle their life routines from one another. And enchantment becomes disenchantment; enchantment with the institution of marriage is not lost as a rule, judging by the high remarriage rate in the

United States, but enchantment with the present marriage is destroyed.

These three expressions of deterioration are correlated and are very likely to operate together as a more general process of marital devolution (Pineo, 1961). Feelings of loneliness typically accompany the process, although Pineo has supplied evidence that loss of satisfaction in marriage is relatively independent of the personal life adjustment of the spouses. It is typical for people to show greater loss of marital satisfaction than loss of personal fulfillment in the course of their marriage, which is to say that one may not be too happy with his marriage and still be reasonably happy! On his deathbed the essayist William Hazlitt, who suffered domestic discord, unrequited love, financial troubles, and ill health throughout his life, is quoted as having said, in all seriousness, "Well, I've had a happy life."

A special temptation for the father issues from the fact that he has broader opportunities to find escape outside of marriage and still be reasonably happy! On his deathbed the Paternal neglect takes two primary forms: the man may withdraw from the daily routines of the household and become emotionally indifferent to his family, or he may attempt to withdraw material support from the household. Of course he could do both. Middle-class neglect is more often of the former variety and apparently presents the lesser problem. It is easier to adjust to a husband who is not much fun to be with, perhaps none at all, than to one who neglects his more utilitarian duties. A sour father who makes a good living, for example, is one thing; a charming father who cannot keep a job is a more difficult matter. (Paternal neglect will be discussed in more detail.)

Marriage, Fathering, and the Job

When men marry they obviously must make some adaptation to the domestic condition. More or less simultaneously they make another adjustment to the job away from home, and it is this occupational role that society is organized to license, supervise, and reward. Fine distinctions can be made concerning the worker's proficiency—a "good man" is paid better than a fairly good man, and for a very good man the sky is the limit—but no such invidious gradations can be arranged for men who excel in the husband and father role. As a result, the man is under great pressure to prepare for work and to conform to company demands. Because his ambitions are vested in occupational success, his striving to get ahead at work is accepted without question. Job skills are cultivated; family roles can be played impulsively. It is not surprising, therefore, that grandfathers—more than grandmothers—often attempt to do things for their grandchildren that they could never do for their own children. They were preoccupied during the course of the earlier parental experience (Neugarten and Weinstein, 1964).

Since men are frequently engrossed in their work as women can be only rarely, and some men find their work distinctly more rewarding than marriage, it is no surprise that men derive relatively less satisfaction from marriage than women and that their needs are less completely gratified by it (Winch, 1952). Arnold Rose (1951) found that the "closeness" of family life, as reported by college students, was strongly associated with the life satisfactions of their mothers, not fathers. Although this may mean that the satisfied mother breeds familial closeness more than the satisfied father, it also suggests that close family relations are more important to women and do in fact give them more pleasure than men. In a study of homosexuality in prison, David Ward and Gene Kassebaum (1964) found that female prisoners require more emotional support than male prisoners, which is one reason homosexuality occurs more frequently in women's prisons. Rose Giallombardo (1966) also found that marriage ties and family groups were of great interest in the female but not in the male prison culture. Among women, difficulties in adapting to prison life are problems of being away from "home and family" to a much greater extent than they are among men. In their concern for family associations, women are even more alert to the implications of divorce than men are; the divorced woman is carefully observed as a possible model by dissatisfied wives, whereas the divorced man is less likely to discuss his divorce experiences with cronies, and his cronies are less likely to give him a chance to do so.

Thus it seems that while estrangement from domesticity leads to despair among women, it is more readily faced with indifference by men. Apparently many men in the middle classes can throw themselves all the more into their work, while those in the lower classes seek male companionship away from home. And some men do without family life altogether; there are no skid rows for homeless women.

Although work away from home contributes to a lower threshold for family indifference among men, employment and occupational success interferes less with an acceptable level of familism for them than it does for women. Nor does such success reduce marriageability for men. Unmarried men tend to be less successful and to have greater employment problems than married men; unmarried women, on the other hand, usually have higher career potential than married women. The successful career woman is less likely to have children than a man with a comparable job; he is not even thought of as a *career* man. Genevieve Knupfer (1966) claims that single men are less happy, less satisfied at work, and generally in poorer spirits than either single or married women, or married men. Divorced men who are doing well are even more likely to remarry than the ones who are less successful; divorced women with good incomes are less likely to remarry (Bernard, 1956). The man can throw himself into his work and still fulfill male obligations at home, mainly because the latter are minimal.

The process of preparation for career success tends to reduce the chances of marriage, and consequently of motherhood, for women. Freshman girls who want to undertake graduate work after college tend to be independent of their parents and aloof to the typical feminine-aspiration formula: success via marriage and the family (Wallace, 1964). Among freshmen boys, however, graduate aspirations appear to be supported by the twin desires of pleasing parents and establishing a family of one's own. High achievement among males conforms to both parental and general social expectations. Such aspirations for the girl are more often nonconformist and perhaps rebellious.

Even if married women work, their primary adjustment is to family and household routines. They are not likely to be absorbed by their work, nor are their future expectations tied to career fulfillment (Turner, 1964). Our social heritage makes it difficult, in many cases impossible, for women to work away from home at careers demanding the lifelong commitment routinely expected of middle-class men. Thus, men are less concerned with family life than women, but more involved in it than women when both are committed to job advancement.

The Autonomy Factor

Women are not only more preoccupied with marriage and parenthood, they grasp the complementary nature of marital and parental activities better than men do. Men separate the two spheres in their thoughts as well as in their actions (Tharp, 1963); thus greater discontinuity exists between husband and father roles than between wife and mother roles. Part of the explanation for this can be deduced from our patriarchal heritage. As members of the subordinate sex, women are alert to the strategies of working through men, the ostensible decision makers, in order to achieve their ends and are therefore more conscious of the need to maintain a certain level of marital accommodation in order to fulfill their child-rearing objectives.

But they are also more dependent upon men in both work and recreational activities. Women rely more on sharing leisure time with their spouses than men do, although they become relatively more independent as they grow older. Mirra Komarovsky (1964) found this pattern in blue-collar marriages, and it is probably just as strong in the middle classes. Mother usually gives priority to her children, but she must not neglect father. Father is less likely to worry about coordinating his husband and father roles because he has not been impressed with the need to do so.

Marriage, for example, does not change the husband's life as much as his wife's (Couch, 1958). One reason husbands can retain greater continuity with their premarital life after marriage is because from their earliest years, they are granted more freedom and privacy, as well as the luxury of more familial disengagement than women. The relatively higher level of family aloofness among men affords one clue to the fact that disillusionment with marriage is not as shattering to them as it is to women (Levinger, 1965).

Male autonomy appears to be among the last vestiges of our Western patriarchal mystique, but its implications for familism are at odds with the traditional expectations associated with patriarchy. Instead of fostering a pattern of vigilance by father concerning the family, it supports an ambivalence concerning his family involvement, a vacillation between his responsibility to participate in family affairs and the family's obligation to respect his wish to be left alone.

One might expect that the man's drive for autonomy would be a source of inflexibility in marriage. However, in a study of Mormon couples, Victor Christopherson (1956) found a tendency for the husband more often than his wife to assume a conciliatory role, or the role of peacemaker, in the event of an argument between them. Clearly, the reconciliation must be initiated by one spouse or the other, and usually one of them assumes this role on a more or less continuing basis. Christopherson presents some evidence to suggest that the male is often capable of rising to the occasion. Perhaps the desire for harmony and male autonomy are not antithetical after all; the one thing most likely to upset the man's sacred routine is marital strife. As long as things are going reasonably well, he is free to do what he has always done, that is, what the family has learned to expect of him.

But evidence clearly indicates that the wife is more likely than the husband to subordinate her personal desires to family goals (Bowerman, 1957). The woman is called upon to adapt to her husband's life pattern: to the man, his work schedule, where he works, what he does, and to the general proposition that she is a helpmeet. It is the wife, not the husband, who finds marriage accommodation a primary life task (Burgess and Cottrell, 1939). Since we still define the woman as keeper of the family retreat, she develops an accommodative pattern in her relationship with her husband and becomes the expressive, compliant member of the family (Stuckert, 1963). The husband's conceptions of marital roles, for example, usually prevail and are especially crucial in the early stages of the marriage. Perhaps it is easier for wives than husbands to live up to their spouses' expectations. Whether it is or not, the wife is in fact more likely to make the accommodation (Hurvitz, 1959).

A corollary of this is the fact that the wife's "aptitude for marriage" is more important than the husband's for the couple's adjustment, and her marital adjustment is especially important for the emotional tone suffusing home life (Stroup, 1956). Jessie Bernard (1964) recently reviewed the argument that marriage is not necessarily best for everyone, noting that some people have greater chances for marital success than others. Both marital and maternal aptitudes vary among women, and perhaps there are those who should not marry at all, but it is much easier for us to admit that some men should not be husbands and fathers. Yet if the adaptability of the husband is of secondary importance in most marriages because of the autonomy permitted him, then the critical segment of the population determining the general level of marital success must consist of its women, and the critical quality they possess is their ability to adjust in marriage to the men they happen to get. It is quite likely that the greater interest in marriage inculcated in girls as they mature pays off in greater sensitivity to marital demands among the nubile female population. They are indeed better equipped to adjust in marriage, as they must, than the men they marry.

The wife must adjust not only to her husband, but to his friends as well. Charles Ackerman (1963) has pointed up the advantage in having "conjunctive affiliations" in marriage, a condition which occurs when the associations of husband and wife are overlapping or identical. A concordance of interests, plans, and values is heightened if the husband and wife are responsive to the same circle of friends. Ackerman further contends that the tendency in human cultures is for affiliations of the wife to be organized in response to the primary demands of her husband's life. Nicholas Babchuk and Alan Bates (1963) provide partial, but convincing, verification for this in their finding that the friends of the husband before marriage, as well as those he adds after marriage, are much more likely to become mutual and close friends of the married couple than are intimates of the wife. The initiation of friendship patterns among married couples is characteristically the husband's prerogative, and it is symptomatic of the discrepancy in adjustment problems of husband and wife in the conventional marriage.

Eleanore Luckey (1960a) found the wife's rapport with her husband's conception of himself to be more crucial for marriage satisfaction than the husband's empathy with his wife's self-concept. Charles Hobart and William Klausner (1959), too, found that wives, accustomed to "giving in" more often, produce scores on marital-adjustment tests that reveal insight into their husbands' behavior; husbands cannot match their wives' performance in this regard. If the wife must make greater adjustments in marriage, it helps for her to know what she is adjusting to.

Women in satisfactory marriages tend to perceive their husbands as more similar to their fathers than less satisfied wives do, but no comparable pattern applies in the case of men (Luckey, 1960b). William Westley and Nathan Epstein (1960b) have also suggested that good family relations depend to an important degree on the attitude of the wife toward her husband, which is a function of the wife's former dependency relationship with her father. Empathy with the husband is of strategic importance for the wife and is enhanced if the husband is like her father, from whom she has quite unconsciously learned so much about men—that is, about men like her father. Since conjugal empathy is less obligatory for the husband, it is not so essential that his wife be a stand-in for his mother.

In a sense, the continuity between the husband's premarital existence and his married life is the autonomy allowed him after marriage. This autonomy is facilitated by a high level of continuity between the father-daughter pattern his wife learned as a girl and the husband-wife pattern she later experiences. We might expect complications from the fact that women are usually more intimately and inflexibly attached to their parents than males are; while sexual frigidity may be accounted for in some wives by the fact that the childhood defenses against infantile sexual desires for the father operate now in reference to the husband, no widespread impairment of the marriage relationship appears to follow (Gray and Smith, 1960). Continuity is a ubiquitous theme in family life, but the point of significance here is that son-to-father continuity follows a different pattern from that of daughter-to-mother, and the greater autonomy granted men is the main reason for this difference.

Father's first task, occurring even before he has children, is to be an effective husband, but a series of events in his life as a growing boy tend to blind him to this fact. Girls are attracted to marriage by romantic appeals and by the inevitable lure of motherhood; underlying the attraction for boys is an erotic inducement that is psychologically divorced from fatherhood and very imperfectly linked to the role of husband. The naïveté of men with regard to family life causes them to react to disappointments in marriage according to a different pattern from that of women. They are apparently less despairing in the midst of marital deterioration because of their indifference and autonomy, and also because they are more engrossed in work away from home.

The greatest difficulty in generalizing about the relationship between the husband's marital adjustment and his performance as a father is the lack of evidence clearly linking the two activities. Nevertheless, it has been argued in this chapter that marriage adjustment is important for the man's parental role and is indeed more important now than ever before. This point of view is not an arbitrary one; it is consistent with the general trends in fathering that have been discussed thus far and with the problems of paternal accommodation to be discussed in Chapter VI.

CHAPTER VI

Paternal Accommodation

The husband is confronted with his first specific paternal role when he and his wife must adjust to the presence of an infant in the household. E. E. LeMasters (1957) was the first to try to prove that "parenthood is a crisis," and Everett Dyer (1963) added further evidence of the critical nature of this stage in the family cycle. More recently, however, Daniel Hobbs (1965) has gathered data suggesting that "crisis" is too strong a term; couples do have troubles adjusting to the baby, but ordinarily the difficulties are not severe unless the child has unusual health problems.

In fact, Hobbs suggests that there may be a "baby honeymoon" lasting between one and two months after the infant is born. (He acknowledges that he got this idea from Harold Feldman and that new parents are expected to be jubilant; it is not easy for people to reveal negative feelings about the arrival of their first baby.) At first the couple is elated: they feel "happy, wonderful, and lucky," and even later they feel that parenthood has made them more mature. But as the infant grows older, they also recognize that they have their work cut out for them. One mother summed up the general lack of preparation for parenthood among young couples: "We knew where babies came from, but we didn't know what they were like" (LeMasters, 1957).

LeMasters reported that fathers were generally more disenchanted at the birth of the first child than mothers, but fathers in Hobbs' study were more likely than mothers to think their marriages had improved after the baby arrived. Dyer found that new fathers were especially disturbed by loss of sleep and the fact that their routines were disrupted, whereas the fathers studied by Hobbs seemed to be more concerned about the financial complications of parenthood. Hobbs makes a strong case in this regard; he suggests that parenthood is a crisis primarily for men of low earning power, and that, as time passes, the economic responsibility of fatherhood is felt ever more acutely. Fathers, much more than mothers, view their relationships with children in economic terms and seem to become more upset by parenting as they are increasingly drawn into it. If they are less disturbed than their wives by the initial appearance of the baby, it is probably because due to their work they can get away from the demanding daily problems more often. But involvement for fathers increases as the children grow older, and they are less able than before to put the recurrent problems of relating to their children out of mind.

Apparently there is no widespread modern counterpart for the couvade found among some nonliterate people, wherein fathers have even more severe reactions to childbirth than do mothers, although many men still have psychosomatic ailments during their wives' pregnancies and at the time of delivery (Wainwright, 1964). In fact, women are often more willing than their husbands to have more children, even though it means more work and greater physiological hardship for them (Rose, 1951). It is the woman who has been pregnant for nine months; she thinks about the baby and her future as a mother almost every day of her pregnancy and may have started thinking about it long before. The father, meanwhile, has been just as busy thinking about other things. The "My Boy Bill" soliloquy in *Carousel* captures in a most engaging way the naïveté and offhanded braggadocio characteristic of the future father's thoughts about parenthood. Recall that the women studied by Helena Lopata (1965) considered the mother role to be the woman's most important one; it outranked the role of wife by an astonishingly wide margin. Men regard neither fatherhood nor husbandhood as their chief role in life and are rather easily annoyed by the inconveniences of both.

The transition to parenthood ushers in a whole new interpersonal situation for the couple (Murrell and Stachowiak, 1965). Inevitably, it creates difficulties; the arrival of the child destroys the two-person pattern of interaction, forcing the couple to reorganize their routines into a triangular arrangement. Childless couples, for example, are likely to have a relatively clear-cut division of homemaking tasks that becomes unsettled and ambiguous with the addition of children (Marchand and Langford, 1952).

From the point of view of congeniality, students of small groups have long considered the dyad a more sanguine combination than the triad, since the latter almost without exception invites coalitions of two members against the third (Simmel, 1959). It also seems possible that the appearance of relatives in the home, which the new baby often attracts, may be more harmful than helpful. Although they come to help, they frequently create problems for the new parents; their very presence may indicate that the young couple is not self-sufficient enough (Hobbs, 1965).

A further complication also appears. The romantic complex, given so much attention in our society and usually subjected to considerable strain after, or even during, the honeymoon, is often dealt a terminal blow by the appearance of the child. Husband and wife now begin to see one another as parents as well as—or instead of—lovers.

Motherhood is usually more damaging to the female's erotic image than fatherhood is to the male's. Thus, once again it is the father whose sex conceptions of his spouse are put to the greater test. He is the one who has isolated sex and romance from parenting during his introduction into the world of heterosexual relations; as we have seen, his wife's attitudes toward sex and romance were very likely fused with visions of family life and mothering from the start. She is the one who is concerned with pregnancy; he has been concerned with sex. One of the reasons she develops a somewhat less inhibited approach to sex relations in the course of marriage (Kinsey, Pomeroy, and Martin, 1948) may be the fact that her sex partner is now the father of her children; but from the man's point of view the mother figure as sex partner evokes, at best, an ambivalent response.

Power and Work in the Household

A satisfactory arrangement of the couple's activities after marriage is based upon some degree of consensus concerning family affairs and the importance of family life itself. This mutuality may extend far beyond daily household matters, but practical problems of the home are the ones of immediate interest. The management of household routines is a particularly difficult problem for the husband and father because his attention is so easily distracted from domestic affairs. The man's task as breadwinner is more likely to be protected from diversions, but even that role suffers if the man works at a dismal job for inadequate wages. Precisely because the male is so weakly involved in family routines as he grows up, he is susceptible to disengagement from or indifference to household affairs as an adult and is the weak link in the family chain.

The key element in father's long-range accommodation to parenthood is his response to the daily problems of decision making and domestic work. These are the core elements in *mutualization* after marriage; they are more crucial for the man's performance as a father than either *idealization* or *enchantment*. Changes over time in the latter two areas affect the father's family adjustment, to be sure, but they are more often influenced than influential. Regardless of the general level of the couple's agreement about things, difficult choices must often be made and a division of work must be established in order to meet the daily needs of the household. It is more important that the couple constantly cope with these two basic problems in a context of mutual respect than that they maintain an intense enchantment with their marriage or a romantic idealization of one another.

Power: Rhetoric and Reality

In Chapters III and IV the rise of the equalitarian marriage was discussed; although that kind of marriage is the ideal, influence is almost always exercised unequally. The more powerful spouse usually denies his power, however, even if the fact that he has it is obvious to others; he may be quite sincere in the belief that he is not a domineering person.

Thus, in the attempt to describe patterns of conjugal authority accurately we face the difficulty of separating rhetoric from reality. C. Wright Mills (1940) once identified the disparity between talk and action as the central methodological problem of the social sciences. It is ubiquitous in the study of any form of social power, since the relationship between ways of speaking and actual behavior is especially precarious where power is at issue (Clifford, 1959). In the lower social classes, for example, the rhetoric of patriarchy remains strong, while in the middle and upper-middle levels the ideal of "democratic decision making" has taken hold (Olsen, 1960). But evidence clearly indicates that the father typically has a higher level of authority in the middle and upper classes than in the lower classes. In the middle classes his influence is most completely diffused throughout family activities.

Moreover, the exercise of power within the family usually occurs in a very complex pattern. For example, when one reads Oscar Lewis' (1959b, 1964) detailed descriptions of the daily life of peasant families in Mexico, the problem of sorting parental behavior into hard-and-fast categories becomes quite apparent. Clichés about family authority are only tenuously related to the daily life of peasants. The problem of classifying families in highly industrialized nations is just as hazardous, but we cannot send field workers to live with them and observe their routines as Lewis did so ingeniously in his anthropological studies. Instead, questionnaires and interviews are used, and we must depend upon what people say, which is not necessarily what they do.

A sensitivity that only experience in the particular family can give is required to tell how the family determines what it will do together—what is to be done this coming Sunday afternoon, what sort of vacation it will take next summer, or whether the entire family will go to the church supper. Certainly the questionnaire technique of studying conjugal power has limitations; spouses are much more likely to agree on whether certain matters have been discussed than on how decisions were made or who made them (Wilkening and Morrison, 1963). Couples also have insight into their way of parceling out the family chores much sooner after marriage than into their pattern of decision making, primarily because of the subtlety involved in the latter. It is usually much easier to determine who does what than who decides what in the family, especially in a society stressing give-and-take in decision making.

Fred Strodtbeck (1952) used the "interaction process analysis" of Robert F. Bales to study decision making by a Mormon couple; Strodtbeck observed them at the task and noted that at least three factors were operating simultaneously: the generalized conceptions of family roles held by the spouses, the pattern of decision making that they had worked out in the past, and the immediate situation. It amounted to a remarkably subtle interaction process. This kind of analysis, it might be added, shows that garrulousness is an important factor in the exercise of influence, other things being equal. It is an equalizer many women possess, but men know the strategy too.

Anne Steinmann (1958) contends that both daughters and their mothers erroneously impute an exaggerated traditionalism to fathers, due mainly to faulty communication between father and the female members of his household. His inarticulateness makes him seem stodgy and authoritarian. David Heer (1962) found that both the husband and wife exaggerate the power exercised by their spouses; the husband tends to regard the wife as more powerful than she will admit, and the wife perceives the husband to be more powerful than he prefers to think he is. Perhaps this is part of the tendency for married people to think they contribute more to the marriage than their spouses and to link the exercise of power with the avoidance of responsibility. Thus, the imputation of power to a spouse can mean that the imputer feels that he submits to the wishes of his spouse in the interest of family harmony and that the person exercising power is being selfish and obstinate. "I let George have his way because he's so stubborn. Otherwise we'd get nothing done." The authoritative spouse is accused, in effect, of giving orders instead of compromising, or instead of doing the necessary work.

Heer's explanation for his finding, however, is based on a "guilt theory" of verbal reporting by domineering women. Since by community standards women are not supposed to have more power than their husbands, "strong" wives feel guilty and deny, or misrepresent, their power. But this hypothesis leaves an important question unanswered: Why don't husbands, responding to an equally plausible "shame theory," refuse to admit that their wives have greater power? A denial would enable them to avoid the shame that such a revelation reflects upon them, since men are certainly not supposed to be dominated by their wives. If Heer is correct, men don't "cover up" as much as women. Perhaps women are more concerned than husbands about the appearance of their marriages and are more likely to disguise the true power pattern in order to make their marriages seem "normal." P. G. Herbst (1952), however, in advocating that the child is an accurate reporter of the conjugal power structure, claims that parents tend to exaggerate the extent of mutuality in their decision making. The persistence of the traditional patriarchal rhetoric may conceal a good deal of egalitarianism, but it is likely that the greater deception works in the opposite direction; we pride ourselves on being more egalitarian than we really are.

Victor Christopherson's (1956) study of patriarchal authority among Mormons is relevant here. To Mormons, patriarchal authority is a divinely instituted practice and is set forth as such in church doctrine; it is necessary in this life as well as the next as a system of family government. Mormons believe that patriarchal authority is as obligatory now as in former times; the father who does not assume leadership in family matters is neglecting his duty, and it is his explicit responsibility to instruct the children in ways of righteousness lest he be held accountable for the ignorance of his children.

But religious matters constitute a special province for the exercise of patriarchal authority. More flexible arrangements are made for other matters. In fact, Christopherson noted a trend away from patriarchy among Mormons, although he believes the shift to have been less marked than for most other groups in American society. The Mormon father uses his wife as a sounding board for tentative opinions; he exercises his paternal privileges with caution and with an eye to what might be willingly accepted. In this way the Mormon rhetoric of patriarchal authority can remain essentially unchanged while its translation into daily activities is modified to meet the requirements of a changing society. The doctrine remains patriarchal, but practice drifts in the direction of egalitarianism, flexibility, and pragmatic compromise.

The following generalization seems plausible: Where the rhetoric of patriarchy remains strong, it is tempered in everyday conduct; where the rhetoric of equality has taken hold, unequal levels of conjugal power are likely to be camouflaged. As Oscar Lewis' study of Mexican peasants illustrates, conjugal power patterns defy easy cataloguing.

The Power Pattern

Although the possibilities may be endless, three alternatives to the husband-dominated marriage have been cited most frequently in sociological literature: marriage dominated by the wife, marriage in which there is continual conflict between husband and wife, and equalitarian marriage (Straus, 1962). We are prone to call equalitarian marriage "democratic," which is perhaps only a glib way of saying we like it. It has also been called "autonomic" marriage by P. G. Herbst (1954), while Daniel Miller and Guy Swanson (1958) call it a "colleague" arrangement. But Murray Straus (1962) contends that researchers often lump equalitarian and conflict patterns together, which may help to explain the contradictory results of research in this area; Straus found that these two types have quite different consequences. Moreover, Donald Wolfe (1962) distinguishes between "syncratic" and "autonomic" marriage patterns: in the former the husband and wife share authority in all areas; in the latter they share in some areas but also maintain separate spheres of influence for certain activities.

Most American marriages fall in the broad category including authority-sharing and conflict-prone marital arrangements. Decisions are traded in a more or less patterned way (Heer, 1963), although there are two kinds of trades: those that are ad hoc, applying in nonrecurrent situations, and those that are incorporated into established routines. Both may provide comforting evidence that the couple is living up to the contemporary ideal of "fifty-fifty" and that the family is democratic. It would be interesting to know how great a discrepancy in the exercise of power can be overlooked by the weaker spouse as long as he is given an occasional chance to wield power, even if only in trivial ways. Few partners in voluntary relationships can find enough satisfaction to keep the affair alive if they have no element of discretion at all, although compensations need not neatly square accounts. The couple that tries to keep a record of such things is already in trouble.

In the early stages of marriage decisions are reached in an ad hoc way, through discussion of a particular problem or as the result of spontaneous reactions in a new situation. The couple does what the circumstances seem to require, according to the relationships they have established with one another and their personal styles. After repeated episodes, decisions are reached on the basis of subtle cues learned in the earlier situations. Decisions become routine, and, as such, unnoticed, as when one spouse defers to the wishes of the other without even thinking about it. No doubt this is the ideal: influence is exercised tacitly and tempers are not stirred.

It may become mother's prerogative, for example, to decide when the children need new shoes and father's to decide when the car needs new tires. But other decisions, such as where to take a vacation, fall in that no man's land in which no member of the household wields unchallenged authority. In these cases decisions must be made by two persons, maybe more, representing various interests, different strategies of influence, and noncomparable claims to priority. "Routine" can no longer handle things; one will is pitted against another, moderated to some extent by a spirit of fair play and the very general ethos of cooperation. Children are rarely hampered by the latter, however, and we have already noted that most persons feel they are more virtuously motivated than their spouses. Thus, when one spouse wins in a dispute of openly conflicting wills, the winner has the resentment of the loser to contend with.

It is at this point that the last vestiges of patriarchy are most operative. If a woman knowingly gives in to her husband's superior will, the chances are reasonably good that she will adjust to her frustration, without undue regrets or recriminations. She would like to have her way, but community opinion enables her to reconcile herself to the dilemma. She may admire, even adore, her firm, strong man. But if a man succumbs to his wife he is much more likely to harbor resentment and to suffer the torments of self-depreciation, despite his conjugal dependence. Patriarchal sentiments no longer determine who wields power in the family, but they still influence our expressive reactions to the power pattern!

There may be countless spouses whose deeper sentiments are violated by family decisions but who have resigned themselves to their fate without realizing how it came about. Beaten down by what seems to be a lost cause, they cannot assert themselves. Responding to the imperfect protective functions of the psyche, they are unable to comprehend the source of their frustration, and only the most sophisticated counseling can uncover the family dynamics at work. Unfortunately, we have no theory of family resignation except that implicit in the traditions of patriarchy. The woman is supposed to be content with her lot, or was at one time; the divorce rate itself reflects the decline of a viable norm of infinite patience. The resigned spouse may now be male or female, and the explanation must be ad hoc.

Theories of Conjugal Power

Several theories concerning conjugal power have been formulated that are useful in explaining known family patterns and also in providing a basis for conjecture about patterns for which we have limited information. One plausible approach stresses the relative involvement of the spouses in different matters and specifies this principle: The spouse who is more concerned about a particular issue will be the more influential in that area (Heer, 1963). Without some sense of excitement about an issue, a person is not likely to command much authority or even try. From such a premise we are not surprised to learn that women are usually more influential in household matters and men are relatively more effective in making major economic decisions.

The same principle can be extended to extrafamilial affairs: the spouse who participates more extensively in social activities outside the home will be more influential in managing relations between the family and the external world (Blood, 1963). Thus, we should expect the husband to be more important in committing the family to community affairs because his employment involves him in a wider social milieu. We should also expect that women, as their interests expand, will have increasing importance in a range of community-welfare activities affecting their children, especially those concerning health, education, and recreation. These are areas of traditional feminine concern, and they offer the most convenient job opportunities for women. If a new trend appears, it will be one in which women enter career fields not traditionally associated with children and nurturance, and we should then expect their community power to match the scope of their work. It remains true even in contemporary society, however, that husbands are allowed greater opportunities than wives to express power drives outside the home, mainly because their career opportunities are more diversified (M. Hoffman, 1963b).

Unfortunately, this theory tells us little about the dynamics of power in those instances in which mother and father disagree and both have an equal desire to have their way. The theory explains *deference*, perhaps, but not influence or power when there is a true conflict of interest.

Beyond the undoubtedly valid principle that domestic power is conditioned by the patterns of interest and involvement of the spouses, conjugal power might be explained in terms of the relative importance or expendability of the spouses. According to Robert Blood and Donald Wolfe (1960), for example, the chief alternatives to tradition as a source of marital influence are the respective "resources" of husband and wife, such as their relative earning abilities. Power accrues to the spouse who has the more imposing or relevant resources, and thus has the greater contribution to make to the family. "Successful" men for example—those with superior earning power—wield greater family authority. Male dominance is directly related to the man's occupational status in the community, and for this reason "patri-dependency" is still an important determinant of mother-father relations in the higher social classes. We should add, however, that, although successful professional men claim considerable influence in the home, as a rule they exercise it with a deft hand and tend to avoid rigid authoritarianism. Less successful men are often more openly assertive, but apparently less influential (Elder, 1965).

In line with the resources theory, any marked discrepancy in the academic achievements of spouses will yield an advantage to the one with the most education; this is another basis for the edge generally held by men in the middle and upper classes. The wife, on the other hand, will have more power than she would otherwise if she works, if she is attractive, or if she is particularly competent as a homemaker, hostess, sex partner, or understanding companion (Heer, 1963).

Herbert Danzger (1964) has added a footnote to the resources theory, incorporating the factor of relative involvement. He argues that the person for whom a goal is most important will spend more time and energy to reach it, but the person who is ambivalent or indifferent is not likely to use even those resources available to him. Thus, resources are important, but only when the desirability of a goal excites the person enough to put his assets to use.

David Heer (1963) has suggested still another and more arresting modification of the resources theory, along lines that are reminiscent of Willard Waller's (1937) famous "principle of least interest" in courtship. Waller observed that the partner who cares least about maintaining a relationship has the greatest control over its activities. (Note that this is not the same as the theory of relative involvement, although the two propositions are not mutually exclusive.) Assuming that both spouses conceive of the possibility of breaking the marital bond, Heer suggests that the power of each is determined by his estimate of the contribution of the other measured against his own opportunities outside the marriage. "The greater the difference between the value to the wife of the resources contributed by her husband and the value to the wife of the resources which she might earn outside the existing marriage, the greater the power of her husband, and vice versa" (Heer, 1963, p. 138). Heer calls this an "exchange value theory"; it has been developed as a more general social theory by Peter Blau (1964). The less successful the husband, for example, the less the wife has to lose by insisting she be given her own way. The discrepancy between satisfactions found in a marriage and those expected in an alternative to that marriage is the measure of conjugal power.

The premise—essential to this theory—that most spouses give some thought to the possibility of divorce is a rather recent historical development. Only in the past fifty or sixty years has it become possible for a large number of American couples to realistically contemplate alternatives to an existing marriage, a trend that reinforces Heer's basic assumption. Divorce is now a feasible alternative to marital misery, although many couples may not allow themselves to consider it even yet, as Robert Blood (1963) has pointed out. But couples do seem to have greater psychological access to divorce nowadays, and many contemplate it without feelings of guilt.

Heer's theory is especially attractive because it explains some things that the "resources theory" cannot handle, such as the fact that mothers of preschool children have less power in the family than they did before the children were born, even though their family contributions are increased. The explanation, congruent with Heer's theory, is that the family alternatives available to these women are now much more restricted. The fact that mothers with more children have less power despite their greater contributions can also be explained by Heer's theory: Their alternative life chances are limited. Why should the historical status of women have risen while their family burdens have diminished unless their chances outside of marriage have improved? Heer's theory helps to explain Judson Landis' (1963) conclusion that unhappy husband-dominated marriages are more likely to lead to divorce than comparable wife-dominated marriages; more promising alternatives ordinarily exist outside of the present marriage for males than for females.

From the same premise we should expect the power of women to be related to their relative numbers in the population. A scarcity of women has long existed in the western American states, which would seem to afford women greater opportunities to remarry and to establish a demographic basis for greater female power. We cannot be certain about the latter point, but divorce rates are indeed higher in the West (Levinger, 1965).

Largely in response to the changing problems of growing children, readjustments are made in the conjugal power pattern during the life cycle of the family, and these can also be explained in terms of Heer's theory. Peter Pineo (1961) found that American husbands tend to become more authoritarian in marriage with the passage of time, but both husbands and wives, particularly in high-income families, become more opposed to authoritarianism as an ideal. Even as the rhetoric of family power becomes more egalitarian, husbands attempt to consolidate and augment their strength. The traditional male-dominant attitude is found most frequently among unmarried couples whose relationships are quite casual. As intimacy increases, the veneer is stripped away (Heiss, 1962). Transition from the single state to marriage customarily marks a further trend toward equalitarianism, as noted by William Dyer and Dick Urban (1958), although married couples are more agreeable to a division of labor with regard to household tasks than single persons are.

But in reality opinions about family power change less during marriage than actual behavior. Pineo's data indicate that ideas about conjugal authority are established early in marriage and change only marginally with the passing years. The initial behavioral tendency during the honeymoon period and before the children are born is toward equalitarianism. After the first child, the wife's power declines as she withdraws into domesticity and the husband's power reaches its peak. The more children the wife has, the more likely is the husband to be dominant (Hoffman and Lippitt, 1960), although children as well as father maintain a constant pressure on overworked mothers. (When children are young, they accuse parents of dictating the conditions of their existence, but from the parents' point of view it seems that children run their parents' lives, especially the lives of young mothers.)

The fact that mothers with little children are at a disadvantage vis-à-vis their husbands raises an interesting point. If a divorce were to occur at this time the husband would have a better chance for remarriage than his wife, but the children would ordinarily be kept by their mother. Hence the mother of young children could gain some leverage in marriage by threatening to take the children from their father; the fact that mothers usually have less power at this stage in marriage seems to reflect a measure of indifference on the part of many fathers toward their children. Nevertheless, we may presume that many a father who has developed a close relation with his children can be intimidated by his wife's threat to pack them off with her if he does not mend his ways, that is, if he does not become more compliant to her wishes.

When her children start school, the mother can be more autonomous and exercise more power because she is better able to handle outside employment; the children can now take care of themselves in many ways and are supervised to a greater extent by the school and other community agencies (Heer, 1963). The mother's gradual resumption of a position of independent influence coincides with her reemergence from the ceaseless responsibilities of mothering (Blood, 1963), and children do report father as "boss" of the family less often as they grow older (Hess and Torney, 1962).

When the children have grown up and left home, the mother is even more completely relieved of mothering responsibilities, propelling her further in the direction of nonfamily social participation. But Heer argues that after her children have been "launched" the mother loses some conjugal power because the sex ratio in her age bracket is not now in her favor; her chances of remarriage are much lower than those of a divorced man of comparable age. Hence, the husband's power rises moderately, as noted also by Robert Blood and Donald Wolfe (1960).

Robert Blood (1963a), however, contends that mothers of children over eighteen who have not left home tend to be particularly possessive, dominating both their husbands and their children. Thus, an important role may unwittingly be played by some fathers; in avoiding subservience to their wives and maintaining their own independence they may contribute to the emancipation of their children. Emotional disturbances in children are among the symptoms that appear when the father's "dependency needs" are excessive—when his wife is the family mainspring and he must turn repeatedly to her for support (Westley and Epstein, 1960b). This problem reflects the persistence of patriarchal sentiments; when they are openly violated, family trouble is hard to avoid.

The Household Division of Labor

The conjugal power pattern that we have discussed overlaps and animates an essential division of labor within the family. Perhaps the most cogent way to link these two kinds of activities is through the concept of *responsibility,* since decision making on important matters inevitably involves an allocation of responsibilities in order to put the decisions into effect. Sometimes decision making is itself a responsibility, assumed by one spouse or the other for a particular matter, but that of course is not the case when the couple pointedly disagree about whose wishes are to prevail.

It is never easy to determine whether responsibility has been "given," "assigned," or simply "taken"; some responsibilities are assumed because both husband and wife, without any conscious thought at all, subscribe to a historical or neighborhood pattern concerning their respective roles. Although current social norms for domestic life are weak and indistinct, which increases the importance of ad hoc arrangements, couples still find reassurance in community standards that legitimize their family habits. In fact, couples are likely to experience strain in marriage to whatever extent their division of labor differs from that practiced by most couples in their immediate social surroundings (Hurvitz, 1960).

Karen Geiken (1964) suggests that family responsibilities can be divided into three categories: *child-care tasks, housekeeping tasks,* and *authority patterns.* She found that the area of greatest sharing among married couples was that of authority patterns; child-care tasks were next, while housekeeping activities were shared least of all. Generally, the more "mental" the task, the greater the extent of sharing between husband and wife; physical tasks are separated and each becomes the permanent prerogative (or burden) of one spouse.

William Dyer and Dick Urban (1958) found greater acceptance among married couples of a division of labor in household tasks than in any other area, as have others. Couples who have no children share tasks to a greater extent than those who have them; much less sharing occurs when the children are over five years of age (Geiken, 1964).

Marvin Olsen (1960) has verified the existence of a pattern we all see in real life and must witness again and again on television commercials: women clean house (mop, vacuum, wax, dust, pick up after family members, wash and dry dishes, etc.) while men are called upon to empty the garbage and make household repairs. The father serves as handyman, consultant, and substitute for mother when she is sick or called away. Wives may feel that it is unfair for them to have to do so much housework while their husbands seem to enjoy soft jobs somewhere else, but unfortunately no *objective* means of calculating the worth of different family chores has yet been devised.

Both boys and girls are taught to think of outside chores—

working in the yard and exterior painting, for example—as husband's work (Dunn, 1960). Farm wives, however, by contrast with those in the cities, are expected to do more of both household and outside chores (Blood, 1958). Moreover, farm fathers are more likely than city men to get help from their wives in their work. While farm wives are helping their husbands, city husbands are more likely to be helping their wives. The closest approximation to the farm pattern in the urban area is found in families where father is a small entrepreneur; his wife, and often his children, assist in what takes on the appearance of a family enterprise. The greater authority of the father under these circumstances is derived from his role as manager or executive in the family business, but both farming and the family business enterprise have declined in importance in the United States.

Two factors operate in tandem to sustain the household division of labor—expediency and habituation. Some tasks must be endlessly repeated, and expediency dictates that the person who is accustomed to the chore perform it on a continuing basis. Thus, the more often a housekeeping task must be performed, the less likely it is that its performance will be shared. Routine tasks become fixed in a division of labor, while tasks occurring infrequently can be shared more or less haphazardly.

Time itself is a factor in apportioning routine tasks. Newly married couples, for example, are more likely to share in managing and spending money since no budgeting of outlays has been settled upon. Once a spending pattern is more or less established, however, they no longer need to consult one another so closely (Geiken, 1964).

Women usually give more thought to daily family functions than their husbands do, and housework takes on a significance for many of them that it can only rarely have for men (Weiss and Samelson, 1958). This is primarily true, of course, for women who are not employed away from home, and even they often remain reluctant. Women are now bombarded with advice to reject housework (Friedan, 1963). Alberta Siegel and Miriam Haas (1963), summarizing research on this point, suggest that working mothers may feel guilty about the possible neglect of their children, but they show very little concern about neglecting their housekeeping tasks. It would appear that housekeeping is an activity that women can abandon without regrets, despite the fact that it has been a primary female role for so long. But, because men have traditionally been less preoccupied with household matters, they must have female guidance as they are called upon to do more work around the house. Hence Russell Lynes, with at least an ounce of truth, can refer to the husband and father as "America's new servant class."

Considering their greater absorption in domestic routines, women quite naturally give more thought to relief from the drudgeries involved and are more likely to want to hire household servants (Rose, 1951). Kathryn Powell (1961) has observed that the role of father may be significantly altered when the mother works, depending on the availability of maids. Most middle-class families in Pakistan, for example, can engage servants to help in the homemaking, especially if the wife is employed outside the home; according to Khalida Shah (1960), this helps to explain why only a minority of both men and women in Pakistan believe that a husband should help with rearing of little children and homemaking, even when his wife works. Most Americans would expect the husband to help.

But it remains typical for adolescent girls to consider homemaking the responsibility of wives, and they are sometimes more traditional in this respect than boys. In a study by Ruth Hartley (1960) girls accepted a rather clear-cut and decidedly traditional division of labor, with homemaking as the woman's duty—and moneymaking as the man's. Boys may actually be more willing to accept child-care activities as legitimate male roles than girls realize, even more willing than many girls think they should be (Hartley and Klein, 1959; Dunn, 1960).

Data collected by Marie Dunn (1960) suggest that adolescent boys and girls have more equalitarian values with regard to child rearing than with regard to any other area of husband-wife activity, which probably reflects their impressions of the reality in their own homes. Dyer and Urban (1958) found that fathers are expected to give about the same attention as mothers are to child-rearing concerns (disciplining, birth planning, playing with the children, planning the children's work, determining the children's use of money) with one important exception: mothers must assume primary responsibilities for the physical care of infants and young children. In a sample of adolescents studied by Charles Bowerman and Glen Elder (1964), the father was reported to be the dominant parent in child-rearing matters as often as the mother, in spite of the fact that mother does most of the actual work; apparently she often finds herself responsible for doing the menial chores without having the stronger voice in "child-rearing policy."

We find greater complexity and ambiguity in the division of responsibilities for family finances than for child rearing or household and outside chores. Harry Sharp and Paul Mott (1956) found that the husband usually selects a new car, the wife buys the family's food, and they try to reach a consensus on going into debt for a new home and deciding where to go on vacations. Marvin Olsen (1960) also found that the purchase of a car is mainly the man's job (although salesmen, and car designers, are quite sensitive to wives' reactions), and the man typically controls insurance buying. But he found men to be somewhat more important than women in deciding where to go on vacations. Mother buys her own clothes, while clothing father is a cooperative task, as clothiers have long known.

Dyer and Urban (1958), however, could find hardly any consistent pattern in the way couples handle spending for different kinds of items—necessities, luxuries, recreation, personal items, savings, investments, and cash holdings. Only one principle seems to apply: Fathers play an important role in the purchase of items requiring a single relatively large expenditure (cars, furniture, appliances), but even here they usually share this role with mothers. Mothers, on the other hand, rather typically make routine family purchases without consulting father in advance (Johannis, 1957a). This seems to be consistent with the image of father as a figure who is important, but in the background; he can be counted on to take an active role only in matters that are of more than routine importance.

Now that there are so many alternative ways of spending our leisure hours, no member of the household can claim responsibility for establishing the family's recreation schedule, and in any case the family spends relatively less free time together. Father has undoubtedly lost prerogatives in this area, although Walter Gerson (1960) suggests that the husband may be more sensitive about the way he uses his leisure time than his wife (a facet of the father's attempt to preserve his autonomy). It is quite possible that mother is more concerned with the *family* recreational pattern than with her own pleasure.

We noted that middle-class husbands initiate more mutual friendships than do wives, and most married people do not maintain strong independent friendships apart from their mutual ones (Babchuk, 1965). Close friends of the male before marriage are more likely to become close mutual friends of the couple after marriage, although the wife plays a larger role in establishing new family friends as the length of marriage increases (Babchuk and Bates, 1963). Nevertheless, women do most of the planning of the couple's home entertainment (Olsen, 1960), and though this may more often involve persons who were originally friends of the husband, it often includes more affairs with the wife's relatives than with the husband's. Her attachment to her parents, for example, is usually stronger (Komarovsky, 1950; Wallin, 1954); she also feels homesick more often than her husband and visits her parents more frequently (Gray and Smith, 1960).

Many fathers have a set of cronies, consisting mostly of work associates, whose activities are separated from family affairs; mothers, on the other hand, are likely to maintain contacts with relatives, neighbors, and women they meet through church and social activities, who, when they get together, talk more about family matters than anything else. The emergence of a crony system among working wives comparable to that among men may have occurred in the twentieth century, although expectations with regard to the roles of wife and mother probably keep it from becoming as strong and as independent as that found among men.

Clearly, recent trends affecting the allocation of tasks within the family favor an overlapping of husband-wife, mother-father activities. In his study of Mormons, who tend to be somewhat conservative in family affairs, Victor Christopherson (1956) noted an increasing participation by husbands in such routine household matters as feeding the children, cleaning house, preparing meals, and related activities. The trend is found in the community at large, but is especially strong among middle-class couples (Olsen, 1960). In the upper classes it is less pronounced. Here much of the work is done by paid help, and only the responsibility for supervision remains, leading to rather distinct spheres of control for men and women. The mother often supervises both indoor and outdoor work while the husband serves as occasional consultant and troubleshooter.

Women in lower-class homes do more housework, of course, since they cannot hire outside help and their husbands cannot be counted on to assume responsibilities that have come to be expected of middle-class fathers. Thus, the reluctant father is most frequently found in the lower classes as is the deliberate withdrawal of male efficiency: the domestic burden falls almost entirely on the wife. Nevertheless, children in the lower classes, collectively, may help out more than those in the middle classes, but only because there are more of them in the average family (Olsen, 1960).

We must recognize that for many matters of both urgency and frequency the household division of labor is far too complex to permit valid generalizations—at least at this time. Religious training is a case in point; the division of labor for the religious training of children is indeterminate, although certain rather superficial tasks may customarily be handled by one parent or the other. Mother, for example, usually packs the children off to Sunday School, but that does not tell us much about her role in establishing lasting religious values. She is also dispatcher and cabby for school children during the week, which does not automatically make her responsible for the children's academic commitment. With respect to education, the processes by which children identify with mother and father and the things each stands for may be more important than the parental division of labor.

Birth Planning

One strategic task confronting the couple at the very outset of their married life is birth planning. In a most complex way it involves both decision making and the division of labor.

In the attempt to explain changes in the birth rate a tendency has long existed to look for new developments in the conditions of motherhood rather than in those affecting fatherhood, but birth planning is obviously a cooperative parental venture. The first mutualization problem of *parenthood* occurs in connection with fertility, which is an implicit consideration when the couple makes plans for buying a home, furnishing it, saving money, and so on. Certainly, planned children are more likely than unplanned children to receive a warm and confident reception by their parents.

Planning involves two primary considerations: how many children to have and how to arrange to have them, about which men and women usually have similar attitudes (Christensen, 1961b). The sex of the child is a secondary matter, as a rule, but it may affect the decision to have another child, due to the desire to have children of both sexes (Freedman, Freedman, and Whelpton, 1960). If the first two babies are girls, for example, the couple may be more willing to have a third child in the hope that it will be a boy.

No one knows the ideal number of children to have from either the father's or the family's point of view, except that it is probably no longer desirable to have a large number. No compelling evidence has been found to indicate that the number of children a man has in and of itself determines his performance as a father. Obviously the demands made upon a man with five sons are different from those made on a man with only one, but one child is not always easier to care for than five. Nevertheless the trend toward smaller families certainly seems to be a pragmatic adaptation to modern conditions, given the availability of cheap, effective, and convenient contraceptives. If the mother is the more diligent parental planner, it is because her life is more totally affected by the size of the family.

The most conspicuous condition affecting birth planning by

the father is his socioeconomic status. Lower-class fathers are less often planners; they *expect* to have children earlier in marriage and are indeed more likely to induce premarital pregnancies. The class factor helps to explain the lack of birth planning among Negroes and also their high rate of premarital pregnancies, but not entirely: there is a greater difference in the rate of premarital conceptions between lower- and middle-class whites than between comparable classes for Negroes (Monahan, 1960). Attitudes toward birth planning that prevail among Negroes are apparently the products of rather general influences upon American Negroes, just as there are rather distinctive subcultural attitudes in the rural population and among Catholics. Inactive Catholics and inactive Protestants have quite similar birth-control patterns, however, and they constitute the majority in both religious groups (Westoff, Potter, and Sagi, 1963).

The pattern whereby couples in the lower socioeconomic levels have the most children antedates modern techniques of birth control. But, at least in recent times, this fact cannot be explained by assuming that they want more children; they do not (Freedman, Whelpton, and Campbell, 1959). Many of their pregnancies are unplanned and unwanted. From the viewpoint of planning-oriented middle-class standards, we should expect reactions of guilt and dejection, but that is not necessarily the case. The lack of guilt, especially among fathers, is itself significant. We tend to exaggerate the problems parents have in adapting, both psychologically and in their daily routines, to a large number of children; this is not to say that couples do not have difficulties that can be almost unbearable, but there are strong pressures upon people to accommodate.

In fact, ambivalence about the use of contraceptives is found in all classes, especially before the first pregnancy (Potter, Sagi, and Westoff, 1962). Many couples are relatively uninterested in contraception until they have their second child or they are approaching the birth limit they have set for themselves. Then the effectiveness with which they control fertility increases sharply (Westoff, Potter, and Sagi, 1963). But in the lower classes indifference to family planning is a pattern; it is the primary reason for the higher birth rate and the frequently sanguine reaction to it.

Planning per se is a fringe concern in the life style of the lower classes, which Lee Rainwater and Karol Weinstein (1960) have described exceptionally well. To the person reared in poverty the world appears to be chaotic and unpredictable, controlled by fate and chance—or by callous big shots. Ingenuousness pervades whatever sense of order exists, and people do not think themselves capable of effective planning in life, especially for long-term goals. They do not know how to plan and they have not been very successful in the management of their personal lives. They find planned *non-parenthood* particularly hard to comprehend. It seems to them an artificial status sought by spurious means and maintained, if at all, against the pressure of natural forces. Not having children when you do not want them becomes a matter of luck for women and married couples, and cunning for single men. The best way for single men to avoid parenthood is simply by not getting caught. If contraceptives are used at all, they are usually the least effective ones; the condom is the favored method of contraception in the working classes.

Lack of planning with regard to fertility is part of a larger complex of ingenuousness with regard to children in general. The pattern can be traced back before the marriage, even to childhood in the unplanned family of the previous generation. For couples who are ineffective family planners, courtship is characterized by general planlessness concerning the couple's prospective life together. There is little or no discussion of future domestic routines and none of contraception (Rainwater and Weinstein, 1960). After marriage, lower-class wives find it difficult to talk to their husbands about common family goals and about the necessity for limiting children in order to accomplish these goals. As a result, such couples have no choice but to reconcile themselves to large families. (In a literal sense, choice has nothing to do with it. We are talking about social patterns that *mold* individual and family choices.)

But if the wife is dissatisfied with the couple's fertility pattern, she can sometimes work out a change with her husband; the husband's dissatisfaction is poorly articulated as a rule and may lead to desertion. Prabha Malhotra and Lilian Khan (1962) suggest as much from data collected in New Delhi, supporting impressions generally reported in American case records. Lack of interest in and *knowledge* about reproduction go together. Women who are effective family planners, for example, have a clearer idea of the separate contributions of sperm and ovum to conception than women who are ineffective do. Lower-class men, on the other hand, seem generally disinterested in the mechanisms of conception; about half of all the men studied (including those who planned families and those who were ineffective in planning) by Rainwater and Weinstein (1960) had no clear idea of what might be involved. Hence the woman's knowledge of reproduction is more important than her husband's. She is the one who is most likely to use effective contraceptives; she initiates discussion on the subject, and her interest is the basis of the couple's joint knowledge about it.

But men in nonplanning marriages tend to be aloof in discussions with their wives, and they share fewer mutual interests with them. They maintain less involved relationships with all members of the family. The sense of separateness in relations with wives among lower-class men contrasts sharply with the emphasis on intimacy projected by middle-class men (Rainwater, 1962; Komarovsky, 1964). Half of the women in J. Mayone Stycos' (1955) Puerto Rican sample reported a virtual absence of activities with their husbands outside the home, and many of the remaining women reported only infrequent or limited mutual interests. Oscar Lewis (1951) found the same pattern in Tepoztlán. Spouses participate in relatively closed social networks that provide a rather independent sense of stability and continuity in life for each. In lower-class Puerto Rican marriages the man may be a hard worker but a casual husband and father—a thorough *macho,* the traditional he-man of Puerto Rican society. The *macho* follows the dictum that the woman belongs in the home, the man in the street, where he proves his masculinity and chases women (Rogler, 1965). American working-class fathers also tend to see child rearing as their wives' responsibility (Kohn and Carroll, 1960; Komarovsky, 1964). The pronounced segregation in marital roles causes considerable difficulty in communication between husbands and wives on almost all matters that are not clearly defined by traditional expectations (Hill, Stycos, and Back, 1959; Rainwater, 1964).

Fathers who are unconcerned about family planning feel that having sex relations is their central right in marriage and that wives are dutybound to make themselves available on demand (Rainwater and Weinstein, 1960). Sex relations between husband and wife under these circumstances become rather impersonal "outlets" and are divorced from the responsibility of parenthood. The father may pride himself on the number of children he has, but may remain indifferent to the quality of his performance as a father. In an anomalous combination of energies and values, fathers who do not plan the size of their families often have a greater desire to become fathers than those who do plan, and derive relatively more satisfaction from whatever social esteem may be attached to fatherhood per se, but they fall short on family commitment and dependability.

Thus, planlessness and indifference to the routines of fatherhood go together; both are related to a lack of preparation for fatherhood. A key goal in the upgrading of the lower-class father, therefore, is to increase his involvement in family planning, which includes much more than the specific duties of birth planning. But the planning of pregnancy, because of its early and strategic place in the life cycle of the family, provides an important basis for general family planning and for an enlarged, more effective role for the father in family affairs. Since birth planning is such an important link to more general family planning, the need for an emphasis on precisely this kind of planning, explained and encouraged in the public school system, should be apparent.

Perhaps we might add that when two critical transitions in life must be accomplished simultaneously the maximum crisis effect is experienced (Rapoport and Rapoport, 1965); for example, when an individual marries at about the same time he graduates from high school, or at the same time he becomes a parent. Therefore it is not surprising that early postmarital pregnancy is typically followed by greater than average marital difficulties. Couples who have children soon after marriage are under exceptional economic pressure, especially if they married at an early age. They find difficulty in accumulating goods and assets, and tend to become discouraged about their chances to cope effectively with life's problems (Freedman and Coombs, 1967). Pregnancy conceived even before the marriage, which occurs quite frequently (Gray, 1960), places an even greater strain on the marriage and seems to be part of a larger "divorce-producing syndrome" (Christensen and Rubenstein, 1956). Premarital pregnancies are associated with younger age at marriage, ignorance of birth-control devices, lower socioeconomic status, brief acquaintanceship, mixed religions, lower educational levels, and minority Negro status (Lowrie, 1965)—all of which are associated with high rates of marriage failure.

It is possible, of course, that many marriages occurring after pregnancy were never intended to last; the only purpose of the ceremony was to legitimize the baby. Therefore the hurried marriage is most likely to occur precisely where premarital pregnancies are most highly condemned (Christensen, 1963). And yet in the places where pressures for a quick marriage are strongest—in the middle classes, for example—the pregnancy will have the most harmful effects. Harold Christensen (1960) found that the most liberal nations, such as Denmark, have the highest levels of premarital pregnancy, but also the least negative consequences. Clark Vincent (1959) concluded from his own studies that "ego involvement" accompanies the sexual relations of middle-class couples to a greater extent than those in the lower classes; he suggests, therefore, that lack of ego involvement may account for the relatively low incidence of divorce among couples of low status whose marriages followed pregnancy.

Strangely, couples who delay marriage after a premarital pregnancy have the most trouble of all, because couples who do not delay were planning marriage anyway (Christensen and Meissner, 1953). It should be clear that a "hurried marriage" in the present context is one in which the couple hurries the *decision* to marry; rushing the ceremony is not as disastrous as making a decision to marry under pressure.

Two points of particular interest emerge from this discussion of the man's adjustment to fatherhood. One concerns his first reactions to the experience of being a father; the other concerns his exercise of power within the family. Fathers are prone to think of parenthood in economic terms and to become more disturbed by the burdens of parenting as they are drawn into closer involvement with their children's daily problems; men with limited earning power are the most thoroughly shaken by these responsibilities. Combining relatively naïve and callous attitudes toward pregnancy and childhood, men in the lower classes are severely handicapped in the task of accommodating to paternity.

The father's exercise of power in the family has proved to be extremely complex. A combination of "resources theory" and "exchange value theory" seems to be particularly useful in explaining historical changes in the relative power of mothers and fathers as well as changes that occur during the life cycle of the family itself. The concept of *responsibility* links the study of power to that of the family division of labor, since both decision making and work involve an assumption of responsibilities. Work is usually divided within the family according to conventional community standards, but the power pattern is much less predictable. In fact, the relatively conventional division of labor found in most homes exerts a powerful influence over family decision making; decisions are much the same whether made by father, mother, or jointly by the two of them because whoever makes decisions usually wants his family to appear "normal." The widespread commitment to an "ideal image" of family life contributes to uniformity in family decision making even though we have no strong community norms regarding who should make the decisions.

CHAPTER VII

Identification With Father

Sexualization refers to a set of closely related processes by which boys learn to assume masculine roles and girls learn the feminine counterparts. It encompasses behavior specifically associated with erotic arousal and release, but much more than that. We know that sexual performance is largely a function of identification with one's sex and that this identification can take many forms, since there are many forms of manhood and womanhood.

We know also that the sequence of physiological events by which boys become men differs from that by which girls become women. But the psychological make-up of each, and its characteristic pattern of behavior, is more easily explained in terms of the processes by which roles are learned than by physiological or growth processes. Perhaps the woman's style of life is dictated more by her physiological functions (child-bearing in particular) and by glandular processes than is that of man, but most of her daily activities, and certainly the differences between female behavior in one culture and that of another, cannot be explained in this way. The maturation or "flowering" approach to sexualization—the "women are women and men are men the world over" approach—has long been outmoded.

Scores of subtle cues nudge little boys toward manhood and little girls toward womanhood, the cumulative effect of which begins to appear very early in life. The pattern is so diffused throughout community activities that it does not depend on any one of its elements, but "culture" must nevertheless be transmitted through the machinery of its parts, and some are more important than others. We shall be concerned here with those aspects of paternal behavior that contribute to the masculinization of boys and the feminization of girls.

Theories of Identification

In the most obvious theory, father is the model of masculinity for his son, while mother is the feminine model for her daughter. Examples of masculinity are seen almost everywhere, but father is the most visible and the most significant male figure for his own children. He is the guide for how men talk, how they express the sentiments of friendship and indignation, what they are interested in, and what they stand aloof from.

The "father as masculine model" hypothesis has greatest analytical power in connection with theories of father-son identification. Although a distinction should be drawn between identification with one's father and identification with one's sex (Lynn, 1966), the former almost inevitably conditions the latter. Moreover, through the concept of identification it becomes possible to extend the role of father to the sex training of daughters. Unfortunately, "identification" is a fuzzy term. Some writers suggest that it is simply the process by which children acquire their parents' attitudes, values, and behavior patterns (Aldous and Kell, 1961). That definition can be improved upon, as we shall see, but it provides a good starting point.

Through intimate association the child gains rapport with his parents and becomes like them in countless ways. He "takes the role of the other," as George Herbert Mead (1934) put it; he develops a conception of himself and of others similar to those held by his parents. One can never by identification with father take his specific role in the family, although fantasies about doing so occur among quite normal boys. But through the father as a model the boy learns to become *a* father in another family. Identification therefore implies the internalization of a *generalized* role pattern (Parsons, 1954).

In Freudian theory the parent is largely responsible for formation of the child's superego, serving as a moral control over his behavior (Freud, 1949). In Eric Berne's (1964) transliteration of Freud, the parent is largely responsible for the "parent ego state" in the child, that is, reproductions within the individual of the ego demands of his parents as perceived by the child. Thus, everyone "carries his parents around inside him."

When the child identifies with a parent the latter becomes an embodiment of what the child would like to be; the child then endeavors to mold his own behavior after the parental model. For example, as part of the process of identifying with his father, the son tries to please him and to imitate his actions. The boy looks up to his father, develops respect and concern for him, is deferential in relations with him, and judges him sympathetically. He acquires an ability to predict his father's actions and reactions subconsciously, and pleasing father becomes a source of personal satisfaction. The child's own actions confirm his similarity to the admired parent, and thus imitative behavior induced by identification becomes intrinsically rewarding (Rau, 1960).

Although a portion of the child's social development is the result of direct and self-conscious training, much of his behavioral repertoire is acquired through this rather "mindless" identification with important adults in his life (Bandura and Hutson, 1961). Certainly the need for identification with someone is apparent; the child in an institution, for example, will very likely identify with some attractive adult whom he sees frequently, whether it be the gardener, dorm parent, staff member, or caseworker. Identification with others is an essential catalytic agent for human learning, and obstinate disruptions of the learning process are most typically caused by abnormalities in just this agency, especially abnormalities in parent-child identification.

Efforts to please parents that are based on fear of retaliation are not products of identification; they provide a weak basis for the inculcation of appropriate sex-linked behavior. The threat of punishment is an ineffective means of discouraging unwanted behavior in the long run precisely because the child often fails to identify with the punitive parent (Sears, Maccoby, and Levin, 1957). Both warnings and retribution are short-term controls; if they have long-term consequences it is only because the individual has been sapped of his ability to act on the basis of inner resources.

Clearly, identification is a powerful means of sustained self-control in behalf of social goals and values. As a result of the child's identification with another person who has already learned to exercise personal control, the child attempts to conduct himself according to prevailing social norms. This promotes appropriate sex styles, but it contributes to all other facets of child development as well. For this reason sexualization is a relatively painless and invisible process, provided that the "normal" parent-child identification is not in some way impaired or corrupted.

It also becomes apparent that identification is not a unilateral endeavor. The child identifies with the parent, and the parent also identifies in certain important respects with the child. We must agree with Talcott Parsons (1958) when he defines identification as the internalization of a reciprocal role relationship, not merely the assumption of "personality traits." Long ago Charles Horton Cooley (1902) pointed out the essentially reciprocal and subjective character of primary relationships such as those involved in identification. Following Cooley's lead, Nicholas Babchuk and Alan Bates (1963) suggest that identification is in fact a "suspended primary group," which may consist of people who have not seen each other for years. When identification linking two people is well established, especially in the cases of husbands and wives, or parents and children, it retains a control function until *both* have died.

During its formative years, father-son identification is thus a two-way process entailing continuous feedback. Father wants his son to do certain things in certain ways and his own behavior is affected by the boy's efforts; father is a dynamic masculine model, not a static one. He, as well as the son, is constantly making adaptations within their mutually compelling relationship. The son becomes like his father in some ways and unlike him in others—unlike him because of the relationship, not in spite of it.

In the literature on child development, the task of the child to make the proper sex identification is usually stressed rather than the parent's effort to facilitate the process, but father's role in his son's groping for manhood is as important as the boy's and cannot be limited to fitful reprimands or occasional advice and encouragement. Our increasing awareness of this truth may be reflected in the greater guilt parents feel nowadays if their children "go wrong" than they once felt. This is characteristically a maternal reaction, however; fathers are still more likely than mothers to enjoy an untroubled parental conscience.

The identification that a father may have with his son is, of course, qualitatively different from the identification that a son has with his father. For one thing, the father is more knowledgeable about what is going on in the course of their interaction; he is able to "step back" occasionally and contemplate the pattern. And he has been a son once himself.

Of course the father does not imitate his son; there can be no intrinsic reward in doing so. The son's imitation of his father, on the other hand, is rewarding to both son and father and is a crucial basis for father's identification with his son. Deference operates in a slightly different, but related, fashion; in a variety of situations the boy respectfully defers to the wishes or to the patently superior judgment of his father, which is ordinarily more rewarding to the father than to the son.

From the child's viewpoint, two kinds of identification can be distinguished: *satellization* and *incorporation* (Ausubel, 1952). In the former the child keys his behavior to the actions of a strong and reassuring parental figure. It is contingent upon the parent's support and acceptance of the child, who is dependent and unable to cope with life alone. The child constantly looks to the parent for guidance and encouragement, and he can therefore slowly develop an inner core of self-esteem and establish an independent basis for managing his own life.

Incorporation occurs when the child accepts parental habits or values because of their capacity to enhance his status, independent of any emotional ties to the parent. Thus, whether the satellization pattern is strong or not, the child will assume some of his parents' qualities by virtue of their visibility and usefulness.

We can also distinguish between expressive and manipulative identification from the father's viewpoint. In expressive identification, father enjoys spending time with his son, makes efforts to please him, develops a positive concern for him, judges his behavior sympathetically, and gains vicarious ego enhancement through the boy's accomplishments. In manipulative identification, father attempts to teach, cajole, or pressure his son to improve his performance, for which father is rewarded if the son shows progress. Needless to say, mother can identify with the son in both expressive and manipulative ways, too, but the boy cannot please mother as readily by being like her; if he is too much like her she will be among the first to show alarm.

Little children can manipulate their parents in only trivial ways. Quite obviously children learn how to "work" their parents, especially daughters vis-à-vis fathers, but they do this for the purpose of getting specific things they want, not to mold the parent into a certain kind of person. Parents may try to live up to their children's expectations, of course, and Jules Henry (1963) has suggested that parents strive to meet their children's demands more frequently than children try to please their parents. In that case the parent is the satellite and the child the star.

But in terms of the "gross identification effort" one must admit that children do indeed work harder than parents. The child, at least the small child, strives to make the grade according to parental wishes in almost all facets of his existence, whereas parental striving to please children is a much more segmented effort. Furthermore, much of the effort of the child is subconscious and occurs in the course of rapid personal development; the very fact that parents are in a stage of life characterized by rather sluggish personality change limits the extent to which they can be modified through identification with their children (Davis, 1940).

We might note that the expressive, as distinguished from manipulative, identification of parents with children is probably more characteristic of American fathers than fathers in most other countries. This type of identification is, in a sense, a peer or brother relationship rather than the traditional father-son pattern. Writers such as Erik Erikson (1950) and Jules Henry (1963) contend that it is one in which father and son are joined in mutual submission under the female yoke. Father is an "imp buddy" to his son; the two may stray from family obligations in hapless fashion, but inevitably succumb to the perseverance and common sense of mother. This pattern seems to reflect the very strong antiauthoritarian pressures in our society. If father has any kind of moral authority in America, it is not so much because he is "father" and thereby enjoys the right to command, but because he is more skilled or more knowledgeable than his children.

Robert Lane (1959) suggests that father-son "identification without affection" is rare in the United States, but, by contrast, has been rather common in Germany. The German son respects his father although he receives little enjoyment from the relationship. Respect for father implies that he is to be honored and deferred to; it is of a piece with respect for one's commanding officer. In this context the son identifies with father, struggles for his approval, and ultimately leaves home to become like his father: a rather demanding and aloof figure, yet effective in his way.

Philip Slater (1961), however, remains unconvinced. He claims that many a German Hausfrau supports her husband's disciplinary measures while he is in sight, exhorting the child to be obedient, but when he leaves she hustles the child off to the kitchen for candy and sympathy, thus making a sharp distinction between what is necessary in public in the presence of authority and what one may do and feel privately in its absence. Slater suggests that this has long been a source of weak paternal identification in the German family; an attempt to overcome the frustration inherent in an incomplete identification with father may even have contributed to the yearning for a powerful national authority.

Identification and the Life Cycle

Because the infant's primary needs are almost always gratified by mother, she is the first object of identification for both sons and daughters (Sullivan, 1953). As basic needs are being met, the infant establishes responses to an entire system of social cues based largely upon maternal dependency, in which mother's presence, her gestures and attitudes, as well as her primary nurturant behavior become pleasurable and rewarding to the child (Sears, 1957). Hence, the first social system of which the child is a part is the little world of mother-child interaction, and mother is the child's primary point of human reference.

When the child is very young he adopts some of his mother's ways because he is unable to distinguish between himself and mother. Later the child develops an identification with mother due to his dependency upon her for care and protection. Still later, there is some loss of identification with mother due to disappointments inherent in the relationship with her. She cannot continue to "baby" the child as he grows older, and a series of role readjustments leads to increasing differences between the identification processes for girls and boys.

In the Freudian view girls develop some hostility toward their mothers, but also fear retaliation in the form of withdrawal of the mother's love. For this reason, mother-daughter identification is imbued with ambivalence. Boys gradually transfer identification from mother to father, largely due to fear of the aggressive male who controls and therefore often frustrates the child. Boys are able to defend themselves against the punishing father by identifying with him, or at least they can more adequately manage their tensions in this way, thus resolving, or containing, the Oedipal problem; attraction to mother is accompanied by conflict with father, and the conflict is relieved through identification with the male figure.

This Freudian formulation is discordant with most recent theories stressing "warmth and affection" as the qualities most likely to promote identification between child and parent. In fact, the Oedipus hypothesis has not fared well when subjected to empirical tests. Freud did not deal adequately with the possibility that the Oedipal conflicts he observed might have been products of a particular kind of social organization rather than a universal human condition (Mead, 1953). He seemed to assume that Oedipal tensions are shared by all people and had their beginnings in primitive family groups; sons banded together to kill and sacrificially eat the father. Later a totem animal, considered taboo, emerged as the paternal substitute. In *Totem and Taboo* (1918) Freud drew heavily upon the ethnographic data assembled by Sir James Frazer, Robertson Smith, and others, especially material on Australia.

But Bronislaw Malinowski (1927), for one, denied the existence of Oedipal conflicts in matrilineal societies. He rejected the universality of the father-son Oedipal conflict, pointing out that in the Trobriand Islands, with which he was quite familiar, discipline was in the hands of the mother's brother, not the father. Malinowski may have taken Freud's point of view too literally, but even if he did not grasp Freud's real meaning, which frequently occurs among Freud's critics, the misunderstanding is symptomatic of the problem: in many respects Freud's work is inherently ambiguous (Hartmann, Kris, and Lowenstein, 1951).

An alternative to the Freudian theory of identification, although clearly derived from it, is one developed by Miriam Johnson (1963). It seems to be more useful than Freud's theory and is supported by an impressive body of empirical evidence. Johnson contends that identification with father—that is, the internalization of a reciprocal role relationship with him—is crucial for producing appropriate sex-role orientations in *both* sons and daughters; she skillfully shows that the processes of identification can be used to explain prevailing social expectations for masculinity and femininity and are also linked to observable community practices.

As in the Freudian approach, the first parental identification of the child according to Johnson is with mother, who is characteristically nurturant and supportive in her relations with both son and daughter. During this early stage, in a love-dependency relationship with mother, the child's first superego principles are established, and in this almost exclusive maternal attachment both sons and daughters learn the fundamental forms of expressive behavior. Although certain basic life habits are being established—eating, sleeping, cleanliness, toilet training—the most pervasive emphasis at this time is security through warm, expressive relationships.

The pattern thus established serves as the basis for a lifelong intimacy with mother, and it is only rarely duplicated in associations with father. The average level of affection will remain higher toward mother than father (Bowerman and Irish, 1962), and she will be preferred more often than father by children of both sexes (Stodgill, 1937; Prince and Baggaley, 1963). Clyde Nunn's (1964) data clearly indicate that both younger and older children consider mother to be the more demonstrative and loving parent; her superior ranking vis-à-vis father is roughly three to one.

Although mother does share common cultural values with father concerning appropriate masculine and feminine behavior, and she may assign chores to her children on the basis of sex, she does not ordinarily make as sharp a distinction in her attitudes toward son and daughter as does father. She is also much less concerned about appropriate sex-typing in her children (Tasch, 1952; Goodenough, 1957; Sears, Maccoby, and Levin, 1957). She neither plays wife to her son nor urges her daughter to "get in there and be a woman" (except in the sense that she expects the girl to show progress in getting her man). Mother tends to think of both sexes as *children*, whom she cares for in the light of her general nurturant and supportive family role. To fathers, on the other hand, the preservation of differences between men and women is usually important; they prefer that sex distinctions be easily recognizable, and they exert a strong and dogged influence upon their development.

This is not to suggest that sons and daughters identify with mother in identical ways; girls generally retain closer, more intimate relations with their mothers than boys do (Bowerman and Irish, 1962) and are encouraged to imitate a much broader range of maternal behavior. David Riesman (1964), for example, notes that boys identify less with their mothers as shoppers than do girls. But Leone Kell and Joan Aldous (1960) found that boys were more likely than girls to have child-rearing values similar to their mothers', perhaps because fathers are so inarticulate in this area; girls, who give more thought to child rearing, have an opportunity to work out orientations for themselves that are somewhat different from their mothers. Because boys think less about parenthood in their teens, the critical years for anticipations of parenting, they are destined to retain more "childish" orientations to the parental role, orientations they acquired subliminally when they were quite young.

Thus on certain issues mother's influence endures more noticeably than that of father, even for sons. Robert Hess and Gerald Handel (1956) suggest that mother may transmit her style of aggressiveness to the children more completely than father, despite the fact that this is usually considered one of father's strongest areas of influence (Sears, Pintler, and Sears, 1946). There is very little similarity between father's pattern of aggressiveness and that of his daughter, while the similarity between father and son in this regard is of a generalized nature found among almost all males, whether they are related or not.

But as the child grows older, identification with father becomes increasingly apparent, accompanied by the sharpening of differences between sons and daughters. In Johnson's analysis, identification with father, coming after the stage of infantile dependency on the mother, is now crucial for the appropriate sexualization of girls as well as boys. Both sons and daughters identify to a greater extent with father than before, but in different ways and according to distinctive father-son and father-daughter patterns.

Relationships between father and daughter tend to be expressive; those between father and son tend to be instrumental (the more so if father's sex adaptation is highly masculine). Girls receive more affection, attention, and praise than boys, especially from father, whereas boys are subjected to greater pressure and discipline, again mainly from father (Bronfenbrenner, 1961a). He wants his daughter to be pretty, nice, likeable, and so on, but he thinks his son should begin to show an ability to hold his own in a man's world. Thus, father typically takes a less demanding and more appreciative attitude toward his daughter than his son, playing husband to the girl and mentor to the boy (Mead, 1953; Johnson, 1963).

Since fathers are both less exacting and more rewarding in their relationships with their daughters, girls rate fathers much higher in nurturance and affection than boys do (Emmerich, 1959a; Johnson, 1963). In fact, girls report a closer relationship to both parents than sons do (Landis, 1960), which is consistent with the proposition that both mother and father maintain expressive ties with daughter, but father, unlike mother, forms a strong instrumental bond with his son.

Father adds a specifically feminine element to the girl's initial expressiveness by appreciating her not simply for being "good," but for being "attractive." Fathers participate in the daily care and protection of girls even more than of boys and fall into the habit of thinking of their daughters as dainty and fragile (Tasch, 1952). In fact, fathers play with their daughters more than mothers do and engage in a pattern of affectionate teasing that girls usually enjoy (Gardner, 1947). A counterpart to this mutually enjoyable flirtation between father and daughter rarely occurs in mother-son relationships, in part of course because the son objects to it so artlessly as he grows older. It reflects upon his masculinity, but it is also forbidden because of the extremely harsh cultural attitudes toward mother-son incest. Intimacies between parents and children of the opposite sex are necessarily limited due to our abhorrence of even the hint of incest, but mother-son taboos are probably the most zealously inculcated restrictions found in human culture.

The consequences of the girl's relationship with her father will, of course, be determined by the kind of person her father is. If he possesses a strong masculine orientation in his interests and attitudes, he is almost certain to encourage the girl's participation in conventional sex-typed activities (Mussen and

Rutherford, 1963). On the other hand, highly masculine boys tend to have highly masculine fathers too. Both the father and mother of the highly masculine boy may have relatively strong masculine leanings, but the very feminine girl is not likely to have had both a feminine mother and a feminine father. Thus it would appear that father is even more important for his daughter's sexualization than mother is for her son's. Mother can, in her relationships with her son, impede the boy's progress toward masculinity, but is limited in her ability to positively inculcate the male orientation. Mother's relationships with her son have *relatively* little influence on the boy's male-female preferences, while the father's personality and behavior appear to be important factors in the daughter's desire to be "feminine." Boys move toward father and away from mother as they grow older, for example, but girls often identify almost as much with father as with mother (Osgood, Suci, and Tannebaum, 1957).

We have no reason to assume that this pattern will be found in all cultures, of course, especially since we know it is variable even within our own. The expressive relationship between father and daughter does not occur as frequently in the lower classes, for example, as in middle classes. Glen Elder and Charles Bowerman (1963) found that in both large and small families lower-class girls experienced more restraint, more paternal direction, and more punitive discipline than lower-class boys, especially when the girls had brothers. In fact, lower-class girls who had brothers were more than twice as likely to report their fathers as autocratic than girls in "all girl" families were; both mother and father were much more likely to be authoritarian with regard to daughter under these circumstances. Thus, the lower-class father seems less likely to give his daughter the pleasure that is inherent in an affectionate expressive relationship, especially if his family includes sons as well as daughters. The presence of boys in the lower-class household may very well serve as a reminder of their danger to wayward girls.

In Negro neighborhoods the pattern is further complicated; male-female distinctions so characteristically found among white youth are much less pronounced. This situation is a corollary of the father's frequent weakness and the Negro mother's assumption of both male and female obligations. The instability of the Negro home as compared with middle-class white families, the higher probability that the Negro mother must contribute to her family's income by working away from home, and the greater likelihood that the Negro father is ineffective or has even deserted, all contribute to a blurring of the distinction between male and female roles (Lott and Lott, 1963).

Of course the more typical expressive relationship between father and daughter in the middle and upper classes, although similar to mother-daughter expressiveness in form, is different in content. Middle-class girls do not express curiosity about sex to fathers as they do to mothers, for example. They don't get frank answers when they do, nor are they given any encouragement to explore specifically female problems in the presence of their fathers (Burchinal, 1960a). Many vital problems the girl must face are thus avoided in relations with her father; these are problems that the girl can ordinarily discuss with her mother. For this reason, expressiveness with father thrives in an almost pure form; with mother it is tempered by practical considerations of daily importance and is thereby given a deeper and more solid foundation.

Mother's expressiveness is also more effective because she is immune to her daughter's "feminine wiles." In fact, in certain ways mother is much more instrumental with her daughter than father can ever be. She is more likely than father, for example, to goad her daughter to make progress toward marriage in dating and courtship affairs. The daughter may need father upon whom to practice a repertoire of social devices and from whom to learn to understand and appreciate masculine interests, but it is mother who pushes her to "get her man" (Henry, 1963). (Both parents put more pressure on girls in courtship than on boys.) It remains generally true, however, that mother is expected to be expressive in her most characteristic functions, whereas father is expected to be both expressive and instrumental. David Riesman (1964) has softened the contrast between parental roles by suggesting that father is in charge of realism, understudied by sentiment, while mother cultivates utopianism, holding practicality in reserve.

The Impetus to Identification

Are there any known explanations for the fact that the quality and intensity of father-child identification differ so markedly from one family to the next? In the search for an answer, characteristics of the parents rather than those of the child are most often studied, and a number of them have been considered by one authority or another to be especially important: the sex of the parent, the parents' respect for one another, the degree to which parents differ from one another, the impressiveness or clarity of each parent's personal qualities, the extent to which the parent's activities overlap those of the child, the power of the parent, and the affection the parent shows for the child.

The explanation most commonly given is that children identify with the parent of the same sex; the implicit assumption here is that sex similarity is the primary basis for parent-child identification (Beier, 1953; Gray and Klaus, 1956; Sears, Maccoby, and Levin, 1957; Emmerich, 1959a). There is considerable empirical evidence in support of this view, and it appeals to common sense: children are usually rewarded for behavior similar to the parent of the same sex and are not rewarded, indeed they may be punished, for acting like the cross-sex parent (Stoke, 1954; Ratzeburg, 1959). Boys almost inevitably perceive themselves to be like their fathers, while girls believe themselves to be more like their mothers (Gray and Klaus, 1956; Kagan, Hosken, and Watson, 1961).

It seems likely that the child will identify most readily with a parent of the same sex if that parent is reasonably self-confident about his own sexual identity. If the girl's mother accepts herself, for example, she provides a more impressive model of femininity for her daughter (McCandless, 1961); the same process probably occurs in father-son identification.

Note, however, that cross-sex identification does not account for femininity in boys or masculinity in girls. Effeminate boys do not consider themselves to be like their mothers, nor do masculine girls think they are like their fathers (Beier, 1953). Effeminacy is more likely to be the product of a damaged father-son relationship than of a strong mother-son bond (recognizing of course that factors other than the parent-child relationships may be involved). The same principle is probably true of masculinity in girls; a strong father-daughter tie does not produce masculinity in girls—the opposite is in fact a greater possibility.

Mother may or may not reinforce the masculinizing effect of father, but the traditional expectation is that she will, especially by the way she shows affection and respect for him. She thereby defines her husband—and the style of life he represents—as worthy of emulation. M. M. Helper (1955) reports that both male and female offspring are more likely to describe themselves as similar to the father if the mother approves of him as a model, while relatively masculine mothers tend to inhibit strong father identification in their sons (Payne and Mussen, 1956). Lucy Rau (1960) suggests that the parents' effectiveness as models is greatly enhanced by a prevailing pattern of agreement between them. We might also add that in promoting a favorable image of father, mother may in turn facilitate the success of father in emancipating the children from herself.

Rau also suggests that the parent's influence as a model depends to a large extent on the clarity, or perhaps salience, of his personal style. The most distinctive qualities of the parent are the ones the child is most likely to incorporate into his own behavior. This is a plausible proposition, but a critical test for it is lacking, and it poses a very difficult research problem: How is *saliency* to be determined? Boys sometimes become like their fathers in terms of marginal, almost "invisible" qualities and yet fail to assume certain of father's ways that are quite apparent to others. In fact, the marginal quality that is transmitted may have been unnoticed by the child, and perhaps both parent and child will deny that either of them possesses it. If the father has a trait that is readily apparent and his son also has it, everyone can agree that the trait has been passed on through the process of identification. But many subtle qualities, and those which are hard to define, go unnoticed. Thus, the clarity theory is reinforced because the saliency factor, upon which the theory is based, deceives the researcher and establishes its own validity.

The clarity theory is rather closely related to one that holds that if the styles of the parents are different and easily distinguished from one another, the son is more likely to identify with his father and the daughter with her mother (Parsons, Bales, *et al.,* 1955). But Irene Josselyn (1956) argues that pressures in contemporary America often lead to grotesque efforts on the part of women to be manlike, and that, in response, men try all the harder to be different in order to establish their masculinity. In striving to close the gap between the sexes, the American mother, emancipated from housework by labor-saving devices, and alienated from it in any case, becomes an unhappy imitation of her husband. At the same time, she treats her husband like a little boy or an awkward helper, thus damaging the child's image of his father. To make matters worse, Josselyn continues, the father tries to hang on to his status by proving his manliness, which he does by inhibiting any signs of femininity, including the tenderness associated with it.

Thus the American child lives in a world dominated by women and receives love only from his mother. Identification with the masculine figure becomes a difficult struggle, and in order to achieve it the boy must give up all similarity to women. Frustrated in his identification effort, he winds up like his misguided father anyway, straining in an uphill battle to distinguish himself as a man. Presumably the predicament would not be so lamentable if the distinction between maternal and paternal styles was unmistakable. Josselyn's is an interesting theory, but unproved.

Following an entirely different line of reasoning, Philip Slater (1961) contends that distinctive parental styles are not advantageous in modern society. If the family is surrounded by a closely knit network of friends, neighbors, and relatives, mother-father differences may be encouraged along with the encouragement of a general separation of the sexes. But when this network is lacking, the family is more effective if parents can maintain closeness and rapport. The children will spend their lives in shifting groups and must internalize their parents' values in order to discipline themselves. If the parents have sharply contrasting styles, each parent evokes a different kind of feeling from the child: this lessens the emotional intensity of family life by reducing the areas of joint activity and thus increasing the psychological distance between family members.

Obviously the child in modern America will identify with both parents to some extent. Since the parents are inevitably different from one another in a number of ways it is to be expected that identification with both of them at the same time creates tension. This tension is alleviated to some extent if the child develops a stronger relationship with one of the parents, and also if he avoids (although this is largely unconscious) incompatible characteristics of the two parents. But Slater seems to be correct; it has become necessary for the child to identify rather strongly with both parents, not just the parent of the same sex. It helps, therefore, if the parents are similar to one another in basic values and orientations, and if they can cooperate intimately with one another in their dealings with the children.

Robert Winch (1962) contends that the greater the number of roles relating the child to his parent, the stronger the child's identification with that parent will be. This is an "overlapping activities theory" and implies that the quality of the parent's performance may not be as important as the way the performance links the activities of the parent to those of the child. It seems reasonable to assume that the more time a son spends with his father, in whatever capacity, the more he will be like him, and this would appear to be true independent of the degree of positive affection between the two; we tend to assimilate the characteristics of those with whom we associate whether we like them or not, a principle that has been observed repeatedly in parent-child relations. But children no longer spend much time *working* with their parents, and they are not likely to spend a great deal of time playing with them if that is not a pleasurable activity. Hence, since the extent of overlapping activities now tends to be a product of choice rather than necessity, it is less a cause than a consequence of father-child identification.

Some writers contend that the child will identify most intensively with a powerful and aggressive parent, and less so with one who is weak and passive (Cava and Rausch, 1952; Hetherington and Brackbill, 1963). Even affection, they suggest, is not as important for identification as forcefulness is. According to this view, children are most likely to identify with those they perceive as powerful, especially the parent who most effectively controls their rewards and punishments. Glen Elder (1963), however, found that in American society both highly autocratic and highly permissive parents are likely to appear unattractive to the child by comparison with the middle-of-the-roader.

A theory of identification based on affection or parental warmth is much more popular these days than the power theory: the child identifies most readily with an affectionate parent. According to this approach, love and affection provide the most consistent and effective incentives for identification (Mowrer, 1950; Stoke, 1954; Gray and Klaus, 1956; Payne and Mussen, 1956; Kagan, 1958; Bronfenbrenner, 1960; Mussen and Distler, 1960). Payne and Mussen, for example, contend that a high degree of identification with father by the son is likely to occur if the boy perceives his father as a highly rewarding, affectionate person. Although sometimes left unstated, it is often assumed that identification stirred by affectionate regard is more intense than that induced by sheer power, and is less likely to be contaminated by ambivalence. Warmth breeds an interpersonal bond without reservations; certainly affection is now defined as an unmitigated good, as the exercise of power in human relationships is not.

Rae Carlson (1963) has thrown some light on the different effects of power and affection in parent-child relations by distinguishing between "threat-based" and "support-based" identification; she found that children identifying with supportive parents were consistently more self-accepting, less dependent on their current social relationships, and more acceptable to their peers. On the other hand, she found no relationship between the *extent* of identification and these measures of personality. One can conclude that it is more useful to know the quality of parental identification than simply "how much," since identification is not a unitary condition and its different forms have different consequences.

"Threat-based" identification is probably most influential when the "support-based" variety fails, and therefore Philip Slater (1961) contends that the child assumes the values of his parent to approximately the same degree that the parent is the source of both nurturance and discipline. Kindergarten boys in a study by Paul Mussen and Luther Distler (1959, 1960) identified most intensively with fathers who were perceived as nurturant and rewarding, but also as powerful sources of punishment. Paul Mussen and Eldred Rutherford (1963) found that highly masculine boys and highly feminine girls perceived their like-sexed parents as significantly warmer, more nurturant, and more affectionate than girls and boys who were rated inferior in appropriate sex-role identification. But among boys, and not girls, the very masculine group saw father as a highly salient and powerful person in their lives; he was a commanding figure in both a rewarding and a controlling fashion. This supports neither a power theory of identification per se nor an affection-giving theory, but more properly a "paternal importance" theory. The father who plays a principal role within the context of family life, especially in terms of both control and affection, is very likely to be an object of strong identification for his son.

Thus, the fact that fathers are accepted more frequently if they are warm and rewarding does not violate the axiom that both sons and daughters identify most completely with the parent of the same sex if the parents play somewhat different and distinctive roles within the family. The mother in the model case will cultivate expressiveness, while the father will moderate his essential instrumentalism by a strong expressive component.

But identification with father is also a function of general cultural patterns, since solidarity among men is more crucial in some societies than others. Lionel Lazowick (1955) argues that the boy's identification with his father is in part a function of the degree of masculine dominance in society. Where men do not prevail over women, the son's identification with father will tend to be weak or ambivalent. Moreover, where male solidarity is a critical matter, group rituals may assist in securing the boy's commitment to masculine standards (Young,

1962). A male initiation ceremony, for example, is sometimes used to dramatize the boy's sex role and to reinforce his identification with the male group and its function, especially when men must hunt together, or work cooperatively in dangerous activities calling for precise and absolutely reliable coordination. The soldier father of a boy growing up in a time of anxious preparation for battle will be an entirely different object of identification and respect than the white-collar father living in a relatively tranquil era of suburban affluence.

We have seen that the father who plays an impressive role within his family's daily routines, in terms of both control and affection, will very likely be an object of strong identification for both his son and his daughter. Under these circumstances the children will find that pleasing father and being like him are intrinsically rewarding. But this poses a problem. An ideal relationship between parent and child would provide the basis for a lifelong bond between them without sacrificing the identity of the child or his ability to explore life for himself. If the father is highly conventional, however, the child as an adult may have difficulty in adapting to new life orientations in a rapidly changing society. It is perhaps for this reason that the expressive facet of father's behavior has been enlarged as his control and disciplinary functions have declined. A warm relationship between father and child, laced with paternal firmness but not authoritarianism, increases the chances that the child will find a sense of security and self-confidence without becoming dependent upon his father for constant guidance.

CHAPTER VIII

Father and the Urge to Manhood

The most distinctive feature of the relationship between the father and his son—the fact that the father typically puts pressure on the boy to be "manly"—can be fully appreciated only when it is seen as an integral part of the pattern of masculine instrumentalism.

Unlike femininity, manliness does not flower in innocence and a sheltered maturation. Professional theory and popular opinion suggest that boys need to be pushed; no comparable prodding is required to promote womanliness. Herbert Barry, Margaret Bacon, and Irvin Child (1957), drawing upon a survey of 110 cultures, report a widespread social pattern in which the girls are nurtured and protected in return for which they are expected to be obedient, while self-reliance and striving are expected of boys, who must prepare themselves to compete for status and prestige outside the home. Thus, becoming a man calls for purposive effort on the part of the growing boy and a shove from his parents or from others in his milieu.

Miriam Johnson (1963) observes that males are urged to "try to be a man," as if they might not make the grade; females are simply told, or reminded, to "be a woman." The girl who strays is wrong-headed; the boy does not *stray*, he *fails*. Margaret Mead (1953) argues that women will readily adapt to motherhood unless they are "outraged" against it. It is their natural fulfillment if the customary growth processes are not violated.

M. F. Ashley Montagu (1953) has added an exotic twist to this subject by placing enormous importance on the fact that boys cannot look forward to childbirth, which he considers the primary act of creation. Hence boys, and men, must compensate. In our terminology, we might say that they are driven to instrumentalism because they are not allowed the fundamental satisfaction of giving birth to another human being. For women, this natural function is enough, or has been throughout most of "man's" past history. Giving birth solves the problem of female purpose and identity, and it enables women to find a life of pleasure in nurturance, protected by the instrumental striving of their husbands. Fathers, along with mothers and peer groups, may prod the boy in his compensatory search, but the underlying propulsion lies in the existential difference between male and female.

It is possible, of course, that greater pressures are exerted upon boys only because social traditions demand them; we are prisoners of the past in so many ways that perhaps this is just one more case of cultural lag. Several writers in recent years, Myron Brenton (1966) for example, have argued that masculinity in the traditional sense of the term is now tragically outmoded. In an earlier social era a push may have been required to make boys into men, but both society and manhood have changed; perhaps we can now let up on our sons as we press for more achievement from our daughters. It is at least possible that the push pattern survives solely as a relic of the past.

Even at very early ages greater demands are made upon boys than girls to conform to the social conventions of male and female behavior (Cava and Rausch, 1952; Gray, 1957; Hacker, 1957), and boys therefore become more apprehensive about not succeeding (Hartley, 1959; Lynn, 1961). The possibility of failure to meet male standards triggers restive and intimidating reactions in both the boy's peers and his elders.

Boys often feel the pressure in kindergarten, while as many as five years in school may elapse before girls are obliged to take definite feminine roles (Brown, 1956, 1957a, 1958). Daniel Brown reports that girls in the elementary-school years are significantly more variable in their sex-role preferences than boys and can be tomboys with social impunity longer than boys can be sissies (if it can be said that boys are ever allowed this alternative).

Boys are constantly reminded that they must avoid feminine behavior and must show signs of being able to cut themselves loose from the world of women that surrounds them. They develop hostility toward girls and things feminine in very early childhood, and the hostility recurs throughout their lives as a fear of being identified with "the enemy." By contrast, anxiety over being like the opposite sex appears to occur among girls and women at only a very low level of intensity.

Certainly girls find greater attraction to male interests and activities than boys have been able to discover in female pursuits. If it is more difficult for girls to assume the feminine role than for boys to adjust to masculinity, as Mirra Komarovsky (1946) and many others have contended, it is probably for this very reason. Girls may be enticed by the advantages of the opposite sex, which have a universal appeal; boys are rarely distracted by any persistent desire to join the girls, although they may retain a covert attraction to the female role because of their identification with mother in early childhood. Both males and females tend to prefer masculine roles, but both tend to retain an underlying feminine identification (Lynn, 1966). Hence girls must reconcile their desires for masculine privileges with the practical demands made upon them to be feminine; boys, on the other hand, are more likely to feel a need to be ever more masculine.

Persistent feminine leanings in the male are usually more problematical than masculine leanings in the female because the former spring from deeper, more anomalous, and more intensive social-psychological conditions (Hartley, 1959). They represent a rather gross distortion of the conventional boyhood pattern; the boy may have received some encouragement to adopt a feminine style, but it is also very likely that he suffered a great deal of embarrassment if he responded to it. Masculine girls, on the other hand, need not face much embarrassment. As women they may have problems, of course, but largely because they were *not* strongly and consistently punished for adopting masculine ways when they were young. In particular, they must cope with subtle discrimination when competing with men. The aggressive career woman, for example, may find that the men with whom she works sabotage her in ways that are just barely noticeable, and they usually do not take her as seriously as they take other men. Perhaps in childhood she was not adequately forewarned about such treatment, although apparently most women have been, which may be why they usually avoid competition with men as they grow older. David Lynn (1966) argues that with increasing age males develop psychological disturbances associated with sex-typing at a more slowly accelerating rate than females.

The *boy culture,* passed on from generation to generation in male peer groups, revels in masculine striving and transmits strong sentiments against feminine ways in general as well as against the particular girls who happen to live in the neighborhood. Boys ceaselessly act out the warrior role, which seems to give them unqualified pleasure; Simone de Beauvoir (1953) once suggested that access to this role has been the key to male supremacy in the battle of the sexes. Rose Giallombardo's (1966) findings are consistent with the definition of the female as nonaggressive; she noted that the roles of violence that emerge in the male prison—those of "wolf," "tough," "gorilla," "hipster," and "ball buster"—are notably absent among female inmates.

The corollary to the male's fear of being feminine, of course, is that of not being fully masculine, and again, compared to the analogous female anxiety, men and boys are the ones who most torment themselves. In her study of female prisoners, for example, Rose Giallombardo could find no circumstances in which inmates were compelled to assert or defend their femininity. In male prisons the inmate *must* prove his manhood when it is called into question, or forever be humbled (and there are many instances in which the man's maleness is in fact put on the line); no comparable situation exists in female prisons. Susan Gray (1957) found that boys showing high levels of masculinity also had high levels of anxiety. Intense masculinity, associated as it is with the suppression of affect and a drive to assert itself, is inherently insecure, *especially if the boy does not have a close relationship with his father.*

Masculinizing forces, like all primary aspects of socialization, are "in the air." But if parents are needed in this pursuit, as they seem to be, father rather than mother is the parent who is supposed to do the prodding. He is the parent who must sternly call attention to behavior that does not measure up to male standards. Mother is more often the consoling parent; she pushes her son occasionally, to be sure, but her métier is usually that of comforter in failure and frustration. Recall that father typically has an expressive relationship with both son and daughter, but with his son he is also strict and demanding, supplying that extra impulse required for the full development of instrumentalism (Johnson, 1963).

Even when mother does inculcate striving in her children, her efforts do not ordinarily spring from an instrumental base. The "press" she exerts is often founded upon limited experience with the kinds of activities in which she would have her children excel. Mother's reading habits, for example, do not appear to be correlated with those of her son or her daughter (Bing, 1963), although she may verbally encourage her children to spend more time with books. Mothers exhort their sons to do well in school as much as fathers, and at Little League baseball games they have been known to yell louder than the men. But the exhortation from mother is of a different order from father's, because she *cannot* be what she goads her son to be. Mother in effect urges the boy to "do well for me."

Father is more critical in his dealings with the boy because he judges by universal standards, and his flattery is usually harder to obtain. He is more often positively involved in the processes of learning male expertise, having participated in similar pursuits as a youth. Mother presents herself primarily as a person who can be pleased by good performance, but who will also be the first to offer solace in defeat. She has little practical advice to offer.

Walter Emmerich (1959a) argues that girls identify with their mothers simply because mother is an adult; boys, on the other hand, identify with father not because he is an adult but because he is a *man* and different from mother. It isn't so much that he is unlike the boy, but that he is male and hence ungirl-like. If Emmerich is correct, an intriguing proposition implicit in his argument would also seem to be true: Boys must learn to identify masculinity as part of the process of identifying with father. They seek rapport with the mature man, and they turn to father rather than mother at least in part because they have been conditioned to want a validation of their own masculinity. Just such a validation is available through paternal identification. Thus, sexualization is a problem-solving process for the boy, whereas it is a lesson-learning process for the girl (Lynn, 1966). The girl learns in detail the female role from her mother; the boy must "figure out" how to be masculine, at least in part because father is not around enough to give detailed instructions. Mother is the parent at hand, and she can only hint at what masculinity is all about.

The typical father-son relationship follows a pattern found in relations between persons of unequal skill, as between teacher and student or master and apprentice. A similar skill disparity does not exist between father and daughter, nor does it exist between mother and daughter. The difference is inherent in the distinction between instrumental and expressive patterns, since the former is often, if not characteristically, a relationship between unequals, whereas expressiveness usually occurs among equals, especially when it involves intimacy and the sharing of confidences. Mother does teach certain things to her daughter, of course—in the kitchen, for example—but within an expressive context in which competitiveness and tension are only weakly developed. The skills mother can impart are not those that ordinarily require arduous practice; they are likely to be mastered by almost any girl, if she is given a chance to learn.

Father, on the other hand, often participates in activities involving motor skills with his son; he serves as an exacting and insistent coach, acting out masculine patterns of aggressiveness. He drills his son continually, repeatedly calling attention to mistakes. There is a mutual awareness between father and son of the need for improvement. Learning male skills involves preparation for bigger and more serious battles to come. Girls learn routine skills once; there is little or no pressure to "train" or to rehearse in order to assure top performance in the big game or at the crucial moment. (Cheerleading, piano lessons, and ballet are minor exceptions, but these are rarely coached by mother.)

It is possible, of course, that the extent to which father actually pushes his son toward masculinity is overstated. In fact, the most crucial determinant of masculinity in young boys is probably the father-son relationship, not any particular activity of the father (Mussen and Rutherford, 1963). The boy's perception of his father as a nurturant and powerful individual is the important thing. The father's apparent efforts to induce his son to be manly are only incidental considerations; effective pressure is built into his routine exchange with the boy.

Nevertheless, fathers usually crack down on their sons for misbehavior and for failure to show signs of progress toward self-sufficiency. The father is more likely to be harsh toward his daughter in an effort to protect her from the dangers that lurk in a man's world. He scolds his daughter occasionally for naïvely inviting trouble, but he is more likely to punish his son physically for being boyish, that is, unmanly (Gardner, 1947).

It is not surprising, then, that ambition patterns differ between males and females. Compared to the ambitious girl, the aspiring boy is more likely to prepare himself for future success through persistent self-improvement and suppression of the urge to be just "one of the boys" (Turner, 1964). Turner points out that the male "deferred gratification pattern" represents an active stance toward long-term success; the boy develops his talents for the sake of future achievement, and he disciplines himself to meet well-known standards of performance, whether in athletics or academic work.

The ambitious girl is more likely to be satisfied with popularity in her immediate social circle. She tries to make herself distinctive (but not distinctive enough to arouse resentment), and she is not strongly committed to a career (Adamek and

Goudy, 1966). The expression of individuality among girls represents a willingness to be slightly conspicuous by being only slightly different—not as different as their talents might allow—which is necessary if girls wish to be noticed and favored at the same time. Ambitious boys use the autonomy permitted them in order to prepare for competition in adult life; any relaxation in their self-discipline becomes a handicap when they must face open competition, as ambitious boys must someday.

Due largely to their unconscious respect for the instrumental orientation and the discipline it requires, boys are actually more tolerant of fathers who restrict their freedom than girls are of mothers who impose restrictions. Girls are more likely to identify with their mothers if the mothers are lenient, while boys will identify with their fathers even when the fathers interfere with their freedom (Aldous and Kell, 1961). Boys apparently regard paternal restrictions upon their freedom as legitimate, although they may strenuously object at the time restraints are imposed; maternal restrictions are more likely to be resented by both boys and girls. We still retain the idea that too much tenderness, especially paternal tenderness, weakens the boy's will, and boys themselves learn to accept this mystique. Thus the expressive mother facilitates her daughter's maternal identification, while the instrumental father at least does not alienate his son. Hence, father can be more instrumental toward his son than mother can be toward her daughter, and the expressive-instrumental division of labor becomes self-perpetuating.

The fact that severely retarded children may acquire some domestic and expressive skills but will not be able to master the instrumental role provides a very plausible explanation for the fact that mothers are more effective with such children (especially boys) than are fathers (Tallman, 1965). Handicapped girls can turn to nonphysical recreation where they are not at a disadvantage, but physical activity is much more highly prized among boys (Richardson, Hastorf, and Dornbusch, 1964). The father of a retarded or handicapped boy is placed in the unhappy position of having superfluous interests and training skills, since he finds little opportunity to serve as model or coach for the child. But such a child may achieve enough mastery of his environment to give the mother the feeling that she has made an important contribution to his well-being.

The fact that relations between father and daughter are primarily expressive also helps to explain why fathers are more influential with daughters who are not career-oriented than with those who actively seek careers (Simpson and Simpson, 1961). By the nature of their relationships with daughters, fathers are not so much teachers and prodders as protectors and appreciators, a pattern that extends to the area of moral development. Throughout the adolescent years of his children father has greater influence on the boy's moral views than on the girl's; mother seems to have roughly equal influence on children of both sexes at this time (Brodbeck, 1954).

William Rushing (1964) found that daughters who have unsatisfactory relations with their fathers have higher career aspirations than those whose relations with their fathers are satisfactory. The reason, he suggests, is that unhappy experiences with father lead to a negative attitude toward men and family life in general; thus the girl becomes relatively more career-oriented and somewhat less drawn to the roles of wife and mother.

Boys, on the other hand, do not react in this way to disaffection with either mother or father. The degree of satisfaction in their relations with parents cannot affect their career aspirations so much because boys are expected to be career-oriented, independent of family adjustments. The daughter is the one who sees career aspirations as an *alternative* to family commitments.

Curiously, father's reading habits may be more closely related to the verbal abilities of his daughter than to those of his son, especially if he is an inveterate reader (Bing, 1963). At first glance, this seems inconsistent with what has just been said; one might expect father's reading habits to be more highly correlated with the son's verbal ability. But it is likely that the "intellectual" father—who is not the most common variety—will enjoy greater rapport with his daughter than with his son, especially when both children are young, since it usually takes boys longer than girls to discover the pleasures of reading. It also takes boys longer to become articulate. Fathers frequently find it easier to discuss things they have read with daughters than with sons, unless the subject is sports or cars.

The Masculine Discontinuity

The skill disparity that characterizes the relationship between father and son while the boy is young gradually diminishes as he grows older. He "catches up" with his father; nothing comparable occurs in the boy's relationship with mother. Greater continuity characterizes the mother-son pattern because of its fundamentally expressive nature, which is a static, not a dynamic, quality. Father pushes his son, but there comes a time when he can push no more; his prodding lingers on only as an unseen motivation in the "suspended primary group" that links the two men—one at his economic peak, the other in his physical prime.

As the boy becomes a man, he assumes the role of his father's social equal, or such tends to be the case in modern society. A deferential relationship may continue, but its earlier quality is transformed, most conspicuously in the area of athletics. The father may drill his son and continue pointing out weaknesses, but at some time during adolescence the boy surpasses his father, who must now simply watch and take vicarious satisfaction if the boy plays well. The father may still prod his son to practice and improve, but at this stage his pressure is likely to be resented—and ineffective to boot.

Girls experience the early years of life within the expressive mode and remain committed to that essential style even when they become wives and mothers. The transition to adult female behavior is probably smoother for the girl because her mother serves as both her earliest socializing agent and as the mature model for her moral behavior. Since love reciprocity—seeking and attaining love by giving it—is the key to feminization of the girl, expressive equality in mother-daughter and father-daughter relationships is a satisfying and durable source of continuity.

Boys begin life within the expressive mode, but must make

an instrumental adaptation later as they become fathers and men in the community of men. The boy establishes a strong relationship with his father only after the primary period of maternal dependency (Grinder, 1964). Both girls and boys have to transfer an expressive attachment from the parent of the opposite sex to an adult of their own age when they grow up, but for the boy love reciprocity is not enough. He must be weaned from his mother and develop a relationship with a woman his own age that is similar in certain respects to the one he has enjoyed with his mother. He must also develop the ability to cope effectively, on the instrumental level, with his nonfamilial surroundings. An abiding identification with father is very useful in this regard. Inevitably some discontinuity must occur for both boys and girls in the transition from childhood to parenthood (Benedict, 1938), but a frequent dilemma for males results from the fact that they tend to be overly dependent upon their mothers and only weakly identified with their fathers.

Daniel Brown (1957b) has suggested several reasons why the boy may fail to make a transitional identification with his father after the period of maternal dependency and before the time to leave home. Fathers who are significantly less effective in the instrumental sphere than their wives, or who are excessively harsh or indifferent, make the son's task particularly difficult. Extreme paternal severity, especially within the context of American "democratic" values, breeds volatile reactions and invites resentment; weakness and indifference, on the other hand, turn father into a nonentity. Father's prolonged absence from home also reduces his impact, and therefore the clarity of masculine patterns, unless there are fairly strong male substitutes for father with whom the boy can identify. In the general case, of course, boys have more opportunity to observe the feminine behavior of mother and other women, at home and school, than the masculine behavior of father and the world of men. In a sense, modern fathers are challenged to simply make an impression on their sons—without being tyrannous or playing the fool.

Although not always recognized as such, the push toward manhood is also a push away from home; we expect our children to be "emancipated," especially our sons. Girls are allowed—even expected—to be more dependent than boys, and any given level of dependency for the boy is likely to be a greater problem for him than a similar amount for the girl; the instrumental orientation calls for the ability to leave home, whereas expressiveness makes no such demand. Thus, the boy in particular must not overidentify with his parents. Boys do not ordinarily find it as difficult as girls to leave home, however, nor do they have as much trouble breaking with their fathers as girls have in working out a mutually satisfying separation from their mothers. This is true at least in part because male relationships, shaped by the instrumental standard, are generally easier to break, and the father-son relationship encompasses the push pattern; it is built around an assumption of discontinuity.

Father and the Drive to Excel

Father, of course, is not the only pushy parent. Mother exerts pressure on her children too, and in some ways her efforts may be more forceful and effective than dad's. She might be the key to upward striving on the part of most children, although current evidence on this point is by no means conclusive.

There is abundant testimony that the successful student usually has a strong self-image, the product of being accepted as a worthwhile person in the course of a series of experiences with success (Cervantes, 1965). High achievers also have the intellectual alertness, vocabulary, and reading ability that extensive interaction with sympathetic parents can supply. David McClelland (1961) contends that uncommon achievement in later life is characteristically promoted by parental pressure for accomplishment in the early years combined with a consistent pattern of parental rewards for each realization of success. The effectiveness of such pressures is enhanced by a high ratio of successes to failures on the part of the child and by a healthy identification with parents, especially mother.

If mother motivates academic striving, it could be simply because she spends more time with the children, although perhaps she also personifies the maximal combination of pressures and rewards, especially in relations with her daughter. Mothers seem to be more effective when they put pressure on their daughters to do well in intellectual pursuits than when they push their sons (Kagan and Freeman, 1963). Charles Werts (1966) found that the "father-model effect" is not generally applicable to girls, who base their career choices on a rather distinctive set of female values. When the mother stresses independence rather than conformity, her impact is greatest for her daughter; when the father stresses independence, the impact is most striking for his son (Norman, 1966).

But it is possible, as Urie Bronfenbrenner (1961b) has suggested, that pressures upon both sons and daughters for achievement are increasingly imposed by mothers, occasioned by a shift in the locus of family power from husbands to wives. Often mothers are now even more involved than fathers in their sons' occupational plans. Lee Burchinal (1960b) found that mothers are more active than fathers in urging both sons and daughters to further their formal education beyond high school, although their inducements are meaningful primarily at the lower levels of the middle class and in the working classes, where going to college is not taken for granted.

In the past, when fathers were more domineering in the home, they were presumed to have a crucial role to play in determining the life goals of their sons, yet the traditional father-dominated family, as found today in most underdeveloped nations, seems especially ill-designed to foster achievement drives in boys. The Brazilian father, for example, tends to stifle his son's efforts to be self-reliant and autonomous. The child learns that only revolt or submission is possible, and submissive, ingratiating obedience is the typical reaction (Rosen, 1962). Reinforcing this pattern, the Brazilian mother is usually deferential toward her husband, but dominating and excessively protective in relationships with her children. Thus, self-reliance is not encouraged by either parent. For boys in particular, paternal domination and maternal overprotection have decidedly enervating effects (Rosen and D'Andrade, 1959).

Moreover, in the Brazilian father-centered home the ambitious son is often perceived as a threat to his father, who reacts to his son's competitive behavior as if it were an expression of aggressiveness. Since aggression against the father is perhaps the most heinous sin in the Brazilian family, children often learn to avoid any appearance of assertiveness in relations with parents or elders.

A few studies specifically suggest that a strong mother-weak father combination is conducive to upward mobility and ambitiousness in the offspring (Bendix and Lipset, 1959). Fred Strodtbeck (1958) has shown, at least for his sample of Jewish and Italian boys, that sons in families in which the father is ascendant tend to have low aspiration drives by contrast with those in mother-dominated families. The less mother and son are subordinated to the father, the greater the disposition of both to believe that the world can be rationally mastered and that the son should risk separation from his family in order to find personal fulfillment. Moreover, warm but strong and assertive mothers, who are greatly concerned with their sons' performance, contribute to a high need for achievement; dominating fathers are less likely to instill strong impulses to accomplishment, at least less likely to instill them in an effective way. The mother often transmits even more of her individual features of aggressive behavior to her children (especially to her daughters) than father does (Hess and Handel, 1956). Little research has yet been done on the social-psychological conditions in the life of the highly motivated, but inept, individual.

It would appear that fathers, especially in the working classes, are frequently more interested in athletic than intellectual success for their sons, whereas mothers stress the importance of academic performance with impressive single-mindedness. During adolescence, the son's youthful and vigorous physical faculties are clearly superior to his father's, just as teen-age girls are likely to be physically more attractive than their mothers. It is at this time that father can best appreciate his son's athletic prowess and renew the fun and excitement of his own adolescence. Unfortunately, witnessing the son's intellectual coming of age cannot provide similar opportunities for camaraderie between father and son (Berger, 1963). Intellectual maturation is a much more private matter and affords little opportunity for mutual rejoicing, nor does it lend itself to public events of a recreational nature, which accounts for the fact that adolescents who are popular heroes are more likely to be athletes than "brains" (Coleman, 1962).

Despite what has been said, there is an impressive array of evidence suggesting that a strong mother is not the decisive parent in inspiring upward mobility in children (Kahl, 1957; Bordua, 1960). Boys from mother-dominated families in one study were impulsive, unfriendly, and generally unsuccessful in their attempts to be influential (L. Hoffman, 1961). Glen Elder (1962a) found that American adolescents who described their mothers as dominant in family decision making tended to rate relatively low in terms of autonomy and academic motivation, and that boys from wife-dominated homes were at the very bottom level in achievement. A study conducted by Lois Gill and Bernard Spilka (1962) among Mexican-American youth suggests that where males are expected to be "strong" in relations with women, wife domination has negative effects on academic achievement, particularly for boys. In another study, both American and West German boys in extremely wife-dominated families were considered by both teachers and peers to be more selfish, incompetent, excitable, and dependent than boys from any other type of family (Devereux, Bronfenbrenner, and Suci, 1962). William Smelser (1963) concluded that downwardly mobile sons were more likely than others to feel that their mothers dominated the home, and high-school dropouts seem to come from homes in which the father is relatively uninfluential (Cervantes, 1965). Murray Straus (1962) found that the mother-dominant family was associated with tense sons who tended to reject their parents, although achievement potential for the sons was relatively high. Sons in father-dominant families, however, had equally high achievement levels, but lower levels of anxiety and parent rejection.

We have come to realize that a major task of the college student is to loosen excessively dependent ties to his parents, and both male and female students are more likely to be dependent upon mother than father. As noted earlier, father-son relations tend to promote instrumental discontinuity while both mother-son and mother-daughter relations lead to expressive stasis. Helping the child transfer from the stage of maternal management of his affairs to self-management becomes a critical role for father, a task that the weak father performs poorly. Charles Bowerman and Glen Elder (1964) suggest that academic motivation is strongest among boys who see their fathers as both head of the family and "democratic" in their relations with the children. The coupling of paternal strength and warmth seems to have the effect of inculcating in boys a flexible, pragmatic type of self-control.

The father's position as a motive force in his children's lives is undoubtedly contingent, however, upon his own status in the larger community (Werts, 1966). Joseph Kahl (1953), for example, contends that the attitudes of parents, particularly of fathers, constitute the chief influence differentiating intellectually capable lower-class boys who aspire to go to college from those who do not. The father who is disappointed with his own life accomplishment "teaches his son that the next step up calls for more education." By contrast, Kahl (1965) argues that upper-class fathers take their success for granted more often and can turn attention to "the higher things of life." They encourage achievement on the part of their sons simply by being what they are, or by having done what they have done. They can assume that their sons will have economic security and therefore advise them to learn to play the piano or enjoy tennis and not concentrate all their attention on preparation for a career. Obviously such men do not disapprove of economic success, but they do not have to think about it all the time. Men who have achieved less success—in a society that puts great emphasis on it—are inclined to keep pushing, both for themselves and their sons.

Kahl's approach acknowledges that the relative impact of mother and father may differ in the various social classes, although his specific conclusions run counter to the findings of other students. Kenneth Keniston (1965), for example, has written about highly intelligent Harvard undergraduates from well-to-do families who are thoroughly alienated and who reject almost all traditional values and commitments. Many of them, he claims, have a fondness for their grandfathers, but they usually prefer mother over father and feel that father has "sold out" for money and success. Sometimes the dynamic father may overwhelm his son, as dramatically portrayed in Saul Bellow's *Seize The Day,* although the "successful father-bewildered son" combination does not seem to be typical of either the upper or the upper middle classes in the United States.

Father's role in establishing the level of ambition in his children does differ markedly from one class to another, however —probably more than mother's role. Robert Ellis and W. Clayton Lane (1963) found father to be the main source of parental support for college attendance in the higher social strata. In the middle and upper classes both fathers and mothers seem to be relatively more important than teachers in encouraging children to strive for high levels of achievement (Gottlieb and Ramsey, 1964). Excellent students from the lower classes, on the other hand, especially girls, receive relatively more support from teachers, and low achievers in these strata get little support from either parents or teachers, certainly little from their fathers. College aspirants from the lower social strata, when compared with those from the same background who do not plan to go to college, are significantly less likely to regard a family member as an "adult ideal" (Douvan and Kaye, 1962).

But even if lower-class parents manage to stimulate high ambition in their children, they are usually in no position to give it effective direction. Youth in these circumstances must receive outside social support and guidance because parental motivation is not enough. They need concrete assistance. Identification with persons outside the family becomes an important source of practical information, not to mention hope. For this reason working-class students whose acquaintances plan to go to college are more likely to make such plans themselves, and an older sibling's college experience is much more influential than it would be for the middle-class child (Krauss, 1964).

In the lower classes the mother's education is often superior to that of the father. When this is the case, in any social class, the mother is overwhelmingly likely to be the primary influence upon the child's decision to continue in school (Ellis and

Lane, 1963). The lower-class father is poorly trained and has neither the social status nor the personal style to be of much help. Although Ralph Turner (1962) found that adolescents in families in which the mother's education exceeded that of the father had relatively high educational aspirations, the father under these circumstances is typically a liability, inhibiting the development of values that might encourage the child to seek a college education (Krauss, 1964).

The working-class mother whose occupational status is higher than her husband's is also likely to exert a strong influence on her children to move up in the world. She, more often than her husband, comes in contact with middle-class persons and has a better opportunity to acquire middle-class values. If her husband's status seems unlikely to improve, she may very well attempt to realize her own aspirations by encouraging her children to develop middle-class interests and objectives (Krauss, 1964). William Bennett and Noel Gist (1964) concluded that both Negro and white mothers in the lower classes are more important than fathers for the educational and occupational aspirations of their children. These mothers are simply more persistent.

The lower-class father often regards his children as "the old lady's" and may be only marginally involved in the most critical child-rearing decisions. His wife not only puts more pressure on the children to get ahead in the world than he does, she puts pressure on him too. He may be dissatisfied with his own attainments, but his discontent is often forced upon him by a wife who is willing, even eager, to remind him of his failures (Ellis and Lane, 1963). She is more likely to be disappointed with the family's lot in life than father, in a more sustained and bitter way, and her reaction to the family's status is most often the catalyst for a change if one is to be made. Apparently lower-class men can accommodate to low social status easier if they are not married; in this stratum marriage rates are in fact lower, and desertion rates are relatively higher.

The foregoing discussion raises a number of questions that cannot yet be answered satisfactorily. The reciprocal nature of mother-father roles is so complex that current methods of investigation are inadequate to the task of disentangling them completely, and perhaps only slight shades of difference in research orientations, or subtle differences in the wording of questions, are sufficient to make one or the other parent seem a bit more important for the urge to excel. Although the evidence clearly eliminates father dominance as a major source of academic effort, especially in the lower classes, mother dominance at that level is not necessarily a handicap. The mother seems to be particularly important in this milieu, but less for the son than for the daughter. The father becomes relatively more important as the social ladder is ascended, but his impact in the upper classes is still undetermined. Certainly the recent search for the sources of achievement motivation—in the family, school, peer group, and community—has not yet resulted in a definitive explanation. Although the relevant evidence has not yet been presented, on one point the record does seem clear: the most generally effective family structure for promoting high aspiration levels is now one in which there is continual, unabated cooperation between father and mother.

In his study of second-generation Italian and Jewish boys in the Boston area, Fred Strodtbeck (1958) found that those who experienced democratic relations with their parents and also reported a condition of equality between the parents were most likely to value independence and achievement. Urie Bronfenbrenner (1961a) found that boys who received neither sufficient discipline nor sufficient love in the home were least likely to receive high ratings on leadership and responsibility in school. Since our prevailing theory holds that fathers stress discipline and mothers stress love, Bronfenbrenner's data suggest the importance of a complementary parental pattern. The assessment of the relative importance of parents as individuals may be beside the point, although Bronfenbrenner himself suggests that paternal behavior related to "leadership" qualities is more variable than mothering, and hence fathers may account for more of the variation among children in this area than do mothers.

Glen Elder (1962a) found that the equalitarian husband-wife structure was associated more consistently with a desire to achieve among adolescents than either the mother-dominant or the father-dominant pattern was. Both extremes had negative effects on the development of ambition and achievement skills. Studying samples from the United States, Great Britain, West Germany, Italy, and Mexico, Elder (1965) found that the likelihood of reaching secondary school was uniformly low among persons who had authoritarian parents, regardless of the pattern of parental decision making. High educational attainment was most prevalent among persons who reported democratic relations with their parents and equalitarian relations between mother and father. Moreover, Elder found that democratic family relations become more important with the emergence of better educational opportunities, whereby an improved school system promotes democratic family relations, and the latter in turn are conducive to higher levels of aspiration in children. This pattern was found in all of the nations studied by Elder, but he added the point that the educational system itself is more important for educational attainment in a population than family structure. The equalitarian family complex can be of help, but only if the community has an adequate school system in which the child can gain a foothold.

It is quite possible of course that the aspirations of children differ qualitatively as well as quantitatively, depending upon the nature of the mother-father relationship. For example, Donald McKinley's (1964) data suggest that sons in families in which the father is the chief source of authority tend to enter technological and scientific occupations, while sons in families in which parents have equal authority more often enter cultural, artistic, and entertainment fields. In families in which the mother is the source of authority, sons are prone to enter occupations in which organizational ability is important. But again there is evidence which, while not contradictory, changes the perspective rather sharply. Robert Rapoport and Edward Laumann (unpublished paper cited in Rapoport and Rapoport, 1965) suggest that the scientific orientation is most likely to be promoted by joint conjugal decision making; science is nonauthoritarian and universalistic in its outlook, they claim—a world view that is facilitated by mother-father cooperation. Nevertheless, one cannot help but think that the values parents express with regard to different fields of interest are at least as important in this regard as the conjugal power pattern per se.

Feminine Restraint

Although there is much to suggest that boys need to be pushed more than girls in the sex-typing process, good sense cautions against exaggeration on this point. If the boy has a problem in switching from the strong mother identification of his early years to an appropriately independent masculine style, the girl's problem is to resist the urge to abandon her restricted and culturally subordinate feminine status in favor of the masculine idiom (Lynn, 1964). The boy needs to be pushed into manliness; efforts are made to confine the girl to the feminine fold and to pull her back into it whenever she strays. The girl's problem is restraint; the boy's problem is drive. The modern girl's dilemma certainly seems to be as great as the boy's and one calling for just as much personal and social energy to produce an effective adult.

At least for the moment the assumption is made that adaptation to prevailing differences between men and women is necessary and worthwhile. To the extent that many modern girls straddle the fence, attempting to have some of the opportunities once reserved for men as well as some of the privileges once reserved for women, their problems of sexualization are probably even greater than those of boys. There is no question but that the few women who try to compete with men, no favors asked, have assumed an extraordinarily hazardous course of action.

Paul Mussen and Eldred Rutherford (1963) argue that boys can acquire masculine behavior and interests more easily than girls can assimilate femininity, partly because the cues for appropriate masculine behavior are more distinct, easier to discriminate, and hence easier to learn. This seems to be true primarily in the sense that it is easier for boys to know how far *not* to go into the female domain. Girls are less sure of how far they can safely proceed in activities regarded as masculine.

Certainly the processes of sexualization are different for the two sexes, and females complain the most—one consequence, perhaps, of their expressive style. Their major problem stems from the ambiguity and arbitrariness of the female role, plus its inferior status. Girls are limited to female expressiveness just as boys are goaded into masculine instrumentality. But there are also certain mannerisms, enthusiasms, and inhibitions that must be acquired by the girl if she wishes to meet the conventional social requirements for femininity. These traits are not acquired automatically; they must be encouraged, even exalted.

Betty Friedan (1963) argues that since the 1940s, the ideal nurtured by American women and their mentors has shifted from the achievement of independence, the fulfillment of careers, and the development of special capacities to an emphasis on feminism itself, on a "feminine mystique." (Their mentors, incidentally, are not only mothers and fathers, but hucksters and corporate interests.) The highest value and only true commitment for women if guided by this mystique is the realization of their own femininity, which is accomplished primarily in the kitchen and the nursery according to Friedan. In an earlier period a collective effort was made by women to escape their ancient role, but now, at the very threshold of a new life, they strive for a singularly female fulfillment more than ever before. Femininity, Friedan contends, is nourished as an end in itself, and its attainment has been raised to a lofty goal. But there is a strong negative valence to this endeavor, since the woman who would be thoroughly female is asked to affirm her femininity by avoiding "unfeminine ways," however attractive they might seem in this day and age. This requires an effort on her part and vigilance by those who would restrain her.

As we have already noted, for some time the girl has been expected to maximize her feminine image in order to enhance her man-getting powers. She must shift from her childhood attachment to father to a more mature expressive relationship with an appropriate adult male. Boys must leave mother, of course, but they are not prodded in courtship in any way comparable to the pressure put upon girls. Although our traditions give men the initiative in seeking dates, it is for this very reason that the female must make herself as attractive as possible. This requires application, and the girl is reminded of the effort she must make by her mother, advertisers, other girls, and song lyrics: to the girl, the whole universe seems to be shouting this indisputable message. Father joins in, but he is usually less active, more subtle, than mother.

Meanwhile, the girl is also called upon to control herself with regard to sex. She must learn to limit her sexual appetite and yet be sexually attractive. She must present herself to males as desirable and approachable, but not as an easy mark. Again, this is not simply a passive stance the girl must take, but an appropriate sex style to be nursed, worked at, and mastered. The boy can be sexually predatory; sex management for the girl involves a more delicate combination of flirtation, release, inhibition, and sensitivity to the changing state of the pair relationship. Father may be helpful as a source of security in this process, but mother is the girl's principal parental confidant. In fact, the girl may learn more that can be useful in this regard from interaction with a slightly older brother than from relations with her father (Kanin, 1957).

Father may have a role to play—perhaps an important one—in developing his daughter's attractiveness to boys, but he is of no help in preparing the girl to get along with women as well as men. Overestimation of the expressiveness of women, especially among men who write on the subject, is probably due in part to the fact that in the presence of men women exaggerate their expressive qualities (Kenkel, 1961). Even among strangers women tend to reveal less of their practical resourcefulness and greater emotionality than men (Leik, 1963). But when women are with other women they assume a more complex, perhaps more natural, style.

For that matter, men may display their most ingratiating congeniality in the presence of women, but the male mode is probably more uniform from one situation to the next than the female mode because men can impress both men and women with their instrumentalism. It does not make much difference who men are with; they press for the masculine image. But women are not likely to enhance the impression they make upon men by calling attention to their more businesslike capabilities. With one another, women may indeed strive for greater instrumentalism as a means of self-protection. Just how their expertise for this all-female milieu is developed we don't know, but father doesn't seem to have much to do with it, and he may not even know much about it—or care.

Parochialism in the Sexualization Process

Assuming that "universalism" is more characteristic of males than females, as we suggested earlier, it follows that the sex training of men is a more worldly process than the sex training of women. The family plays a direct and forceful role in the sexualization process of girls, while the extrafamilial world is more important for boys; it is also generally more supportive of masculine styles (Bushong, 1938; Mussen and Rutherford, 1963). Both father and mother are relatively less significant for the boy's sex typing because the impact of the community outside the family looms so much larger for him. Thus, feminization is a highly parochial process, while masculinization is influenced by much broader and more diffusive pressures. And throughout their lives males can therefore be enlisted in the pursuit of social causes and abstract principles, unrelated to narrow family concerns, which are virtually incomprehensible to most women.

One index of female provincialism is the fact that the mental health of girls seems to be more related to the quality of affection between girls and their parents than is that of boys (Nye, 1957b). Family disorganization has long been considered a more likely cause of emotional disturbance and role confusion among girls than boys (Caldwell, 1930; Weeks, 1940). Girls are expected to perform more household chores than boys, partly because such routine tasks are considered woman's work, but also because it is assumed that boys will be engaged in external affairs, such as sports, which cut into the hours that could otherwise be spent at home.

Not all of the evidence, however, leads to the same conclusion. E. E. LeMasters (1957) found that boys suffer more severe damage than girls when their parents' marriage fails and is not terminated by divorce. John Ball (1962) found that boys from broken homes showed even greater neurotic (especially depressive) tendencies than girls.

Nevertheless, if other things are equal the daughter is probably a more discriminating student than her brother of their parents' life together and a more sensitive reflector of family anguish. If the boy reacts in a volatile way to family disorder, it is likely that he has failed to adapt to the male peer culture and the aloofness to family matters that it engenders. In fact, his awkwardness among other boys may itself be a result of disabling family relations (L. Hoffman, 1961). The girl's reaction to family stress is less likely to be influenced by her relations with other girls, but, when it is, the process appears to work in the opposite direction; the girl who is strongly integrated as a member of a female group is likely to be all the more concerned about any signs of trouble in her parents' marriage. The main reason, of course, is that girls frequently talk to one another about family affairs, while boys concern themselves with other things. Hence a tentative hypothesis can be proposed: Family tranquility is the basis for an effective cosmopolitanism among boys, giving them a sense of security from which to embark upon their exploration of the nonfamily world; among girls, on the other hand, family tranquility promotes a parochialism centered in the female peer group and familism itself.

Indeed, girls are more like their mothers than boys are like their fathers, and the sex identification of boys as compared with girls seems to be less closely related to the sex typing of either parent (Angrilli, 1960; Gray and Klaus, 1956; Gray, 1959). Robert Hess and Gerald Handel (1956) found that girls resemble their mothers in aggressive characteristics much more than any other adult, male or female, but no comparable pattern exists among boys. In full support, David Lynn (1962) suggests that men identify with a cultural stereotype of the masculine role, but women tend to identify with their own mothers, who serve as very specific models.

All these findings are consistent with the hypothesis that the family is more important for the girl's sexualization than for the boy's. The immediacy of the mother's role in the home is readily grasped by the daughter, but the son finds difficulty in identifying with his father. The father is often away from home, and the boy is cut off from his father's occupational role. Girls, molded in a more parochial way, are more similar to their household model. Boys are allowed to be different, or are at least subject to a greater variety of models, and hence there is a greater chance for them to escape the local mold. In fact, boys learn appropriate sex behavior by sheer trial and error to a greater extent than do girls.

This hypothesis, of course, does not imply that boys are grossly unlike their fathers. Hess and Handel (1956) found father and son to be quite similar, as a rule, if for no other reason than that they both reflect male patterns of aggression. Susan Gray (1959) found that in her sample of college students both males and females were more often like the parent of the same sex than the other parent. In fact, the behavior of boys fulfills the boys' image of what their fathers want them to be more frequently, it would seem, than the behavior of girls can match the girls' image of what their mothers prefer (Fauls and Smith, 1956). But this is quite consistent with the more cosmopolitan masculine pattern. The father can actively encourage and appreciate a son who grows up to be quite different from himself; the mother typically prefers a daughter who is more confined and inhibited than many contemporary daughters wish to be, especially those in their late teens.

Father, Son, and the Peer Group

Although parents usually exercise extensive controls over their teen-age offspring, the discipline exerted by the adolescent's age mates typically applies even more forcefully to the immediate concerns of the teen-ager's life (Slocum, 1963). James Coleman (1962) contends that the youth culture, operating primarily through the medium of the peer group, is often more powerful than parents are, although the methods Coleman used to reach this conclusion have been seriously challenged (Berger, 1963). Adolescents certainly seem to become highly dependent on the peer group when they leave the preadolescent stage of life, and they remain so until they reach the late teen years. Talcott Parsons (1963) has argued that the prominence of the youth culture, by contrast with its place in other societies, is one of the hallmarks of the American social system; its power and saliency are of much less significance in most European societies.

But David Epperson (1964) reports that teen-agers in the

United States are not any less anxious to receive parental approval than younger children. A comparison of the impact of peer groups in different cultures must in fact be considered problematic at the present time. The real test of any generation comes, of course, after it has been submitted to the trials of responsibility; its adolescence is of little historical significance. And when responsibility is taken, the parental code, not the teen-ager code, is inevitably invoked. David Riesman (1964) notes that adolescents may go through a stage of other-direction and identity-diffusion in what seems like overdependence upon peers, but that when they reach adulthood they are released from many of the peer-group dictates, and values reflecting parental influences reappear. Perhaps this is a reactivation of what Nicholas Babchuk and Alan Bates (1963) call the "suspended primary group." Identification between parents and children is a primary relationship, even after years of separation, as Charles Horton Cooley (1902) noted long ago in his discussion of the subjective character of primary groups. The vitality of the parent-child bond is only submerged temporarily, or camouflaged, during adolescence.

Nevertheless, during this stage the peer group does become extremely important to young people, and the relative influence of their parents is characteristically reduced. Teen-agers want parental approval, but they sense a need for colleague approval as never before. In a sense, modern youth socializes itself during adolescence, as Friedrich Tenbruck (1962) has argued. For the boy in particular the influence of the "outside world" is channeled very extensively through the male peer group, which, by comparison with the female group, acts quite independently of family controls. Even in groups of their own choosing, girls are relatively easily managed by mothers, although there is no question but that peer-group values have an impressive effect on both sexes, sometimes overriding parental expectations (Carlson, 1963).

Close friends of their own age, for example, seem to be more important in determining whether boys will want to continue their education than the peers of their sisters are; girls are influenced to a greater extent by parents (McDill and Coleman, 1963), although the parental influence continues to have a stronger overall influence than the peer group even for boys (Simpson, 1962). Peers are certainly more crucial for the sexualization of the boy than for his sister, and it is very possible that father himself is less important in the determination of his son's masculinity than the peer group is. Evidence clearly indicates that boys learn more about sex from the gang than from father, and less from father than either boys or girls learn from mother (Ramsey, 1953). It is not that the peer group is inherently a more powerful socializer, but that father is frequently absent at the critical moment when guidance is needed. The boy picks up bits and pieces of information and misinformation about sex, often within a context of swaggering male superiority, from age mates whose sources of information are often unreliable (Hartley, 1959).

The more global reach of the male world has the effect of overwhelming and thereby lessening father's influence on his son. Father's role as a masculine model, for example, is tempered by the peer group. Father and the male gang work rather independently of one another upon the boy and often at cross-purposes; mother and the girl's age mates work hand in hand. As a result, the impact of the male group may not reinforce the style and general direction of father's influence.

In fact, when boys are little, male groups are influenced more by mother than father. The mother's advantage is again her constant presence; even working mothers probably have more frequent contact than fathers with their young sons' play groups. Mothers—almost always those who are not employed—are used as den leaders for cub scouts; when boys graduate into scouting men are used more prominently in positions of leadership, but mother often remains the parent who is close at hand when the work for the merit badge is being done. As male peer groups are progressively emancipated from maternal control, they usually provide for their own management, and the role of father is notable principally for its insignificance.

Nevertheless, the father may be of considerable importance for his son's acceptance within the peer group because the father, as the object of his son's identification, promotes a patterning of masculine habits that can foster, or undermine, the boy's standing with other boys. Indeed, the primary advantage of adequate sex socialization for young boys is peer adjustment. Susan Gray (1957) found that boys who rated high in acceptance by their peers showed a high degree of appropriately sex-typed behavior. It has often been assumed that peer adjustment is associated with strong sex identification (Lynn and Sawrey, 1959), and the latter, as we have seen, is a function of identification with father. Donald Payne and Paul Mussen (1956) found that boys who were strongly identified with their fathers were more calm and friendly in interpersonal relations than boys who were less thoroughly identified. F. N. Cox (1962) has also provided support for the hypothesis that a positive attitude toward the parent of the same sex is an important condition for the establishment of competent and warm relationships with peers. Lois Hoffman (1961) found that, for boys, warm companionship with the father is clearly related to peer-group adjustment. Positive affection for and interaction with the mother does not have the same effect, although it may contribute to the boy's fondness for other children and to being liked by them in return. A positive relationship with the father is not only conducive to these qualities but to self-confidence, assertiveness, and proficiency in the peer group.

The quality of the daughter's relationship with her father, on the other hand, is not very helpful in predicting her social adjustment, nor is the girl's relationship with her mother an important clue. M. M. Helper (1955) found that boys who model themselves after father in a rather conspicuous way are likely to register a high level of social acceptance and adjustment in high school, but the same does not apply to girls who are very much like their mothers. Susan Gray (1959) made a similar discovery. Boys, she found, who think they are like their fathers rather than their mothers are regarded more favorably by their peers, while girls who see themselves as being like their mothers are, if anything, regarded less favorably. What is important for girls is an affectionate relationship with mother, in which they can feel free and spontaneous in her presence, not an imitative relationship. (This, incidentally, is not inconsistent with the observation made earlier that girls tend to be more like their mothers than boys are like their fathers. Boys, in fact, are given greater freedom by their fathers to be different from themselves than mothers extend to daughters, mainly because fathers are busy with other things.)

Roger Burton (1961) suggests that joining a gang in America is similar to the initiation tests of manhood in some other societies. Little boys are forced into close contact with women and compelled to obey and learn from them. They are protected, bossed, and even excelled in feats of strength by women. Exposed almost exclusively to the influence of mothers, female teachers, and sisters—the principal spokesmen for nice, respectable behavior—the growing boy tends to identify "goodness" with femininity (Hacker, 1957). Engaging in "bad" behavior acquires the function of denying the boy's femininity and therefore is an assertion of masculinity; such behavior is at least one motivational factor in juvenile delinquency (Cohen, 1955; Parsons, 1947).

If contemporary girls are unsuccessful in finding a sex identity, it is because they are ambivalent about the desirability of assuming a highly feminine pattern, not because of any inherent discontinuity in feminine training. To boys, on the other hand, getting rid of feminine ways is like a weeding-out process. Father can help the boy to become independent of mother, but father's larger task is to promote the boy's emancipation from women in general and from the characteristic feminine style of life, without loss of a fundamental respect for it. Father represents contact with reality and the facts of life in the nonfamily world, and the maintenance of close relations between father and son can help to keep the teen-age boy's "reality testing"—part of which is his search for the limits to what he can get away with—in check.

Nevertheless, the American boy often tries to prove his manhood through gang behavior, and as Frederick Thrasher (1927) suggested long ago, the less adequate the parental controls in the boy's life, the more likely he is to respond to the gang pattern. Satisfying or pleasant experiences within the family increase the intensity of its relationships, leading to a greater probability that the family's characteristic style will be adopted; acceptance of the family culture thus tends to promote greater selectivity in relations with peers, leading to a choice of friends who conform to the prevailing values of the family (Stanfield, 1966). In similar fashion, Glen Elder (1962b) suggests that teen-agers are more likely to emulate their parents and associate with other adolescents who are approved by their parents if the latter can keep lines of communication open and make their point of view clear.

There is good reason to believe that freeing the adolescent too early and too completely from emotional ties to his parents can be dangerous. Ivan Nye (1952), for example, is doubtful that adolescent groups by themselves can supply the necessary emotional security. They are too unstable, "brittle," and brief in duration. The boy who must rely on the peer group is particularly susceptible to any negative impact it may have. The available evidence does suggest that a severe break in father-son relationships is associated with a higher rate of delinquency, perhaps in part because the break itself reflects a failure to internalize parental values (Bandura and Walters, 1958), but also because it suggests both an instrumental and expressive failure on the part of father. Consistent discipline by the father within a context of generally satisfying family relations reduces the probablity of delinquency even if the boy is actively involved in a "gang" (Glueck and Glueck, 1950; Stanfield, 1966). James Bieri and Robin Lobeck (1959) found that among their sample of college undergraduates those who rated average or above in "authority acceptance" perceived themselves to be most like their fathers, while those who resisted authority considered themselves to be more like their mothers and to be relatively closer to their mothers.

If girls are more immune than boys to neighborhood delinquency patterns, as Erdman Palmore and Phillip Hammond (1964) indicate, once again it is probably because the home environment is so much more important in their lives. Harwin Voss (1966) found a somewhat similar pattern among boys and girls in Honolulu; boys, moving both physically and psychologically farther from home, are more susceptible to non-family pressures.

The family and peer group are in a sense competing with one another for the allegiance of boys in high-delinquency neighborhoods. In the case of girls, the competition is much less pronounced. Thus, an erratic or lax father is more detrimental in the lower classes because of the delinquent alternatives in the neighborhood (Stanfield, 1966), and, as we have noted earlier, this is precisely where the problem father is most likely to be found.

Lower-class boys are tutored by slightly older boys and are likely to model themselves after leaders within the local group. They tend to develop submissively dependent relationships with their contemporaries and psychological distance from their fathers (and from adults in general). Although they have greater physical and social freedom than middle-class boys, it is often accompanied by an intense fear of parents and feelings of rejection by them (Maas, 1951). If the lower-class boy can attend a predominantly middle-class school, he naturally has a better opportunity to identify with the middle-class peer culture (Wilson, 1959; Krauss, 1964). But delinquent repeaters in the lower classes are much more likely than nondelinquent boys to consider their families unattractive; middle-class repeaters report better parent-adolescent adjustment even when such variables as broken home, size of family, maternal employment, and rural-urban residence are held constant (Nye, 1951; Gold, 1963). Ralph Epstein (1963) observed that his middle-class subjects retained significantly more memories of their parents and relatively less of their teen-age peers than subjects from the lower classes did. He tentatively explained his discovery by the fact that middle-class parents supervise their children's activities more frequently and more carefully, but the data also indicate stronger relations with parents and comparatively weaker ones with peers. Obviously the lower-class father has limited economic and social resources, which reflect upon the attractiveness of his family and household life.

An advantage held by the middle-class father is the fact that he usually becomes a stronger masculine model for his son as the boy grows older because of the social value attached to his work. Blue-collar work is appealing to little boys in both the lower and middle classes, but it becomes less impressive as they mature. Little boys of all status levels enjoy watching carpenters, demolition crews, automobile mechanics, firemen, and so on, and they admire the things these men do. But the middle-class father's white-collar career, although not appreciated by small children, becomes increasingly meaningful to the growing middle-class boy. William Dyer (1958) found that attitudes of children toward their fathers' work are generally similar to the views held by their parents, and that children from white-collar families are more often pleased with their fathers' work even before they reach adolescence than those from blue-collar families. But the fact remains that it is easier to identify with the blue-collar father in childhood than in adolescence, especially when we recognize that it takes quite some time to learn the many subtle values in modern society that maintain the prestige of "low energy" types of work.

If the lower-class boy identifies too strongly with his father, especially in occupational and educational terms, his prospects for upward social mobility are thereby circumscribed. If, on the other hand, he is oriented toward mobility, he will probably develop a way of life that estranges him from his father. The distance between them is not necessarily a measure of hostility or antagonism, but of interest and sensitivity. Even if the father takes pride in the boy's progress, which is likely enough, the gap remains.

Expressiveness Between Father and Son

Although the instrumental nature of father's association with his son is typically the key to their relationship, an expressive affinity often characterizes their relations too. For all the pressure father exerts upon his son, as a rule he is closer to the boy than to his daughter; the girl is almost inevitably on more intimate terms with her mother because of their mutual feminine interests (Bowerman and Irish, 1962). As a model for male expressiveness, father serves as an example of how men handle friendships, how they make small talk, how they tell jokes, how they convert light conversations into more serious matters, how they display affection toward women, and so on. He helps his son convert expressiveness into the male mold after it has first been established in experiences with mother and the female idiom. Thus, the boy must be weaned away from mother in both instrumental and expressive spheres.

Glen Elder (1961) found that adolescent boys wanted to

spend time with and do things with their fathers much more than with mothers, and Ruth Tasch (1952) has noted that when boys reach the age of six there is a tendency for fathers to engage in more activities with their sons than with their daughters, a tendency that grows stronger over the years. Father is able to exchange certain kinds of confidences with his son simply because they are of the same sex (Babchuk and Bates, 1963); thus he plays the expressive role of confidant.

It should be added, however, that inhibitions in conversation between father and son are more prevalent and more impenetrable than are those between mother and daughter. In fact, girls seem to be less reserved with both parents than are boys. Paul Landis (1960) has noted, for example, that girls appear to be more open and candid in discussing their dates with parents than boys are; this fact reflects the greater underlying expressiveness of the female style, which we have stressed all along.

Perhaps the boy needs to be pushed toward an appropriate expressive style just as much as he is pushed toward instrumentalism, and more than most boys in fact are. We noted earlier that boys are prodded by general social pressures to think about their future occupational life rather than about any imminent family commitment, and that the expressive pattern that they develop in relationships with girls is often exploitatively oriented to "making out" in sex relations. The boy's instrumentalism, turned to career preparation, is in admirable harmony with community desires, at least in the middle classes, but the thrust of his expressive life tends to be directed toward objectives that are not approved. He cultivates a strong work affirmation, yet the emotional promise of family life is often left underdeveloped. If there is no comparable imbalance between expressiveness and instrumentalism among girls, it is probably because the two modes are rather automatically united for them, and both are given meaning by a conspicuous commitment to familism. When imbalance does occur among girls, it is likely that expressiveness is cultivated at the expense of the girls' career talents. Among boys the danger is that instrumentalism will be overemphasized, leaving their expressive lives underdeveloped in adulthood.

The observations of almost all students of the family indicate that males tend to have relationships with women similar to those experienced by their fathers. Eleanore Luckey (1960b) found that men who had satisfactory marriages were more likely to have identified strongly with their fathers than men whose marriages had deteriorated. Women who had favorable marriages, however, had not identified with their mothers more frequently than other women.

The boy *needs* to identify with father in order to achieve a workable masculinity in terms of both affection and practicality; the girl's identification with mother is not quite as necessary because of the lesser demands of femininity and also because of its more elementary expressive qualities. Thus, although girls are subject to more parochial training than boys, femininity itself is not as dependent upon mother-daughter identification as masculinity is upon father-son identification.

The pressure exerted upon boys starts at an early age, and father, because of his instrumental style, is the parent more inclined to prod. Although the need for the boy to become committed to an instrumental purpose in life has been stressed, the danger is that in the process his expressive life will become impoverished. Among girls the greater danger is that their expressive qualities will be developed in an instrumental vacuum —clearly a problem for many modern women. Perhaps the best thing the modern father can do is to avoid the temptation to exaggerate traditional female roles and values, especially during the adolescent years when girls are so prone to abandon the ambitions of their early girlhood.

A tentative hypothesis is proposed, the validity of which is supported by almost all available evidence: Family tranquility and paternal identification are the bases for an effective cosmopolitanism among boys, giving them a sense of security from which to embark on their exploration of the nonfamily world; among girls, however, family tranquility (somewhat independent of maternal identification) promotes parochialism centered in the female peer group and familism itself.

CHAPTER IX

Father-Child Conflict

Father has never been conspicuous for his willingness to indulge immaturity; mother is the patient parent. Tension between father and his children has many sources, but the most common sources stem from the failure or inability of children to live up to the stern father's expectations. Either he sets his standards too high or the children are slow for their age. Almost inevitably the father will find shortcomings in his children's behavior; unfortunately, they are imperfect disciplinary subjects, and so in turn they develop exasperating ways of coping with father. Thus, the father-child relationship becomes a very complex one early in the child's life.

The relationship is further complicated by mother's response, and by the fact that, independent of father's disciplinary efforts, he may not be able to live up to the expectations that his children set for him. He is the source of demands at first, but as the children grow older the demands they make upon him may become even more exacting than his own.

Almost all available evidence indicates that children have greater conflict with father than mother. They consistently perceive their mothers more favorably (Hawkes, 1957) and look upon father as the principal generator of fear (Becker and Krug, 1964). Arnold Rose (1959) found that college students, both male and female, had a greater willingness to express fondness for mothers than for fathers. Jerome Kagan (1956) found that children considered mothers to be friendlier, less punitive, less dominant, and less threatening than fathers. Both boys and girls in a study by Jerome Kagan, Barbara Hosken, and Sara Watson (1961) regarded fathers as stronger, larger, darker, and less nurturant. Adolescents in a study by Ivan Nye (1952) manifested higher levels of adjustment to their mothers than to their fathers. John Anderson (1946) found that girls criticize both parents more reliably and more frequently than boys, and mothers are criticized more often than fathers. But when frequency of contact between parent and child is constant, Anderson found, fathers were criticized three times more frequently than mothers.

All these studies lend support to the proposition that conflict with father usually damages his image more than conflict with mother can damage hers. Mother-child relations seem to run smoother. It is possible, however, that children look more favorably upon mother simply because she spends more time with them and satisfies their physical and emotional needs, not because of greater conflict with father. Father's image could be interpreted as that of an outsider rather than as a conflict maker. Many of the terms attributed to him in Kagan and Watson's study, for example, resemble those attributed to "foreigners" in cross-cultural attitude studies.

The important thing is that almost any unpleasant incident involving mother is soon followed by a resumption of cooperative interaction. Conflict with her occurs most often in connection with daily affairs involving a constant give-and-take and is easily absorbed by the more important fact that the child's daily needs are in fact being met. The pattern reflects a state of open rapport between mother and the children, as Patricia Maxwell, Ruth Connor, and James Walters (1961) indirectly suggested in their study. They found that mothers and adolescents perceive parental behavior quite similarly, whereas fathers do not. The children develop some insight into mother's problems through their daily exchanges with her, just as mother gains insight into the children's frustrations.

Conflict with father, on the other hand, is less routine, more disjunctive, and not as easily resolved. It often concerns unusual matters because father is drawn into the toughest situations, the ones mother has been unable to handle. Very few parents report that father alone takes responsibility for his children's discipline (Eron, Walder, *et al.*, 1963); usually both parents or the mother alone assume this burden. Since he has no backlog of experience in child-management problems, his very involvement is "symptomatic" of crisis. If he is called upon, the situation is imbued with a special atmosphere: his presence at this time is somewhat comparable to a doctor who is paying a sick call, although father's diagnosis is rarely the result of calm, professional reflection.

His reactions are characteristically intemperate because he is a poor judge of what can reasonably be expected of the child. Mother knows the difference between an extraordinary problem and a routine one, as father does not, and adjusts her reactions accordingly. This may help to explain why father seems to express greater anger toward the child—at least he appears to his children to be angry more often than mother, and he more often than she is disliked for his occasional outbursts of rage (Henry, 1963).

It is quite possible that the wrath displayed by father—when he simply puts his foot down, talks much louder than usual, and shows that he really means business—does settle matters for the time being, but unless he makes some effort to convey his love and respect at other times the child will tend to look upon him as an imperious figure to be obeyed when aroused, but otherwise an object of limited significance. Thus, Walter Emmerich (1959b) found that children in his study were more likely to attribute to their mothers behavior that Emmerich called "facilitative behavior," whereas fathers were more apt to be cited for "interfering behavior." Father is an occasional source of frustration and interference, indeed he is more notable in this role than in any other, but as such he tends to evoke obedience without respect, while mother inspires only routine forms of conflict within a larger framework of mutual affection.

Conflict with father follows a pattern that is difficult to arrest, often leading to a *vicious* rather than a *beneficent cycle* in parent-child relations (Hallowitz and Stulberg, 1959). In the former, behavior by the child is annoying or intolerable and the parental reaction leads to further noxious behavior by the child, the classic condition of self-extending conflict. In a beneficent cycle, the parental reaction to the child's nuisance behavior is by and large warm and accepting, or somehow appropriate, which leads to more acceptable behavior by the child.

We noted earlier that father tends to be more instrumental in his orientation to life than mother; he looks for signs of potential success in his children and shows less tolerance for attributes that might disqualify them for success outside the family. At the same time, he is usually anxious to get on with his own work, while mother is primarily interested in the household routines, of which maintaining peace with the children is a part. Father worries less about satisfying day-to-day relations and tends to judge his children by the "universal," unbending standards he meets away from home. For this reason mother often intercedes for him in behalf of family harmony. Her role as an intermediary between father and the children becomes greater as father loses his traditional claims to the role of "head of the household" and finds himself in the position of a rather arbitrary and weak authority. Mother's job is not so much to see that his demands are met as to devise ways of cooling tempers and avoiding prolonged tension.

Father as Disciplinarian

More than parents may realize, children consider both parents to be frustrators and intruders, and they talk more often about the disciplinary efforts of parents than about their kindness, sympathy, or affection (Anderson, 1946). Mothers are in fact more aggressive toward their children than the children are allowed to be in return, and children usually consider punishment inflicted by their mothers to be harsher than their mothers think it is (Morgan and Gaier, 1956). This pattern seems to be even more true in relations between father and children.

In some respects parents are like managers in organizations, who tend to be complacent insofar as their managerial effectiveness is concerned. Theodore Caplow (1964) argues that each level of management exaggerates its own success compared to lower levels in the same hierarchy. Officers overestimate their effectiveness when comparing themselves to enlisted men, teachers do the same thing when comparing themselves to students, and employers feel superior to their employees; each ranking group tends to be cut off from information that might challenge or undermine its self-esteem. Parents also overrate their competence, and for similar reasons; their children are not in a position to judge effectively or correct them. But parents are in a particularly shielded position because there is no superior over them to exercise a chastening influence. Father is the most isolated authority of all; he may supervise his wife in her role as mother, but she is less likely to reciprocate, partly because she is inhibited by patriarchal traditions and partly because the onus of parenthood is primarily on her.

But parents do have a much better perspective than their offspring on their relations with the children and on their effectiveness as parents as well. As Kingsley Davis (1940) noted, the relationship between parents and children is an *asymetrical* one. Parents were children once themselves, and they have usually given more than casual thought to the problems of both parents and children; children have no previous experience with parenthood and can have only a limited understanding of the problems parents face. In a sense, children may "study" their parents, but they do not study *parental roles,* and they do not appraise their parents in a very self-conscious way. The insight they occasionally show surprises us precisely because it is so unexpected.

Parents frustrate their children largely in the interests of the whole family; children frustrate parents because they are not yet socially mature and cannot think in terms of the whole family. Obviously parents must attempt to govern their children, and the children cannot be expected to understand why they are treated as they are. That is precisely what it will take time and discipline for them to learn. Hence some parent-child conflict is inevitable.

How great it will be depends in part on the type of discipline parents use. A helpful distinction in this regard can be made between *jural controls* and *moral controls*. Jural controls are used to enforce a set of rules; such controls make clear to the child that there are rules to be obeyed, whether he likes them or not. Moral controls refer to efforts, usually verbal, to get the child to adopt some set of values by which to govern himself, independent of external threats or regulations. Almost all parents use both strategies at one time or another, but fathers tend to favor jural controls whereas mothers find moral controls particularly attractive.

Clyde Nunn (1964), for example, found that fathers are more likely than mothers to form "coalitions with God" as a means of managing their children (jural control). They claim supernatural sanctions for their authority. Fathers also lean toward coercion and corporal punishment, while mothers more characteristically use reasoning and verbal methods (moral controls). Fathers think of child rearing primarily in disciplinary terms (Johannis, 1957b).

Cora Martin and Alexander Clark (1966) found that mothers were more likely than fathers to use sanctions that encourage the child to reflect on his own behavior (moral control). Mothers seem to view incidents in which their children have behaved improperly as learning situations, wherein the mother's responsibility is not just to control behavior but to "build character." Fathers on the other hand often try to overwhelm the child, perhaps because they have a better chance of succeeding. There is even a difference between father and mother in what they discipline for. Fathers stress conformity (jural control); they strive to have their children act like other children and are more alarmed if they are unusual in any way (Nunn, 1964; Tallman, 1965).

Since mother asks the child to be "good" rather than merely obedient, she suggests to the child that he must surely be "bad" if he has to be disciplined. Father says to the child, "You must not do this, it is against the rules." The child need not think there is anything wrong with himself since he has merely violated a rule that is external and perhaps arbitrary. Father also withholds privileges more often than mother, which makes the child mad at father, not at himself. The response of the child to mother's moralistic approach is likely to be, "What is wrong with me?" To father's jural approach it is, "What's wrong with the lousy rules?" To which father replies, "Rules are rules. Do as I say." Although father is the prime superego figure in our literary imagery, mother's control efforts may have an even greater effect because the child is more likely to direct his anger inward upon himself when mother is the chief disciplinarian.

If father plays this role, the child tends to channel his anger toward targets outside of himself; this is especially true of sons since daughters can more easily be beaten down by paternal authority (although those who cannot readily attract our attention). Wesley Becker and Ronald Krug (1964) found that girls with punitive, legalistic fathers tend to be withdrawn and distrustful, both in the presence of their parents and in the schoolroom, although this would seem to be true primarily when the mother sets a model of submissiveness.

Generally speaking, a parent who uses severe punishment to control the aggression of boys succeeds in curtailing it only when they are in his presence. When boys are punished severely, the *frustrating* effect of the punishment seems to overcome the *inhibiting* effect, and they become more aggressive than they would otherwise be (Eron, Walder, *et al.*, 1963). Temperate punishment, carefully tailored to the problem at hand, is much more effective in the long run.

But father in particular is prone to overthreaten, perhaps in part because of the prevailing masculine tendency to inhibit expressiveness and to deal harshly with transgressors, but also because he has less sensitivity to the degrees of threat required to accomplish his purpose. Mother is closer to the children and is more likely to adjust her threats to the requirements of each situation.

Her very style in this regard tends to serve as a moral control. Elliot Aronson (1966) has demonstrated that when a child is severely threatened he is likely to comply with the threatener's wishes because of the latter's superior power; the child can easily rationalize his own submissiveness since he has simply succumbed to an irresistible force. If the threat is only mild, however, the child has a greater need to account for his compliance by convincing himself that he is doing the right thing, and he therefore internalizes moral values that can justify his behavior. As a consequence he is likely to abide by these values in the future, even in the absence of external threats. Thus, the dilemma, or "cognitive dissonance," induced by a mild threat leads to the development of inner controls even more effectively than severe threats do precisely because the latter create no moral dilemma. Aronson implies that although coercive controls are useful in establishing self-control, they must not be so great that they "blot out" any sense of moral conflict for the child. But that is the kind of coercion father tends to use.

Both jural and moral controls have been overemphasized in the preceding discussion. In reality, it would appear that the child develops appropriate *self* controls more through identification with his parents than in response to the disciplinary tactics they happen to use. Thus, a third source of child management, operating independently of jural and moral discipline, consists of *identification controls.* For the most part these do not operate at the conscious level and hence do not involve deliberate discipline. The child imitates his parents to some extent because he identifies with them and tries to please them for the same reason. The child who, through identification, internalizes the expectations of his parents at an early age requires very little external discipline; he controls himself.

As we noted in Chapter VII, the most effective paternal identification is suffused with expressive warmth between father and child. The qualities of "love and affection" are now encouraged at least in part because they are believed to foster a willingness to cooperate in children; they are not advocated for sentimental reasons alone (M. Hoffman, 1963a). But fathers seeking close relationships with their children mix affection with any number of other qualities. The combination arrived at may or may not be conducive to the kind of identification that leads to self-control on the part of the child. Since the size of the family has been reduced and the love theme is given ever stronger endorsement, parents themselves may develop an inordinate need for affection from their children and have been known to compete for the love of the child. The notion that there should be a warm, loving relationship between parents and children emerged historically as a corollary of the emphasis on love between man and woman as the basis for marriage. Love became "good" for children, but also an exciting emotional gratification for both parents and children; it has a life of its own independent of any theory of child rearing. As is always true of sacred qualities, it is both a means to an end and an end in itself.

Today children obviously have greater leverage in domestic power struggles and may sometimes control their parents as much as they themselves are controlled. Parents who repeatedly resort to coercive methods to manage their children reveal their own expressive failure, while the challenge to be successful in an expressive way turns out to be a particularly disturbing blow to the father's traditional strategy of jural control.

The Arbitrary Old Man

Occasionally even now a father may successfully play the role of patriarch in the classical sense of the term, but more often his attempt to be a strong authority figure leads to failure and frustration. The chances for success are not good because paternal authority, exercised in the spirit of patriarchy, tends to be transparently arbitrary in the contemporary setting. Perhaps it has always been essentially dogmatic, but not capricious; in the past father's authority was usually reinforced by a network of community supports. His demands thus seemed to be based upon the wisdom of the ages, and that is precisely what is now lacking.

The authority of father is most effective when he operates within a set of guidelines that both he and his wife follow. If other adults—teachers, parents in the neighborhood, respected guests—subscribe to similar guidelines, the parents' control is further strengthened. Paternal authority then has a resonance that arbitrary or idiosyncratic control can never achieve, and children will almost invariably recognize and respond to it. To children it will seem that there is some higher necessity to the father's decisions; each decision has the overwhelming impact of inevitability.

Parental rules that reflect community standards are also more likely to be followed and seem to enhance the effectiveness of parents. Walter Slocum (1963) contends that families that emphasize social participation and conformity with prevailing social standards have a broader influence over their offspring than those who convey the impression of indifference toward these social values. This has been most convincingly shown with regard to educational attainment. When the family is indifferent or antagonistic toward the local educational system, there is little or no incentive for children to do well or even to continue in school (Bertrand, 1962). And under these circumstances paternal authority is weak and ineffective.

Our contemporary problem arises because many of the activities of youth—dating and dancing patterns, for example—are no longer subject to community norms with which the father is fully familiar. In the modern, mobile family, father does not represent a known community of adults (Slater, 1961). Fewer traditional problems occur to which he can give an authoritative solution, and many situations arise that are as new to him as to his children. Father himself is often looking for some higher source of wisdom to guide him through the endless choices he has to make. In fact, children tend to expect more wisdom of father than he can even pretend to have, although adolescence is usually reached before they realize the full extent of their disillusionment.

The modern father is a miracle worker only to little children. A painless transition from the miracle worker (mythical) stage of fatherhood to the "ordinary-man" stage appears increasingly more difficult to make, although it has never been easy, and in some cultures even unnecessary. Perhaps ideally, family members retain some of the trappings of the illusion even though all concerned know better. Thus one of the "little myths" of everyday family life can persist, providing a measure of satisfaction for all.

But in a society in which great changes take place during the life cycle of the individual, the father inevitably becomes old-fashioned in the eyes of his children (Davis, 1940). There is nothing absolutely new about this of course; parents have always been considered old-fashioned by their children, and they in turn have felt that the younger generation was abandoning everything worthwhile—but this tendency has been aggravated. References to father as "the old man" become particularly poignant as a result. The term connotes both derision and endearment, and it captures our ambivalence about the arbitrary father.

In adolescence young people begin to spot the inconsistencies and absurdities that are inevitable in any society, but that are perhaps worse and surely more visible in a nation whose youth are encouraged to be critical and to think objectively. Whereas parents are given greater autonomy than adolescents, the parents are not particularly exploratory. They have made their peace with the toughest social problems and are no longer as eager for reform as they may once have been. The youthful idealism they once had was molded in a different social context by events unfamiliar to their children—in a different "political generation," to use Harold Lasswell's phrase. Their idealism has long since been diluted by an accommodation to slight or imagined corrections of the abuses they once challenged. Under these circumstances parents may not only seem to be out of date to their children, but fraudulent as well.

As noted earlier, one of the chief reasons for the rise of permissiveness has been the breakdown of the feeling that we know just what to encourage and what to discourage in our children's behavior. Strong positions in the present setting seem dogmatic and arbitrary because they can be challenged. Father makes pronouncements he cannot justify according to any set of rules or recognized body of principles. "No, you can't wear lipstick." "Yes, you can go to the show." "No, you can't have a new basketball." Father desperately needs a wife who will support his pronouncements, but this very fact reveals his dilemma. His edicts receive little corroboration except from his wife, and her ability to undermine his authority is often greater than the father's corollary potential; he needs her more than she needs him.

The tendency toward arbitrariness is of course characteristic of both paternal and maternal authority, and it helps to explain why parents complain so much about difficulties in disciplining their children (Isambert, 1961). But the perseverance of the notion that father should be forceful can lead him to revel in arbitrariness in a manner that mother is likely to avoid. She is too intimately involved in daily routines and has too much to lose. The idea that he should exercise his will autonomously, demanding members of his family to adapt to his wishes, however peremptory, is a persistent part of the syndrome of male assertiveness.

Father at least occasionally feels that he should be a respected, perhaps revered, authority in his own household, a man of substance and strength in the still viable conception of a powerful father. Hence he may submit to the temptation to make decisions affecting others in his family in the most controversial areas. As we have seen, his wife may invite him to participate in only the most difficult situations. This provides the man with a means of acting out his image of himself, but judgments made in an ad hoc way, in complicated situations, and in a rapidly changing society, simply invite evasion and, ultimately, mockery. To his bewildered and inconvenienced offspring the willful father seems like an intruder from some foreign land.

Father-Son Conflict

Almost all available evidence points to the fact that fathers encounter more sustained and intense friction with their sons than with their daughters. Both parents have greater problems with boys than girls, but mother has *relatively* greater trouble with her daughter, and thus the difference in the degree of conflict with girls as against boys in her case is not so great. Boys in one study reported significantly more aggressive and hostile behavior toward their fathers than girls did, although the researchers pointed out that boys are allowed to be more aggressive than girls before steps are taken to stifle their contentiousness (Lansky, Crandall, *et al.*, 1961). Arnold Rose

(1951) found that college males were somewhat more willing to express dislike for both parents than coeds were.

On the other hand, Yi-Chuang Lu (1952) could find no significant differences between male and female conflicts with their parents. Thus, continuing belief in the proposition that father has more conflict with son than daughter is based less on empirical consensus than on prevailing theories about differences in father-son and father-daughter relationships.

Because father is more demanding in relations with his son, and more aggressive toward him, he generates more aggression toward himself from the boy. It has been monotonously reported that the more children are punished for aggression by their parents, the more aggressive they tend to become. Boys are in general more aggressive than girls, and once their aggressiveness passes the level of tolerance they are punished more severely than girls, especially by their fathers (Eron, Walder, *et al.*, 1963).

Father's behavior also leads to more diverse and unpredictable responses on the part of sons than daughters (Becker and Krug, 1964), partly because the combative and aggressive behavior so prevalent among boys is characteristically volatile, but also because boys are usually allowed to express themselves in a wider range of activities. Mother makes no greater demands on son than daughter, if as many, and she is less likely to provoke unequal levels of aggression in her children. There are, of course, rather diffuse cultural pressures toward nurturance, obedience, and responsibility in girls, and toward self-reliance and achievement in boys (Barry, Bacon, and Child, 1957), but father seems to reflect this differential pressure much more than mother.

It is not that father is partial to daughters, although his behavior is sometimes interpreted in that way, but rather that his relationship with them follows a distinctive pattern. No good theory of parental preference for one sex or the other exists at the present time. Children probably accept both parents, knowing no others, in a much more naïve way than parents can accept their offspring. Parents have acquired stereotypes of "good" and "bad" children (for which there are no counterparts in the images children have of their parents) but the stereotypes that parents hold do not make children of one sex consistently more attractive than children of the other. The parental preference for one child over another is ad hoc. (A prejudice in favor of male babies persists to some extent, but it does not necessarily result in a preference for the growing boy if there is also a girl in the household.)

Father-son conflict is greater in part because of the "amplifying effect" of the son's identification with his father. In the large, patriarchal family of former times social distance often tempered hostility toward the parent: the father belonged to an entirely different social world than his children. In the contemporary family hostility is tempered in the opposite way: by reducing social distance and keeping relationships free and easy. But father's overt disciplinary efforts become all the more provocative as a result. Sears and others (1953) found that punishment from mother will have a greater effect upon her daughter than her son because of the daughter's greater identification with mother. It seems to follow that a comparable amount of punishment from father would affect sons more than daughters, although we have no proof of this point as yet. The general principle is this: Almost any coercive control from a parent with whom the child identifies has a more disturbing impact than a comparable effort from a more neutral or distant parent.

Parent-child relationships are extremely complex, of course, and the way fathers relate to their daughters may in turn influence their interchange with sons. Boys who have a brother but no sister, for example, are apt to be more strictly controlled by the father than boys with a sister, but no brother (Koch, 1955). Generally speaking, if a boy has a sister he will be less closely controlled, but the girl will be even more carefully watched than if she had no brother (Elder and Bowerman, 1963). The nurturant attitude that father usually displays toward his daughter seems to promote a similar nurturant relationship with his son, and the greater demands that he makes upon his son as part of the characteristic father-son pattern lead to greater pressures upon his daughter. Moreover, the girl who has a brother is more resistant to parental controls than the girl who does not, apparently because she picks up elements of the masculine pattern from her brother.

One might assume that the father who has children of both sexes would emphasize femininity in the girl and masculinity in the boy, while the father with children of only one sex would blend expressive and instrumental expectations into one pattern. If the father had only a daughter, for example, he might be expected to encourage her to cultivate elements of both male and female life styles. Evidence, however, does not support this supposition. In a family with both a son and a daughter, neither extreme masculinity nor extreme femininity is encouraged, and the excesses of the more typical father-son and father-daughter patterns are also likely to be avoided.

As discussed earlier, both boys and girls are confronted by a more punitive father in the lower socioeconomic levels. Here the stress upon father's disciplinary role persists, and he is more often called upon to impose constraints upon his children than to perform any other parental act, although paternal severity is more variable from one family to the next at this level than at any other (Bronfenbrenner, 1961a). Only the mother is expected to be consistently supportive, and working-class mothers encourage their husbands to be tough, if nothing else. But working-class fathers seem to play well neither the directive role their wives would have them play nor the more highly supportive role (Kohn and Carroll, 1960), and they are less likely to exert family leadership than fathers in middle-class families (Blood and Wolfe, 1960). Thus, the power of the lower-class father in conjugal relations tends to be relatively unimpressive, but in most cases his son views him as the parent who makes the final decisions concerning the boy's behavior (Bowerman and Elder, 1964).

Donald McKinley (1964) contends that the lower-class father often expresses his status frustrations by being hostile and severe to his son; although rare, it is also at this level that the child is most likely to be beaten brutally—"battered-child syndrome." Father's aggressiveness is displaced from the "power and reward structure of industrial society" to the powerless child, although he may turn to sex, peer-group activities, or even exaggerated patriotism to compensate for his lack of occupational success. Fathers who enjoy greater autonomy in their work, and hence less frustration, show less hostility toward their children. The lower-class father may not rule his family, but he usually tries to dominate his son.

This helps to explain why Martin Gold (1963) found that lower-status families are "less attractive" to their sons than middle-class families are to theirs. The lower-class boy tends to be alienated from life in general and from family life in particular when he reaches maturity. As a consequence of paternal severity, his identification with father is weak. By contrast, admiration and identification with father in the higher social levels is much greater, and father's authority is more willingly accepted (McKinley, 1964), although both boys and girls of high status who are severely punished for aggression by their fathers tend to be extremely aggressive (Eron, Walder, *et al.*, 1963). It is possible that the key to alienation among lower-class boys is deficiency in father-son relations, although they have many other reasons for becoming disgusted and bitter. Certainly adversity in the father-son relationship seems to loom much larger in this context than mother-son troubles.

In some respects the situation appears to be rather similar for lower-class girls, who are punished more severely by their fathers for aggression than are girls of higher social status (Eron, Walder, *et al.*, 1963). Lower-class fathers take particular pride in their daughters' respectability and are reluctant to delegate much responsibility to them (Elder and Bowerman, 1963). Restrictive and punitive controls over girls in lower-class families, especially in large families, combined with the girls' relatively meager opportunity for social advancement through education, frequently lead to an early exodus from school, early entry into the labor market, and early marriage (Burchinal, 1959; Elder and Bowerman, 1963).

Oversolicitous fathers in the higher social classes, on the other hand, often contribute to a "Brahmin problem," leaving their daughters at a disadvantage in the marriage market (Scott, 1965). These young ladies expect to receive in courtship the same extravagant favors and attention that their well-placed fathers were able to give them. They prefer to marry men whose status is at least as high as their own, but for these men they must compete against women who are less demanding and of lower social status. Thus the bond between father and daughter, which is the result of distinctive child rearing and courtship patterns, remains much stronger in the higher-status brackets.

Although they meet with occasionally severe discipline, girls in the lower classes are freer from controls in the normal course of events than girls in middle and higher social strata (Elder, 1962b). They tend to identify relatively strongly with their mothers because women in the lower classes have greater social and economic equality with their husbands. This fact serves as a focal point for the unique lower-class pattern, the consequences of which are most notable in Negro families. In one study, Negro daughters were found to be less conformist in their behavior than white girls, which was attributed to the fact that the Negro father is absent so much of the time (Iscoe, Williams, and Harvey, 1964). Mother is the chief source of authority and receives relatively little disciplinary assistance from her husband. The Negro girl can get away with nonconformity more easily than white girls, and as she grows up she becomes much more independent than her brother in dealing with members of the white community.

The latter fact is not due merely to the absence or indifference of the father, however; he is unavailable to both son and daughter. It is more likely due to the relatively high status of Negro women vis-à-vis Negro men. The Negro mother is a stronger model for her daughter than the Negro father is for his son because of the more stable economic position of women in the Negro community. Thus, despite their nonconformity, Negro girls are distinctly superior in school achievement and show fewer "neurotic tendencies" than Negro boys do (Ball, 1962).

Returning to general patterns of father-son conflict, it might be argued that fathers have more conflict with sons than daughters simply because girls accept authority more readily than boys do. Helen Koch (1955), for example, found girls to be more obedient and less quarrelsome, less revengeful, and less insistent upon their rights than boys. Boys in her study were less inhibited in expressing anger, although the girls were more tenacious of purpose. In a study of fourteen-, fifteen-, and sixteen-year-olds, Tuma and Livson (1960) found girls to be slightly more compliant to authority than boys. Indirectly, Miriam Johnson (1963) has suggested that girls can be controlled by rather straightforward methods, while boys are less responsive to the direct approach. Psychological discipline, which capitalizes on affectionate relations between parent and child, is most effective in establishing moral codes for both sexes, she concludes, but especially for sons. The identification process, with its attendant subtleties, is less necessary for the control of girls. Urie Bronfenbrenner (1961a), on the other hand, contends that boys tend to suffer from lack of direct controls, while girls are more likely to suffer from too much discipline. It could be, of course, that boys are less often subjected to direct controls precisely because they are so hard to control.

In a cross-cultural study of the Philippines, Japan, and the United States, patterns of parental authority were found to differ consistently between the sexes; in each case males were allowed greater freedom than females (Smith, Ramsey, and Castillo, 1963). This double standard was accepted by both sexes in all three countries, although it proved most acceptable in Japan and least acceptable in the United States. Curiously, the girls in all three countries were willing to grant significantly more freedom to both sexes than the boys were. They accorded more freedom to their own sex than boys did, but also more freedom to young men than would be extended by boys themselves. One is tempted to conclude that girls are encouraged to develop an optimistic, even unrealistic, rhetoric of freedom; males demand more freedom in actual practice, but remain quite conscious of the limitations to which they must submit.

We are all aware that the double standard is closely associated with restrictions upon female sexual behavior. Girls are restricted because of the insistent danger of premarital pregnancy, and in most cases they acknowledge the need for this control. There are fairly strong cultural sanctions for controlling boys during preadolescence, but teen-age boys are given a broad range of freedom—enough to get many of them into trouble. They may be punished very severely on occasion, but considerable latitude is still left for reality testing. We take fewer chances with girls and preadolescents of both sexes (Toby, 1957).

The fact that boys are given greater freedom may itself lead them into situations that cause conflict with their fathers. For example, males seem to deviate more from the political positions of their parents than girls do (Middleton and Putney, 1963). This may be a source of conflict with fathers, but it is also a consequence of the greater freedom granted to boys in the first place. It would seem that, other things being equal, the greater the freedom permitted a child, the greater likelihood of friction with father. We allow greater freedom to children now than in the past; if we do not always experience greater conflict and hostility it is because we are more tolerant of youth who are not carbon copies of ourselves, and thus, as so often happens, other things are not equal.

Conflict as the Children Mature

It seems reasonable to assume that parents may be able to meet the needs of their children more capably during certain phases of the children's lives than others. A father, for example, may lack the flexibility to grow as a parent along with the physical and social growth of his children (Bell, 1958). Yet both mothering and fathering seem to be rather continuous processes; a foundation is laid when the children are small, and the relationship assumes an ever more predictable pattern as the sequence of parent-child experiences unfolds. A person cannot be expected to suddenly fail as a parent or to blossom all at once because of some age-specific talent or by "taking thought." If there is an exception to this rule, it seems most likely to be the mother who is in her element with infants but becomes ineffectual as they mature. By contrast, the father is more likely to improve as a parent as the children grow older.

Speculation on the latter point may be wishful thinking, however, based on the fact that greater demands are actually made upon the father as his sons grow older. Numerous studies have shown that parents tend to be more involved in the rearing of children of their own sex than those of the opposite sex (Bronfenbrenner, 1961b); as the children mature this pattern becomes increasingly necessary because of the parent's sex-linked experiences in life. Many of the problems faced by older adolescent boys, for example, are best understood by fathers who have gone through similar experiences themselves, as suggested by the recurrent plea of perplexed mothers to their husbands, "Please talk to your son. I can't seem to reach him." If the father fails in response to this appeal it may be because he does not summon up enough effort, since he quite often has the potential rapport.

With the birth of each new child, mother's attention is diverted to the infant, and father is called upon to help out with the older children. As the children mature and their range of activities expands, father is more often involved in decisions that concern their sense of dignity and independence, and the mode of his relationship with them tends to become more threatening.

This is especially true in the father's relationship with his son; the mother, on the other hand, tends to become relatively more threatening in the eyes of her daughter (Kagan, 1956). The father in Mexican-American families presents a rather exaggerated example of this change. He may drop his dignity to cradle an infant or small child, care for its physical needs, even crawl on his hands and knees in play, but with the onset of puberty the authoritative role of father becomes clear. The man assumes the position of distant, perhaps dignified, master (Madsen, 1964). The son may respect and obey him, but his abiding affection is reserved for mother.

Martin Hoffman (1963a), after reviewing the research on parental control techniques, concluded that paternal discipline is relatively unimportant when the children are little, but assumes an increasing significance as they approach and enter adolescence. Strangely, however, father is not necessarily perceived as the dominant parent more often than before; evidence on this point is equivocal. Walter Emmerich (1961) found that between the ages of six and ten children consider the father to be the more powerful parent, but when they are either younger or older the mother fares better. In a study of children between the ages of seven and fifteen Robert Hess and Judith Torney (1962) also found that father was less often reported as "boss" as the children matured. But Jerome Kagan (1956) found a consistent tendency for older children to be more likely than younger ones to view the parent of the same sex as more dominant and punitive, and Charles Bowerman and Glen Elder (1964) concluded that older adolescents are more likely to regard father as the final authority in the household.

Clearly there is no consensus here. As the children mature, father tends to take a more prominent role in discipline, but he may not appear to be more powerful. It seems likely that children perceive the parental-dominance pattern more accurately as they grow older, in part because they gain greater rapport with their parents (Bowerman and Irish, 1962). Father's more frequent involvement in the discipline pattern does not mean that he is the stronger parent, nor does it necessarily make him seem more potent. It is quite possible that father often becomes involved in the discipline problems of his children under circumstances that call attention to his ineffectuality rather than to his power. He is drawn in at the most difficult time, for it is as the children reach preadolescence and adolescence that they most openly resent parental discipline and are most likely to rebel against it in a sustained way.

The children also participate in more activities away from home as they grow older, and as their activities in school, church, youth organizations, and peer groups increase, their status within the family rises (Blood, 1963). Jules Henry (1963), among others, has pointed out that adolescents want very badly to grow up and to be treated as adults, but they establish their own criteria for identifying and validating maturity. Doing things with their parents and complying with their parents' wishes have low priority for adolescents.

The most intense period of conflict seems to come in the first stages of adolescence, perhaps at the age of thirteen or fourteen (Hurlock, 1959). In classroom essays the majority of the author's students have repeatedly cited these two ages as most troublesome, although the reasons given are not exclusively conflicts with parents. Edward Clifford (1959) found that as the adolescent advances through his teens, discipline problems diminish. But contrary evidence is also available. Ivan Nye (1952) divided adolescents into four groups—young boys from twelve to fourteen, older boys from fifteen to seventeen, young girls from twelve to fourteen, and older girls from fifteen to seventeen—and found the older boys to be most conflict-prone; they registered the poorest adjustment to their parents. The other three groups ranked about the same by Nye's measure.

Perhaps these discrepancies are illusory, however. The author is inclined to believe that the toughest period for parent-child conflict—hard conflict rather than the petty disputes that characterize the early years of childhood—usually occurs in the first years of adolescence. After the disruptions of this period, patterns of accommodation are usually worked out. The conflict continues, perhaps even deepens, but a better understanding of its nature is achieved and a reasonably satisfactory modus vivendi is established. The reason more conflict may seem to exist later in adolescence is because the child is now better able to verbalize his adjustment problems. Although family patterns are more stable, any lack of adjustment is more clearly and forcefully articulated by the family members involved, and conflict thus appears to be greater than it really is.

We have noted that the status of children rises during adolescence. It rises still higher when they go to college, take jobs, and marry, but these pursuits pull them away from home so completely that conflict with father diminishes. Thus peak father-child conflict seems to occur most often in the early stages of adolescence.

The Moderation of Conflict

Kingsley Davis (1940) once argued that societies in which merit is the basis for status engender a high level of conflict between youth and their elders. Thus, in primitive societies conflict is minimal because age is the primary basis for prestige and power. In peasant societies, status is ascribed by birth, and so again contention between generations is not pronounced. More recently, however, formal education and talent have become primary sources of social status; if Davis is correct we would expect to find greater conflict between fathers and sons in the contemporary setting.

In reality father-child conflict in the United States is probably minimal when viewed in historical and cross-cultural perspective. Davis' hypothesis about conflict between generations may be true in a general sense, but the battles are not characteristically waged within the family. Younger men may compete against older men at large, but only rarely against their own fathers. Indeed, where the success theme is strong, fathers actually take pride in seeing their sons eclipse them (Schorr, 1962). Moving up the social ladder also tends to reduce association, and hence conflict, among family members (Merton, 1957; Ellis and Lane, 1963). Thus, expansive opportunities for physical and social mobility help to keep tensions in check in the United States, although improved chances of this nature are characteristic of most industrial nations.

Of even greater importance is the American father's relative weakness. Alan Valentine (1963) contends that fathers are even too unsure of themselves nowadays to write letters of advice to their grown-up sons; he demonstrates that this has not always been the case. Ample evidence attests that non-authoritarian fathers, such as those found in the United States, have relatively little conflict with their children. One study, comparing American and the more traditional Italian parental values, found that American parents tend to be child-centered, stressing the child's own development and gratifications, whereas Italian parents seem more adult-centered, emphasizing the child's conformity to adult standards (Pearlin and Kohn, 1966). Paul Landis and Carol Stone (1952) reported that parent-teen-age relationships were distinctly superior in democratic as compared to authoritarian families. Yi-Chuang Lu (1952) found that the more dominant the father is in the family, the more conflict he has with both son and daughter and the less attachment they have to him. Even the relationship between grandfathers and their grandchildren is closer and more affectionate in cultures where the grandparents have relatively limited familial powers (Sweetser, 1962). Power and authority breed social distance, and the American father is neither authoritative nor powerful by world standards.

Nor does the American father have many children to manage. The more children there are, the more trouble they can cause, thus inviting disciplinary efforts to prevent disturbance, and harsher reactions when trouble occurs. Ivan Nye (1952) found that the fewer the children, the better the adolescent-parent adjustment, a pattern that prevailed in all social classes. Parents can give each child more attention in small families, and one or two children rather than four or five makes it easier to satisfy the children's economic needs without sacrificing new cars, homes, education, and a variety of parental wishes. Children in small families are also more likely to have been planned and are therefore more welcome when they arrive.

In fact, it is quite possible that in the small American family damaged father-son relations are more likely to lead to apathy than to any form of rebellion. Robert Lane (1959) argues that the American culture discourages revolt against the father because he is not allowed to dominate in the first place. Under such permissive child-rearing circumstances, rebellion would be superfluous. Lane suggests that where father-son relations have been damaged in the United States the son is not likely for that reason to develop a critical attitude toward authority figures; he is more likely to become indifferent toward them. Lane particularly notes the low level of political awareness in America, which may in fact reflect the low saliency of politics among American fathers. He argues that quitting school as a form of rebellion against parental controls is the American youth's equivalent of joining a radical political movement in Europe. Germany provides a rather sharp contrast. Both Lane and Erik Erikson (1958) contend that German sons are subject to much greater provocation against paternal discipline than boys in America are.

. . .

Nevertheless, conflict with father, though less frequent than with mother, is more likely to become part of a vicious cycle. Father tends to think of child rearing as essentially a discipline problem and relies heavily on jural controls, striving to get his children to comply with "the rules." But paternal authority tends to be transparently arbitrary in contemporary society, especially when it is exercised in the spirit of patriarchy. In the past father's authority was reinforced by a network of community supports, and thus it seemed to be based on the wisdom of the ages. In a rapidly changing society father often finds himself in situations that fathers never faced in the past, and he is as uncertain as his offspring in making decisions.

Perhaps for this very reason father-child conflict is minimal in the United States. The American father is too weak and American society too permissive for father to be the source of truly bitter hostility. It is possible that he is more often resented for his weakness, or viewed as an object of sympathy, than hated for his tyranny. If Americans have unusually free spirits, it may well be because they are neither beaten down by their fathers nor forced to exhaust childhood energies fighting them.

CHAPTER X

Fatherlessness

Ideally each child lives with both a father and a mother; the absence of either is presumed to have an adverse effect upon the child's personality, and he also misses the pleasure normally associated with having two loving parents. Graham Blaine (1963) contends that one of the most terrifying and pervasive unconscious fears harbored by children is that they will be abandoned by one or both of their parents. In a sense, one of father's duties is simply to stick around, although his absence is almost always symptomatic of more than an unwillingness to stay at home.

For the boy, the father image has mythic qualities whether his father is a gallant figure or manifestly unheroic; almost all fathers can lay claim to at least some of the archetypal stuff associated with paternity. A search for the father as hero or for some symbol of male triumph lingers on, propelled by the universal stresses of sonship perhaps, but also by a theme running through virtually all cultures—the ideal of a brave, omniscient father and a singular father-son, hero-acolyte relationship. The son's lifelong search for father, Telemachus in search of Ulysses, appears much more often in poetry and novels than any quest by daughter, and consequently it is a more frequent topic in literary criticism. Leslie Fiedler (1960), for example, referring to the "eternal comedy of fathers and sons," seems as much obsessed by it as by the writers he attempts to judge. The boy who has never seen his father, or who has seen him very infrequently, is the prime candidate to conduct a lifelong search for "the man."

We have noted that father is the "weak link" in the family system, and, as such, the degree to which fathers are able to meet general social expectations is a good index of the health of both the family system and the general social structure. Judson Landis (1962a), for example, has indicated that the feeling of closeness to the father by children is a more accurate index of family integration than the feeling of closeness to the mother. If children are devoted to their fathers, they are very likely to be close to their mothers as well, but an intimate relationship with the mother is an unreliable index of close father-child relations; a common corollary of distance between the child and his mother is equal or greater distance between the child and his father.

Thus, a breakdown of the mothering role is the most critical factor in family disintegration, but a strong father reflects the existence of the most thoroughly integrated family. (If the children are closer to the father than to the mother it can mean that she has abdicated her role or is simply unable to function adequately in relations with her children; it may also mean that she is a tyrant.) But mother is usually the crucial parent for maintaining the basic essentials of a nurturant family life. Therefore, the father is not so much the key to minimal parental adequacy as he is the potential source of maximal family vigor.

But it is not uncommon for one-parent families to be unstable and to know chronic adversity (Willie and Weinandy, 1963), and the majority of them are families in which the father is absent. Fortunately, the loss of father appears to have considerably less damaging effects than the loss of mother (Nye, 1952), which is not surprising in the light of our earlier designation of mother as "the primary parent." About 10 percent of the children in the United States are living with only one parent, and approximately one-third of the nonwhite children are in that category (Chilman and Sussman, 1964). Roughly 4 million American women rear children without a father in the household (Ilgenfritz, 1961), whereas less than one-sixth that many fathers are attempting to manage children alone. Indeed, quite a few of the mother-only families in the lower social classes have one mother and more than one father, none of whom remain at home and provide for the family in a dependable way.

The pattern of fatherlessness almost constitutes a subculture, although to call it that without qualification would be misleading. William Stephens (1961) found that the family consisting of only mother and children tends to perpetuate itself; 50 percent of the solo mothers in his sample had themselves had mothers who were reared in mother-only families. That is not enough to earn the designation "subculture," but it does indicate a nonrandom, patterned continuity in fatherlessness from one generation to the next. Peter Kunstadter (1963) has also noted that the "matrilocal" family—a residential kin group in which no male performs the role of husband-father in a regular way—may be institutionalized in some societies. Its relatively frequent occurrence among Negroes in the United States can only be explained in terms of the special historical conditions experienced by this minority group.

The Mother's Response

Most mothers are more concerned about their children than about their husbands, as we have mentioned before, yet most of them will readily admit that father comes in quite handy in the rearing of children. Presumably the woman who is a wife first and a mother second will be most painfully distressed by the loss of her husband. But the husband's absence creates a number of problems even if the wife considers his departure the answer to all her prayers. Some difficulties may simply be due to the lack of a male companion (assuming there is no early remarriage). We usually take it for granted that the mother will have a man around to help her meet certain kinds of problems, since a number of practical matters assume crisis proportions without the knowledge and skills that a husband can ordinarily supply. The woman may also fear going to certain places alone, and hence the father's absence restricts both her life space and that of her children.

A child who has never known his father is likely to create a vivid image of him, if not of fatherhood itself, by the way his mother acts toward males in general. A negative, disdainful image of the father himself is often hard to avoid (Wylie and Delgado, 1959). In the case of divorce, some animosity is usually directed toward the father in connection with his visits to the children, yet if he does not visit, bitterness can be expected (Ilgenfritz, 1961). Solo mothers sometimes express a free-floating hostility toward men; both divorced and widowed women often feel that men regard them as "fair game" for sex relations.

The child will also pick up ideas about his father from personal experiences with the older males he encounters. In an extended family system, many male relatives are usually available who can substitute for father, but not in the American small-family arrangement. The solo mother faces a problem in finding men to portray masculine ways to her children that are compatible with her own life style. Many writers have advised mothers to try to convey a "wholesome attitude" about father when he is absent and to make certain that the children have regular contacts with a congenial male relative or some other positive father substitute. Thus, it has become rather common for solo mothers to search for ways to bring men into their children's lives—uncles, grandfathers, scout leaders, fathers of friends, corner policemen, and so on. A monthly journal is published, *Parents Without Partners,* in which among other things advice is exchanged on finding such stand-ins for father.

The solo mother is often ambivalent toward the child, perhaps because she is trying to be both mother and father at the same time. Howard Wylie and Rafael Delgado (1959) suggest that the mother whose husband is absent is prone to imagine that the boy is just like his father and, as a result, the mother-son relationship becomes intense, highly sexualized, and hostile. They found that solo mothers often have trouble controlling boys; if both father and son are aggressive types, the boy's aggressiveness is particularly frustrating. Thus, sex education, a common problem for solo mothers, is further strained. But another reason that the solo mother has difficulty managing the child is because her disciplinary efforts, based on the judgment of only one person, seem arbitrary to the child; mother and father operating in tandem tend to strengthen and legitimize one another's decisions (Glasser and Navarre, 1965).

Moreover, an important component in the mother's capacity to discipline her children is derived from the authority attached to the father figure. Fathers usually regard themselves as more self-sufficient than mothers and are much less likely than mothers to feel the need for help from others in dealing with their children (Littman, Curry, and Pierce-Jones, 1957). Mothers often use the threat of paternal action as a control device ("Wait 'til your father gets home."), however unrecommended this may be by child-rearing experts. In this way father's association with his children extends the limits of mother's disciplinary activity, even though he is not home most of the day (Eron, Walder, *et al.*, 1963). The solo mother is therefore at a disadvantage because she is almost the exclusive source of punishment for her children. If it does nothing else, the absence of father simply removes one source of authority in the home. Although the "domesticated" father is generally more democratic than the one who is frequently away from home (Crain and Stamm, 1965), parents tend to take a more severe position in child rearing jointly than individually, and they usually resolve their differences by taking a more exacting rather than a more permissive position (Putney and Middleton, 1960).

The mother in a fatherless home may also have trouble maintaining a sense of security for her children because she is more likely to reveal anxiety in dangerous situations. She tends to be more excitable than the mother living with her husband, especially if some loss of her self-esteem is associated with the father's absence (Ilgenfritz, 1961). This fact calls attention to one of father's functions in his fulfillment of the "sturdy-oak pattern." He is more likely than the mother to portray "calmness in the face of danger," which is a general security function for the children and a masculinizing function for the son as well.

Although his mere presence is not sufficient to this task, the father has a role to play in keeping the mother from developing an exaggerated and tense emotional relationship with her children. The solo mother's loneliness, or her fear of loneliness, can become a problem with serious implications for her children. Both solo fathers and mothers are characterized by a frustrating sense of incompleteness and sometimes by a sense of failure and guilt (Freudenthal, 1959). Normally the father is a companion, an emotional support, and a love object for his wife. In his absence the mother may seek these highly desired qualities from her children, whether the husband actually supplied them or not. As a consequence she tends to overprotect the children, increases their dependency upon her, and burdens them with adult problems. She is likely to "absorb" an only son, an obsessive concern that is not necessarily appreciated by the child, nor is it always—perhaps not even usually—taken for love; Alan Crain and Caroline Stamm (1965) found that both boys and girls whose fathers were absent rated their mothers as less "loving" than those whose fathers were present. As many counselors have noted, children must become emancipated from their infantile love-dependency relationship with the mother in order to "grow up," and the problem is more difficult if the father is not present to help. If nothing else, he can deflect some of the mother's emotional energy from the children.

For the son in particular, the father has an opportunity to ally himself with the child's efforts to become free of his mother's apron strings. The father himself may find an avenue of escape in this alliance, although the teaming of father and son against the female hegemony may lead to some rather picaresque activities, and there is certainly no guarantee that the father's presence will promote a healthy emancipation. Herbert Hendin (1964) contends that one reason that people in Denmark are vulnerable to depression and suicide is their intense dependence upon the mother, in spite of the father's presence. His contention should by no means be taken as an established fact, but it does call into question the importance of the father's presence in the home as a buffer against maternal dependence. In one study no differences could be found in the dependency levels of boys whose fathers were absent and those whose fathers were in residence (McCord, McCord, and Thurber, 1962).

It is apparent that the mother raising her children alone may be forced to seek employment if she was not already working at the time of the father's departure. Solo mothers have about as many children to look after as those sharing responsibilities with their husbands, but on the average they have less than half as much income (Chilman and Sussman, 1964). Three out of every four families receiving "aid to families with dependent children" have no father in the home. Nevertheless, the fact that the mother must work is not necessarily a disadvantage. In a small sample of children living with mothers only, Ivan Nye (1959) found that children whose mothers were employed appeared to be somewhat better adjusted than those whose mothers were not. The full significance of this is not yet clear, but it does suggest that we should be cautious about assuming that the solo mother's employment per se is harmful to the children.

In fact, none of the problems of the solo mother that have been mentioned thus far necessarily impair the overall performance of women in their capacity as mothers. Ivan Nye (1957a) found no evidence that children with solo parents have more adjustment problems than those in unhappy, unbroken homes, although quite a bit of evidence from other sources suggests that problems do arise. The point of immediate significance is that the child is not the only one who reacts to the special conditions of the one-parent family; the solo parent reacts too, and this reaction becomes a part of the child's milieu. Many mothers whose husbands are gone do in fact rise to the occasion.

Reasons for Father's Absence

The wife's reaction to her husband's absence or to the reasons for his departure may be more critical in the lives of the children than the mere fact that the father is gone. There are five major possibilities, each with its own set of implications:

death, desertion, divorce, prolonged or periodic separation, and nonmarriage (the man may never have become a part of the household in the first place). Most research, unfortunately, has been limited to exploration of the effects of death and divorce; very little information is available about deserting, separated, and unmarried fathers.

Both death and divorce represent painful experiences for members of the family, but the loss of the father by death is usually less traumatic over an extended period of time (Russell, 1957; Glickman, 1954). The mother and her children will of course experience almost unbearable sorrow when the father dies, but in most cases bereavement passes quickly enough for the children. A sense of guilt sometimes accompanies the death of a family member, even among children, which can be the basis for an extended reaction (Isaacs, 1945).

The father's death occasions the loss of his presence, but usually no damage to his esteem. He may in fact gain greater symbolic respect in death. Raymond Illsley and Barbara Thompson (1961) found that the death of father had little adverse effect upon the children, unlike his absence due to separation or divorce. Jessie Bernard (1956) contends, however, that the entrance of a new parent tends to have a troubling effect after the original one's death, a benign effect after divorce. The proud image of the deceased father thus may become a problem. Charles Bowerman and Donald Irish (1962) support this contention; the adjustment of children to stepparents is better after divorce than death, they say, at least in part because of the invidious comparisons posed by the latter.

In theory divorce is more tolerable than death because of its voluntary nature. Some time ago Joanna Colcord (1932) called attention to the possible advantages of voluntary over unintentional family dissolutions. She inferred that people can adjust better to a situation of their own choosing than to one over which they have no control. But this is probably a spurious argument. Although divorce may be mutually desired by the parents, the couple most certainly did not choose the conditions that made them want divorce in the first place. It is one thing to voluntarily choose a desirable situation in life, another to "voluntarily" want out of a bad one. One must conclude that the concept of voluntarism is of little help to us here. Children want a father, usually the one they've got; it is not they who favor divorce. For that matter, we often find it easier to adjust to situations that cannot be avoided than to conditions of our own choice. The fact that children have little option in the matter is probably a good thing, which can also be said for the fact that they are usually allowed little choice in deciding which parent they will live with in the case of divorce (Blaine, 1963).

A widow has her hands full explaining the father's death to her children, especially to young children. But divorce presents an even more difficult problem; little children are often unwilling to accept it, and they find the idea that their father will not return as a regular member of the household almost incomprehensible (Cohen, 1960; Ilgenfritz, 1961). His occasional visits may only complicate matters.

Thus, divorce increases the emotional distance between children and their fathers (J. Landis, 1960b). Children live with their mother in most cases and tend to accept her views, usually negative, about the missing man. An atmosphere of guilt and ambiguity surrounds the concept of father, a limbo status involving awkward conflicts of loyalty for the child and uncertainties of affection (Faris, 1948). Even if the father is unknown, as in the case of children of unwed mothers, the realization that he is alive and "out there," or may be alive, raises an identity problem. A positive image of the father in the case of desertion, divorce, separation, or paternity out of wedlock is hard to maintain, even though it may never be overtly stated that he is a scoundrel. We know very little about what mothers actually say or do to characterize these men; an occasional reference or a noticeable rigidity when his name comes up may be the only clues.

The deserting father probably regrets the loss of his children more than that of his wife (Hill and Becker, 1942), and perhaps he regrets the loss of his role as parent more than that of husband. Although a desire to escape from the burdens of fatherhood may have been an important factor in his desertion, dissatisfactions with the wife and her inability to compensate for problems in the husband's life are usually more important. Jacob Zukerman (1950) has suggested that extramarital sex and drinking are the two leading reasons why men desert, but these are at least in part functions of the man's relations with his wife. Zukerman argues that an impressive number of men hesitate to leave home until after the children are old enough to take care of themselves and suggests that there is something to the notion that a man approaching his forties should be watched. One might wonder, however, whether that possibility has even occurred to many people. (Deutsch and Goldston [1960], incidentally, have reported several instances of wives deserting disabled husbands, but no cases of a disabled married woman with children being deserted by her husband.)

The deserting father tends to be of low socioeconomic status; there is an impressive body of literature on this subject, some of it mildly reserved (Kephart, 1961). If the deserting father has any significant status in the community he will be easily apprehended (and there will be good reason to pursue him), unless he flees leaving all social ties behind. The fact that the man of status would be able to fulfill his obligations to wife and children if caught is crucial. It is often questionable, however, whether deserting husbands and fathers, family fugitives, are worth catching. They can no longer safely flee to the frontier or even to the anonymity of the metropolis, but social workers and civil authorities remain reluctant to insist that they support their wives and children; as a rule, they *cannot* insist, and the most apparent alternative, imprisonment, seems pointless (Monahan, 1958). In the middle classes, of course, the greater likelihood is that standard divorce procedures will be followed in order to clarify financial matters, protect the children, and permit legal remarriage. Both divorced and widowed mothers are more likely to have formal support arrangements for themselves and their children than mothers in families broken by desertion.

Not much is known about unmarried fathers, mainly because of their inaccessibility. Studies of unwed mothers outnumbered those of unmarried fathers by about twenty-five to one (Vincent, 1960). High rates of illegitimate fathering are believed to be found among groups that are weakly committed to prevailing social norms (Goode, 1960a, 1961a; Bock, 1964). We know very little about public attitudes toward these men other than that the mothers, not the fathers, are the objects of shame and ostracism. There is a widespread feeling that the responsibility for pregnancy is the girl's because she, rather than the boy, is supposed to restrain herself sexually. About half of the high-school youth in a study by Bernice Moore and Wayne Holtzman (1965) agreed that the girl who becomes pregnant before marriage has only herself to blame; the liability is hers and the boy is, for all practical purposes, exonerated. When the father of the child refuses to marry the girl he will usually argue that he was not the only male who had relations with her, and that "she knew what she was doing" (Vincent, 1960). Most members of one teen-age gang interviewed in Chicago said the only difference they could see between the young man who had fathered an illegitimate child and one who had not was that the latter was lucky (Short, Strodtbeck, and Cartwright, 1962).

In premarital sex relations boys do in fact take the precaution of using condoms more often than girls use diaphragms, jellies, or pills, at least in the working classes (Rainwater and Weinstein, 1960) and probably in the middle classes too; perhaps taking such precautions alleviates the boys' guilt feelings. Girls are reluctant to use contraceptives because to do so would amount to premeditated defection from "the code" forbidding premarital sexual intercourse. Hence when girls indulge, they must do it on "impulse." They may have thought about having sex relations before going on a date and perhaps even decided to let nature take its course, but as Christopher Jencks (1964) has pointed out, to go so far as to prepare for contraception in advance requires a stronger sense of rebellion against mores than most girls possess. Consequently this is an area in which the structuring of social relations to prevent one kind of "evil," premarital sex, increases the chances of yet another, premarital pregnancy. (Use of "the pill" could alter this dilemma if it served some purpose in addition to that of contraception. Then it could be taken without implying that the girl was going to engage in sex relations.)

Not only is little known about unmarried fathers, but much of what we think we know may be inaccurate. Clark Vincent (1960) collected data that do not substantiate the notion that the annual crop of 300,000 unmarried fathers are much older or much better educated than the females they impregnate; Vincent contends that homogamy prevails in both legitimate and nonlegitimate unions. In a study of unwed mothers who kept their children, Mignon Sauber (1966) found that about three out of five mothers were still in contact with the fathers and one-third of them had lived with the father during the first eighteen months after the infant's birth. The longer the mother and father had known each other before conception, the longer they continued to have contacts after the birth of their child. Many of the fathers voluntarily gave financial support both during pregnancy and during the first eighteen months after birth; no other source of support was as steady as that from the father!

In a most unusual, and questionable, switch, Vincent comes to the defense of the unmarried father; he states that it is often the woman who is the exploiter, using sex and then pregnancy to gain love and affection. Most illegitimate pregnancies, he argues, are not the result of casual affairs; many of the fathers do care about the child and register guilt feelings. But the fact that the girl was willing to trade sex for affection, or merely attention, hardly qualifies as exploitation. Although premarital sex is a two-way process, it is the female who usually suffers the most degrading and burdensome consequences.

Effects on Children

Many efforts have been made to determine the effects of the absence of father upon children. Studies of the consequences for sons are most numerous, and fatherlessness does indeed seem to be most damaging to boys. As we have seen, however, much depends on the way mother handles the situation after father is gone. The age of the children is also a factor (Langner and Michael, 1963). Graham Blaine (1963) says that one of the most traumatic periods to lose a parent through death or divorce is between the ages of three and six. Mary Leichty (1960) found that relatively few males whose fathers had been away from home when the boys were between the ages of three and five developed a strong identification with their fathers or chose their fathers as an ego ideal. Benjamin Spock (1962) also says that a child can thrive on a mother's love during the first three years of life, but after that he will need a flesh-and-blood father or a strong paternal image.

Both theory and research suggest that sex identification will pose particular difficulties for the fatherless boy (Winch, 1949). John Nash (1965) concluded that boys reared for the first five years in the absence of a father figure often fail to acquire the masculine attitudes held by most other boys. William Stephens (1961) also found greater femininity in sons from mother-child families than in those from intact families. In the former case mothers showed a relatively high level of "maternal seductiveness" toward the son, as indicated by their jealousy of the boy's girl friends and by the son's anxiety about sex. Roger Burton (1961) argues that boys from father-absent homes have fantasy lives very much like those that are typical of girls; other researchers had earlier found that the fantasies of fatherless children tend to be less aggressive and more idealistic than those with fathers (Sears, Pintler, and Sears, 1946). James Bieri (1960), too, contends that fatherless boys identify poorly with their sex; they tend to describe themselves as being similar to their mothers and characterize the father as a person who is dominated by women (Bach, 1946). Eleanor Maccoby (1962) found that boys whose fathers were absent when they were between the ages of one and five performed better on verbal than on analytical tests, whereas most boys excelled on the latter. G. A. Milton (1957) also found that boys separated from their fathers scored relatively poorly on problem-solving tests, tests on which boys generally perform better than girls.

The degree of masculinity or femininity exhibited by a child may be no problem in and of itself, however; we have very little direct evidence of the effect of fatherlessness upon the behavior of persons in critical situations, nor is there consensus on the definition or measurement of maleness and femaleness.

But David Lynn and William Sawrey (1959), along with Roger Burton, suggest that father-absent boys are more *insecure* in their masculinity, at whatever level, leading to rather excessive forms of compensatory behavior and a more intense striving for male identity. Their masculine performance is often awkward and contrived; it is not a spontaneous expression of the self independent of efforts to impress others. In particular, fatherless boys often suffer from an immoderate need to impress females. Claude Bartlett and John Horrocks (1958) suggest that this is part of a more general pattern: adolescents from homes where one parent is deceased tend to compensate for lack of recognition and response from adults by striving for affection from members of the opposite sex.

Various problems other than sex identification per se have also been associated with fatherlessness. Richard Palmer (1960) found that children with "behavioral problems" were more likely to have had extensive separations from fathers than the children in his control group, particularly when the separations had been in the early period of the child's life. In their study of sons of Norwegian fathers, Lynn and Sawrey (1959) found that boys who were away from home for prolonged periods of time showed symptoms of poorer personality adjustment, greater immaturity, and poorer peer-group adjustment than either boys whose fathers were present or girls whose fathers were absent. In the case of young children, but not adolescents, Walter Mischel (1961) found that a significantly greater proportion of fatherless children were impulsive and chose immediate rewards over those that must be delayed.

Although these studies suggest that aggressive behavior among fatherless boys is excessive, the bulk of the evidence points in the opposite direction. A number of researchers have indicated that boys from father-absent homes tend to be less aggressive, more submissive, more dependent, and more willing to accept authority than those from intact homes (Bach, 1946; Sears, Pintler, and Sears, 1946; Stolz, 1954; Lynn and Sawrey, 1959; Bieri, 1960; Bronfenbrenner, 1961a). Fatherless girls, on the other hand, are likely to show more than the ordinary amount of aggressiveness. Father is presumed to be a model for masculine aggressiveness and also a more persistent source of frustration than mother, especially for boys. The son is more likely to be overly aggressive and antisocial if there is a severe disruption in the father-son relationship and father does *not* leave home (Gordon, 1962). But the amount of aggression displayed by a child is usually less important than its quality; the role of father is to model the proper way to be aggressive, not simply the degree of aggression.

Various studies have suggested that a relationship exists between fatherlessness and delinquent behavior (Stephens, 1961; Andry, 1962). Homes in which the father is not present produce more than their proportion of both male and female delinquents, but this is also true of homes in which a father is present, yet fails to function as head of the household (Barker and Adams, 1962). Although some writers continue to claim a positive value for the intact home as such (Weinberg, 1964), evidence is accumulating that the quality of family life is of greater significance than, and independent of, its formal structure. John Clausen (1961) claims that a disproportionate number of prostitutes, drug addicts, unwed mothers, and other deviants come from homes lacking a *stable* male head, which are different from homes where father is absent. William Goode (1961b) cites evidence indicating that the delinquency rate is higher for those whose parents are separated or divorced than it is for those who have lost a parent by death. But Sheldon and Eleanor Glueck (1950) as well as Joan and William McCord (1958) contend that divorce itself does not cause delinquency; the crucial variable in accounting for juvenile misconduct is the absence of a generally stable home environment, rather than the specific absence of father. Divorced mothers in one sample worried about the effects of divorce upon their children, but most of them thought their children's lives had improved after divorce (Goode, 1956). In fact, the proportion of gang delinquents seems to be higher among boys whose parents quarrel frequently but remain together than among those whose fathers are absent (McCord, McCord, and Thurber, 1962).

We can distinguish, then, between a *structural* and a *psychological* breach in the family, since members of the conjugal group need not be physically separated in order to be estranged from one another (Smith, 1955). The degree of deterioration in marriage is an almost useless basis for the prediction of divorce. Ivan Nye (1957a) found that children in broken homes showed less psychosomatic illness, less delinquent behavior, and better adjustment to parents than children in unhappy, unbroken homes did, although in both cases the children were found to have made rather poor adjustments with other children. The children living in mother-only households scored relatively high in satisfactory parent-child relationships. Judson Landis (1962b) also found significant differences between children of happy unions as opposed to children of unhappy marriages, whether the parents were divorced or not; differences between children from the divorced and those from the unhappy nondivorced marriages were few indeed.

Citing further evidence for this point of view, Lee Burchinal (1964) contends that we would do well to study the processes parents use to minimize traumas for their children and to assist their adaptation after family schism. An exaggerated concern for the formalities of family stability distracts us from the more appropriate search—that is, for the best solution to the children's problems. In fact, the differences in parent-child relations between nondelinquents and delinquent repeaters that have been identified in the literature are often unreliable (Gold, 1963). Many habitual delinquents do not live in derelict homes; they do things with their parents, talk to them about their problems, and want to be like their fathers. The lack of a father may contribute to the child's delinquency, of course, and the father's absence may signify family disorganization, but the most appropriate generalization we can draw is that the void father's absence makes reflects even deeper community disorders.

Moreover, since fathers who remain members of the household may do their children harm as well as good, their presence can very well be a mixed blessing. The lower-class Negro boy, for example, whether his father is at home or in flight, is surrounded by delinquent opportunities (and invitations to prolonged idleness) that are only rarely found in the middle classes. The plight of the Negro family, its undependable father and its neighborhood style, can all be traced directly to a pattern of economic deprivation. There is no point in blaming dad. If any further evidence is needed, Catherine Chilman and Marvin Sussman (1964) point out that there are many more children living in extreme destitution with *both* parents than there are with mother alone.

Perhaps we should distinguish between the role of actual fathers within the family unit and the concept or institution of fatherhood as it is portrayed in the community at large. References to fathers and paternity are made in many social contexts in the United States; children who do not have fathers are by no means unaware of fatherhood, which is the main reason they sense that something is missing in their lives. The distinction between the role of a particular father and the concept of fatherhood helps to explain why the loss of father may be so problematical at the time it occurs, yet need not be a persistent source of grief or maladjustment. If a boy loses a father who was not a dependable guardian of his welfare—even a child beater—the boy may still be traumatized since he is supposed to have a father. On the other hand, the existence of father's image in so many places in our society means that the boy will not be denied knowledge of fatherhood or the masculine style, and that he will learn many of the things his own father would have taught him.

Our distinction between the role of the particular father and the institution of fatherhood is basic to any discussion of possible substitutes for father or alternative institutional arrangements for the rearing of children. A father in the household may not be necessary; but it is possible, indeed likely, that there is no adequate substitute for the *institution* of fatherhood, that is, certain minimum institutional expectations for persons who are classified as "fathers."

Stepfathers

Although the solo mother has problems, a stepfather will not necessarily solve them, and he sometimes makes matters worse. Of course not all natural fathers are effective either. Joseph

Perry and Erdwin Pfuhl (1963) could find no significant differences in the adjustment of children in homes in which the father was absent and those in homes in which there had been a remarriage.

Nevertheless, there is some evidence suggesting that children from broken homes may make better social and emotional adjustments when they live with just their mother than with mother and a stepfather. Unhappily, both "stepparent" and "stepchild" are words with predominantly negative connotations; as William Smith (1953) has observed, the latter term has come to be applied to almost anything that is mistreated or neglected. One study concluded that both sons and daughters whose divorced or widowed parent remarried scored lower on tests of mental health than those whose remaining parent did not remarry (Langner and Michael, 1963). A study by Ivan Nye (1952) revealed better adjustment among adolescents in broken homes with mother only than in mother-stepfather homes. Children in homes with a mother and stepfather may have only slightly less affection for their mothers than children who live in unbroken homes do, but the level of affection toward stepfathers is often markedly lower (Bowerman and Irish, 1962). The stepfather is also more likely than the real father to be regarded as a rival for the mother's affection (Podolsky, 1955), suggesting that stepsons in particular may have identification problems. Stepdaughters, however, generally manifest even more extreme reactions toward their parents than do stepsons, and children are closer to both natural and stepparents of the same sex than to those of the opposite sex.

Nevertheless, stepfathers may do better in comparison with the natural parent than stepmothers, although the evidence is equivocal (Langner and Michael, 1963). Jessie Bernard (1956) has called attention to the fact that the stepmother seems to be able to win the biological father to her point of view in child-rearing matters more easily than the stepfather can influence the mother, probably because both mothers and stepmothers are more involved in the children's affairs. Substitutes for father are in fact easier to find than those for mother, although certainly not because of the sex ratio; women of the appropriate age actually outnumber men. The stepfather's advantage is the nature of father's role: it is not as demanding as the maternal role; a major part of the father's function is implicit in the symbolism attached to his mere presence. The mother's role is less symbolic and more active, and she is therefore harder to replace. Charles Bowerman and Donald Irish (1962) found that stepmothers do in fact have more difficult roles than stepfathers and that the general level of affection toward stepmothers is quite low. In our folklore the cruel, callous stepmother is known to all; no comparable stereotype exists for stepfather.

We noted earlier that stepfathers greatly outnumber stepmothers, which may also have something to do with their greater success. Being more common, society gives them more assistance; the fact that they are not so unusual also means that they are more likely to find social acceptance as well as effective models to follow.

One reason for caution in assessing the impact of the stepfather, however, is that there are a number of conditions closely associated with stepfatherhood that may have a stronger impact on the children than stepfathers themselves. Social class is an example. Stepfathers are more prevalent in the lower classes and hence any research that links misconduct in children to stepfatherhood may be grossly misleading (Glueck and Glueck, 1950; Barker and Adams, 1962).

The same research problem is found in the case of foster fathers, although their social characteristics seem to follow an altogether different pattern in terms of social class, race, age, and so on. H. David Kirk (1964) has pointed out that adoptive parents also have different expectations about parenthood than natural fathers do. He contends, for example, that unlike natural fathers, who often prefer sons because they can carry on the family name, adoptive fathers more typically want daughters. Kirk notes that the role of adoptive parent is plagued by inconsistencies and ambiguities. People in the community often regard adoption, while perfectly acceptable in the abstract, as an inferior and slightly stigmatizing alternative to the enchantment of natural parenthood; such attitudes are not uncommonly held by adoptive parents themselves.

Nevertheless, foster parents are probably less likely to be problem parents than natural progenitors are, since they are a selective group and ordinarily do not have more children than they want. Note, however, that adoptive standards, such as those set by the Child Welfare League of America, tend to be relaxed for "hard-to-place" children (Woods and Lancaster, 1962). Almost 90 percent of all adopted children are white, but 60 percent of all illegitimate babies are colored. Negro middle-class couples are surprisingly reluctant to adopt Negro children. We could very well give more thought to changing legislation to allow the placement of children in one-parent homes.

There are many reasons why the woman in a fatherless home may be expected to have greater than average difficulties in her mothering role: loneliness, loss of self-esteem, problems in finding father substitutes, the retention of a negative image of father, problems in controlling the children and handling sex training, the likelihood that she will show greater anxiety in critical situations, the possibility that she will "overabsorb" her children and that she will have to go to work if she was not already working. But we have seen that many women are capable of exceptional compensatory effort. Fatherlessness can be a critical problem, but almost all communities provide the solo mother with means to maintain a healthy image of both father and the masculine role. If we have special difficulties in the United States in this regard—and there is no way to be sure that our problems are unusual—it is not because of a high rate of fatherlessness, but because the masculine style is now in the process of extraordinary change.

PART THREE

The Breadwinner

CHAPTER XI

The Breadwinner: Work and Fatherhood

The breadwinner task is unquestionably father's key responsibility in the United States. It lies at the core of our ideology of fatherhood, fuzzy as that may be. It constitutes the effort that most thoroughly satisfies the man's family obligation: he is the instrumental leader of the household primarily because he is accountable for its economic well-being. The father's activity as breadwinner has long been established as the chief embodiment of his masculinity; his success in this role is the cornerstone of his self-esteem. In a money economy, the more money father makes the greater his family potential, and economic largesse thus provides the basis for the expansiveness of the man's domestic role.

Both sexes acknowledge this fact. In a study of women, Helena Lopata (1965) reported that 64 percent considered the breadwinner role to be the father's most important function; husbanding and child rearing ranked a poor second and third. The overwhelming majority of adolescent boys agree that men must earn an adequate living if they are to receive love and respect from their families, while an unrealistically large number of both boys and girls expect that, when they marry, the wife will remain unemployed or will work for only a short period of time (Dunn, 1960; Christensen, 1961a). The corollary to such emphasis on the male breadwinner role is suspicion of women who work; this suspicion is reinforced by an occupational structure that penalizes women when they do work.

Margaret Mead (1953), for example, argues that the male role of provider has persisted throughout history, only temporarily disrupted by very special circumstances; she infers that the role is natural, good, and inevitable. In taking this position, she seems to suffer a failure of vision. She suggests that an economic system in which each family has its own budget based on the work or earning power of the male provider is a standard component of any humane society and that if the state or some other agency undermines the family budget system, we shall become like ants or bees and lose our birthright as human beings. This is sophisticated, if rather unique, conservatism indeed. Mead asserts that men must be the economic caretakers of the family, but she also prefers to minimize the differences between men and women. Thus she poses a dilemma, one "we must learn to resolve." In her defense, it should be said that the gross inconsistencies we often find in this area of study reflect the underdeveloped state of social theory as it applies to family life in general and parenting in particular; we have an urge to retain the family as we have always known it, but we would like to overhaul it too.

In traditional societies, the structure of work and domestic activities are bound together; each is unambiguously an extension of the other. In modern social science we recognize that the two activities are related to one another, but in both our business and our psychological accounting we assign them separate spheres. Economists study work, familists study the family, and scholars in the two camps rarely read each other's publications. An exception occurs with regard to the employment of women; when women work most students are alerted at once to the unavoidable family implications (Caplow, 1954). Only the work of men is isolable from domestic matters, although its relevance may become fairly prominent in the early stages of marriage and at retirement. Another period of relatively conspicuous interdependence occurs when there is a severe depression; then the relationship between work and family life becomes too obvious to ignore (Rapoport and Rapoport, 1965).

The man's work life and his domestic life can be regarded as two aspects of the same role set. His employment is both a role in the occupational system and a representative role in the kinship system, since he works not only for his "firm" but also for his family, and his family responsibility is discharged primarily by doing well on the job (Parsons, 1954). The man's work influences the daily habits of members of his family both directly and indirectly. The social life of children is affected by the way their father's behavior at home is directly responsive to the demands of his job, and, in a larger sense, by the total orientation of the man's life to his work career, which was usually molded long before he had children or was even married. Every occupation has a prevailing order and style, although some are more unusual and problematic than others—the culturally charged atmospheres of preachers and policemen come to mind. Small businessmen, like small farmers, often feel justified in asking for help from members of the family or may simply assign work to them as if they were employees.

There are also correlates of occupational status, in particular the pattern of acquaintances made possible by the father's job. Men typically adjust their lives to the patterned behavior of their colleagues; work associates become significant figures in the father's life and constitute a reference group from which people in other lines of work are relatively isolated. The father's income and the life style of his colleagues provide a basis for his sense of family responsibility, or lack of it in some cases. Neither the wages nor the work associates of men (especially of Negroes) in the lower socioeconomic levels contributes to a pattern of family concern, and it is not surprising that they are not very "responsible" as fathers (Olsen, 1960). Thus, occupation not only determines income, it conditions its use.

Family wealth based on the father's work also establishes certain functional limitations to fathering. There are many things a poor father cannot do for and with his children that are well within the reach of wealthy fathers. Still another dimension of the father's occupation is the time it allows for fathering, and wages are poorly correlated with hours. Upper-middle-class occupations, for example, usually provide favorable income, but limited time. Nor are the longer hours that the professional man gives to his work dictated by the formal requirements of the job; they are self-imposed because of the work discipline the man exacts of himself. Professional work can be defined in various ways, but one measure is the extent to which it requires continuous reflection by the man concerning his own performance; another is the extent to which, once some level of self-discovered competence is reached, new goals come into view requiring still further effort. If such work is taken seriously, perhaps just the least bit seriously, it drains energy from family life and parental concerns and the man's work becomes his passion. Arnold Green (1946) has argued, however, that the middle-class father's concern for social status leads to ambivalence toward his children independent of any compulsion to improve his job competence.

Nevertheless, work as a positive area of personal commitment declines in importance as one descends the status hierarchy because the nature of the job loses its intrinsic appeal (Rapoport and Rapoport, 1965). Thus, work at the lower socioeconomic levels entails limitations in income and life style, but relatively more time and independence for family affairs. Robert Dubin (1956) has suggested that mechanization in the factory system robbed the manual worker of the strong sense of ego involvement that craftsmen once had and has led workers to develop a greater interest in domestic activities. Although this observation has never been proved, it is at least possible that reduction of the workweek along with the rationalization of labor may have had a domesticating effect upon fathers. The contemporary trend toward the professionalization of work would seem to exert pressure in the opposite direction.

Father can spend leisure moments with his children in various ways. Some of this time is routine, as when father customarily spends fifteen minutes or so with the children just before they go to bed; some of it is catch-as-catch-can, as when father happens to have a few extra moments in the morning and spends it with the children. We can also distinguish between the small segments of time father occasionally spends with his children and the larger blocks of time he may devote to them on weekends or vacations. It appears that fathers in the less demanding occupations actually have more time in the course of an ordinary week to spend with their children; men in lines of work requiring greater commitment are likely to postpone relations with their children until larger blocks of time are available, time that they can set aside specifically for the family. But a problem is posed by this practice; fathers who hope to make up for lost time with their children are often disappointed, primarily because they have not established rapport with them in the daily, routine relationships. Such fathers tend to expect too much of these occasional spurts of paternity and show frustration if the children fail to appreciate their efforts. Even if a rather elaborate event should be a great success, a week on the ski slopes perhaps, father may still have regrets and guilt feelings unless the day-to-day relations are kept up.

Not much is known about the direct effect of occupational styles on fatherhood. James Bossard (1953) found that children have negative reactions to their father's work depending on the clothes he must wear, the products he handles, and the extent to which it keeps him away from home, but that the nature of the work itself is usually beside the point. In theory it would seem that men who are treated with dignity at work will tend to treat their families with dignity. The behavior of father at home may compensate for frustrations at the office, just as neglect of his family may be justified by success at work. Leonard Pearlin and Melvin Kohn (1966) found that fathers' parental values are strikingly related to their occupational circumstances. For example, fathers who are closely supervised in their work tend to value obedience in their children more than those who are given greater autonomy; the latter stress self-control.

But truly systematic information about the influence of most occupations upon fatherhood is lacking. In place of carefully collected data, we are surrounded by folklore; we have all heard of the rebellious preacher's son and the trials of the farmer's daughter, and we can guess at the special difficulties faced by the children of undertakers, traveling salesmen, and butchers. The film "Cheaper By the Dozen" caricatured an industrial time-study expert who organized his family according to professional prescriptions he had devised for the office. Conceivably, there are soldiers who run their families like platoons, computer technicians who program their families as they do machines, and boxers who use physical violence at home (Rapoport and Rapoport, 1965). But no coherent body of knowledge is available for these occupations, let alone the countless other run-of-the-mill jobs.

Father's work is significant primarily because it is the basis for the family's social status and, therefore, its style of life. An enormous body of sociological literature corroborates this observation, which is demonstrated daily in our personal experience. Although father's occupation is not the only source of the family's wealth, for most families it is the most important source. It establishes the family budget for basic household items and the amount of discretionary income available to the family. Nor is this the case only in "capitalistic" societies; the existence of some kind of family budget keyed to the income or productiveness of father's work is found in virtually all societies.

Fatherhood and Work Styles

Since the variety of work men engage in has become so great, we can only hope to discover the influence of the most general kinds of employment upon fathering. Men who work primarily with things, for example, seem to place a high value on obedience in children but are not disposed to value self-control very highly; men who work mainly with ideas tend to stress self-control and to devalue obedience; men whose work consists essentially of dealing with people fall somewhere in-between (Pearlin and Kohn, 1966). An explanation of this pattern is apparent enough: the manipulation of ideas is necessarily under the direct control of the individual, while the manipulation of things is more easily standardized and regulated by others. Handling people is a much more ambiguous task. Thus the nature of the father's work may condition his attitude toward a significant aspect of child rearing.

A useful distinction might also be made between fathers who perform rather complete, self-integrated tasks and those who engage in highly segmented, assembly-line work. Urie Bronfenbrenner (1958) has suggested that the personality characteristics of children have some correlation with the degree to which their fathers can see the outcome of their work, judge its quality, and therefore, in some way, judge themselves. In some occupations, and perhaps more generally in certain societies or historical eras, the self-esteem of each man has been a function of his craftsmanship, and the relationship between the man's work and his identity is passed on from father to son, generation after generation. Evidence in support of this approach is much too limited to warrant generalizations for most occupations, however.

The distinction between entrepreneurial and bureaucratic occupations has been used with somewhat greater success. Daniel Miller and Guy Swanson (1958) contend that the family breadwinner in entrepreneurial families is engaged in a type of work that involves risk taking and he therefore tends to promote innovative and individualistic values within his family. (Miller and Swanson studied mothers, however, not fathers.) Children in such families are encouraged to be rational, to exercise self-control, to develop self-reliance, and to assume an "active, manipulative stance toward their environment." It is implied that the father not only verbally favors such an approach to life, but in subtle ways is also likely to act it out in the presence of his wife and children, who therefore come to regard it as "the way."

The breadwinner in bureaucratic families, on the other hand, engages in work that involves relatively little risk; he therefore tends to avoid speculative ventures, and his family becomes oriented to security and the standards of welfare that bureaucracy provides. Children in such families are encouraged to be accommodative rather than competitive in response to challenging situations and are allowed to be spontaneous rather than calculating in expressing their impulses.

Strong support for the Miller-Swanson theory has not been forthcoming, but there is some evidence in its favor. Upholding the proposition that entrepreneurial and bureaucratic families are indeed different in child rearing and family practices, Martin Gold and Carol Slater (1958) found that women in the former have less influence in making family decisions, place a higher value on motherhood, and prefer larger families than women in bureaucratic families. Curiously, the entrepreneurial mothers appear to be more traditional, despite the innovative qualities attributed to their husbands.

An intriguing similarity exists between Miller and Swanson's entrepreneurial-bureaucratic distinction and one used by Herbert Barry, Irvin Child, and Margaret Bacon (1959) in a series of cross-cultural studies. The latter claim that pastoral and agricultural societies are organized to inhibit inventive and individualistic tendencies; in such societies faithful adherence to routine usually provides the best assurance of a stable food supply, and the fathers are aware of this. Therefore a fear of innovation is engendered and child training reflects an emphasis upon conformity and obedience. In hunting and fishing societies, on the other hand, individual inventiveness is at a premium. Innovation is less dangerous and often quite useful, so initiative and self-reliance are more likely to be encouraged in childhood training. One is left with the impression that, with the rise of industrialism on an advanced agricultural base, especially when industrialism is accompanied by entrepreneurial "capitalism," fathering patterns emerge that are similar in certain respects to those found in hunting and fishing societies. But as large corporations are formed and the welfare state grows, fathering tends to become more like that in pastoral and agricultural societies.

Perhaps we should point out, however, that the growth of the modern bureaucratic nation is a social form *sui generis,* and that fathering thus takes absolutely new forms despite the appearance of similarities to earlier ones. One of the major new developments stems from the fact that the modern nuclear family maintains fewer contacts with its larger circle of kinsmen (as we discussed in Chapter III). This seems to be true of entrepreneurial (Kosa, Rachiele, and Schommer, 1960) as well as bureaucratic families, and it is occurring in countries with even stronger historical kinship ties than our own. Ezra Vogel (1963), for example, argues that in Japan the emergence of large-scale business and government bureaucracy has created a new basis for the economic and social security of the salaried middle classes. Japanese industrial organization has incorporated a paternalistic feature: appointment to a salaried position is tantamount to the acquisition of tenure in the firm. Men working for salaries enjoy a regular income, security, and substantial leisure time. Their earnings and fringe benefits rise sharply with the length of their service, and, except for extreme incompetence or misbehavior, dismissal is very unlikely. The primary source of group membership and identification for the salaried man has shifted to the firm, and the claims of his kin group no longer have the force of duty or the authority of social and economic power.

In the modern industrial society with its general emphasis upon security through bureaucratic loyalty the entrepreneurial-bureaucratic distinction is tenuous. The truly entrepreneurial family has become an anomaly, but the value attached to innovation has gained favor even as bureaucracies have expanded. In studies by Melvin Kohn (1959, 1963), differences between entrepreneurial and bureaucratic families such as those suggested by Miller and Swanson were not found. As a result, and in the light of the differences that his study did point up, Kohn argues that there is greater significance and utility in distinguishing between middle- and working-class occupations—broadly speaking, between white-collar and blue-collar work—whose differential effects upon the behavior of parents are striking.

Kohn, like Miller and Swanson, contends that the pattern of child rearing found in most homes is implicitly oriented toward the type of future the children will have, a future comparable to that of the parents' current social position. David Aberle and Kaspar Naegele (1952), for example, observed that fathers in a middle-class suburb evaluated their children's behavior in terms of the aggressiveness and competitiveness expected in their own occupational world, despite their explicit contention that the two spheres should be kept quite distinct. Thus, fathers regard the characteristics essential to their work as virtues, not simply means to occupational goals. In Italy, for example, where it is hardly likely that daughters will have occupational careers comparable to their fathers', the same relationship exists between the fathers' occupational experiences and the values they encourage for their daughters and for their sons (Pearlin and Kohn, 1966). Thus, occupational experiences not only contribute to the father's view of his occupational world, but to his view of the social world in general.

From this basic premise Kohn argues that childhood experiences in the middle and working classes are different because the children's futures in the work world are different; values conditioned by life in the two classes produce distinctive child-rearing practices and usually result in successful adaptations to different ways of life. Kohn's point of view assumes only minimal social mobility; if parental roles are competently performed, children will grow up to take their parents' places, reenacting the status of their elders in the community and preserving equilibrium in the larger society.

Ephraim Mizruchi's (1964) data on the middle and higher classes suggest that parents in both classes tend to view success in terms of the intrinsic qualities of the job along with its general status in the community. They are willing to take some risks in order to achieve impressive results and are concerned with the nature of the task and its challenge to their abilities. Moreover, since minimal levels of respectability and material success can usually be taken for granted, middle-class parents can be more supportive of their children than working-class parents, who are anxious about cleanliness, neatness, and obedience (Kohn and Carroll, 1960).

Thus, middle-class children are more likely to become prepared for work requiring high levels of self-discipline, and Kohn argues that their parents place a high value on self-direction when the children are young. It is of primary importance to these parents that the child be able to decide for himself how to act and that he have personal resources to implement his decisions. Working-class parents, on the other hand, stress conformity to external standards and are themselves quite willing to give obedience, obedience to "authority," in return for security and respectability; this is especially common among the fathers (Martin and Clark, 1966). Nor is this pattern peculiarly American; the concern for obedience among the American working classes is even more apparent in the values of the Italian working classes (Pearlin and Kohn, 1966).

Kohn contends that the working-class parent is likely to respond to the immediate consequences of his child's misbehavior, while the middle-class parent often makes allowances for the child's intentions, judging the case in terms of a broader, more future-oriented perspective. Middle-class parents are more alert to the long-range effects of their child-rearing efforts and are also closer students of the relationship between the work they do and the kinds of training needed by their children (Oeser and Hammond, 1954). This may be one reason why upper-middle-class couples have a more favorable outlook on life after their children are grown (Deutscher, 1964); they have a greater sense of accomplishment with regard to the rearing of their children.

But the extent to which middle-class parents are conscious of the long-range effects of their daily child-rearing efforts remains open to debate. Cora Martin and Alexander Clark (1966) found that most parents, even those in the middle classes, think less about the future in dealings with their children than we have suggested thus far. They tend to judge their children's behavior primarily in terms of its suitability to the immediate situation. Most parents, they contend, want ten-year-olds to act like ten-year-olds and will be quite satisfied if they do; the future will have to take care of itself. Nevertheless, the definition of ten-year-old behavior is different in the middle classes than it is in the working classes.

According to Kohn and Carroll (1960), working-class fathers are much less likely than middle-class fathers to see child rearing as part of their parental duties. The working-class father is not very sensitive to the state of his children's "happiness," and he rarely encourages "curiosity." In fact, middle-class mothers want their husbands to be as supportive as themselves, and the men usually share their wives' point of view. Differences between middle- and working-class fathers in this connection are substantially larger than differences between mothers in the two classes (Bowerman and Elder, 1964).

It is possible, of course, that the psychological distance between parents in the lower classes is transmitted from one generation to the next through very general processes of social learning and may not be, strictly speaking, a function of the father's occupation. Psychosocial dynamics in the routine of lower-class life contribute to the preservation of such patterns. For example, Gerald Handel and Lee Rainwater (1961) contend that the basic style of interpersonal relations within the lower-class family conditions the child to see the world as unloving and unpredictable. His ability to communicate and to make common cause with others is therefore limited, often resulting in emotional isolation. Since in many cases the lower-class girl's father has not been an integrated part of the household during her childhood, she does not develop the early psychic basis for a close relationship with a man that might be transferred to her husband (Rainwater, 1964). Yet such daughters tend to marry earlier than women whose fathers enjoy higher status, in part because the establishment of a new family is an attractive refuge from just this pattern of "socialized loneliness."

It should be added that the sexes in the lower classes differ in their chances of achieving "success" because of differences in the meaning of success for adult men and women. Girls typically can anticipate a future of marriage and motherhood, however imperfect, and a great many of them will meet some acceptable criterion of success, regardless of the hardships they may encounter. For lower-class boys, on the other hand, aspirations for marriage and fatherhood are not enough: indeed, lower-class boys do not look forward to such roles, as we have seen. In the eyes of society, a good job and adequate income are the prime masculine objectives. Consequently boys in the lower strata, Negro boys in particular, face barriers to the achievement of their assigned goals that are almost insurmountable compared to those confronting girls (Palmore and Hammond, 1964).

Job aspirations of lower-class boys are not very high, but the boys do aspire to a higher level than that reached by their fathers as a rule (Rosen, 1956; Empey, 1956; Strodtbeck, 1958). The lower the ranking of the father's job, the greater the discrepancy between his job and the one aspired to by his son. As a result, the lower-class boy often strives for an occupational level beyond his reach. Moreover, the young working-class male, upon entering the labor market, receives little financial assistance from his father, less than either men or women in the middle classes, and less than women in the lower classes. It is paradoxical, of course, that the neediest parents and their children are least likely to be assisted by grandparents (Beyrer and Tevald, 1956), and once again the lower-class father is the one who is most often forced to manage without parental support (Adams, 1964).

Perhaps differences in parental behavior between the social classes have been narrowing somewhat over the past quarter of a century, as Urie Bronfenbrenner suggested in 1958, but the class system itself and the role of father within it have by no means disappeared, nor do they show any signs of disintegration. Mirra Komarovsky (1964) contends that the entry of skilled and semi-skilled workers into the middle classes through higher income has been *un*accompanied by the adoption of middle-class manners and tastes. The working-class style of life—its values, attitudes, and institutions—remains in many respects distinct. And of course it is still difficult for middle-class child-rearing strategies to be implemented by parents who lack middle-class resources.

Family Crises and Social Class

The term "family crisis" is necessarily broad; it refers to a great range of possible troubles, some rather trivial, others potentially disastrous. It appears that crisis proneness increases as the family's socioeconomic position declines, that is, as father's occupation becomes more precarious and his earning power drops below the level needed to cover the most common family emergencies. There is more frequent family disorganization in the lower social classes because of poverty and its consequences: exploitation, callousness, brutalization, and so on (Hobart, 1963). The middle classes are spared much of this.

Although unemployment may hit people who have certain personality traits more often than others, it is most closely correlated with job specialties; men with limited skills are the ones most frequently laid off, furloughed, or simply "out looking for work." Unemployment obviously poses a problem for the married man's family and possibly a crisis. Several studies during the depression of the 1930s concluded that when father is out of work he experiences a substantial loss of respect and authority as head of the family *only* if poor marital adjustment preceded the discharge; unemployment by itself does not undermine father's position (Angell, 1936; Cavan and Ranck, 1938; Komarovsky, 1940). It also seems likely that loss of a job in the lower classes is less critical than it is in the middle classes, at least partly because it is so common, which is all the more true during a depression.

Families in the lower classes have more than their share of troubles, but if crises are approached from a strictly subjective point of view any image of a higher serenity in the middle classes must be dispelled. According to Earl Koos (1950), middle-class families actually recognize more family crises in their lives than lower-class families do, primarily because they are more alert to situations that require quick remedial action. Koos stresses the family's perception of the crisis situation and the fact that middle-class families are quicker to realize that they are undergoing unusual strain. The quality of marital adjustment, for example, is probably less conspicuous in the lower classes because couples face so many critical economic problems that divert attention from their marriages. In the middle classes marital troubles are likely to be recognized as such; hence there is a greater chance that steps will be taken to resolve them.

Because middle-class couples have more self-ascribed crises, they are more likely to resolve them. They respond to critical situations more promptly and effectively, often with some added benefit. The crisis is not something from which they merely recover; it is a springboard to better things. The lower classes are at a disadvantage because they are prone to become inured to the crises in their lives, thus failing to improve and adapt. A key to this pattern is the father's benumbed comprehension of alternative family possibilities; the very training, especially college training, that would have prepared him for higher-status work roles would probably have given him greater insight into his family problems.

The Educational Factor

A strong case might be made for the proposition that the differences between middle- and working-class fathering are caused not so much by the father's work as by his formal education. Yet Melvin Kohn (1963) argues that the latter constitutes only one aspect of the life style of the different social classes; it is important to be sure, he maintains, but parental behavior is deeply rooted in the more encompassing life conditions of status groups. Pearlin and Kohn (1966) found that among men in similar occupations, educational achievement was weakly and inconsistently related to parental values. Thus, they contend that occupation rather than education accounts for most of the major differences in fathers' values.

Possibly so. But increasingly the various work specialties men follow are entered only after years of educational preparation; young children are given a common basic training, and as they grow older the things they study are progressively differentiated. Courses taken in the later stages of education become the basis for each individual's career and may be as important as his occupational milieu or that of his parents in determining the fathering style that he subsequently enacts. Of course, the boy's formal education takes little account of his future roles as a father. An enormous imbalance exists between facilities for training men to become workers and those for training them to become fathers. Since formal education has very little to say or teach about parenting, its influence may inevitably be imperceptible (Brim, 1962).

Nevertheless, there does seem to be a general correlation

between the amount of education parents have received and their expectations for their children. Persons with greater educational attainment hold higher hopes for their children and such parents are more likely to seek escape from the parental role if their children cannot be expected to fulfill their expectations. The more educated the father, for example, the more disappointed he will be if he has a retarded child and the less interest he will show in the child (Downey, 1963). The more education parents have, the sooner they are likely to place a subnormal child in an institution, provided a suitable one is available. A general principle seems to apply: The higher the level of educational achievement of parents, the more discontented they will be with the responsibility for rearing children of limited educability.

Yet it seems likely that the more education parents have, the greater their understanding of children will be. Parents with advanced formal training tend to have greater insight into the reasons for their children's behavior and are more tolerant of immaturity and childishness. One study concluded that the higher the socioeconomic level of the mother, the more likely she will be to feel that the sexual problems of her children are comprehensible and that they can be easily handled (Kantor, Glidewell, *et al.*, 1958). Among the poor, it is usually not even considered appropriate for parents to acknowledge a need for sex education for their children (Rainwater, 1964). These contrasting orientations seem to be based more on the knowledgeability of parents than on occupational considerations per se.

Upper-middle-class parents devote more time to teaching things to their children in a number of different ways. We may expect instruction to vary in terms of type of activity, of course, since lower-class parents know more about some things than middle-class parents do, but the "urge to teach" and to see learning occur are stronger among the more educated. An interesting comparison of parent-child interaction was made at two beaches, one frequented by upper-middle-class families and the other by stable working-class families. The study revealed that parents spent more time teaching their children to swim at the upper-middle-class beach; parents at the other beach used relatively more of their time playing with the children and commanding obedience, or pleading for it (Smart, 1964).

One must acknowledge, however, that in a contest between the man's educational attainment, his occupation, and his family experiences in childhood, the latter is most likely to be the primary determinant of his adaptation to fathering. We are confronted with a complicated intergenerational effect: the father's education is the basis for his occupation and that career provides the major institutional setting for the family life he leads, which in turn is the primary basis for his son's orientations to fathering, work, and family life. As the boy matures, his educational and occupational accomplishments will reflect his childhood family experience; these accomplishments constitute the major social capital for his adult family life, which then becomes the primary basis for *his* son's paternal orientation.

The Farmer as Father

A few words about the farm father are in order, though he is a fading image in American life. Much has been written on the effect of rural life on the family, but very little on the specific influence of farm work on fatherhood. Most men in the world are still peasants who live in villages and are engaged in subsistence farming; their family life has been studied rather extensively. As fathers, they appear to be very much alike the world over. But the American farmer is no peasant—he never has been—even though conditions in rural areas have remained until recent times somewhat like those that sustain patriarchal practices in peasant societies.

The rural American father is usually pictured as a rather stern authority in his household, a man who keeps his distance in relationships with both his wife and the children. Traditional paternal values once may have been useful in rural areas, but Robert Blood and Donald Wolfe (1960) argue that "tradition" is an ineffective basis for decision making in the modern family, even in rural areas. They claim that the farm husband no longer has greater conjugal power than the average American male. City-family practices and values have undoubtedly had time to penetrate rural areas in the United States, and farming fathers are now often subject to these new social pressures.

Nevertheless, the rural population lags behind in child-rearing techniques and generally adheres to less flexible and less permissive practices (Bronfenbrenner, 1958); for example, urban teen-agers tend to be more egalitarian about husband-wife roles in marriage than rural adolescents are (Dunn, 1960). James Coleman (1962) found rural and small-town youth more likely to conform to parental wishes than students living in metropolitan areas, who are relatively susceptible to the commands of the peer group.

Farm fathers are not all alike, of course, but the main drawback in distinguishing between rural and urban life is not *rural* diversity; an even bigger problem is the heterogeneity of work in the city, along with the fact that farm life is no longer the prototype for family life in America. The farm family now has access to a style of life very much like that of most city families, and farming itself has become a thing apart; it does not engulf the family and determine its daily routines as it once did, except in the case of people on poor, small-family farms (Beers, 1937). On prosperous farms mother and the children can come and go just as they do in town, responding to the very same pressures (including those from television commercials).

For some time it has been the destiny of many children born in the country to abandon agriculture (or simply to ignore it) in favor of city life, and perhaps farm fathers have gradually adjusted to the change. But as a rule they still want their sons to remain on the farm and, unlike their wives, are in no hurry to prepare their sons for life in the city. In a swiftly changing environment, the farm father becomes somewhat less helpful in training his son for farm life itself, because so much of his lore must become obsolete. When farm children move to the city, father's ways are even less useful as a guide to life. In particular, the farm father is not a strong influence for educational achievement; for generations American farmers have cultivated a suspicion of formal schooling, and it is only recently that they have accepted the word of professors on agricultural matters. Even today the more engrossed the family is in farming, the lower the academic performance and aspiration level of its children. When they abandon farming, farm boys follow different occupational patterns from city boys, and those who could undoubtedly make the grade in college are much less likely to plan to enter college than boys of comparable ability in urban areas (Sewell, 1964).

For those boys from rural areas who do find success at school, mother is usually the influential parent; it would appear that she has been more responsive to changing opportunity structures than father and is more realistic in her judgment of future possibilities for her children. If the American mother has been more perceptive in this connection than mothers in most other countries, which is a plausible generalization, it is probably because women in America have always had a relatively greater role to play in planning for their children; they have had better opportunities for mobility and generally higher status vis-à-vis the men in their lives. The mother's disillusionment with farm life, or her attraction to other life styles, conditions the way she will handle academic striving in her children. Indirect evidence of this is given in a study by Prodipto Roy (1961): he found that when city mothers work away from home their children's school achievement may be adversely affected, but when rural mothers are employed, their children usually do even better in school.

Lee Burchinal (1960b) found that fathers on farms were much less frequently involved in their daughters' occupational plans than fathers in towns and cities were, although farm mothers rallied on this issue just as much as urban mothers. By contrast with fathers on the farm, city fathers have considerably more rapport with daughters during their early years. As a result, urban fathers may now be even more important than mothers for the development of their daughters' verbal abilities, and perhaps for general cognitive development as well (Bing, 1963). The modern father can make a major contribution to the educability of his daughter by *not* exaggerating the traditional female roles, especially during the adolescent years when girls are so prone to retrench the intellectual ambitions they had earlier acquired. Fathers in the city are either more flexible in relations with their daughters or their inflexibility is rather easily neutralized by other environmental forces.

The father's occupational achievement has become the cornerstone for his success both as a father and as a man. Men adjust their life styles to their employment, and they both consciously and unconsciously prepare their children to do the same general type of work upon which they must depend. Since fathers in the lower classes are confronted with relatively frequent job crises, they are likely to have recurrent family crises.

Whether the man's occupation or his education is more important in determining his fathering style remains a moot point, but increasingly the various formal educational programs that boys follow are the basis for the occupational differences among them. As the boy matures, his educational accomplishments reflect his childhood family experiences and constitute the primary "economic capital" for his adult family life, which then becomes the basis for his own son's paternal orientation. The family can help the child to do well in school, but once he shows educational promise there are countless careers he can pursue that are unlike his father's. In a former time, differences in fathering from one generation to the next were limited by the fact that the kinds of work men could do were limited. Now the variety of work is almost limitless and fathers are correspondingly more variable. Nevertheless, similarities among fathers are based increasingly upon the underlying similarities in their formal education.

CHAPTER XII

Transformation of the Breadwinner

Fatherhood is an extremely conservative institution, but for some time the role and function of the male breadwinner has been undergoing a significant transformation in America, a corollary of two sweeping trends: the rise of the welfare state, and the increasing employment of women away from home.

In many ways, welfare legislation has had the effect of undermining or simply by-passing the family budget. Traditionally, consumers' goods and services have been allocated in accordance with expenditures from the family purse, but welfare programs have established a variety of procedures that operate independently of domestic funds. Public assistance is directed in particular to the family whose breadwinner is inadequate, but a number of social programs have emerged that make the adequacy of the male figure irrelevant. The public school system, for example, was not designed to help poor families alone, but to provide services to all families, independent of their ability to pay.

Although the father's income still usually constitutes the family's basic resource in America, in many cases the wife now earns approximately half of the family income. In fact, there are now many instances in which she earns more than half.

Since 1960, two-income families have become more numerous than those with only one breadwinner, and the trend continues. Women have always worked, of course, but in earlier times employment away from home was largely, and certainly ideologically, a male function.

Both the increase in female employment and the rise of the welfare state have occurred in response to general changes in industrial-urban conditions, and they have inevitably contributed to a reassessment of the father's breadwinner role. Strangely, however, this reassessment is rarely undertaken in a very self-conscious manner. Lack of both public and professional concern for the impact of social trends upon fatherhood seems to be but another indication of the low saliency of the role of father in social theory and reform strategy.

Female Ambivalence

Today wives and mothers work away from home more than in the past, at least in part because they used to be able to earn money even while they were at home; now that is rarely possible (Rollins, 1963). The opportunity structure has changed, which is part of a trend toward the realignment and lessening of differences between male and female roles. Fluctuations in social attitudes toward working women in America have been traced from alarmed opposition in the late nineteenth century to widespread acceptance of the employment of single and childless women today, accompanied by a continuing worry about working mothers (Smuts, 1959). Mildred Weil (1961) found that, in general, employed women in recent times feel that neighbors approve of their decision to work as long as their children are adequately cared for, and among many Americans there is no objection to mother working at all (Sussman, 1961). Nevertheless, some public disapproval is still directed toward the mother of young children and the mother who devotes her primary attention to a career; the feeling persists that a mother who creates a full life for herself outside the home may be cheating her children, if not her husband.

Implicit here is the retention of a "fire-department ideology of mothering": mother should be available at all times to meet any emergency. By contrast, working mothers in the Soviet Union, due in part to postwar labor shortages, are given rather enthusiastic as well as practical social support (Mace, 1961).

Although many American wives and mothers work, in the majority of cases both men and women still hold to some extent the idea that "woman's place is in the home" (Hurvitz, 1961; Gover, 1963). An unstated corollary of this belief is the notion that if women must work, they should not compete directly with men. Talcott Parsons, Robert Bales, *et al.* (1955) minimize the importance of the occupational role of the wife for this reason; they contend that men and women do different kinds of work and hence are not rivals for status. But the working wife continues to be perceived as a threat by many men in our society, especially those whose wives do not work (Axelson, 1963). When the wife works, marriage accommodation itself seems to prompt the husband's approval (Gianopulos and Mitchell, 1957). The male fear of competition from women is not based solely on myth. It has been shown that the income of men is indeed decreased as women compete with them in particular occupational markets (Hodge and Hodge, 1965), although it probably is not competition per se that decreases wages, but the impact of cultural definitions of female employment (Taeuber, Taeuber, and Cain, 1966).

Since housewife and mother roles are preferred for women, it is considered distasteful and perhaps dangerous to upgrade their occupational status. Apparently there is a fear of mass defections from maternal responsibility. Perhaps there is also a hidden suspicion that the woman's employment is symptomatic of a subversive attitude toward motherhood. Certainly when the man works it is not evidence that he rejects fatherhood, but rather proof of his paternal rectitude.

Working mothers do in fact desire and have fewer children than nonworking mothers (Nye, 1959; Siegel and Haas, 1963). But there is no evidence that they take employment because they are uninterested in or hostile toward their children. Curiously, if the family is small, employed mothers actually report more satisfaction from the maternal role than mothers who do not work (Nye, 1963). In a London study Pearl Jephcott, *et al.* (1962) found that the money married women earn is most often used to improve the *family's* standard of living, especially to provide advantages for the *children.* Many mothers may work to earn pocket money for themselves, but it would appear that the traditional mothering expectations channel the woman's earnings into buying things for her children or for the family (Glenn, 1959). Occupational commitment does not always or even usually come first in the lives of these women. It is more likely that the occupational role will be neglected than the maternal role (Peterson, 1961), although employers rarely complain that women neglect their work because they are mothers (Conyers, 1961). Working mothers may very well feel some guilt in connection with their employment and therefore try all the harder to be good mothers (Powell, 1961; Jephcott, *et al.,* 1962); no comparable evidence exists suggesting that they try harder to be model wives!

An inevitable consequence of our set of beliefs about the justification for female employment is the fact that women earn less money than men when they work. Women are frequently willing to work for peanuts because they do not conceive of themselves as breadwinners and are often grateful for the little they are paid. It enables marginal consumption under circumstances in which *things* are more highly valued than *time.* Viola Klein (1961) has pointed out that most married women in Britain feel that the money they earn is a means of increasing their standard of living, not just a means of keeping the wolf from the door. The desire for more consumer goods instead of more leisure time leads to both moonlighting and the working wife.

As they grow up, girls are methodically shunted into "women's work," that is, work considered to be of secondary economic importance. The pattern is not simply a product of hiring and firing practices, nor of our system of determining wages, but part of a much more general social process. During their childhood training girls experience a process of preparatory acquiescence to the system, or ambivalence about it: since they have only limited access to sources of information (not at school perhaps, but in their family and community "sheltering"), they undergo a trivialization of verbal ability, despite their superior scores on verbal aptitude tests. These conditions produce a lack of self-confidence about ability to work, which reduces the woman's participation in the most challenging career fields. Girls are progressively weeded out; those who are able scholars are not encouraged to fully exploit their talents and prefer to be remembered for their outstanding scholarship less and less as they grow older. The opposite is true for boys (McDill and Coleman, 1963). Jessie Bernard (1964) argues that academic women are overrepresented in low-prestige colleges and in colleges that emphasize different functions from those undertaken at the elite universities not because women are discriminated against, but because their life styles are more compatible with such institutions.

By the time adolescence is reached, young people are quite aware of sex distinctions in the ranking of occupations (McKee and Sheriffs, 1964). Although most American girls assume that they will work at some time during adult life, they do not think in terms of full-fledged careers. In Ralph Turner's (1964) sample of senior high-school girls, for example, very few even considered a choice between career and homemaker roles. The choice, on which they were evenly divided, was between having or not having a serious career *in addition to* the conventional domestic duties.

As might be expected, more adolescent girls than boys anticipate having a part-time job during their lifetime. Young girls expect to be employed more than boys expect them to be (Christensen, 1961a), but they also plan to abandon the labor force earlier than their male cohorts. A large percentage of girls expect to be "retired" within ten years after high-school graduation. They do not plan to graduate from college as often as boys and seem to look forward to it for other than professional training (Christensen, 1961a). They are less likely to take out loans for their education than young men are; both the girl and her father are hesitant to saddle some future husband with repayment of such an advance because women are not really considered to have a future in this regard (Rossi, 1964).

Confirming this pattern, Ralph Turner (1964) concluded

that the problem of women's ambition is inherently more complex than that of men. It is conditioned by a delicate interplay between family, work, and educational goals. Women maintain the hope that their material expectations will be fulfilled through their husbands' careers. Thus, educational ambition for women becomes a vehicle for the pursuit of intrinsic rewards rather than the means to a career in the breadwinner sense of the term. They are unlikely to become career-oriented unless they have been influenced by some unusually compelling set of conditions (Simpson and Simpson, 1961). Even the people they turn to for advice when making career decisions are different from those to whom noncareerists usually turn; the career-oriented rely less on parents and peers and more on professional models at school or in the community.

Because of our conceptions of femininity, the woman can win greater social approval and face less role conflict through full-time marriage and motherhood than through a career. An example is found in the realm of science; our common conception of the scientist and the housewife are worlds apart (Motz, 1961). The general role definitions and values associated with scientist and housewife in American society contradict rather than complement each other. As a result, it is difficult to imagine how a woman could be a scientist and a housewife at the same time. That is not to say that it cannot happen, but it is not easy.

In fact, the housewife role in the upper middle classes has itself taken on the coloration of a career. Here one finds an executive-wife pattern quite at odds with the standard career-girl pattern. Its duties include care for the home, husband, and children, but it also entails other obligations: to manage one's daily routine so that the husband can have a portion of the wife's time; to entertain his business associates and their mutual friends; and to participate in social and civic affairs (Whyte, 1956; Helfrich, 1961). This alternative, an attractive one it would seem, is open only to certain women of course, and it has no counterpart among the options available to men.

Thus, although working wives and mothers are increasing in both absolute and relative numbers, there is a lag in the development of social structures facilitating their recruitment for prestigious jobs. The performance of important work and mothering may be mutually exclusive, but, whether this is true or not, the assumption that it is assures that the two will not be mutually undertaken, except in rare circumstances.

The employment of women in the United States therefore remains essentially a supplementary economic activity, not in terms of its importance in our economic system but from the point of view of the typical family budget. Working women are essential to society, but their remuneration is nevertheless approximately half of that for male work. Both Negro and white women are in fact losing ground to men in terms of pay, or seem to be, although the process is less rapid among Negroes (Batchelder, 1964).

Female Employment and Domestic Power

Although the employment of mother leaves unchanged the amount of influence husband and wife exert over each other, the need to make family decisions remains as great or perhaps greater than ever before. Thus, a redistribution of authority in the direction of a more equalitarian balance usually occurs, and a larger percentage of the woman's wishes are likely to be honored (Blood, 1958; Hoffman and Lippit, 1960). Where traditional attitudes toward family authority prevailed before marriage, a shift toward less conservatism typically follows marriage in two-income families (Blood and Hamblin, 1958). The working mother often loses some power in the area of household decisions, but gains in the area of major financial transactions involving such things as the purchase of a car, a home, or insurance (Middleton and Putney, 1960; Nye and Hoffman, 1963).

If the wife has a better job than her husband, she will very likely have greater power—and apparently more marital difficulties, mainly because her occupational advantage violates the assumption that father will be the breadwinner (Roth and Peck, 1951; Gover, 1963). Conversely, the greater the discrepancy between the status of the husband's work and that of his wife's, the greater the husband's power will be (Heer, 1958) and the more likely it is that the wife will be employed only for the intrinsic value of her work. Nevertheless, the higher the social level of the family, the greater the husband's resentment of his wife working (Blood and Wolfe, 1960).

In the lower classes the employment of the wife at a higher wage than her husband is fairly common, and the lower the status of the husband's work, the more likely it is that the wife will seek employment (Rossman and Campbell, 1965). Certainly this is often true in Negro neighborhoods, where women earn more in comparison with their menfolk than white women do (Batchelder, 1964). Although this pattern may not contribute significantly to the marital difficulties of Negro and lower-class couples (since there are other important reasons for trouble), we do know that there are exaggerated interpersonal problems. In fact, dissatisfaction with the wife's work by either husband or wife is clearly related to poor marital adjustment, and Ivan Nye (1961) contends that both types of dissatisfaction occur more often in the lower classes.

There is no widely-acclaimed theory explaining why women should gain greater conjugal power when they work, but Lois Hoffman (1960) has suggested four plausible reasons.

First, the wife who works for wages can legitimately claim greater control over the money she has earned, and her control of income is used, implicitly or explicitly, to wield power in the family.

Second, a higher value is attached to the role of wage earner in society than to that of housewife, thus justifying greater power for the employed wife.

Third, an independent supply of money emboldens the influence of the working woman because she is less dependent on her husband and could, if necessary, support herself in the event of the dissolution of the marriage. In terms of the "least-interest theory," she has relatively less desire to maintain the relationship because of her independence, and thus she wields greater power. Similarly, David Heer (1963) has used an "alternative family resources theory of conjugal power" to explain the historical rise in the status of women. Women today, he contends, have more satisfying alternatives to an existing marriage than were available in the past because of the greater accessibility of jobs outside the home. In a similar way James Coleman (1966) would explain the decline in the rigidity of premarital sex codes. As women become less dependent upon men, there is less need for them to be inhibited with regard to sex.

And last, outside employment affords an opportunity for broader and more satisfying social interaction than the housewife role does. This in turn may lead to an increase in the wife's power due to the development of social skills that are useful in influencing her husband; the development of self-confidence; and more frequent interaction with men, which may result in the feeling that remarriage is feasible.

None of Hoffman's points, incidentally, should be interpreted to mean that the working wife's "personality" is altered. Personality differences do not seem to be produced in any systematic way by employment among women and hence do not account for any greater influence in decision making that working wives might have (Heer, 1963). It remains possible, of course, that women who work may have had distinctive personality patterns even before they started working, although strong evidence in support of this proposition has yet to be found.

It has also been suggested that the women who work tend to be less conventional than those who are confirmed housewives (Gover, 1963); hence, one could argue that any changes in domestic relations associated with female employment may be a product of unconventionality rather than employment per se. But this begs the question; it does not explain why orthodoxy among women is on the wane. Does the fact that more women are working have something to do with it?

The conditions that promote female employment may very well affect all women, whether they work or not. As in the case of the decline in rural-urban differences with the growth of cities, there is a "milieu effect" as more women work. The changing organization of work, for example, breeds greater heterogeneity in the population in terms of work skills and requires an upgrading of the average educational level. More women go to school longer, and it must be expected that some will advance farther than their boyfriends and husbands. One would expect wives who have completed more schooling than their husbands to have an edge in conjugal disputes, as research by Johannis and Rollins (1959) has verified; working mothers are indeed more likely than nonworking mothers to be better educated than their husbands (Rossman and Campbell, 1965). But regardless of which spouse has more education, the fact that men and women have similar educational influences in an industrial society contributes to greater equality in decision making.

The increased number of women who work may also change female conceptions of men's work, and perhaps even of masculinity itself. When women work beside men the traditional mystery that once imbued male skills is laid open to observation, and no doubt both the men and the skills lose some of their impressiveness in the process. Throughout history men have contrived to keep their work activities secret from women, and even today employed women are often kept ignorant of some aspects of the male work pattern. Nevertheless, many women have now had an opportunity to see men on the job, in offices and factories as well as in schools and clinics. They still act dutifully impressed in face-to-face relations with the boss, but in private they have been known to express skepticism. It is almost impossible to keep much from secretaries and nurses (although female public-school teachers often seem to be as naïve about the real workings of the masculine world as were housewives in times past). If the luster and magical endowment of male work activity depended on an exaggeration of the skill required, men have now been found out. One thing that working women must surely learn, however, is that men outrank them in promotability and earning potential. Perhaps this "mystery" is most gracefully resolved by acquiescing to the proposition that men belong to a wholly different status universe; women thus need compare themselves and their progress only with other women.

Before leaving the subject of the impact of the wife's employment upon family power patterns we should at least acknowledge that the wife's power does not automatically fluctuate in response to changes in her husband's social position; it is responsive to a rich and elusive combination of social and psychological factors (Middleton and Putney, 1960). As we have seen, the *pattern* in the exercise of power is what changes as more women work away from home.

Lois Hoffman (1960), for example, points out that the trend toward sexual equality in both conjugal power and generalized social status is not as simple as our most convenient formulations suggest. She found that, in general, the working wife has more power at home than the nonworking wife, but only if she is able to overcome a prevailing female tendency toward ambivalence about male dominance. If she remains ambivalent on this issue, her domestic power may even be reduced. Working wives who endorse male dominance gain status by working, and so do those who completely reject it; those who are caught in-between do not.

It is easy enough to explain why women who reject male dominance will have high status when they work, but why do working wives who endorse male dominance have greater power? Perhaps one explanation is that such women are likely to work only because of economic necessity. They are literally forced to work, and thus their husbands are not deserving of the deference due to men in general. Hoffman did indeed find that women who were working out of economic necessity wielded more family power than women working for other reasons; she did not find, however, that women who endorsed male dominance were more likely to cite economic necessity as the reason they worked.

Another question is also raised: Why do wives who are ambivalent about male dominance have relatively low status at home? A plausible explanation is that their ambivalence reflects a conflict between what they are led to believe should prevail in male-female power relations by their work milieu and that which they actually experience at home. They may be subject to stronger-than-average male controls at home and it is hard for them to reconcile this domestic pattern with the things they hear from the girls at the office. The fact that they are dominated by their husbands, yet work under circumstances that suggest they should not be, renders them ambivalent. If this theory is correct, ambivalence is not the cause of low conjugal status, but a product of that status in combination with the woman's position at work.

Work at Home and Away

Putting aside the still murky issue of conjugal power, we find a clearer picture concerning household work: The sharing of domestic tasks by husbands and wives is not only more frequent but usually a more congenial occurrence when both are employed. The husband assumes some of the domestic activities once performed by his wife, and he becomes involved in making decisions about things that could not claim his attention before (Blood, 1958; L. Hoffman, 1960; Weil, 1961; Siegel and Haas, 1963). The various home chores become less sharply defined as either man's or woman's work, and the husband's working philosophy shifts toward a greater acceptance of domestic equality between the spouses (Blood and Hamblin, 1958; Heer, 1958; Blood and Wolfe, 1960; Axelson, 1963). His conversion seems to be more pronounced when his wife works full time than when she works only part time (Geiken, 1964).

With the assumption of greater responsibilities by husbands when their wives work, our domestic ideology is quietly modified and a bloodless revolution occurs, unnoticed, in millions of homes. The new pattern is not lost on the children, however, who perceive it as the natural order of things. In the majority of cases both adolescent boys and girls now agree that the responsibility for homemaking should be shared if the wife works outside the home (Dunn, 1960), and elementary-school girls whose mothers work consider the sharing of household activities to be more appropriate than do girls whose mothers do not work (Hartley and Klein, 1959; Hartley, 1961). Boys become more dependent and obedient when the mother works, and the masculine side of the family reflects a generally diminished status (L. Hoffman, 1963). By contrast, daughters of working mothers are more independent, self-reliant, aggressive, dominant, and disobedient; in short, they act more like little boys (Siegel, Stolz, *et al.*, 1963). The grandparents also respond to this transition; when the mother works, the grandmother often assumes some of her duties, and the grandfather in turn undertakes some of the grandmother's previous roles (Nimkoff, 1962).

The majority of problems mentioned by employed women in connection with their work seems to involve lack of time (Clover, 1962). Clearly it becomes more difficult for the husband whose wife is employed to escape to his chair after a day's work. Not only is his wife now working away from home just as he is, but the hours of his own workday have been reduced by contrast with an earlier era. Should he turn to television within sight and hearing of his wife at work in the kitchen, she is reminded not only of his ease but of the many chores that need attention: picking up, baby tending, garbage emptying, and so on. Robert Blood (1965), with remarkable restraint, observes that "the existence of so much work to be done and of a man so potentially available to do it seems likely to create in the mind of the wife a tendency to invite her husband's participation in these chores."

Even the community routines of women are altered as they go out to work; they are not likely to do a variety of things in the neighborhood that nonworking wives customarily have time to do. Working mothers devote less of their free moments to chatting with neighbors, telephoning friends, visiting people, attending parties, playing cards, and watching television (Nye, 1958). Along with many others, Bruno Bettelheim (1964) contends that the role of full-time wife and mother is no longer absorbing or rewarding enough to fill out thirty or more years of a woman's life, unless she spends the first part of it in repeated pregnancies. As a consequence, unemployed women often overinvest in their husbands and children, especially their children, and they expect to be compensated for this emotional expenditure. Since the husband and children have no emotional need for mother that is commensurate with her need for them, they cannot meet her demands; the emotional conflict that results is destructive to the well-being of all.

The woman who does not work may in fact become over-involved in the management of her home and reflect a psychological need to keep the husband out of *her* sphere (Rossi, 1964). If she is able and alert, she must have some means of expressing her own self-worth, and father is thus subtly urged into a subordinate role as mother's helper—the father who does not know best. In such a case, tasks that earn relatively little recognition are delegated to father or the children, while mother reserves the more complex tasks for herself (Johannis, 1958). If, on the other hand, mother is employed and has a sense of fulfillment away from home, both she and her husband may find a very gratifying shift in the balance of feeling within the family. Needless to say, employment does not necessarily give the woman a sense of fulfillment, but then it cannot guarantee that for men either.

Resistance to sharing certain household tasks occurs even when the wife works, however. Although a democratizing trend is discernible, Everett Dyer (1958) found that some traditional work orientations remain in two-income families, especially the woman's role in housekeeping. One study concluded that equalitarianism has evolved quite conspicuously in the area of child rearing, decision making, and recreation roles, but is significantly less apparent with regard to certain household tasks and financial matters (Dyer and Urban, 1958). Kitchen work, housecleaning, and the persistent need for "straightening up" are chores only slowly adopted by men, even when their wives work.

Evidence of resistance has been found in other countries too. In Russia, for example, where sex equality in the form of nondiscriminatory work opportunities has been rather substantially realized, husbands nevertheless remain reluctant to share domestic duties (Mace and Mace, 1963). Even in Russia, however, a *trend* toward household collaboration is apparent. Raissa Khalfina (1964) contends that the Mace report is somewhat misleading and that Soviet husbands do give considerable assistance to their wives. In the evenings, they wheel baby buggies in public gardens, go shopping, take the older children for walks, and lend a hand with the household work.

Of course in the United States the availability of paid domestic help modifies the problem of housework, although working mothers rely only somewhat more on such assistance than nonworking mothers do (Siegel and Haas, 1963). Kathryn Powell (1961) found that more household tasks are performed by maids and other adults in the families of working mothers than in the families of full-time homemakers, but only when the oldest child is of preschool or elementary-school age. The sex of the children also seems to be a relevant factor. Alice Hubert and Joseph Britton (1957) found that fathers assume more responsibilities for household tasks if they have sons than if they have daughters. If the mother works and there is a daughter in the household, the latter may very well lighten the mother's load, thereby relieving father of much responsibility. As every mother knows, and as the contemporary father is learning, a son is more likely to add to the domestic burden than to assist in easing the load.

But even on this point available evidence suggests that children are more likely to participate in the management of the home when their mother works than they otherwise would (Siegel and Haas, 1963); this would seem to be true at least to some extent for both sons and daughters. Prodipto Roy (1961) found that both boys and girls of employed mothers did more housework, although only a little more. The social life of the children was just as full and they seemed to have about as much spare time as children of nonemployed mothers.

The Sexual Convergence

One frequently hears that the classic differences between masculinity and femininity are vanishing as men and women take on similar roles in the labor market. Robert Odenwald (1965) argues with shocked concern that the sexes are disappearing, that we are moving toward a one-sex society in which male and female distinctions will be only faintly discernible. The result, he contends, is the proliferation of serious social and personal ills, such as homosexuality, alcoholism, illegitimacy, and narcotics addiction. His alarm is contrived and his argument grossly overstated, although it is true that we must now live with greater sexual ambiguity, which heightens the perennial problems of personal identity and integrity.

More soberly, Robert Blood (1965) argues that the old asymmetry of male-dominated, female-serviced family life is being replaced by a new symmetry, one which is reflected in the contemporary relationships between males and females at almost all age levels. One recent study, for example, concluded that children between the ages of ten and thirteen are now mingling quite freely with members of the opposite sex; that there is less hostility between boys and girls at this age level, less withdrawal, stronger and more frequent romantic interests, and a greater range of friendships (Broderick and Fowler, 1961). Boys can now gain a kind of psychological rapport with girls that was virtually impossible in the past. Even dating and courtship codes have been modified with the decline of the double sex standard. After the stage of aggressive, although superficial, antigirlism in the elementary-school period, boys now undergo a rather sharp transformation and are less inclined to approach girls from a predatory point of view. The trend extends even to old age; although Ruth Cavan (1962) has argued that the elderly male must now learn to be a slightly masculinized grandmother, Bernice Neugarten and Karol Weinstein (1964) suggest that the newly emerging grandparent styles are neuter in gender.

The sexual convergence in America becomes all the more evident in cross-cultural comparisons. Japanese children, for example, perceive distinctive family roles for each parent, whereas American children find it difficult to make such sharp distinctions (Matsumoto and Smith, 1961). In particular, the Japanese father is pictured as a much more formidable authoritarian figure than the American father. On the other hand, the roles of mother and father in the Israeli Kibbutzim seem to be even less differentiated than in America (Kaffman, 1961).

The vectors for the two sexes are not of corresponding strength and direction in this sexual rapprochement, however, since it consists primarily of an expansion of the female role into formerly male territory. Masculinity has encompassed a much larger part of the total range of human activity throughout history, and therefore women have more room into which to expand. They have been the inhibited sex; freedom for them is a new thing, and only a handful of women have actually tasted the satisfactions that are available. A measure of femininity may be lost as women enter fields once closed to them, of course, but girls have less valuable qualities to give up than boys do, at least in terms of contemporary values. In fact, the rewards for femininity have always been minimal in a society steeped in centuries of patriarchy. Opportunities to claim rewards formerly reserved for men are still limited, but those made unequivocally available are quickly snapped up.

Men find no comparable inducements to seek the honors available to women. The pay-off is limited and punishment is the greater likelihood (although we don't rib "sissies" as much as we used to). A new tolerance is undoubtedly associated with the rise of the middle classes and the fact that most men in these strata establish their status through low energy, non-physical skills. (Men in the aristocratic and elite classes have long had access to effeminate manners.) But the issue is really academic; for boys, identification with the masculine role provides all the satisfaction most males could want. The most rewarding strategy for girls is to retain flexibility in order to claim whatever masculine prerogatives they may be permitted (Webb, 1963).

But more is at stake in the present transformation than the relative desirability of masculine and feminine traits. We have noted that the dominant feminine mode is expressiveness and the masculine mode, instrumentalism. In terms of cultural vitality, there is probably greater advantage to be gained in the female shift toward instrumentalism than in a male shift toward expressiveness, although there are many good reasons for encouraging the latter. The man's expressive work in the grandfather stage of life now looms larger than it did in the past; it has also become a "middle-age" phenomenon to a much greater extent, continuing into old age (Neugarten and Weinstein, 1964). It is the leisure in fathering that comes to the fore when we turn our attention to the future, since we may presume that the time men spend at work will be reduced and discretionary time increased. Men can profit from a bit more concern for the sharing of intimate confidences in interpersonal relations, even at the risk of substituting subjective cliquishness for the more "ideal" instrumental standards of objectivity and discipline. But the greater gain in an objective society stressing high standards of personal and organizational accomplishment is most likely to be found in upgrading instrumentalism among women. It is odd that women have tended to become alienated from motherhood just as men show signs of being reintegrated within the family. For women, the separation of home and work is a relatively new condition.

Women need to participate in the world of masculinity not only for their own good, but for that of men. If for no other reason, women must be educated in order to improve the milieu of their male companions, as John Stuart Mill recognized long ago. The convergence of sex styles has been prompted by fundamental and irreversible changes in society, but it is possible to encourage these changes without giving equal encouragement to a transformation of sex roles. The technological roots of our culture are very similar to those of the Soviet Union, for example, but it is already apparent that in the coming century the Soviets are likely to eclipse us in the development of nontraditional female talents. This is but another case in which cooperation with the inevitable would seem to be advisable, and thus, for all the dangers we might cite, sexual convergence calls for our support, not our reservations.

Although convergence is not self-generating, once it gains momentum it does seem to supply resources for its own progress. Aggressive women make it easier for those who follow, and they establish new horizons that are reflected in intergenerational mother-daughter patterns. The more education the mother has, for example, the more likely her daughter is to be aggressive, achievement-oriented, and heterosexually active (Kagan and Moss, 1962). The more educated the mother, the more likely it is that her daughter will cultivate both expressiveness and instrumentalism, or the version of instrumentalism that worldly women are permitted to cultivate.

As a result of sexual convergence, father seems to become less important in the process of sexualization per se, and his son's identification with him loses some of its former importance since the boy no longer needs to develop a pronounced masculine point of view. By the same token, effective masculinity itself becomes much more subtle and more difficult to master; a crude exaggeration of the male style will no longer suffice. Fathers no longer have a stereotyped task, and their "homework" is by no means cut and dried. The man's job is to complement his wife in terms of the unique capacities of the couple and to make a domestic contribution in terms of his own view of life. Ideally he reflects certain elements of the masculine perspective even though that perspective lacks sharp definition.

The contemporary father necessarily becomes much more intimately involved in the lives of his children, thereby reinforcing and enhancing the mother's role in their lives. As parents become similar, balancing both expressive and instrumental functions, they become more absorbed in the entire range of parental concerns. If the contemporary middle-class child is more completely manipulated than the child of an earlier era—and he is—it is due to the parents' zealous concern for the child's welfare, not because of a "will to power" over the younger generation.

In a sense, both masculinity and femininity are being enlarged. It may be inevitable that the cultures of men and women will differ, as Margaret Mead (1953) has observed, but the greater the scope of each and the more each impinges on the other, the better off both will be. Mead ardently contends that every effort, every strategy, should be used to minimize the differences between the sexes and to maximize the range of human activities for all men and women. Sexual convergence is an expansion process that stands to enrich the lives of all.

Perhaps we should add, however, that convergence per se is no virtue; the fact that women do more things like men, or with men, may be good or bad depending on what the men themselves are doing. The forces that are enlarging the range of female behavior are also enlarging the range of male behavior, and although diversity may be desirable in and of itself, there are dangers whenever the life space of individuals undergoes rapid expansion. Novelty itself becomes an attraction, and lack of experience with the new roles guarantees a measure of insecurity and fumbling in the process of trial and error.

Thus, as women enter male domains they share men's problems. Both men and women find themselves struggling with divergent tendencies—those of instrumentalism versus expressiveness, that is, strength, fortitude, and willfulness versus tenderness, sympathy, and compliance. Men have trouble balancing the two tendencies even though, collectively, they have had generations of experience. They are now caught between the "soft," sympathetic codes governing home life and the "hard," categorical rules of the office and the factory.

Women approach these values from their heritage of maternal nurturance, men from their heritage of masculine determination. Myron Brenton (1966) argues that we continue to judge masculinity by standards set long before the Victorian era, leaving many men crippled by rigidity and a fear of emotional commitment. In the traditional pattern they are not only called upon to be tough, but they are often encouraged to equate silence with strength; thus they lose the ability to talk about their feelings openly with trusted friends, counselors, or even wives. The fact that woman is caught between traditional and modern roles is now widely acknowledged, but the dilemma is man's as well.

The old pattern of male-dominated, female-serviced family life is slowly being replaced by a new and more symmetrical pattern. Greater equality is reflected in a great many changes in the relationships between men and women at almost all age levels. The changes in the sexes are not equal, however, since they occur most frequently as an expansion of the female role into formerly male territory. From the point of view of the economy this may be a good thing, since technological progress can be advanced more by a female shift toward instrumentalism than by any male shift in the direction of expressiveness. From the point of view of the individual and his family, however, the encouragement of male expressiveness is just as important. In fact, the range of both masculinity and femininity is being enlarged, since the very forces that increase the scope of female behavior also broaden that of men.

But the fact that women do more things like men, or with them, is not necessarily desirable; it depends on what the men themselves are doing. It is too early to tell how the appearance of women in the labor force in large numbers will change the quality of family life, or whether it will have much impact upon the quality of life and work in the community. So far most employed women have found careers only in subordinate positions, not in policy-making roles.

PART FOUR

Prognosis

CHAPTER XIII

Fatherhood and the Emerging Family

Any forecast concerning fatherhood must be based upon certain assumptions about trends in the family, but there are overwhelming difficulties in predicting family developments because the family is not a self-contained social system, nor is it subject to strategies of legislative and administrative control. Although lip service is repeatedly given to the family's irreplaceable value to society, laws passed each year rarely deal directly with the family. Legislators attend to other matters, obliquely affecting family life to be sure, but in unformulated or unanticipated ways. Nor are corporations any more concerned than the legislature; they view the family as a sales target. The courts are usually more solicitous of domestic needs, but are not in a strategic position to initiate new and important family legislation.

Changes in the family are ultimately responsive to the most fundamental, and least supervised, changes in society. Yonina Talmon (1964) has observed that almost the entire social channeling of our selection of mates occurs as an unintended, unforeseen, or even undesired consequence of institutional arrangements made for other purposes. Trends toward earlier marriage and a higher marriage rate, for example, reflect this unsponsored, in a sense accidental, drift, with obscure implications for father; but, as we shall see, the changes that are occurring do seem to be related to the underlying transformation of the breadwinner role.

Various scholars have attempted to appraise the future of the family by more reliable means than humanistic reflection or intuition. Reuben Hill (1964), for example, has sought to pinpoint family trends through the intergenerational study of the family; more specifically, through the study of three generations within particular families. On the basis of his research he predicts greater overall family effectiveness, enhanced professional competence among those who work with family problems, improved economic well-being for the family, better family-life planning, and greater communication among family members. His two most questionable predictions concern the family's overall effectiveness and progress in communications. They emerge as hopes, not objective projections. Even if we could be assured that both trends have actually emerged in the past fifty years, it is impossible to know what kind of effectiveness will be required in the world of the future; certainly the entire matrix of communications in modern society is in a state of transformation, bearing unknown implications for husband-wife interaction. Hill's profile of the future freezes the non-family world and projects recent family trends in an otherwise static society, but that is something forecasts almost always do.

Charles Hobart (1963) has also written about the kind of family that can be expected to flourish in a society that is increasingly affluent in consumption and bureaucratic in management. He is optimistic that greater stress will be placed on "being" rather than "doing" within the family, on expressive rather than instrumental bonds, and that there will be a warmer, richer family center to life. He contrasts his view with that of Barrington Moore (1960), who contends that the family of the future will have to become more bureaucratized, just as everything else in society has responded to the principles of efficiency and rational organization.

Moore's position is easily misinterpreted. He correctly recognizes that as society becomes increasingly bureaucratized, aspects of the family must also succumb, yet essential aspects of family life can remain unbureaucratized as they always have. Indeed, there are no known strategies for bureaucratizing family intimacies as yet, only for surrounding them with greater comfort and with more effective labor-saving devices.

No intention is made by either Hobart or Moore to belittle the role of the family. Although it has receded in scope in modern society, it still remains the most meaningful social unit for most of the world's people—more meaningful than the corporation, the neighborhood, the political party, the church, the city, or the nation. Its universality is derived from the immediate satisfactions it offers and from its effectiveness in coping with daily problems. Nothing has come along to replace it, although other social agencies do have an increasing appeal; the nation-state, for example, has become relatively more important, but it cannot carry a primary symbolic load for many, perhaps not even for most, people. Hobart sees the family of the future as the basic source of affection and meaning in life, but one whose material subsistence is to be provided for by countless bureaucratically ordered, nonfamily agencies.

Hobart's point of view seems to reflect the mainstream of current thinking among American students of family life. But there is something that we tend to ignore, perhaps because it is so pervasive in our lives: the family-budget ethic, which is linked in America to the rhetoric of capitalism and private enterprise. This ethic, modified here and there over time though retained in essence, fosters opposition to government assistance to the family as an economic unit and to any enlargement of the public sector of our economy, except as it may be designed to strengthen or assist the private sector. The concepts of freedom, justice, and personal integrity, which are written into this ideological package, define for the individual an important dimension of his self-concept. As this ethic applies to man the father, each adult male is responsible for the economic well-being of his family, and he therefore takes pride in his success as a family provider and suffers if he is inept.

The successful man is not eager to share the rewards of his good fortune with men who fail, and the greatest prerogative of success is to be able to dispense its bounty to one's family and heirs. Paternal largesse has therefore been established as a carefully graded privilege the world over. Compounding the misfortunes of the unsuccessful man is the fact that his failure is a family tragedy, not merely a personal one. The lower-class child inevitably has trouble; if his father should leave home, as he very well may, the child's basic problem remains because public assistance is absolutely minimal (McKeany, 1960), an inherent consequence of the family-budget ethic and one that seems natural enough to those who have been reared in its discipline.

The Welfare Ethic

In a smaller way, however, Americans retain a humanitarian, welfare ethic, one that is also deeply rooted in our national experience and that is currently propelled by powerful political and economic forces. The welfare ethic is diffusive and can encompass anything from small acts of kindness to "wars on poverty." In its most vital form it promotes social arrangements by which each person is given the means and the encouragement to realize his own potentialities. We now recognize that the key to "equal opportunity" is the elimination of arbitrary advantages accorded to some children and denied to others; the perseverance of patterned inequality is always rooted in a status system by which some parents can provide opportunities for their children not available to all.

The contemporary effort to equalize life chances has led to the development of governmental programs in health, education, and welfare, with little thought of challenging the morality implicit in the family-budget system. But clearly the *equal-opportunities ethic* and the *family-budget ethic* clash. Welfare programs are usually oriented to the needs of family units, and they are most often designed to help families in which the father is inadequate, setting standards for services and consumption independent of the family's "ability to pay."

An inevitable consequence is that efforts are made to promote only those welfare services that do not openly challenge the family budget system. The latter is deeply entrenched, and its requirements take precedence over those specified by the welfare ethic. Thus family health and welfare services in the United States are essentially ameliorative rather than reformative or preventive (Robinson, 1963). A coherent welfare program is retarded by retention of the "each-family-for-itself" orientation in the dominating private sector of our economy, a veritable handicap system in the competition for status. If it can be argued that the greatest obstacle to man's rapport with humanity is status seeking, the basis for this isolation is the tradition of the family budget and its almost universal appeal to familism, with father as the key to the family's status.

The tenacity of the "father-as-breadwinner" doctrine prevents the resolution of problems of both the working mother and the modern welfare state. It is the basis for the supplementary character of mother's earning power, and it serves as the moral explanation by which to justify the unhappy state of those in the lower classes. In accordance with the ethic of paternal enterprise, one can logically resolve most social problems by saying, "If men would just do an honest day's work for an honest day's pay, we should not have all this misfortune."

The disabled father is not held responsible for his inadequacy as a breadwinner, of course, but the burden falls on his wife's shoulders. The discrepancy between what is expected of him and his potential fulfillment is enormous, much greater than would be the case for the disabled mother. Disability reduces father to a position that is antithetical to the expectations of adult men held by both the man and his wife.

An inverse relationship seems to exist between the father's breadwinner function and the progress of the welfare state and also between the breadwinner function and the expressive, "primary-group" functions of the family. Curiously, however, emphasis on the breadwinner has been displaced but the breadwinner role has not; thus father is psychologically tied to a role whose ethical validity is not nearly as strong as it once was. Men worry excessively about their earning power, but the satisfactions to be gained from "making good" are often insufficient to relieve the anxieties associated with striving.

It is possible that a modification of the breadwinner ethic

might help to free parents from their obsession with the success potential of their children. It could be argued, for example, that we have made parenthood too close, too exclusive, and too isolated a function. A leading student of both American and Russian family life, David Mace (1962) contends that the Russian child learns in crèche and nursery to adjust to the wider life of the community as well as to the more circumscribed life of the home. Is it possible, he asks, that American parents, even good parents, cannot prepare their children for community living because the home provides a setting so distant from and so unlike the community at large? Do parents give their children not only security, but an exaggerated sense of their own importance and a limiting life style as far as community welfare is concerned?

In contrasting American parents with those in the Israeli Kibbutzim, Howard Halpern (1962) has explored similar questions. He contends that Americans are less generous in their relationships with both their own children and the larger community. Kibbutzim parents, on the other hand, have been so absorbed by the Kibbutz itself that, although they have countless hours of warmth, laughter, and fun with their children, they do not share the potentially deeper bond based on inconvenience, frustration, and even misery of growing up together in a home. Both Halpern and Mace suggest that nations with different cultural experiences have much to learn from one another as we search for new ways of expanding the sense of identity among children to include a larger share of the human race.

A worry of long standing in the United States is that community or public assistance to parents (not counting occasional charitable gestures from people of good will) undermines their desire to work and their sense of parental responsibility as well, despite solid evidence to the contrary. The Canadian family-allowances system, for example, has in no way diminished parental efforts in behalf of children, nor has it diminished the efforts of voluntary agencies to cope with family problems (Madison, 1964). The system has not been accompanied by any of the disastrous effects prophesied by its opponents, nor has it resulted in the proliferation of large families among the chronically dependent sections of the population or among Catholics.

In an economy capable of affluence even in wartime, a modification of the family-budget ethic, geared to the wages of father, is no longer hypothetical. A feasible modification might be likened to that which has already affected paternal authority. Fathers still have power over their children, but arbitrariness in its use is cushioned by a variety of specialized authorities now able to influence the life of the family. Even the socialization role of the family, and that of its father, has been declining; father's role in child rearing and his role as breadwinner may in fact decline together. Although father's difficulties in the lower classes and among nonwhites may be ameliorated by economic and social reform, the prime obstacle to decisive improvement is the breadwinner emphasis itself. A great many of our social problems can be alleviated only by altering the extremes of the breadwinner system so that a problem father will not necessarily produce a problem family, and a self-perpetuating one at that.

Three feasible changes exemplify the possibilities. First is the establishment of a truly public school system, one in which no assumptions need be made concerning supplementary home finances, facilities, or experiences. All books and supplies, all study accommodations, including travel, might well be furnished at public expense. Every effort could be made to guarantee that whatever is available in the best schools would be available in all and that schools in favored residential areas would not have superior facilities and teachers, as is currently the case. Even the quality of students in schools must be similar if they are to offer equal opportunities; in fact, the quality of the student body may be more important than any other factor in determining the effectiveness of a school (Coleman, *et al.*, 1966).

Moreover, the age for entering school might very well be lowered. Growing knowledge of the plasticity of the human nervous system and of critical periods in development indicates that it is idle to talk about a society of equal opportunity as long as children are abandoned solely to their families during their most impressionable years. There is overwhelming evidence that this venerable custom is primarily responsible for the relative fixity of the social-class structure. And, as Robert Morison (1967) has pointed out, it seems increasingly unlikely that a complex, demanding society can rely exclusively on the haphazard educational procedures provided by home environments during the most teachable years of life, the first six.

The principal fear of those who would keep agencies of society out of the toddler's life seems to be that community controls over growth and development will reduce the freedom of the individual and, in the long run, produce a colorless, conformist society. But we all know that the most educated people are the ones who are least conformist and most innovative; the greatest conformist in all history has been the unlettered peasant. The real point of bringing education to the child at the earliest possible age is not to induce conformity but to cultivate the plasticity and adaptability of the human nervous system (Morison, 1967). Perhaps it is even possible in a single generation to rear healthy and alert children whose social and psychological orientation to life is entirely different from that of their parents, as suggested by the Kibbutzim experiences in Israel (Neubauer, 1965).

Another possibility is the establishment of a *first-class* network of public-health clinics for children, first-class in the sense that parents capable of paying extra could find no better facilities anywhere. Such an arrangement is well within the resource capacity of the United States in peacetime, although we still assume that people who are willing to pay extra should receive better health care, even for their children.

A third reform worthy of renewed consideration is the elimination of the inheritance of great wealth accumulated during the father's lifetime. The first two changes would resolve most of the social dilemmas now posed by the family-budget ethic, but several inequities would persist unless this third step was taken. One, for example, is the advantage wealthy young men now have in waging expensive political campaigns, without which election to the most important political offices has become increasingly difficult. Independently wealthy men have proved to be very useful public servants throughout American history, but their status has been based on unequal opportunity. As Emile Durkheim (1892) observed, the transmission of wealth by will is the last and most durable form of hereditary transmission.

Of course none of these changes will be made in the near future, although the trends are generally favorable. After all, people are not overwhelmingly committed to true equality of opportunity; many defer to the privileged classes, some revere them. The possibilities are mentioned here to call attention to the nature and implications of the family-budget system as it exists today. Even if these three modifications were made, life chances would still not be perfectly equal, but inequality would no longer be flagrantly perpetuated. Moreover, workers would still be paid unequal wages, so the family-budget system could be preserved in a restricted way. Some families would have more to spend than others, and those with similar incomes could plan their expenditures in dissimilar ways.

Certainly the distinction between the entrepreneurial family and the bureaucratic family, discussed in Chapter XII, has become more and more meaningless. We have learned that the bureaucratic family is every bit as budget conscious, and status conscious, as the entrepreneurial family, and we cannot conceive of a bureaucracy that does not rank its incumbents by function, grading their pay by rank. One will find no suggestion of a budgetless family here.

It is a mistake to think that the father's chief role must inevitably be that of breadwinner. It is also a mistake to think that the demise of his historical function as provider renders him obsolete. Even if he were relieved of his obligation to supply his children with the basic material resources for survival and the power to determine their social status, his work would be cut out for him. Helen Hacker (1957), for example, contends that the man's need to be free of doubts, uncertainties, or insecurities—his need to be "strong"—is the greatest burden of masculinity. Strength, of course, connotes many things, and the breadwinner emphasis is simply one interpretation, or distortion, of its many meanings. But the urge to be a *man* is felt in all cultures; if the wage-earner role is not glorified, other proofs of manhood will surely be established, and men will continue to serve as models for boys.

John Mogey (1957) was probably on the right track when he recognized that a reintegration of father in the family is occurring, after disasters in the early stages of the industrial revolution, in response to the trend toward an affluent, suburban life, and in association with the upgrading of work in general. As economic security reaches a larger part of the population, the father becomes more active in the family and is psychologically closer to both his wife and his children. We may very well be witnessing the establishment of an altogether new kind of family and a new basis for family stability.

In a sense, the family has become more important to father, even as he has become relatively less important to the family. Once father was the prime agent of family strength; now he is often reliant upon it, especially for emotional sustenance (Mogey and Morris, 1960). A system seems to be emerging in which an important function of the family is to guarantee the highly skilled male a sense of interpersonal security. The family becomes the key to father's endurance as a skilled organism in the bureaucratic world. Impersonal forms of bureaucratic organization replace the kinship network as the strategic principle for work and social effort, and the small family becomes the man's emotional "home base" in the process. Indeed, the rise of romantic love as a family affair has accompanied the rise of modern bureaucratic organization.

Thus, father is ideally an integrated member of the family and, as such, an agent of family and social stability, but he is also a source of value, of productivity, to society. As such, he stands in need of all the support that his family and the community at large can provide.

BIBLIOGRAPHY

Abel, Theodore, Jane Belo, and Martha Wolfenstein. *An Analysis of French Projective Tests*. Palo Alto: Stanford University Press, 1954.

Aberle, David F., Urie Bronfenbrenner, Eckhard H. Hess, Daniel R. Miller, David M. Schneider, and James N. Spuhler. "The Incest Taboo and the Mating Patterns of Animals," in William J. Goode (ed.), *Readings on the Family and Society*. Englewood Cliffs, N. J.: Prentice-Hall, 1964.

———, and Kaspar D. Naegele. "Middle-Class Fathers' Occupational Role and Attitude Toward Children," *American Journal of Orthopsychiatry*, 1952, 22:366–378.

Ackerman, Charles. "Affiliations: Structural Determinants of Differential Divorce Rates," *American Journal of Sociology*, 1963, 69:13–20.

Ackerman, Nathan W. *Psychodynamics of Family Life*. New York: Basic Books, 1958.

Adamek, Raymond J., and Willis J. Goudy. "Identification, Sex, and Change in College Major," *Sociology of Education*, 1966, 39:183–199.

Adams, Bert N. "Structural Factors Affecting Parental Aid to Married Children," *Journal of Marriage and the Family*, 1964, 26:327–331.

Adams, Elsie B., and Irwin G. Sarason. "Relation Between Anxiety in Children and Their Parents," *Child Development*, 1963, 34:237–246.

Ainsworth, Mary D. "The Effects of Maternal Deprivations: A Review of Findings and Controversy in the Context of Research Strategy," in *Deprivation and Maternal Care: A Reassessment of Its Effects*. Geneva: World Health Organization, 1962.

Albrecht, Ruth. "The Parental Responsibilities of Grandparents," *Marriage and Family Living*, 1954, 16:201–204.

Aldous, Joan. "A Study of Parental Role Functions," *The Family Life Coordinator*, 1961, 10:43–44.

———, and Leone Kell. "A Partial Test of Some Theories of Identification," *Marriage and Family Living*, 1961, 23:15–19.

Allen, Dean A. "Anti-Femininity in Men," *American Sociological Review*, 1954, 19:591–593.

Amatora, Mary. "Analysis of Certain Recreational Interests and Activities and Other Variables in the Large Family," *Journal of Social Psychology,* 1959, 50:225–231.

Anderson, John E. "Parents' Attitudes on Child Behavior: A Report of Three Studies," *Child Development,* 1946, 17:91–97.

Andry, Robert G. "Parental and Maternal Roles and Delinquency," in *Deprivation and Maternal Care: A Reassessment of Its Effects.* Geneva: World Health Organization, 1962.

Angell, Robert C. *The Family Encounters the Depression.* New York: Scribner, 1936.

Angrilli, Albert F. "The Psychosexual Identification of Pre-school Boys," *Journal of Genetic Psychology,* 1960, 97:329–340.

Apple, Dorrian. "The Social Structure of Grandparenthood," *American Anthropologist,* 1956, 58:656–663.

Aronson, Elliot. "Threat and Obedience," *Trans-action,* 1966, 3, pp. 25–27.

Ausubel, David P. *Ego Development and the Personality Disorders.* New York: Grune & Stratton, 1952.

Axelson, Leland J. "The Marital Adjustment and Marital Role Definitions of Husbands of Working and Nonworking Wives," *Marriage and Family Living,* 1963, 25:189–195.

Babchuk, Nicholas. "Primary Friends and Kin: A Study of the Associations of Middle-Class Couples," *Social Forces,* 1965, 43:483–493.

———, and Alan P. Bates. "The Primary Relations of Middle-Class Couples: A Study in Male Dominance," *American Sociological Review,* 1963, 28:377–384.

Bach, George R. "Father Fantasies and Father-Typing in Father-Separated Children," *Child Development,* 1946, 17:63–80.

Ball, John C. *Social Deviancy and Adolescent Personality: An Analytical Study with the MMPI.* Lexington: University of Kentucky Press, 1962.

Bandura, Albert, and Aletha C. Hutson. "Identification as a Process of Incidental Learning," *Journal of Abnormal and Social Psychology,* 1961, 63:311–318.

———, and Richard H. Walters. "Dependency Conflicts in Aggressive Delinquents," *Journal of Social Issues,* 1958, 14:52–65.

Bardis, Panos D. "Influence of Family Life Education on Sex Knowledge," *Marriage and Family Living,* 1963, 25:85–88.

Barker, Gordon H., and William T. Adams. "Comparison of the Delinquencies of Boys and Girls," *Journal of Criminal Law, Criminology, and Police Science,* 1962, 53:470–477.

Barry, Herbert, III, Margaret K. Bacon, and Irvin L. Child. "A Cross-Cultural Survey of Some Sex Differences in Socialization," *Journal of Abnormal and Social Psychology,* 1957, 55:327–332.

———, Irvin L. Child, and Margaret K. Bacon. "Relation of Child Training to Subsistence Economy," *American Anthropologist,* 1959, 61:51–63.

Bartemeier, Leo. "The Contribution of the Father to the Mental Health of the Family," *American Journal of Psychiatry,* 1953, 110:277–280.

Bartlett, Claude J., and John E. Horrocks. "A Study of the Needs Status of Adolescents from Broken Homes," *Journal of Genetic Psychology*, 1958, 93:153–159.

Baruch, Dorothy. "A Study of Reported Tension in Interparental Relationships as Co-existent with Behavior Adjustment in Young Children," *Journal of Experimental Education*, 1937, 6:187–204.

———, and Annie J. Wilcox. "A Study of Sex Differences in Pre-school Children's Adjustment Co-existent with Interparental Tensions," *Journal of Genetic Psychology*, 1944, 64:281–303.

Batchelder, Alan B. "Decline in the Relative Income of Negro Men," *Quarterly Journal of Economics*, 1964, 78:525–548.

Bates, Marston. *Animal Worlds*. New York: Random House, 1963.

Bayer, Alan E., and F. Ivan Nye. "Family Life Education in Florida Public High Schools," *Marriage and Family Living*, 1964, 26:182–187.

Beauvoir, Simone de. *The Second Sex*, Dorothy F. Beck (trans.), H. M. Parsley (ed.). New York: Knopf, 1953.

Beck, Dorothy F. "The Changing Moslem Family of the Middle East," *Marriage and Family Living*, 1957, 19:340–347.

Becker, Wesley C., and Ronald S. Krug. "A Circumplex Model for Social Behavior in Children," *Child Development*, 1964, 35:371–396.

———, Donald Peterson, and Leo Hellmer. "Factors in Parental Behavior and Personality as Related to Problem Behavior in Children," *Journal of Consulting Psychology*, 1957, 23:107–118.

Beers, Howard W. "A Portrait of the Farm Family in Central New York State," *American Sociological Review*, 1937, 2:591–600.

Behlmer, Reuben H. "Family Life Education Survey," *Marriage and Family Living*, 1961, 23:299–301.

Beier, E. G. "The Parental Identification of Male and Female College Students," *Journal of Abnormal and Social Psychology*, 1953, 48:569–572.

Beigel, Hugo G. "The Evaluation of Intelligence in the Heterosexual Relationship," *Journal of Social Psychology*, 1957, 46:65–80.

Bell, Richard Q. "Retrospective Attitude Studies of Parent-Child Relations," *Child Development*, 1958, 29:323–338.

Bendix, Reinhard, and Seymour Martin Lipset. *Social Mobility in Industrial Society*. Berkeley: University of California Press, 1959.

Benedict, Ruth. "Continuities and Discontinuities in Cultural Conditioning," *Psychiatry*, 1938, 1:161–167.

Bennett, John W., and Iwao Ishino. *Paternalism in the Japanese Economy: Anthropological Studies of "Oyabun-Kobun" Patterns*. Minneapolis: University of Minnesota Press, 1963.

Bennett, William S., and Noel P. Gist. "Class and Family Influences on Student Aspirations," *Social Forces*, 1964, 43:167–173.

Benson, Purnell. "The Interests of Happily Married Couples," *Marriage and Family Living*, 1952, 14:276–280.

Berelson, Bernard, and Gary A. Steiner. *Human Behavior*. New York: Harcourt, Brace & World, 1964.

Berger, Bennett M. "Adolescence and Beyond," *Social Problems*, 1963, 10:394–408.

Bernard, Jessie. *Remarriage*. New York: Dryden, 1956.
———. *Academic Women*. University Park: Pennsylvania State University Press, 1964.
Berne, Eric. *Games People Play*. New York: Grove, 1964.
Berreman, Gerald D. "Pahari Polyandry: A Comparison," *American Anthropologist*, 1962, 61:60–75.
Bertrand, Alvin L. "School Attendance and Attainment: Function and Dysfunction of School and Family Social Systems," *Social Forces*, 1962, 40:228–233.
Bettelheim, Bruno. "Women: Emancipation Is Still to Come," *The New Republic*, November 7, 1964, pp. 48–58.
Beyer, Glenn H. "Living Arrangements, Attitudes, and Preferences of Older People," in Clark Tibbitts and Wilma Donahue (eds.), *Social and Psychological Aspects of Aging*. New York: Columbia University Press, 1962.
Beyrer, J. Benjamin, and Edward Tevald. "Responsibilities of Grandparents of Children Receiving Aid to Dependent Children," *Social Service Review*, 1956, 30:428–435.
Bieri, James. "Parental Identification, Acceptance of Authority and Within-Sex Differences in Cognitive Behavior," *Journal of Abnormal and Social Psychology*, 1960, 60:76–79.
———, and Robin Lobeck. "Acceptance of Authority and Parental Identification," *Journal of Personality*, 1959, 27:74–87.
Bing, Elizabeth. "Effect of Childrearing Practices on Development of Differential Cognitive Abilities," *Child Development*, 1963, 34:631–648.
Blaine, Graham B. "The Children of Divorce," *The Atlantic*, March, 1963, pp. 98–101.
Blake, Judith. *Family Structure in Jamaica*. New York: Free Press, 1961.
Blau, Peter M. *Exchange and Power in Social Life*. New York: Wiley, 1964.
Blau, Zena S. "Exposure to Child-Rearing Experts: A Structural Interpretation of Class-Color Differences," *American Journal of Sociology*, 1964, 69:596–608.
Blood, Robert O., Jr. "The Division of Labor in City and Farm Families," *Marriage and Family Living*, 1958, 20:170–174.
———. "The Measurement and Bases of Family Power: A Rejoinder," *Marriage and Family Living*, 1963, 25:475–477. (a)
———. "The Husband-Wife Relationship," in F. Ivan Nye and Lois W. Hoffman (eds.), *The Employed Mother in America*. Chicago: Rand McNally, 1963. (b)
———. "Long-Range Causes and Consequences of the Employment of Married Women," *Journal of Marriage and the Family*, 1965, 27:43–47.
———, and Robert L. Hamblin. "The Effect of the Wife's Employment on the Family Power Structure," *Social Forces*, 1958, 36:347–352.
———, and Donald M. Wolfe. *Husbands and Wives: The Dynamics of*

Married Living. New York: Free Press, 1960.
Blumberg, Leonard, and Robert R. Bell. "Urban Migration and Kinship Ties," *Social Problems*, 1959, 6:328–333.
Bock, Philip K. "Patterns of Illegitimacy on a Canadian Indian Reserve: 1860–1960," *Marriage and Family Living*, 1964, 26:142–148.
Bordua, David J. "Educational Aspirations and Parental Stress on College," *Social Forces*, 1960, 38:262–269.
Bossard, James H. S. *Parent and Child*. Philadelphia: University of Pennsylvania Press, 1953.
———, and William Carter. "Large and Small Families—A Study in Contrast," *Journal of the American Society of Chartered Life Underwriters*, 1958–1959, 13:221–240.
Bott, Elizabeth. *Family and Social Network*. London: Tavistock Publications, 1957.
Bowerman, Charles E. "Adjustment in Marriage: Over-All and in Specific Areas," *Sociology and Social Research*, 1957, 41:257–263.
———, and Glen H. Elder, Jr. "Variations in Adolescent Perception of Family Power Structure," *American Sociological Review*, 1964, 29:551–567.
———, and Donald P. Irish. "Some Relationships of Stepchildren to Their Parents," *Marriage and Family Living*, 1962, 24:113–121.
Bowlby, John. *Maternal Care and Mental Health*. Geneva: World Health Organization, 1952.
Brace, C. L., and M. F. Ashley Montagu. *Man's Evolution*. New York: Macmillan, 1965.
Brenton, Myron. *The American Male*. New York: Coward-McCann, 1966.
Brieland, Donald. "Uses of Research in Recent Popular Parent Education Literature," *Marriage and Family Living*, 1957, 19:60–65.
———, and Christine G. Brieland. "A Parent Education Project in Pakistan," *Marriage and Family Living*, 1957, 19:348–351.
Briffault, Robert. *The Mothers*. New York: Macmillan, 1931.
Brim, Orville G., Jr. "Changes and Trends in Child-Rearing Advice," *Child Study*, 1959, 36:23–27. (a)
———. *Education for Child Rearing*. New York: Russell Sage Foundation, 1959. (b)
———. "Evidence Concerning the Effects of Education for Child Rearing," in Robert F. Winch, Robert McGinnis, and Herbert R. Barringer (eds.), *Selected Studies in Marriage and the Family*. New York: Holt, Rinehart and Winston, 1962.
———, Roy W. Fairchild, and Edgar F. Borgatta, "Relations Between Family Problems," *Marriage and Family Living*, 1961, 23:219–226.
Brodbeck, A. J. "Learning and Identification: IV. Oedipal Motivation as a Determinant of Conscience Development," *Journal of Genetic Psychology*, 1954, 84:219–227.
Broderick, Carlfred B. "Family-Life Education Versus Reality," *Marriage and Family Living*, 1964, 26:102–103.
———. "Social Heterosexual Development Among Urban Negroes and

Whites," *Journal of Marriage and the Family*, 1965, 27:200–203.
———, and Stanley E. Fowler. "New Patterns of Relationships Between the Sexes Among Preadolescents," *Marriage and Family Living*, 1961, 23:27–30.
Bronfenbrenner, Urie. "Socialization and Social Class Through Time and Space," in Eleanor E. Maccoby, Theodore M. Newcomb, and Eugene L. Hartley (eds.), *Readings in Social Psychology*. New York: Holt, Rinehart and Winston, 1958.
———. "Freudian Theories of Identification and Their Derivatives," *Child Development*, 1960, 31:15–40.
———. "Some Familial Antecedents of Responsibility and Leadership in Adolescents," in Luigi Petrullo and Bernard Bass (eds.), *Leadership and Interpersonal Behavior*. New York: Holt, Rinehart and Winston, 1961. (a)
———, "The Changing American Child," *Journal of Social Issues*, 1961, 17:6–18. (b)
Brown, Daniel G. "Sex-Role Preference in Young Children," *Psychological Monographs*, 1956, 70:1–19.
———. "Masculinity-Femininity Development in Children," *Journal of Consulting Psychology*, 1957, 21:197–203. (a)
———. "The Development of Sex-Role Inversion and Homosexuality," *Journal of Pediatrics*, 1957, 50:613–619. (b)
———. "Sex-Role Development in a Changing Culture," *Psychological Bulletin*, 1958, 55:232–242.
Burch, William R., Jr. "The Play World of Camping: Research into the Social Meaning of Outdoor Recreation," *American Journal of Sociology*, 1965, 70:604–612.
Burchinal, Lee G. "Mothers' and Fathers' Differences in Parental Acceptance of Children for Controlled Comparisons Based on Parental and Family Characteristics," *Journal of Genetic Psychology*, 1958, 92:103–110.
———. "Adolescent Role Deprivation and High School Age Marriage," *Marriage and Family Living*, 1959, 21:378–384.
———. "Sources and Adequacy of Sex Knowledge Among Iowa High-School Girls," *Marriage and Family Living*, 1960, 22:268–296. (a)
———. "What About Your Daughter's Future?" *Iowa Farm Science*, 1960, 14:9–10. (b)
———. "Differences in Educational and Occupational Aspirations of Farm, Small-Town, and City Boys," *Rural Sociology*, 1961, 26:107–121.
———. "Characteristics of Adolescents from Unbroken, Broken, and Reconstituted Families," *Marriage and Family Living*, 1964, 26:44–51.
———, Glenn R. Hawkes, and Bruce Gardner. "Marriage Adjustment, Personality Characteristics of Parents and the Personality Adjustment of Their Children," *Marriage and Family Living*, 1957, 19:366–372.
Burgess, Ernest W., and Leonard S. Cottrell. *Predicting Success or Failure in Marriage*. New York: Prentice-Hall, 1939.

———, and Harvey J. Locke. *The Family*. New York: American Book Company, 1953.
Burton, Roger V. "The Absent Father and Cross-Sex Identity," *Merrill-Palmer Quarterly*, 1961, 7:85–95.
Bushong, Eugene. "Family Estrangement and Juvenile Delinquency," *Sociology and Social Research*, 1938, 18:76–84.
Calderwood, Deryck. "Differences in the Sex Questions of Adolescent Boys and Girls," *Marriage and Family Living*, 1963, 25:492–495.
Caldwell, Bettye M., and Julius B. Richmond. "Programmed Day Care for the Very Young Child—A Preliminary Report," *Journal of Marriage and the Family*, 1964, 26:481–488.
Caldwell, Morris Gilmore. "Home Conditions of Institutional Delinquent Boys in Wisconsin," *Social Forces*, 1930, 8:390–397.
Cancian, Francesca M. "Interaction Patterns in Zinacanteco Families," *American Sociological Review*, 1964, 29:540–550.
Caplow, Theodore. *The Sociology of Work*. Minneapolis: University of Minnesota Press, 1954.
———. *Principles of Organization*. New York: Harcourt, Brace & World, 1964.
Carlson, Rae. "Identification and Personality Structure in Pre-adolescents," *Journal of Abnormal and Social Psychology*, 1963, 67:566–573.
Cava, E. L., and H. L. Rausch. "Identification and the Adolescent Boy's Perception of His Father," *Journal of Abnormal and Social Psychology*, 1952, 47:855–856.
Cavan, Ruth Shonle. "Self and Role in Adjustment During Old Age," in Arnold M. Rose (ed.), *Human Behavior and Social Processes*. Boston: Houghton Mifflin, 1962.
———, and Katherine Howland Ranck. *The Family and the Depression*. Chicago: University of Chicago Press, 1938.
Cervantes, Lucius F. "Family Background, Primary Relationships, and the High-School Dropout," *Journal of Marriage and the Family*, 1965, 27:218–223.
———. "The Isolated Nuclear Family and the Dropout," *Sociological Quarterly*, 1965, 6:103–118.
Chance, M. R. A. "The Nature and Special Features of the Instinctive Social Band of Primates," in Sherwood L. Washburn (ed.), *Social Life of Early Man*. New York: Wenner-Gren Foundation, 1961.
Chilman, Catherine, and Marvin B. Sussman. "Poverty in the United States in the Mid-Sixties," *Journal of Marriage and the Family*, 1964, 26:391–395.
Chrisman, Oscar. *The Historical Child*. Boston: Richard G. Badger, 1920.
Christensen, Harold T. "Cultural Relativism and Premarital Sex Norms," *American Sociological Review*, 1960, 25:31–39.
———. "Lifetime Family and Occupational Role Projections of High School Students," *Marriage and Family Living*, 1961, 23:181–183. (a)
———. "Pregnant Brides—Record Linkage Studies," in Evelyn M. Duvall and Sylvanus M. Duvall (eds.), *Sex Ways—In Fact and Faith*

New York: Association Press, 1961. (b)
———. "Child Spacing Analysis Via Record Linkage: New Data Plus a Summing Up From Earlier Reports," *Marriage and Family Living*, 1963, 25:272–280.
———, and Hanna H. Meissner. "Premarital Pregnancy as a Factor in Divorce," *American Sociological Review*, 1953, 18:641–644.
———, and Bette B. Rubenstein. "Premarital Pregnancy and Divorce: A Follow-up Study by the Interview Method," *Marriage and Family Living*, 1956, 18:114–123.
Christopherson, Victor A. "An Investigation of Patriarchal Authority in the Mormon Family," *Marriage and Family Living*, 1956, 18:328–333.
Clausen, John A. "Drug Addiction," in Robert K. Merton and Robert A. Nisbet (eds.), *Contemporary Social Problems*. New York: Harcourt, Brace & World, 1961.
Clifford, Edward. "Discipline in the Home: A Controlled Observational Study of Parental Practices," *Journal of Genetic Psychology*, 1959, 95:45–82.
Clover, Vernon T. "Net Income of Employed Wives with Husband Present," *Studies in Economics and Business*, Texas Technological College, 1962, pp. 1–35.
Cohen, Albert K. *Delinquent Boys*. New York: Free Press, 1955.
———. "The Study of Social Disorganization and Deviant Behavior," in Robert K. Merton, Leonard Broom, and Leonard S. Cottrell, Jr. (eds.), *Sociology Today*. New York: Basic Books, 1959.
Cohen, Dorothy H. "Children of Divorce," *Parents Magazine*, August, 1960, pp. 46–47.
Colcord, Joanna C. "Discussion of 'Are Broken Homes a Causative Factor in Juvenile Delinquency,'" *Social Forces*, 1932, 10:525–527.
Coleman, James S. *The Adolescent Society*. New York: Free Press, 1962.
———. Letter to the Editor, *American Journal of Sociology*, 1966, 72:217. (a)
———, *et al. Equality of Educational Opportunity*. Washington, D.C.: U. S. Government Printing Office, 1966. (b)
Conyers, J. E. "Exploratory Study of Employer's Attitudes Toward Working Mothers," *Sociology and Social Research*, 1961, 45:145–156.
Cooley, Charles Horton. *Human Nature and the Social Order*. New York: Scribner, 1902.
Coon, Carleton S. *The Origin of Races*. New York: Knopf, 1962.
Corbin, Hazel. *Getting Ready To Be A Father*. New York: Macmillan, 1944.
Couch, Carl J. "The Use of the Concept 'Role' and Its Derivatives in a Study of Marriage," *Marriage and Family Living*, 1958, 20:353–357.
Cox, F. N. "An Assessment of Children's Attitudes Towards Parent Figures," *Child Development*, 1962, 33:821–830.
Crain, Alan J., and Caroline S. Stamm. "Intermittent Absence of Fathers and Children's Perceptions of Parents," *Journal of Marriage and the Family*, 1965, 27:344–347.

Croog, Sydney H., and Peter Kong-Ming New. "Knowledge of Grandfather's Occupation: Clues to American Kinship Structure," *Journal of Marriage and the Family*, 1965, 27:69–77.

Current Population Reports. "Lifetime Occupational Mobility of Adult Males: March 1962," Series P-23, No. 11, May 12, 1964.

Dager, Edward Z., Glenn A. Harper, and Robert N. Whitehurst. "Family Life Education in Public High Schools: A Survey Report on Indiana," *Marriage and Family Living*, 1962, 24:365–370.

Danzger, M. Herbert. "Community Power Structure: Problems and Continuities," *American Sociological Review*, 1964, 29:707–717.

Davis, Kingsley. "The Sociology of Parent-Youth Conflict," *American Sociological Review*, 1940, 5:523–535.

Davis, Maxine. *Sexual Responsibility in Marriage*. New York: Dial Press, 1963.

Day, Lincoln H. "Patterns of Divorce in Australia and the United States," *American Sociological Review*, 1964, 29:509–522.

Deutsch, Cynthia P., and Judith A. Goldston. "Family Factors in Home Adjustment of the Severely Disabled," *Marriage and Family Living*, 1960, 22:312–316.

Deutscher, Irwin. "The Quality of Postparental Life: Definitions of the Situation," *Marriage and Family Living*, 1964, 26:52–59.

Devereux, Edward C., Jr., Urie Bronfenbrenner, and George J. Suci. "Patterns of Parent Behaviour in the United States and the Federal Republic of Germany: A Cross-National Comparison," *International Social Science Journal*, 1962, 14:488–506.

Dobzhansky, Theodosius. "Changing Man," *Science*, 1967, 155:409–415.

Douvan, Elizabeth, and Carol Kaye. "Motivation Factors in College Entrance," in Nevitt Sanford (ed.), *The American College: A Psychological and Social Interpretation of the Higher Learning*. New York: Wiley, 1962.

Downey, Kenneth J. "Parental Interest in the Institutionalized, Severely Mentally Retarded Child," *Social Problems*, 1963, 11:186–193.

Dubin, Elisabeth R., and Robert Dubin. "The Authority Inception Period in Socialization," *Child Development*, 1963, 34:885–898.

Dubin, Robert. "Industrial Workers' Worlds," *Social Problems*, 1956, 3:131–142.

Dunn, Marie S. "Marriage Role Expectations of Adolescents," *Marriage and Family Living*, 1960, 22:99–104.

Durkheim, Emile. Lecture on the family (1892), recorded by Marcel Mauss, translated by George Simpson, "A Durkheim Fragment," *American Journal of Sociology*, 1965, 70:527–536.

Duvall, Evelyn M. "Conceptions of Parenthood," *American Journal of Sociology*, 1946, 52:193–203.

———. "Teenage Boys and Family Living," *Marriage and Family Living*, 1961, 23:49.

———. "How Effective Are Marriage Courses?" *Journal of Marriage and the Family*, 1965, 27:176–184.

Dybwad, Gunnar. "Fathers Today: Neglected or Neglectful?" *Child Study*, 1952, 29:3–5.

Dyer, Everett D. "Some Trends in Two-Income Middle-Class Urban Families," *Southwestern Social Science Quarterly*, 1958, 39:125–132.

———. "Parenthood as Crisis: A Re-Study," *Marriage and Family Living*, 1963, 25:196–201.

Dyer, William G. "Parental Influence on the Job Attitudes of Children from Two Occupational Strata," *Sociology and Social Research*, 1958, 42:203–206.

———, and Dick Urban. "The Institutionalization of Equalitarian Family Norms," *Marriage and Family Living*, 1958, 20:53–58.

Eggers, Oscar. "The Future of the American Family," *Bulletin on Family Development*, 1960, 1:1–4.

Ehrmann, Winston. *Premarital Dating Behavior*. New York: Holt, Rinehart and Winston, 1959.

Elder, Glen H., Jr. "Family Structure and the Transmission of Values and Norms in the Process of Child Rearing." Unpublished Ph.D. dissertation. Chapel Hill, N. C.: University of North Carolina, 1961.

———. *Adolescent Achievement and Mobility Aspirations*. Chapel Hill, N.C.: The Institute for Research in Social Science, 1962. (a)

———. "Structural Variations in the Child Rearing Relationship," *Sociometry*, 1962, 25:241–262. (b)

———. "Parental Power Legitimation and Its Effect on the Adolescent," *Sociometry*, 1963, 26:50–65.

———. "Family Structure and Educational Attainment: A Cross-National Analysis," *American Sociological Review*, 1965, 30:81–96.

———, and Charles E. Bowerman. "Family Structure and Child-Rearing Patterns: The Effect of Family Size and Sex Composition," *American Sociological Review*, 1963, 28:891–905.

Elder, Joseph W. "National Loyalties in a Newly Independent Nation," in David E. Apter (ed.), *Ideology and Discontent*. New York: Free Press, 1964.

Ellis, Albert. *Sex and the Single Man*. New York: Lyle Stuart, 1963.

Ellis, Robert A., and W. Clayton Lane. "Structural Supports For Upward Mobility," *American Sociological Review*, 1963, 28:743–756.

Emmerich, Walter. "Parental Identification in Young Children," *Genetic Psychological Monographs*, 1959, 60:257–308. (a)

———. "Young Children's Discrimination of Parent and Child Roles," *Child Development*, 1959, 30:403–419. (b)

———. "Family Role Concepts of Children Ages Six to Ten," *Child Development*, 1961, 32:609–624.

Empey, LaMar T. "Social Class and Occupational Aspiration: A Comparison of Absolute and Relative Measurement," *American Sociological Review*, 1956, 21:703–709.

English, O. Spurgeon, Max Katz, Albert E. Scheflen, Elliot Danzig, and Jeanne Speiser. "Preparedness of High School and College Seniors for Parenthood," *A.M.A. Archives of Neurology and Psychiatry*, 1959, 81:469–479.

Epperson, David C. "A Re-Assessment of Indices of Parental Influence in *The Adolescent Society*," *American Sociological Review*, 1964, 29:93–96.

Epstein, Ralph. "Social Class Membership and Early Childhood Memories," *Child Development*, 1963, 34:503–508.

Erikson, Erik H. *Childhood and Society*. New York: Norton, 1950.

———. *Young Man Luther*. New York: Norton, 1958.

Eron, Leonard D., *et al.* "Comparison of Data Obtained from Mothers and Fathers on Childrearing Practices and Their Relation to Child Aggression," *Child Development*, 1961, 32:457–472.

Eron, Leonard D., Leopold O. Walder, Romolo Toigo, and Monroe M. Lefkowitz. "Social Class, Parental Punishment for Aggression, and Child Aggression," *Child Development*, 1963, 34:849–867.

Farber, Bernard. *Family Organization and Crisis*. Lafayette, Ind.: Society for Research in Child Development, 1960.

———. "Marital Integration as a Factor in Parent-Child Relations," *Child Development*, 1962, 33:1–14.

———, and Julia L. McHale. "Marital Integration and Parents' Agreement on Satisfaction with Their Child's Behavior," *Marriage and Family Living*, 1959, 21:65–69.

Faris, Robert E. L. *Social Disorganization*. New York: Ronald Press, 1948.

Fauls, Lydia Boyce, and Walter D. Smith. "Sex-Role Learning of Five-Year-Olds," *Journal of Genetic Psychology*, 1956, 89:105–117.

Fiedler, Leslie A. *No! In Thunder*. Boston: Beacon Press, 1960.

Foster, June E. "Father Images: Television and Ideal," *Journal of Marriage and the Family*, 1964, 26:353–355.

Francis, Roy G. "Family Strategy in Middle-Class Suburbia," *Sociological Inquiry*, 1963, 33:157–164.

Freedman, Deborah S., Ronald Freedman, and Pascal K. Whelpton. "Size of Family and Preference for Children of Each Sex," *American Journal of Sociology*, 1960, 46:141–146.

Freedman, Ronald, and Lolagene Coombs. "Childspacing and Family Economic Position," *American Sociological Review*, 1967, 31:631–648.

———, P. K. Whelpton, and Arthur A. Campbell. *Family Planning, Sterility and Population Growth*. New York: McGraw-Hill, 1959.

Freilich, Morris. "The Natural Triad in Kinship and Complex Systems," *American Sociological Review*, 1964, 29:529–540.

Freud, Sigmund. *Totem and Taboo*, A. A. Brill (tr.). New York: Moffat, Yard, 1918.

———. *Group Psychology and the Analysis of the Ego*, James Strachey (tr.). New York: Liveright, 1949.

Freudenthal, Kurt. "Problems of the One-Parent Family," *Social Work*, 1959, 4:44–49.

Friedan, Betty. *The Feminine Mystique*. New York: Norton, 1963.

Friedman, Leonard J. *Virgin Wives: A Study of Unconsummated Marriages*. Springfield, Ill.: Charles C. Thomas, 1962.

Fritz, Charles E. "Disaster," in Robert K. Merton and Robert A. Nisbet (eds.), *Contemporary Social Problems.* New York: Harcourt, Brace & World, 1961.

Furstenberg, Frank F., Jr. "Industrialization and the American Family: A Look Backward," *American Sociological Review,* 1966, 31:326–337.

Gardner, L. P. "An Analysis of Children's Attitudes Toward Fathers," *Journal of Genetic Psychology,* 1947, 70:3–28.

Garner, Ann M., and Charles Wenar. *The Mother-Child Interaction in Psychosomatic Disorders.* Urbana: University of Illinois Press, 1955.

Geiken, Karen F. "Expectations Concerning Husband-Wife Responsibilities in the Home," *Journal of Marriage and the Family,* 1964, 26:349–352.

Genné, William H. *Husbands and Pregnancy.* New York: Association Press, 1956.

Gerson, Walter M. "Leisure and Marital Satisfaction of College Married Couples," *Marriage and Family Living,* 1960, 22:360–361.

Giallombardo, Rose. "Social Roles in a Prison for Women," *Social Problems,* 1966, 13:268–288.

Gianopulos, Artie, and Howard E. Mitchell. "Marital Disagreement in Working-Wife Marriages as a Function of Husband's Attitude toward Wife's Employment," *Marriage and Family Living,* 1957, 19:373–378.

Gill, Lois J., and Bernard Spilka. "Some Nonintellectual Correlates of Academic Achievement Among Mexican-American Secondary School Students," *Journal of Educational Psychology,* 1962, 53:144–149.

Glasser, Paul H., and Lois N. Glasser. "Role Reversal and Conflict Between Aged Parents and Their Children," *Marriage and Family Living,* 1962, 24:46–51.

———, and Elizabeth Navarre. "Structural Problems of the One-Parent Family," *Journal of Social Issues,* 1965, 21:98–109.

Glazer, Nathan, and Daniel P. Moynihan. *Beyond the Melting Pot.* Cambridge: M.I.T. Press, 1963.

Gleason, George. *Horizons for Older People.* New York: Macmillan, 1965.

Glenn, Hortense M. "Attitudes of Women Regarding Gainful Employment of Married Women," *Journal of Home Economics,* 1959, 51:247–252.

Glick, Paul C. "The Life Cycle of the Family," *Marriage and Family Living,* 1955, 17:3–9.

———. *American Families.* New York: Wiley, 1957.

Glickman, Esther. "Problems in Child Placement," *Social Science Review,* 1954, 28:279–289.

Glueck, Sheldon, and Eleanor Glueck. *Unraveling Juvenile Delinquency.* Cambridge: Harvard University Press, 1950.

Goffman, Erving. *The Presentation of Self in Everyday Life.* Garden City, N. Y.: Doubleday, 1959.

———. *Encounters: Two Studies in the Sociology of Interaction.* Indianapolis: Bobbs-Merrill, 1961.

Gold, Martin. *Status Forces in Delinquent Boys.* Ann Arbor: Institute for

Social Research, University of Michigan, 1963.

———, and Carol Slater. "Office, Factory, Store—And Family: A Study of Integration Setting," *American Sociological Review*, 1958, 23:64–74.

Goode, William J. *After Divorce*. New York: Free Press, 1956.

———. "The Theoretical Importance of Love," *American Sociological Review*, 1959, 24:38–47.

———. "Illegitimacy in Caribbean Social Structure," *American Sociological Review*, 1960, 25:21–30.(a)

———. "A Theory of Role Strain," *American Sociological Review*, 1960, 25:483–496.(b)

———. "Illegitimacy, Anomie and Cultural Penetration," *American Sociological Review*, 1961, 25:910–925.(a)

———. "Family Disorganization," in Robert K. Merton and Robert A. Nisbet (eds.), *Contemporary Social Problems*. New York: Harcourt, Brace and World, 1961.(b)

———. *World Revolution and Family Patterns*. New York: Free Press, 1963.

Goodenough, Evelyn W. "Interest in Persons as an Aspect of Sex Difference in the Early Years," *Genetic Psychology Monographs*, 1957, 55:287–323.

Goodsell, Willystine. *A History of Marriage and the Family*. New York: Macmillan, 1934.

Gordon, Ira J. *Human Development from Birth through Adolescence*. New York: Harper & Row, 1962.

Gottlieb, David, and Charles Ramsey. *The American Adolescent*. Homewood, Ill.: Dorsey Press, 1964.

Gouldner, Alvin W. *Enter Plato*. New York: Basic Books, 1966.

Gover, David A. "Socio-Economic Differential in the Relationship Between Marital Adjustment and Wife's Employment Status," *Marriage and Family Living*, 1963, 25:452–458.

———, and Dorothy G. Jones. "Requirement of Parental Consent: A Deterrent to Marriage?" *Marriage and Family Living*, 1964, 26:205–206.

Gray, Horace. "Marriage and Premarital Conception," *Journal of Psychology*, 1960, 50:383–397.

Gray, Robert M., and Ted C. Smith. "Effect of Employment on Sex Differences in Attitudes Toward the Parental Family," *Marriage and Family Living*, 1960, 22:36–38.

Gray, Susan W. "Masculinity-Femininity in Relation to Anxiety and Social Acceptance," *Child Development*, 1957, 28:203–214.

———. "Perceived Similarity to Parents and Adjustment," *Child Development*, 1959, 30:91–107.

———, and Rupert Klaus. "The Assessment of Parental Identification," *Genetic Psychology Monographs*, 1956, 54:87–114.

Green, Arnold M. "The Middle-Class Male Child and Neurosis," *American Sociological Review*, 1946, 11:31–42.

Greenfield, Sidney M. "Love and Marriage in Modern America: A

Functional Analysis," *Sociological Quarterly*, 1965, 6:361–377.

Gregory, Ian. "Studies of Parental Deprivation in Psychiatric Patients," *American Journal of Psychiatry*, 1958, 115:432–442.

Grinder, Robert E. "Relations Between Behavioral and Cognitive Dimensions of Conscience in Middle Childhood," *Child Development*, 1964, 35:881–891.

Gross, Edward, and Gregory P. Stone. "Embarrassment and the Analysis of Role Requirements," *American Journal of Sociology*, 1964, 70:1–15.

Hacker, Helen Mayer. "The New Burdens of Masculinity," *Marriage and Family Living*, 1957, 19:227–233.

Hallowitz, David, and Burton Stulberg. "The Vicious Cycle in Parent-Child Relationship Breakdown," *Social Casework*, 1959, 40:268–275.

Halpern, Howard. "Alienation from Parenthood in the Kibbutz and America," *Marriage and Family Living*, 1962, 24:42–45.

Handel, Gerald, and Lee Rainwater. "Working-Class People and Family Planning," *Social Work*, 1961, 6:18–25.

Harlow, Harry F. "The Nature of Love," *American Psychologist*, 1958, 13:673–685.

———, and Robert R. Zimmerman. "The Development of Affectional Responses in Infant Monkeys," *Proceedings of the American Philosophical Society*, 1958, 102:501–509.

Harris, Irving D. *Normal Children and Mothers*. New York: Free Press, 1959.

Hartley, Ruth E. "Sex-Role Pressures and the Socialization of the Male Child," *Psychological Reports*, 1959, 5:457–468.

———. "Children's Concepts of Male and Female Roles," *Merrill-Palmer Quarterly*, 1960, 6:83–91.

———. "Sex Roles and Urban Youth: Some Developmental Perspectives," *Bulletin of Family Development*, 1961, 2:1–12.

———, and Armin Klein. "Sex-Role Concepts Among Elementary-School-Age Girls," *Marriage and Family Living*, 1959, 21:59–64.

Hartmann, Heinz, Ernst Kris, and Rudolph M. Lowenstein. "Some Psychoanalytic Comments on Culture and Personality," in George B. Wilbur and Warner Muensterberger (eds.), *Psychoanalysis and Culture*. New York: International Universities Press, 1951.

Havighurst, Robert J. "The Social Competence of Middle-Aged People," *Genetic Psychology Monographs*, 1957, 56:297–373.

Hawkes, Glenn R. "The Child in the Family," *Marriage and Family Living*, 1957, 19:46–51.

———, Lee Burchinal, and B. Gardner. "Size of Family and Adjustment of Children," *Marriage and Family Living*, 1958, 20:65–68.

Heer, David M. "Dominance and the Working Wife," *Social Forces*, 1958, 36:341–347.

———. "Husband and Wife Perceptions of Family Power Structure," *Marriage and Family Living*, 1962, 24:65–67.

———. "The Measurement and Bases of Family Power: An Overview," *Marriage and Family Living*, 1963, 25:133–139.

Heiss, Jerold S. "Degree of Intimacy and Male-Female Interaction," *Sociometry,* 1962, 25:197–208.
Helfrich, Margaret L. "The Generalized Role of the Executive's Wife," *Marriage and Family Living,* 1961, 23:384–387.
Helper, M. M. "Learning Theory and the Self-Concept," *Journal of Abnormal and Social Psychology,* 1955, 51:184–194.
Hendin, Herbert. *Suicide and Scandanavia.* New York: Grune & Stratton, 1964.
Henry, Andrew F. "Sibling Structure and Perception of the Disciplinary Roles of Parents," *Sociometry,* 1957, 20:67–74.
Henry, Jules. *Culture Against Man.* New York: Random House, 1963.
Herbst, P. G. "The Measurement of Family Relationships," *Human Relations,* 1952, 5:3–30.
———. "Family Living—Patterns of Interaction," in O. A. Oeser and S. B. Hammond (eds.), *Social Structure and Personality in a City.* London: Routledge & Kegan Paul, 1954.
Herrmann, Robert O. "Expectations and Attitudes as a Source of Financial Problems in Teen-age Marriages," *Journal of Marriage and the Family,* 1965, 27:89–91.
Hess, Robert D., and Gerald Handel. "Patterns of Aggression in Parents and Their Children," *Journal of Genetic Psychology,* 1956, 89:199–212.
———, and Judith V. Torney. "Religion, Age, and Sex in Children's Perceptions of Family Authority," *Child Development,* 1962, 33:781–789.
Hetherington, E. M., and Yvonne Brackbill. "Etiology and Covariation of Obstinacy, Orderliness, and Parsimony in Young Children," *Child Development,* 1963, 34:919–943.
Hill, Reuben. "The Returning Father and His Family," *Marriage and Family Living,* 1945, 7:31–34.
———. "Education for Marriage and Parenthood in the United States." Paper presented to the Social Scientists' Advisory Meeting, sponsored by the Social Security Administration, June 20, 1960.
———. "The American Family of the Future," *Marriage and Family Living,* 1964, 26:20–28.
———, and Howard Becker. *Marriage and the Family.* Boston: Heath, 1942.
———, J. M. Stycos, and Kurt W. Back. *The Family and Population Control.* Chapel Hill, N.C.: University of North Carolina Press, 1959.
Hilsdale, Paul. "Marriage as a Personal Existential Commitment," *Marriage and Family Living,* 1962, 24:137–143.
Hobart, Charles W. "Disillusionment in Marriage and Romanticism," *Marriage and Family Living,* 1958, 20:156–162.
———. "Commitment, Value Conflict and the Future of the American Family," *Marriage and Family Living,* 1963, 25:405–412.
———, and William J. Klausner. "Some Social Interactional Correlates of Marital Role Disagreement, and Marital Adjustment," *Marriage and Family Living,* 1959, 21:256–263.

Hobbs, Daniel F., Jr. "Parenthood as Crisis: A Third Study," *Journal of Marriage and the Family*, 1965, 27:367–372.

Hockett, Charles F., and Robert Ascher. "The Human Revolution," *Current Anthropology*, 1964, 5:135–147.

Hodge, Robert W., and Patricia Hodge. "Occupational Assimilation as a Competitive Process," *American Journal of Sociology*, 1965, 71:249–264.

Hoffman, Lois Wladis. "Effects of the Employment of Mothers on Parental Power Relations and the Division of Household Tasks," *Marriage and Family Living*, 1960, 22:27–35.

———. "The Father's Role in the Family and the Child's Peer-Group Adjustment," *Merrill-Palmer Quarterly*, 1961, 7:97–105.

———. "Effects on Children: Summary and Discussion," in F. Ivan Nye and Lois Wladis Hoffman (eds.), *The Employed Mother in America*. Chicago: Rand McNally, 1963.

———, and R. Lippitt. "The Measurement of Family Life Variables," in P. H. Mussen (ed.), *Handbook of Research Methods in Child Development*. New York: Wiley, 1960.

Hoffman, Martin L. "Childrearing Practices and Moral Development: Generalizations From Empirical Research," *Child Development*, 1963, 34:295–318. (a)

———. "Personality, Family Structure, and Social Class as Antecedents of Parental Power Assertion," *Child Development*, 1963, 34:869–884. (b)

Hollingsworth, Bruce. "An Analysis of a Sample of County Welfare Families with a Record of Pregnancy Causing Increases in Welfare Expenditures." Unpublished Master's thesis. Denton: North Texas State University, 1966.

Homans, George C. *Sentiments and Activities*. New York: Free Press, 1962.

Horowitz, Michael M., and Sylvia H. Horowitz. "A Note on Marriage in Martinique," *Marriage and Family Living*, 1963, 25:160–161.

Hotchner, A. E. *Papa Hemingway*. New York: Random House, 1966.

Hubert, Alice G., and Joseph H. Britton. "Attitudes and Practices of Mothers Rearing Their Children from Birth to the Age of Two Years," *Journal of Home Economics*, 1957, 49:208–219.

Hurlock, Elizabeth B. *Developmental Psychology*. New York: McGraw-Hill, 1959.

Hurvitz, Nathan. "The Index of Strain as a Measure of Marital Satisfaction," *Sociology and Social Research*, 1959, 44:106–111.

———. "The Measurement of Marital Strain." *American Journal of Sociology*, 55:610–615.

———. "The Components of Marital Roles," *Sociology and Social Research*, 1961, 45:301–308.

———. "Control Roles, Marital Strain, Role Deviation, and Marital Adjustment," *Journal of Marriage and the Family*, 1965, 27:29–31.

Ilgenfritz, Marjorie P. "Mothers on Their Own—Widows and Divorcees,"

Marriage and Family Living, 1961, 23:38–41.

Illsley, Raymond, and Barbara Thompson. "Women From Broken Homes," *Sociological Review,* 1961, 9:27–54.

Inkeles, Alex. "Social Change and Social Character: The Role of Parental Mediation," in Neil J. Smelser and William T. Smelser (eds.), *Personality and Social Systems.* New York: Wiley, 1963.

Isaacs, Susan. *Fatherless Children.* London: New Education Fellowship, 1945.

Isambert, Andre. "Personal Maturity and Parent Education," *Marriage and Family Living,* 1961, 23:154–159.

Iscoe, Ira, Martha Williams, and Jerry Harvey. "Age, Intelligence, and Sex as Variables in the Conformity Behavior of Negro and White Children," *Child Development,* 1964, 35:451–460.

Jacobson, Alver H. "Conflict of Attitudes Toward the Roles of the Husband and Wife in Marriage," *American Sociological Review,* 1952, 17:146–150.

Jencks, Christopher. Review of Gael Greene's *Sex and the College Girl, The New Republic,* April 4, 1964.

Jephcott, Pearl, with Nancy Sears and John H. Smith. *Married Women Working.* London: G. Allen, 1962.

Johannis, Theodore B., Jr. "Participation by Fathers, Mothers, and Teenage Sons and Daughters in Selected Family Economic Activity," *Coordinator,* 1957, 6:15–16. (a)

———. "Participation by Fathers, Mothers, and Teenage Sons and Daughters in Selected Child Care and Control Activity," *Coordinator,* 1957, 6:31–32. (b)

———. "Participation by Fathers, Mothers and Teenage Sons and Daughters in Selected Household Tasks," *Coordinator,* 1958, 6:61–62.

———, and James M. Rollins. "Teenager Perceptions of Family Decision Making," *Coordinator,* 1959, 7:70–74.

Johnson, Miriam M. "Sex Role Learning in the Nuclear Family," *Child Development,* 1963, 34:319–333.

Jordan, Thomas E. "Research on the Handicapped Child and the Family," *Merrill-Palmer Quarterly,* 1962, 8:243–260.

Josselyn, Irene M. "Cultural Forces, Motherliness, and Fatherliness," *American Journal of Orthopsychiatry,* 1956, 26:264–271.

Kaffman, Mordecai. "Evaluation of Emotional Disturbance in 403 Israeli Kibbutz Children," *American Journal of Psychiatry,* 1961, 117:732–738.

Kagan, Jerome. "The Child's Perception of the Parent," *Journal of Abnormal and Social Psychology,* 1956, 53:257–258.

———. "The Concept of Identification," *Psychological Review,* 1958, 65:296–305.

———. "American Longitudinal Research on Psychological Development," *Child Development,* 1964, 35:1–32.

———, and Marion Freeman. "Relation of Childhood Intelligence, Maternal Behaviors, and Social Class to Behavior During Adolescence," *Child Development,* 1963, 34:899–911.

———, Barbara Hosken, and Sara Watson. "Child's Symbolic Conceptualization of Parents," *Child Development*, 1961, 32:625–636.

———, and Howard A. Moss. *Birth to Maturity: A Study in Psychological Development*. New York: Wiley, 1962.

Kahl, Joseph A. "Educational and Occupational Aspirations of 'Common Man' Boys," *Harvard Educational Review*, 1953, 23:186–203.

———. *The American Class Structure*. New York: Holt, Rinehart and Winston, 1957.

———. "Some Measurements of Achievement Orientation," *American Journal of Sociology*, 1965, 70:669–681.

Kammeyer, Kenneth. "The Feminine Role: An Analysis of Attitude Consistency," *Journal of Marriage and the Family*, 1964, 26:295–305.

Kanin, Eugene J. "Male Aggression in Dating-Courtship Relations," *American Journal of Sociology*, 1957, 63:197–204.

Kantor, Mildred B., John C. Glidewell, Ivan N. Mensh, Herbert R. Domki, and Margaret C. Gildea. "Socio-Economic Level and Maternal Attitudes Toward Parent-Child Relationships," *Human Organization*, 1958, 16:44–48.

Kaplan, Max. "The Uses of Leisure," in Clark Tibbitts (ed.), *Handbook of Social Gerontology*. Chicago: University of Chicago Press, 1960.

Kauffman, J. Howard. "Interpersonal Relations in Traditional and Emergent Families Among Midwest Mennonites," *Marriage and Family Living*, 1961, 23:247–252.

Kaufman, Dorothy B. "Cooperative Nursery Aids Family Living Classes," *Marriage and Family Living*, 1961, 23:396–399.

Kell, Leone, and Joan Aldous. "Trends in Child Care Over Three Generations," *Marriage and Family Living*, 1960, 22:176–177.

Keniston, Kenneth. *The Uncommitted*. New York: Harcourt, Brace & World, 1965.

Kenkel, William F. "Traditional Family Ideology and Spousal Roles in Decision Making," *Marriage and Family Living*, 1959, 21:334–339.

———. "Sex of Observer and Spousal Roles in Decision Making," *Marriage and Family Living*, 1961, 23:185–186.

Kephart, William M. *The Family, Society, and the Individual*. Boston: Houghton Mifflin, 1961.

Kerckhoff, Richard. "Teaching Ethical Values Through the Marriage Course: A Debate, Con," *Marriage and Family Living*, 1957, 19:330–334.

Khalfina, Raissa O. Review of David Mace and Vera Mace, *The Soviet Family*, *Journal of Marriage and the Family*, 1964, 26:367–370.

Kinsey, Alfred C., Wardell B. Pomeroy, and Clyde E. Martin. *Sexual Behavior in the Human Male*. Philadelphia: Saunders, 1948.

Kirk, H. David. *Shared Fate*. New York: Free Press, 1964.

Kirkendall, Lester A., O. Hobart Mowrer, and Thomas Poffenberger. "Sex Education of Adolescents: An Exchange," *Marriage and Family Living*, 1960, 22:317–332.

Kirkpatrick, Clifford. *The Family*. New York: Ronald Press, 1955.

Kitsuse, John I., and Aaron V. Cicourel. "The High School's Role in Adolescent Status Transition," in B. J. Chandler, L. J. Stiles, and J. I. Kitsuse (eds.), *Education in Urban Society*. New York: Dodd, Mead, 1962.

Klein, Viola. "Working Wives," summarized in *Marriage and Family Living*, 1961, 23:387.

Knupfer, Genevieve. Reported in the *Dallas Morning News*, March 11, 1966, p. 48.

Koch, Helen L. "Some Personality Correlates of Sex, Sibling Position and Sex of Siblings Among Five- and Six-Year-Old Children," *Genetic Psychology Monographs*, 1955, 52:3–50.

Kohn, Melvin L. "Social Class and Parental Values," *American Journal of Sociology*, 1950, 64:337–351.

———. "Social Class and the Exercise of Parental Authority," *American Sociological Review*, 1959, 24:352–366.

———. "Social Class and Parent-Child Relationships: An Interpretation," *American Journal of Sociology*, 1963, 68:471–480.

———, and Eleanor E. Carroll. "Social Class and the Allocation of Parental Responsibilities," *Sociometry*, 1960, 23:372–392.

Komarovsky, Mirra. *The Unemployed Man and His Family*. New York: Dryden, 1940.

———. "Cultural Contradictions and Sex Roles," *American Journal of Sociology*, 1946, 52:184–189.

———. "Functional Analysis of Sex Roles," *American Sociological Review*, 1950, 15:508–516.

———. *Women in the Modern World*. Boston: Little, Brown, 1953.

———. *Blue-Collar Marriage*. New York: Random House, 1964.

Koos, Earl L. "Class Differences in Family Reactions to Crisis," *Marriage and Family Living*, 1950, 12:77–78.

Kosa, John, Leo D. Rachiele, and Cyril O. Schommer, S. J. "Sharing the Home with Relatives," *Marriage and Family Living*, 1960, 22:129–131.

Krauss, Irving. "Sources of Educational Aspirations Among Working-Class Youth," *American Sociological Review*, 1964, 29:867–879.

Kronhausen, Phyllis, and Eberhard Kronhausen. *Sex Histories of American College Men*. New York: Ballantine Books, 1960.

Kunstadter, Peter. "A Survey of the Consanguine or Matrifocal Family," *American Anthropologist*, 1963, 65:56–66.

Landis, Judson T. "Religiousness, Family Relationships, and Family Values in Protestant, Catholic, and Jewish Families," *Marriage and Family Living*, 1960, 22:341–347. (a)

———. "The Trauma of Children When Parents Divorce," *Marriage and Family Living*, 1960, 22:7–13. (b)

———. "A Re-examination of the Role of the Father as an Index of Family Integration," *Marriage and Family Living*, 1962, 24:122–128. (a)

———. "A Comparison of Children from Divorced and Nondivorced

Unhappy Marriages," *The Family Life Coordinator,* 1962, 11:61–65. (b)

———. "Social Correlates of Divorce or Nondivorce Among the Unhappy Married," *Marriage and Family Living,* 1963, 25:178–180.

Landis, Paul H. "Research on Teen-Age Dating," *Marriage and Family Living,* 1960, 22:266–267.

———, and Carol L. Stone. *The Relationship of Parental Authority Patterns to Teenage Adjustments.* Agricultural Experiment Station Bulletin No. 538. Pullman: State College of Washington, 1953.

Lane, Robert E. "Fathers and Sons: Foundations of Political Belief," *American Sociological Review,* 1959, 24:502–511.

Langner, Thomas S., and Stanley T. Michael. *Life Stress and Mental Health.* New York: Free Press, 1963.

Lansky, Leonard M., Vaughn J. Crandall, Jerome Kagan, and Charles T. Baker. "Sex Differences in Aggression and Its Correlates in Middle-Class Adolescents," *Child Development,* 1961, 32:45–58.

Lantz, Herman R. "Nervous Stability of Parents as Reported in a Psychiatric Sample of One Thousand," *Marriage and Family Living,* 1958, 20:69–72.

Lazowick, Lionel M. "On the Nature of Identification," *Journal of Abnormal and Social Psychology,* 1955, 51:175–182.

Leavitt, Harold J. "Ignorance, Success, and Innovation," *Trans-action,* 1965, 2:31–32.

Leichty, Mary M. "The Effect of Father-Absence During Early Childhood Upon the Oedipal Situation as Reflected in Young Adults," *Merrill-Palmer Quarterly,* 1960, 6:212–217.

Leik, Robert K. "Instrumentality and Emotionality in Family Interaction," *Sociometry,* 1963, 26:131–145.

LeMasters, E. E. "Parenthood as Crisis," *Marriage and Family Living,* 1957, 19:352–355.

Le Play, Pierre Guillaume Frédéric. *Les Ouvriers Europeens.* Paris: 1879. Abridged adaptation by C. C. Zimmerman and M. F. Frampton, *Family and Society,* based on the translation of S. Dupertuis. New York: Van Nostrand, 1935.

Leslie, Gerald R., and Kathryn P. Johnsen. "Changed Perceptions of the Maternal Role," *American Sociological Review,* 1963, 28:919–928.

Levinger, George. "Marital Cohesiveness and Dissolution: An Integrative Review," *Journal of Marriage and the Family,* 1965, 27:19–28.

Levy, Marion J., Jr. *The Family Revolution in Modern China.* Cambridge, Mass.: Harvard University Press, 1949.

Lewis, Oscar. *Life in a Mexican Village.* Urbana, Illinois: University of Illinois Press, 1951.

———. "Family Dynamics in a Mexican Village," *Marriage and Family Living,* 1959, 21:218–226. (a)

———. *Five Families.* New York: Basic Books, 1959. (b)

———. *Tepotzlán: Village in Mexico.* New York: Holt, Rinehart and Winston, 1962.

———. *Pedro Martínez*. New York: Random House, 1964.

Littman, Richard A., John Curry, and John Pierce-Jones. "Where Parents Go for Help," *Coordinator*, 1957, 6:3–9.

Litwack, Lawrence. "An Examination of Ten Significant Differences Between Juvenile Recidivists and Non-Recidivists," *Journal of Educational Research*, 1961, 55:132–134.

Litwak, Eugene. "Geographic Mobility and Extended Family Cohesion," *American Sociological Review*, 1960, 25:385–394. (a)

———. "Occupational Mobility and Extended Family Cohesion," *American Sociological Review*, 1960, 25:9–21. (b)

Lopata, Helena Z. "The Secondary Features of a Primary Relationship," *Human Organization*, 1965, 24:116–123.

Lorenz, Konrad. *On Aggression*. New York: Harcourt, Brace & World, 1966.

Lott, Albert J., and Bernice E. Lott. *Negro and White Youth: A Psychological Study in a Border-State Community*. New York: Holt, Rinehart and Winston, 1963.

Lowrie, Samuel H. "Early Marriage: Premarital Pregnancy and Associated Factors," *Journal of Marriage and the Family*, 1965, 27:48–56.

Lu, Yi-Chuang. "Parental Role and Parent-Child Relationship," *Marriage and Family Living*, 1952, 14:294–297.

Luckey, Eleanore Braun. "Marital Satisfaction and Congruent Self-Spouse Concepts," *Social Forces*, 1960, 39:153–157. (a)

———. "Marital Satisfaction and Parental Concept," *Journal of Consulting Psychology*, 1960, 24:195–204. (b)

———. "Family Goals in a Democratic Society," *Journal of Marriage and the Family*, 1964, 26:271–278.

Lynn, David B. "The Husband-Father Role in the Family," *Marriage and Family Living*, 1961, 23:295–296.

———. "Sex-Role and Parental Identification," *Child Development*, 1962, 33:555–564.

———. "Divergent Feedback and Sex-Role Identification in Boys and Men," *Merrill-Palmer Quarterly*, 1964, 10:17–23.

———. "The Process of Learning Parental and Sex-Role Identification," *Journal of Marriage and the Family*, 1966, 28:466–470.

———, and William L. Sawrey. "The Effects of Father-Absence on Norwegian Boys and Girls," *Journal of Abnormal and Social Psychology*, 1959, 59:258–262.

Maas, H. S. "Some Social Class Differences in the Family Systems and Group Relations of Pre- and Early Adolescents," *Child Development*, 1951, 22:145–152.

McCandless, Boyd R. *Children and Adolescents*. New York: Holt, Rinehart and Winston, 1961.

McClelland, David C. *The Achieving Society*. Princeton, N. J.: Van Nostrand, 1961.

Maccoby, Eleanor E. "Differential Cognitive Abilities," U. S. Office of Education, Cooperative Research Project No. 1040, 1962.

McCord, Joan, and William McCord. "The Effect of Parental Role Model on Criminality," *Journal of Social Issues,* 1958, 14:66–75.

———, William McCord, and Emily Thurber. "Some Effects of Paternal Absence on Male Children," *Journal of Abnormal and Social Psychology,* 1962, 64:361–369.

McDill, Edward L., and James Coleman. "High School Social Status, College Plans, and Interest in Academic Achievement: A Panel Analysis," *American Sociological Review,* 1963, 28:905–918.

Mace, David R. "The Employed Mother in the U.S.S.R.," *Marriage and Family Living,* 1961, 23:330–333.

———. "Some Reflections on the American Family," *Marriage and Family Living,* 1962, 24:109–112.

———, and Vera Mace. *The Soviet Family.* Garden City, N. Y.: Doubleday, 1963.

McKeany, Maurine. *The Absent Father and Public Policy in the Program of Aid to Dependent Children.* Berkeley: University of California Press, 1960.

McKee, John P., and Alex C. Sheriffs. "The Differential Evaluation of Males and Females," *Journal of Personality,* 1957, 25:365–371.

———, and Alex C. Sheriffs. "Men's and Women's Beliefs, Ideas, and Self-Concepts," *American Journal of Sociology,* 1964, 64:356–363.

McKinley, Donald Gilbert. *Social Class and Family Life.* New York: Free Press, 1964.

Madison, Bernice. "Canadian Family Allowances and Their Major Social Implications," *Marriage and Family Living,* 1964, 26:134–141.

Madsen, William. *The Mexican-Americans of South Texas.* New York: Holt, Rinehart and Winston, 1964.

Malhotra, Prabha, and Lilian Khan. "Factors Favoring Acceptance of Family Planning Among Women Attending Some New Delhi M.C.W. Centers," *Journal of Family Welfare,* 1962, 8:1–18.

Malinowski, Bronislaw. *Sex and Repression in Savage Society.* New York: Harcourt, Brace & World, 1927.

Manis, M. "Personal Adjustment, Assumed Similarity to Parents, and Inferred Parental Evaluations of the Self," *Journal of Consulting Psychology,* 1958, 22:481–485.

Mann, David, Luther E. Woodward, and Nathan Joseph. *Educating Expectant Parents.* New York: Visiting Nurse Service of New York, 1961.

Marchand, Jean, and Louise Langford. "Adjustments of Married Students," *Journal of Home Economics,* 1952, 44:113–114.

Marshall, Hermine H. "Behavior Problems of Normal Children: A Comparison Between the Lay Literature and Developmental Research," *Child Development,* 1964, 35:469–478.

Martin, Cora A., and Alexander L. Clark. "Social Class and Parental Values: A Critical Reappraisal." Paper presented to the *Southwestern Sociological Society,* New Orleans, 1966.

Matsumoto, Misao, and Henrietta T. Smith. "Japanese and American Children's Perception of Parents," *Journal of Genetic Psychology,* 1961, 98:83–88.

Maxwell, Patricia Henderson, Ruth Connor, and James Walters. "Family Member Perceptions of Parent Role Performance," *Merrill-Palmer Quarterly*, 1961, 7:31–38.

Mead, George Herbert. *Mind, Self and Society*. Chicago: University of Chicago Press, 1934.

Mead, Margaret. *Male and Female: A Study of the Sexes in a Changing World*. New York: Morrow, 1953.

———. Interview in *U. S. News and World Report*, May 20, 1963, pp. 48–50.

———. In "People," *Time*, February 17, 1967, p. 42.

Merton, Robert K. *Social Theory and Social Structure*. Rev. ed. New York: Free Press, 1957.

Middleton, Russell, and Snell Putney. "Dominance in Decisions in the Family: Race and Class Differences," *American Journal of Sociology*, 1960, 55:605–609.

———, and Snell Putney. "Student Rebellion Against Parental Political Beliefs," *Social Forces*, 1963, 41:377–383.

Miller, Daniel R., and Guy E. Swanson. *The Changing American Parent*. New York: Wiley, 1958.

Mills, C. Wright. "Methodological Consequences of the Sociology of Knowledge," *American Journal of Sociology*, 1940, 46:316–330.

Milton, G. A. "The Effects of Sex-Role Identification Upon Problem-Solving Skills," *Journal of Abnormal and Social Psychology*, 1957, 55:208–212.

Mischel, Walter. "Father-Absence and Delay of Gratification: Cross-Cultural Comparisons," *Journal of Abnormal and Social Psychology*, 1961, 63:116–124.

Mizruchi, Ephraim H. *Success and Opportunity*. New York: Free Press, 1964.

Mogey, John M. "A Century of Declining Paternal Authority," *Marriage and Family Living*, 1957, 19:234–239.

———. "Marriage Counseling and Family-Life Education in England," *Marriage and Family Living*, 1961, 23:146–154.

———, and Raymond Morris. "Causes of Change in Family Role Patterns," *Bulletin of Family Development*, 1960, 1:1–10.

Monahan, Thomas P. "Family Fugitives," *Marriage and Family Living*, 1958, 20:146–151.

———. "Premarital Pregnancy in the United States: A Critical Review and Some New Findings," *Eugenics Quarterly*, 1960, 7:133–146.

Montagu, M. F. A. *The Natural Superiority of Women*. New York: Macmillan, 1953.

Moore, Barrington. "Thoughts on the Future of the Family," in Maurice R. Stein, Arthur J. Vidich, and David M. White (eds.), *Identity and Anxiety*. New York: Free Press, 1960.

Moore, Bernice M., and Wayne H. Holtzman. *Tomorrow's Parents*. Austin: University of Texas Press, 1965.

Morgan, Lewis Henry. *Ancient Society*. Chicago: Charles H. Kerr, 1877.

Morgan, Patricia K., and Eugene L. Gaier. "The Direction of Aggression in the Mother-Child Punishment Situation," *Child Development*, 1956, 27:447–457.

Morison, Robert S. "Where Is Biology Taking Us?" *Science*, 1967, 155: 429–433.

Moss, J. Joel, and Marian Myers MacNab. "Young Families," *Journal of Home Economics*, 1961, 53:829–834.

Motz, Annabelle Bender. "The Roles of the Married Woman in Science," *Marriage and Family Living*, 1961, 23:374–376.

Mowrer, O. Hobart. "Identification: A Link Between Learning Theory and Psychotherapy," in O. Hobart Mowrer, *Learning Theory and Personality Dynamics: Selected Papers*. New York: Ronald, 1950.

Muller, Hermann J. "Genetic Progress by Voluntarily Conducted Germinal Choice," in Gordon E. Wolstenholme (ed.), *Man and His Future*. Boston: Little, Brown, 1963.

Murdock, George P. "Family Stability in Non-European Cultures," *Annals of the American Academy of Political and Social Science*, 1950, 272:195–201.

Murrell, Stanley A., and James G. Stachowiak. "The Family Group: Development, Structure, and Therapy," *Journal of Marriage and the Family*, 1965, 27:13–18.

Mussen, Paul H., and Luther Distler. "Masculinity, Identification, and Father-Son Relationships," *Journal of Abnormal and Social Psychology*, 1959, 59:350–356.

———, and Luther Distler. "Child-Rearing Antecedents of Masculine Identification in Kindergarten Boys," *Child Development*, 1960, 31:89–100.

———, and Eldred Rutherford. "Parent-Child Relations and Parental Personality in Relation to Young Children's Sex-Role Preferences," *Child Development*, 1963, 34:589–607.

Nash, John. "The Father in Contemporary Culture and Current Psychological Literature," *Child Development*, 1965, 36:282–293.

Neubauer, Peter D. (ed.). *Children in Collectives*. Springfield, Ill.: Charles C. Thomas, 1965.

Neugarten, Bernice L., and Karol K. Weinstein. "The Changing American Grandparent," *Marriage and Family Living*, 1964, 26:199–204.

Nimkoff, Meyer F. "Changing Family Relationships of Older People in the United States During the Last Fifty Years," in Clark Tibbitts and Wilma Donahue (eds.), *Social and Psychological Aspects of Aging*. New York: Columbia University Press, 1962.

———, and Russell Middleton. "Types of Family and Types of Economy," *American Journal of Sociology*, 1960, 56:215–225.

Norbeck, Edward, Donald Walker, and Mimi Cohen. "The Interpretation of Data: Puberty Rites," *American Anthropologist*, 1962, 64:463–485.

Norman, Ralph D. "The Interpersonal Values of Parents of Achieving and Nonachieving Gifted Children," *Journal of Psychology*, 1966, 64: 49–57.

Nunn, Clyde Z. "Child-Control Through a 'Coalition with God,'" *Child Development*, 1964, 35:417–432

Nye, F. Ivan. "Adolescent and Parent Adjustment—Socio-Economic Level as a Variable," *American Sociological Review,* 1951, 20:341–349.

———. "Adolescent-Parent Adjustment: Age, Sex, Sibling Number, Broken Homes, and Employed Mothers as Variables," *Marriage and Family Living,* 1952, 14:327–332.

———. "Child Adjustment in Broken and in Unhappy Unbroken Homes," *Marriage and Family Living,* 1957, 19:356–361. (a)

———. "Some Family Attitudes and Psychosomatic Illness in Adolescents," *Coordinator,* 1957, 6:26–30. (b)

———. "Employment Status and Recreational Behavior of Mothers," *Pacific Sociological Review,* 1958, 1:69–72.

———. "Employment Status of Mothers and Adjustment of Adolescent Children," *Marriage and Family Living,* 1959, 21:240–244.

———. "Maternal Employment and Marital Interaction: Some Contingent Conditions," *Social Forces,* 1961, 40:113–119.

———. "Personal Satisfactions," in F. Ivan Nye and Lois W. Hoffman (eds.), *The Employed Mother in America.* Chicago: Rand McNally, 1963.

———, and Lois W. Hoffman (eds.). *The Employed Mother in America.* Chicago: Rand McNally, 1963.

Oakes, Don. "The Principal Views the Family-Life Program," *Marriage and Family Living,* 1963, 25:108–109.

Odenwald, Robert P. *The Disappearing Sexes.* New York: Random House, 1965.

Oeser, O. A., and S. B. Hammond. *Social Structure and Personality in a City.* London: Routledge & Paul, 1954.

Ogburn, William F., and Meyer F. Nimkoff. *Technology and the Changing Family.* New York: Houghton Mifflin, 1955.

Olsen, Marvin E. "Distribution of Family Responsibilities and Social Stratification," *Marriage and Family Living,* 1960, 22:60–65.

Opler, Morris E. *Village Life in North India.* Chicago: Delphian Society, 1950.

Osborne, Ruth Farnham. "Boys and Family-Life Education," *Marriage and Family Living,* 1961, 23:50–52.

Osgood, C., G. Suci, and P. H. Tannebaum. *The Measurement of Meaning.* Urbana: University of Illinois Press, 1957.

Paivio, Allan. "Childrearing Antecedents of Audience Sensitivity," *Child Development,* 1964, 35:397–416.

Palmer, Richard C. "Behavior Problems of Children in Navy Officers' Families," *Social Casework,* 1960, 41:177–184.

Palmore, Erdman B., and Phillip E. Hammond. "Interacting Factors in Juvenile Delinquency," *American Sociological Review,* 1964, 29:848–854.

Parsons, Talcott. "The Kinship System of the Contemporary United States," *American Anthropologist,* 1943, 45:22–38.

———. "Certain Primary Sources and Patterns of Aggression in the Social Structure of the Western World," *Psychiatry,* 1947, 10:167–181.

———. "The Father Symbol: An Appraisal in the Light of Psychoanalytic and Sociological Theory," in Lyman Bryson, Louis Finkelstein, R. M. MacIver, and Richard McKeon (eds.), *Symbols and Values.* New York: Harper & Row, 1954.

———. "Social Structure and the Development of Personality: Freud's Contribution to the Integration of Psychology and Sociology," *Psychiatry,* 1958, 21:321–340.

———. "The School Class as a Social System," in Robert E. Grinder (ed.), *Studies in Adolescence.* New York: Macmillan, 1963.

———. *Social Structure and Personality.* New York: Free Press, 1964.

———, Robert F. Bales, *et al. Family, Socialization and Interaction Process.* New York: Free Press, 1955.

Paulme, Denise (ed.). *Women of Tropical Africa.* Berkeley: University of California Press, 1963.

Payne, Donald E., and Paul H. Mussen. "Parent-Child Relations and Father Identification Among Adolescent Boys," *Journal of Abnormal and Social Psychology,* 1956, 52:358–362.

Pearlin, Leonard I., and Melvin L. Kohn. "Social Class, Occupation, and Parental Values: A Cross-National Study," *American Sociological Review,* 1966, 31:466–479.

Perry, Joseph B., Jr., and Erdwin H. Pfuhl, Jr. "Adjustment of Children in 'Solo' and 'Remarriage' Homes," *Marriage and Family Living,* 1963, 25:221–223.

Peterson, Donald R., Wesley C. Becker, Donald J. Shoemaker, Zella Luria, and Leo A. Hellmer. "Child Behavior Problems and Parental Attitudes," *Child Development,* 1961, 32:151–162.

Peterson, Evan T. "The Impact of Maternal Employment on the Mother-Daughter Relationship," *Marriage and Family Living,* 1961, 23:355–361.

Phadke, A. M. "Psychological Aspects of Impotence," *Journal of Family Welfare,* 1958, 4:77–84.

Phillips, Derek L. "Rejection of the Mentally Ill: The Influence of Behavior and Sex," *American Sociological Review,* 1964, 29:679–687.

Phillips, E. L. "Parent-Child Similarities in Personality Disturbances," *Journal of Clinical Psychology,* 1951, 7:188–190.

Pierce, Joe E. *Life in a Turkish Village.* New York: Holt, Rinehart, and Winston, 1964.

Pineo, Peter C. "Disenchantment in the Later Years of Marriage," *Marriage and Family Living,* 1961, 23:3–11.

Plotnicov, Leonard. "Nigerians: The Dream Is Unfulfilled," *Trans-action,* 1965, 3:18–22.

Podolsky, Edward. "The Emotional Problems of the Stepchild," *Mental Hygiene,* 1955, 39:49–53.

Potter, Robert G., Jr., Philip C. Sagi, and Charles F. Westoff. "Improvement of Contraception During the Course of Marriage," *Population Studies,* 1962, 16:160–174.

Powell, Kathryn S. "Maternal Employment in Relation to Family Life," *Marriage and Family Living,* 1961, 23:350–355.

———. "Family Variables," in F. Ivan Nye and Lois W. Hoffman (eds.), *The Employed Mother in America.* Chicago: Rand McNally, 1963.

Prince, Alfred James, and Andrew R. Baggaley. "Personality Variables and the Ideal Mate," *The Family Life Coordinator,* 1963, 3:93–96.

Purdue Opinion Panel. *Future Parents' Views on Child Management.* Report of Poll No. 53. January 1959. Lafayette, Indiana: Purdue University.

Putney, Snell, and Russell Middleton. "Effect of Husband-Wife Interaction on the Strictness of Attitudes Toward Child Rearing," *Marriage and Family Living,* 1960, 22:171–173.

———, and Russell Middleton. "Rebellion, Conformity, and Parental Religious Ideologies," *Sociometry,* 1961, 24:125–135.

Quarantelli, Enrico L. "A Note on the Protective Function of the Family in Disasters," *Marriage and Family Living,* 1960, 22:263–264.

Rainwater, Lee. "Social Status Differences in the Family Relationships of German Men," *Marriage and Family Living,* 1962, 24:12–17.

———. "Marital Sexuality in Four Cultures of Poverty," *Journal of Marriage and the Family,* 1964, 26:457–466.

———, and Karol Kane Weinstein. "A Qualitative Exploration of Family Planning and Contraception in the Working Class," *Marriage and Family Living,* 1960, 22:238–242.

Ramsey, Glenn V. "The Sex Information of Younger Boys," in Jerome M. Seidman (ed.), *The Adolescent: A Book of Readings.* New York: Dryden Press, 1953.

Rapoport, Rhona. "Normal Crises, Family Structure, and Mental Health," *Family Process,* 1963, 2:68–80.

Rapoport, Robert, and Rhona Rapoport. "Work and Family in Contemporary Society," *American Sociological Review,* 1965, 30:381–394.

Ratzeburg, F. "Parental Identification in Young Children," *Genetic Psychology Monographs,* 1959, 60:257–308.

Rau, Lucy. "Parental Antecedents of Identification," *Merrill-Palmer Quarterly,* 1960, 6:77–82.

Reiss, Paul J. "The Extended Kinship System: Correlates of and Attitudes on Frequency of Interaction," *Marriage and Family Living,* 1962, 24:333–339.

Richardson, Stephen A., Albert H. Hastorf, and Sanford M. Dornbusch. "Effects of Physical Disability on a Child's Description of Himself," *Child Development,* 1964, 35:893–907.

Riesman, David. *Abundance For What?* Garden City, N. Y.: Doubleday, 1964.

Robbins, Lillian Cukier. "The Accuracy of Parental Recall of Aspects of Childhood Development and of Child-Rearing Practices," *Journal of Abnormal and Social Psychology,* 1963, 66:261–270.

Robins, Lee N., and Miroda Tomanec. "Closeness to Blood Relatives Outside the Immediate Family," *Marriage and Family Living,* 1962, 24:340–346.

Robinson, Marion O. "Community-Wide Planning for Family Health and Welfare," *Marriage and Family Living,* 1963, 19:198–203.

Rodman, Hyman. "Marital Relationships in a Trinidad Village," *Marriage and Family Living,* 1961, 23:166–170.

Rogers, Everett M., and Hans Sebald. "A Distinction Between Familism, Family Integration, and Kinship Orientation," *Marriage and Family Living,* 1962, 24:25–30.

Rogler, Lloyd H. "A Better Life: Notes from Puerto Rico," *Trans-action,* 1965, 2:34–36.

Rollins, Mabel A. "Monetary Contributions of Wives to Family Income in 1920 and 1960," *Marriage and Family Living,* 1963, 25:226–227.

Rose, Arnold M. "The Adequacy of Women's Expectations for Adult Roles," *Social Forces,* 1951, 30:69–77.

———. "Acceptance of Adult Roles and Separation from Family," *Marriage and Family Living,* 1959, 21:120–126.

Rosen, Bernard C. "The Achievement Syndrome: A Psychocultural Dimension of Social Stratification," *American Sociological Review,* 1956, 21:203–211.

———. "Socialization and Achievement Motivation in Brazil," *American Sociological Review,* 1962, 27:623–624.

———, and Roy C. D'Andrade. "The Psychosocial Origins of Achievement Motivation," *Sociometry,* 1959, 22:185–218.

Rosenstiel, Edith E., and Harold E. Smith. "The Growth of Family Life Education in Illinois," *Marriage and Family Living,* 1963, 25:109–111.

Rossi, Alice S. "A Good Woman Is Hard to Find," *Trans-action,* 1964, 2:20–23.

Rossman, Jack E., and David P. Campbell. "Why College-Trained Mothers Work," *Personnel and Guidance Journal,* 1965, 43:986–992.

Roth, Julius, and Robert F. Peck. "Social Class and Social Mobility Factors Related to Marital Adjustment," *American Sociological Review,* 1951, 16:478–487.

Roy, Prodipto. "Maternal Employment and Adolescent Roles: Rural-Urban Differentials," *Marriage and Family Living,* 1961, 23:340–349.

Rushing, William A. "Adolescent-Parent Relationships and Mobility Aspirations," *Social Forces,* 1964, 43:157–166.

Russell, I. L. "Behavior Problems of Children from Broken and Intact Homes," *Journal of Educational Sociology,* 1957, 31:124–129.

Ryder, Norman B. "The Cohort as a Concept in the Study of Social Change," *American Sociological Review,* 1965, 30:843–861.

Sahlins, Marshall D. "The Social Life of Monkeys, Apes and Primitive Men," in Morton H. Fried (ed.), *Readings in Anthropology.* Vol. II. New York: Crowell, 1959.

Salisbury, Richard F. *From Stone to Steel.* New York: Cambridge University Press, 1962.

Saroyan, William. "Sons and Fathers," *The Reporter,* September 24, 1964, pp. 52–53.

Sauber, Mignon. "The Role of the Unmarried Father," *Welfare in Review,* 1966, 4:15–18.

Schaefer, George, and Milton Zisowitz. *The Expectant Father.* New York: Simon and Schuster, 1964.

Schaller, George B. *The Year of the Gorilla.* Chicago: University of Chicago Press, 1964.

Schapiro, Meyer. "On the Relation of Patron and Artist: Comments on a Proposed Model for the Scientist," *American Journal of Sociology,* 1964, 70:363–369.

Schilling, Margaret. "Evaluation in a Family Education Program," *Marriage and Family Living,* 1961, 23:297–299.

Schneiderman, Leonard. "Value Orientation Preferences of Chronic Relief Recipients," *Social Work,* 1964, 9:13–18.

Schonell, Fred J., and B. H. Watts. "A First Survey of the Effects of the Subnormal Child on the Family Unit," *American Journal of Mental Deficiency,* 1956, 61:210–219.

Schorr, Alvin L. "Current Practice of Filial Responsibility," in Robert Winch, Robert McGinnis, and Herbert Barringer (eds.), *Selected Studies in Marriage and the Family.* New York: Holt, Rinehart and Winston, 1962.

Schwarzweller, Harry K. "Parental Family Ties and Social Integration of Rural to Urban Migrants," *Journal of Marriage and the Family,* 1964, 26:410–416.

Scott, John Finley. "The American College Sorority: Its Role in Class and Ethnic Endogamy," *American Sociological Review,* 1965, 30:514–527.

Sears, Robert R. "Identification as a Form of Behavioral Development," in Dale R. Harris (ed.), *The Concept of Development.* Minneapolis: University of Minnesota Press, 1957.

———, Eleanor E. Maccoby, and Harry Levin. *Patterns of Child Rearing.* Evanston, Ill.: Row, Peterson, 1957.

———, Margaret H. Pintler, and Pauline S. Sears. "Effect of Father Separation on Pre-School Children's Doll-Play Aggression," *Child Development,* 1946, 17:219–243.

———, *et al.* "Some Child-Rearing Antecedents of Aggression and Dependency in Young Children," *Genetic Psychology Monographs,* 1953, 47:135–234.

Sewell, William H. "Social Class and Childhood Personality," *Sociometry,* 1961, 24:340–356.

———. "Community of Residence and College Plans," *American Sociological Review,* 1964, 29:24–38.

Shah, Khalida. "Attitudes of Pakistani Students Toward Family Life," *Marriage and Family Living,* 1960, 22:156–161.

Sharp, Harry, and Paul Mott. "Consumer Decisions in the Metropolitan Family," *Journal of Marketing,* 1956, 21:149–156.

Sheldon, Henry D. *The Older Population of the United States.* New York: Wiley, 1958.

Short, James F., Jr., Fred L. Strodtbeck, and Desmond S. Cartwright. "A Strategy for Utilizing Research Dilemmas: A Case from the Study of Parenthood in a Street-Corner Gang," *Sociological Inquiry,* 1962, 32:185–203.

Siegel, Alberta E., and Miriam B. Haas. "The Working Mother: A Review of Research," *Child Development,* 1963, 34:513–542.

———, Lois M. Stolz, Ethel A. Hitchcock, and Jean Adamson. "Dependence and Independence in Children," in F. Ivan Nye and Lois W. Hoffman (eds.), *The Employed Mother in America.* Chicago: Rand McNally, 1963.

Silber, Earle, Stewart E. Perry, and Donald A. Bloch. "Patterns of Parent-Child Interaction in a Disaster," *Psychiatry,* 1958, 21:167–195.

Simmel, Georg. Kurt H. Wolf (ed.), *Georg Simmel, 1858–1918.* Columbus: Ohio State University Press, 1959.

Simpson, Richard L. "Parental Influence, Anticipatory Socialization, and Social Mobility," *American Sociological Review,* 1962, 27:517–522.

———, and Ida Harper Simpson. "Occupational Choice Among Career-Oriented College Women," *Marriage and Family Living,* 1961, 23:377–383.

Slater, Philip E. "Parental Role Differentiation," *American Journal of Sociology,* 1961, 67:296–308. (a)

Sliepcevich, Elena M. Study described by Elizabeth Force in "A Nationwide Study of Health Instruction in the Public Schools," *Journal of Marriage and the Family,* 1965, 27:96.

Slocum, Walter L. *Family Culture Patterns and Adolescent Behavior.* Agriculture Experiment Station Bulletin No. 648. Pullman: Washington State University, 1963.

Smart, Susan. "Social Class Differences in Parent Behavior in a Natural Setting," *Marriage and Family Living.* 1964, 26:223–224.

Smelser, William T. "Adolescent and Adult Occupational Choice as a Function of Family Socioeconomic History," *Sociometry,* 1963, 4:393–409.

Smith, Philip M. "Broken Homes and Juvenile Delinquency," *Sociology and Social Research,* 1955, 39:307–311.

Smith, Robert J., Charles E. Ramsey, and Gelia Castillo. "Parental Authority and Job Choice: Sex Differences in Three Cultures," *American Journal of Sociology,* 1963, 69:143–149.

Smith, William Carlson. *The Stepchild.* Chicago: The University of Chicago Press, 1953.

Smuts, Robert W. *Women and Work in America.* New York: Columbia University Press, 1959.

Sopchak, Andrew L. "Parental 'Identification' and 'Tendency Toward Disorders' as Measured by the MMPI," *Journal of Abnormal and Social Psychology,* 1952, 47:159–165.

Spaulding, Charles B. "Relative Attachment of Students to Groups and Organizations," *Sociology and Social Research,* 1966, 50:421–435.

Spock, Benjamin. "The Child With One Parent," *Ladies' Home Journal,* July, 1962, pp. 30–31.

Spuhler, J. N. "Somatic Paths to Culture," in J. N. Spuhler (ed.), *The*

Evolution of Man's Capacity for Culture. Detroit: Wayne State University Press, 1959.

Stanfield, Robert E. "The Interaction of Family Variables and Gang Variables in the Aetiology of Delinquency," *Social Problems,* 1966, 13:411–417.

Steinmann, Anne. "Lack of Communication Between Men and Women," *Marriage and Family Living,* 1958, 20:350–352.

Stephens, William N. "Judgment by Social Workers on Boys and Mothers in Fatherless Families," *Journal of Genetic Psychology,* 1961, 99.59–64.

Stodgill, Ralph M. "Survey of Experiments of Children's Attitudes Toward Parents: 1894–1936," *Journal of Genetic Psychology,* 1937, 51:293–303.

Stoke, S. M. "An Inquiry Into the Concept of Identification," in W. E. Martin and C. B. Stendler (eds.), *Readings in Child Development.* New York: Harcourt, Brace & World, 1954.

Stolz, Lois M. *Father Relations of War-Born Children.* Stanford: Stanford University Press, 1954.

Straus, Murray A. "Conjugal Power Structure and Adolescent Personality," *Marriage and Family Living,* 1962, 24:17–25.

———. "Power and Support Structure of the Family in Relation to Socialization," *Journal of Marriage and the Family,* 1964, 26:318–326.

Streib, Gordon F. "Intergenerational Relations: Perspectives of the Two Generations on the Older Parent," *Journal of Marriage and the Family,* 1965, 27:469–476.

Strodtbeck, Fred L. "The Interaction of a 'Henpecked' Husband with His Wife," *Marriage and Family Living,* 1952, 14:305–308.

———. "Family Interaction, Values and Achievement," in David C. McClelland *et al., Talent and Society.* New York: Van Nostrand, 1958.

Stroup, Atlee L. "Marital Adjustment of the Mother and the Personality of the Child," *Marriage and Family Living,* 1956, 18:109–113.

Stuckert, Robert P. "Role Perception and Marital Satisfaction—A Configurational Approach," *Marriage and Family Living,* 1963, 25:415–419.

Stycos, J. Mayone. *Family and Fertility in Puerto Rico.* New York: Columbia University Press, 1955.

Sullivan, Harry Stack. *The Interpersonal Theory of Psychiatry.* New York: Norton, 1953.

Sussman, Marvin B. "The Help Pattern in the Middle-Class Family," *American Sociological Review,* 1953, 18:22–28.

———. "Needed Research on the Employed Mother," *Marriage and Family Living,* 1961, 23:368–373.

———, and Lee G. Burchinal. "Kin Family Network: Unheralded Structure in Current Conceptualizations of Family Functioning," *Marriage and Family Living,* 1962, 24:231–240.

Sweetser, Dorrian Apple. "The Social Structure of Grandparenthood," in R. F. Winch, Robert McGinnis, and H. R. Barringer (eds.), *Selected*

Studies in Marriage and the Family. New York: Holt, Rinehart and Winston, 1962.

Taeuber, Alma F., Karl E. Taeuber, and Glen G. Cain. "Occupational Assimilation and the Competitive Process: A Reanalysis," *American Journal of Sociology*, 1966, 72:273–289.

Tallman, Irving. "Spousal Role Differentiation and the Socialization of Severely Retarded Children," *Journal of Marriage and the Family*, 1965, 27:37–42.

Talmon, Yonina. "Mate Selection in Collective Settlements," *American Sociological Review*, 1964, 29:491–508.

Tasch, Ruth J. "The Role of the Father in the Family," *Journal of Experimental Education*, 1952, 20:319–361.

Taylor, G. Rattray. *Sex in History*. London: Thames and Hudson, 1953.

Tenbruck, Friedrich H. *Jugend und Gesellschaft*. Freiburg: Rombach, 1962.

Tharp, Roland G. "Dimensions of Marriage Roles," *Marriage and Family Living*, 1963, 25:389–404.

Thrasher, Frederick M. *The Gang*. Chicago: The University of Chicago Press, 1927.

Toby, Jackson. "The Differential Impact of Family Disorganization," *American Sociological Review*, 1957, 22:505–512.

Townsend, Peter. *The Family Life of Old People*. London: Routledge & Kegan Paul, 1957.

Tuma, Elias, and Norman Livson. "Family Socioeconomic Status and Adolescent Attitudes Toward Authority," *Child Development*, 1960, 31:387–399.

Turner, Ralph H. "Some Family Determinants of Ambition," *Sociology and Social Research*, 1962, 46:397–411.

———. "Some Aspects of Women's Ambition," *American Journal of Sociology*, 1964, 70:271–285.

Valentine, Alan (ed.). *Father to Sons*. Norman: University of Oklahoma Press, 1963.

Vernon, Glenn M., and Jack A. Boadway. "Attitudes Toward Artificial Insemination and Some Variables Associated Therewith," *Marriage and Family Living*, 1959, 21:43–47.

Vincent, Clark E. "Trends in Infant Care Ideas," *Child Development*, 1951, 22:199–209.

———. "Ego Involvement in Sexual Relations: Implications for Research on Illegitimacy," *American Journal of Sociology*, 1959, 65:287–295.

———. "Unmarried Fathers and the Mores: 'Sexual Exploiter' as an Ex Post Facto Label," *American Sociological Review*, 1960, 25:40–46.

Vogel, Ezra F. "The Marital Relationship of Parents of Emotionally Disturbed Children: Polarization and Isolation," *Psychiatry*, 1960, 23:1–12.

———. "The Democratization of Family Relations in Japanese Urban Society," *Asian Survey*, 1961, 1:18–24.

———. *Japan's New Middle Class*. Berkeley: University of California Press, 1963.

———, and Norman W. Bell. "The Emotionally Disturbed Child as a Family Scapegoat," *Psychoanalysis and the Psychoanalytic Review,* 1960, 47:21–42.

Voss, Harwin L. "Socio-Economic Status and Reported Delinquent Behavior," *Social Problems,* 1966, 13:314–324.

Wainwright, William H. "Fatherhood as a Precipitant of Mental Illness," *Scientific Proceedings in Summary Form,* American Psychiatric Association, 1964, pp. 96–97.

Wallace, Walter L. "Institutional and Life-Cycle Socialization of College Freshmen," *American Journal of Sociology,* 1964, 70:303–318.

Waller, Willard. "The Rating and Dating Complex," *American Sociological Review,* 1937, 2:727–734.

Wallin, Paul. "Cultural Contradictions and Sex Roles: A Repeat Study," *American Sociological Review,* 1950, 15:288–293.

———. "Sex Differences in Attitudes to 'In-Laws': A Test of a Theory," *American Journal of Sociology,* 1954, 59:466–469.

———, and Howard M. Vollmer. "Marital Happiness of Parents and Their Children's Attitudes to Them," *American Sociological Review,* 1953, 18:424–431.

Ward, David A., and Gene G. Kassebaum. "Homosexuality: A Mode of Adaptation in a Prison for Women," *Social Problems,* 1964, 12:159–177.

Warner, W. Lloyd, and James C. Abegglen. *Big Business Leaders in America.* New York: Harper & Row, 1955.

Washburn, Sherwood L. "Speculations on the Interrelations of the History of Tools and Biological Evolution," *Human Biology,* 1959, 31:21–31.

———, and Irven DeVore. "Social Behavior of Baboons and Early Man," in Sherwood L. Washburn (ed.), *Social Life of Early Man.* New York: Wenner-Gren Foundation, 1961.

Webb, Allen P. "Sex-Role Preferences and Adjustment in Early Adolescents," *Child Development,* 1963, 34:609–618.

Wechsler, H. "Conflicts in Self-Perceptions." Unpublished Ph.D. dissertation. Cambridge: Harvard University, 1957.

Weeks, H. Ashley. "Male and Female Broken Home Rates by Types of Delinquency," *American Sociological Review,* 1940, 5:601–609.

Weil, Mildred W. "An Analysis of the Factors Influencing Married Women's Actual or Planned Work Participation," *American Sociological Review,* 1961, 26:91–96.

Weinberg, Carl. "Family Background and Deviance or Conformity to School Expectations," *Marriage and Family Living,* 1964, 26:89–91.

Weiss, Robert S., and Nancy Morse Samelson. "Social Roles of American Women: Their Contribution to a Sense of Usefulness and Importance," *Marriage and Family Living,* 1958, 20:358–366.

Werts, Charles E. "Social Class and Initial Career Choice of College Freshmen," *Sociology of Education,* 1966, 39:74–85.

Westley, William A., and Nathan B. Epstein. "Family Structure and Emotional Health: A Case Study Approach," *Marriage and Family Living,* 1960, 22:364–365. (a)

———, and Nathan B. Epstein. "Parental Interaction as Related to the Emotional Health of Children," *Social Problems*, 1960, 8:87–92. (b)

Westoff, Charles F., Robert G. Potter, Jr., and Philip C. Sagi. *The Third Child: A Study in the Prediction of Fertility*. Princeton: Princeton University Press, 1963.

Whyte, William H., Jr. *The Organization Man*. New York: Simon and Schuster, 1956.

Wilkening, E. A., and Denton E. Morrison. "A Comparison of Husband and Wife Responses Concerning Who Makes Farm and Home Decisions," *Marriage and Family Living*, 1963, 25:349–351.

Williams, Robin M., Jr. *American Society*. 2nd ed. New York: Knopf, 1965.

Willie, Charles V., and Janet Weinandy. "The Structure and Composition of 'Problem' and 'Stable' Families in a Low-Income Population," *Marriage and Family Living*, 1963, 25:439–446.

Wilson, Alan B. "Residential Segregation of Social Classes and Aspirations of High-School Boys," *American Sociological Review*, 1959, 24:836–845.

Winch, Robert F. "The Relation Between the Loss of a Parent and Progress in Courtship," *Journal of Social Psychology*, 1949, 29:51–56.

———. *The Modern Family*. New York: Holt, Rinehart and Winston, 1952.

———. *Identification and Its Familial Determinants*. Indianapolis: Bobbs-Merrill, 1962.

Wolfe, Donald M. "Power and Authority in the Family," in Robert F. Winch, Robert McGinnis, and Herbert R. Barringer (eds.), *Selected Studies in Marriage and the Family*. New York: Holt, Rinehart and Winston, 1962.

Wolfenstein, Martha. "Fun Morality, An Analysis of Recent American Child-Training Literature," in Margaret Mead and Martha Wolfenstein (eds.), *Childhood in Contemporary Cultures*. Chicago: University of Chicago, 1955.

———. "Death of a Parent and Death of a President: Children's Reactions to Two Kinds of Loss," in Martha Wolfenstein and Gilbert Kliman (eds.), *Children and the Death of a President*. New York: Doubleday, 1965.

Woods, Sister Frances Jerome, and Alice Cunningham Lancaster. "Cultural Factors in Negro Adoptive Parenthood," *Social Work*, 1962, 7:14–21.

Wrong, Dennis. "The Oversocialized Conception of Man in Modern Sociology," *American Sociological Review*, 1961, 26:183–193.

Wylie, Howard L., and Rafael A. Delgado. "Pattern of Mother-Son Relationship Involving the Absence of the Father," *American Journal of Orthopsychiatry*, 1959, 29:644–649.

Wylie, Philip. *Generation of Vipers*. New York: Holt, Rinehart and Winston, 1942.

Yarrow, Marian Radke. "Problems of Methods in Parent-Child Research," *Child Development*, 1963, 34:215–226.

———, Helen Trager, and Jean Miller. "The Role of Parents in the Development of Children's Ethnic Attitudes," *Child Development,* 1952, 23:13–53.

Young, Frank W. "The Function of Male Initiation Ceremonies: A Cross-Cultural Test of an Alternative Hypothesis," *American Journal of Sociology,* 1962, 67:379–396.

Zelditch, Morris, Jr. "Role Differentiation in the Nuclear Family: A Comparative Study," in Talcott Parsons and Robert F. Bales (eds.), *Family, Socialization and Interaction Process.* New York: Free Press, 1955.

Zimmerman, Carle C. *Family and Civilization.* New York: Harper & Row, 1947.

Zukerman, Jacob T. "A Socio-Legal Approach to Family Desertion," *Marriage and Family Living,* 1950, 12:83–84.

INDEX